THE
SYSTEM
IS THE
SECRET

PROVEN WAYS TO
IMPLEMENT THE SYSTEMS
THAT WILL
TRANSFORM AND GROW
YOUR BUSINESS

BY
JAMES KARL BUTLER
HOST OF THE
SOUND LAWS OF SUCCESS PODCAST

DEDICATION:
To my beautiful wife Heather,
and my five precious children
who are each my eternal inspiration

and

To inspiring entrepreneurs everywhere
who push through failures, disappointments, and challenges
to get to the next step on their journey to success.

This publication is designed to provide accurate and authoritative information in regard to the subject matter covered. It is sold with the understanding that the publisher is not engaged in rendering legal, accounting, or other professional service. If legal advice or other expert assistance is required, the services of a professional should be sought.

Butler, James Karl
The System is the Secret: Proven Ways to Implement the Systems that Will Transform and Grow Your Business
ISBN: 978-0-578-125350
1. *Business*
2. *Success*

What Others Are Saying About *The System is the Secret*

"*The System is the Secret* is such a valuable book for entrepreneurs. It details how to build sixteen of the most critically important systems that will help you run your business more profitably. As GKIC Retail Marketer of the Year, Jim knows how to build systems. He has built four companies from the start-up to $1million+ mark. He showed us his inbound and outbound lead flow systems at a Peak Performance meeting and I was quite impressed by the detail of his business systems. If you need to have better and more efficient systems in your business, get and apply what's in this book!"—Lee Milteer, author of *Success is an Inside Job*, www.milteer.com

"BY FAR the best book I've read on this subject. Butler explains not only the reasons why every business MUST put systems into place, but also provides step-by-step guidance and real-world fill-in-the-blanks charts to help every small business owner, entrepreneur and sales professional improve his or her income and remove stress and uncertainty."—Steve Sipress, Founder and CEO, Successful Selling Systems, Inc.

"*The System is the Secret* is an extraordinary and must-read (and implement) blueprint for business success in the 21st century. Long gone are the days of ad-hoc marketing efforts and customer management. Jim Butler knows the essential keys to success in this day and age are grounded in the owner's ability to systematize and automate their business. The book you're holding in your hands shows you exactly how to do this and profit from it."—Michael Capuzzi, Founder of CopyDoodles.com

"Jim Butler does a brilliant job addressing what holds so many business owners back...getting systems done and implemented. Well Done Jim! This book will help a lot of business owners!" —Eric Lofholm, author of *The System*

"I can't imagine attempting to grapple with the concept of business systems without *The System is the Secret*. What Jim has compiled here is a must-read for every entrepreneur. And the best part is, he doesn't just tell you what to do but reveals how to do it each and every step of the way. Make an investment in your future and get this book."--Jeff Brown, Award-winning Broadcaster and Host of Read to Lead Podcast

"Holy Cow! I just finished reading Jim's new book and have to tell you I have a stack of notes and ideas I'm going to implement immediately. The content in Jim's book is amazing and logically laid out. It's a fascinating read with real-life practical advice. He's a true marketing genius. As a serious marketing student myself, I have to tell you that I learned a tremendous amount from his book. Not only that, but I found his book so helpful and useful that I intend on buying a few boxes of his books to give as gifts to my VIP clients and marketing friends. If you want to take your marketing and your business to the next level, you need to read, study and implement Jim's content...it's that good!"—Gerry Oginski, Esq., Founder, Lawyers Video Studio

"If you own a business and don't have all the customers or clients you want, grab a copy of *The System is the Secret*, and study it cover to cover. Inside you'll find out how to apply Michael Gerber's admonition in *The E-Myth* to work ON your business instead of IN it. Jim Butler takes the mystery out of developing a sustainable, profitable business by giving you the exact steps you need for putting the right systems in place. As you respond to the thought-provoking questions, assessments and worksheets included in the book, you'll never think about your business in the same way again. And if you apply the insights you get, you should see positive results in your marketing, sales and bottom line."--Meredith Bell, President, Performance Support Systems, Inc.

"This book is filled with many hidden gems that can be transformative to any business. *The System Is The Secret* is a book worth mining for the many gems of entrepreneurial wisdom. I consider it one of my newest go-to references for transforming any business and leading the driven entrepreneur to a lifestyle of financial liberation."—Walter Bergeron, serial entrepreneur, best-selling author, Marketer of the Year

"In *The System is the Secret* Jim Butler has provided the KEY power and clarity desperately needed by freedom seeking ADD riddled entrepreneurs. I'm fond of the quote "Freedom is born of wise structure." Get *The System is the Secret* and let Jim guide you into levels of control and freedom you may not have previously dreamed possible."—Jay Henderson, Founder, Real Talent Hiring, Inc.

"There are 7 questions that when you answer them they will change everything - I know I grow million dollar companies again and again - using systems of course - the cool thing is that everyone - including you - can too - this book is an essential part of that simple process..."—Mike Crow, Founder, Millionaire Inspector Community & Coach Blueprint, Senior Manager, TexInspec

"*The Secret is the System* is a <u>great</u> book for business owners. Butler hits the nail right on the head. As a printer, direct mailer and marketing services company, we have a lot of moving parts in our business and it is absolutely critical that systems are followed to ensure that mistakes aren't made and that we keep our clients happy. This is the best book on systems creation I have ever seen. Get it, study it, and implement its powerful principles." --George R. Platt. President, Harty Integrated Solutions.

"I know and associate with some of the brightest marketers in the world and Jim is one of the sharpest I've ever met. He is a true student of sales and marketing and is one of the smartest business people I've had the pleasure of knowing. I've witnessed firsthand how he has developed his business over the years. Although it's difficult to do one thing well, Jim successfully branched out from a successful bridal business into dress designing, manufacturing, private labeling and coaching to others in his industry. In his spare time he has written several superb books on marketing that can help any business owner to increase their profitability. He has done all this through superb marketing, massive implementation and by creating and using the necessary systems to run his businesses. In this book he finally reveals the strategies and systems that are the backbone of his phenomenal success. I don't know of any business owner or entrepreneur that could not benefit massively from this book."—Grant Miller, CEO, Sun Your Buns

"Butler's laser focus on studying, testing and refining systems for business has made him the authority on the subject. In "The System is the Secret", he gives away his best strategies and tactics that he's used with high paying clients for years. Get this book!"—Brian Horn, CoFounder of Authority Media Group, LLC

"In his book, "The System is the Secret", author Jim Butler shares an important question that every business owner should be able to answer: *Can you leave your business for a year or more and return to find it more profitable and running better than when you left it?*" In my over-20 years of consulting entrepreneurial and professional businesses, my observation is that the best run businesses are those run on 'consciously' created systems that run 'unconsciously.' Everything runs like clockwork. Every situation; every possible problem that comes up; every scenario has a system in place to handle it. The extraordinary businesses that I've witnessed not only have systems, but "systems within systems". Every part of the system is organized in order, and every process is defined in detail. Every possible problem has been thought through and a solution is known and practiced by all who follow the system. I have not found a book so thorough and so important on this topic... until now. Jim Butler has written "THE" handbook on the essentials to

creating successful systems for your business."-Craig Valine, Marketing
Performance Strategist

"There is no way to build a million dollar business without systems. James nailed
the segment for every business in this book. It is more like a blueprint with every
form, template needed for business growth. My absolute favorite is Section III
Implementation because Ideas make entrepreneurs feel good, but implementation
makes money. The ultimate success book, every entrepreneur should read!"--
Richelle Shaw, The $100 Million Dollar Woman, Entrepreneur, Consultant,
Author of *The Million Dollar Equation*

"Jim Butler has taken his personal experience in building four successful
companies and the wisdom of other great minds and focused this book on a
critical success factor for any business – systems. If you are serious about building
a business that meets and exceeds your goals this book will give you a predictable
and disciplined path to success. Systems aren't always sexy, but they will get us the
results we need. This book can be your playbook for systems – and business –
success."-Kevin Eikenberry, Chief Potential Officer of The Kevin Eikenberry
Group and one of the world's 100 top leadership and management thinkers
according to Inc.com

"There is no shortage of books offering business advice. Trouble is, many are
written by authors who simply re-hash information gleaned from others.
Thankfully that is NOT the case with *The System is the Secret*. For growth-
oriented entrepreneurs, this book is where 'the rubber meets the road' –
containing advice, wisdom, and information worth millions. James Butler has
created and built several million dollar businesses from the ground up and in this
book you'll not only learn what to do, but equally as important, what not to do. Do
yourself a favor and lock the door, turn off the phone and start reading this book.
"--Jim Palmer – The Dream Business Coach, www.GetJimPalmer.com

"A lot of the work our firm does with dentists and specialists revolves around
building customized marketing products and programs. I've discovered that in the
end it's all about getting a system in place and having all of the spokes of your
marketing wheel filled with activity to bring you more business. Jim Butler's book
The Secret is the System is the best and most comprehensive approach to systems
development that I've ever seen. I would highly recommend that you get it, study
it and apply it in your business to get better results now."—Kathy Jiamboi,
President, Creativedge Marketing

"As a small business coach, I teach individuals and organizations how to "Dream, Plan, Execute, and Soar." This is the best book I've seen on how to plan and execute better systems within a business. Get this book so you can follow the clearly outlined steps and plan so you can soar to new heights with your business and achieve your dreams."--Patrick Snow, Professional Speaker, International Best-Selling Author of *Creating Your Own Destiny* and *Boy Entrepreneur*

"For years I have made it point to drive home the importance of building and running a business on proven systems to my clients. Finally a simple step-by-step book on why systems are crucial to a company's success and more importantly, real action steps on how to do it. Not only does Jim talk about it, but he has actually done it more than once proving his methods are duplicable. If you have been skipping this step in your business, I highly suggest you read this book from cover to cover, it will be the best thing you can do for your bottom line!"--Vicki Irvin, CEO Superwoman Lifestyle www.VickiIrvin.com

CONTENTS

INTRODUCTION

My name is James Karl Butler and thank you so much for purchasing and reading my book *The System is the Secret*! I look forward to spending time with you as you read, study, and apply the principles I'll share with you over the pages ahead. My goal is to share with you the secrets I've learned of how to build, improve, and strengthen the systems in your business that can take you to the next level in your growth. Most entrepreneurs know they need to build systems and this book will outline and teach you how to build better systems for your business. I'll share insights from my own entrepreneurial pursuits and will share with you the mistakes we've made along the way so you can learn what works and what doesn't. I'll also share contagious stories of inspiration to help motivate you to take action to spread more of the secret sauce that will build your business on the way to success.

As I'm writing this, I have built five companies. Our first business (a retail bridal store) grew from $0 to over $1,000,000 a year in sales in three years. We grew another retail business from $0 to over $1,000,000 in just over 18 months. To date, I have grown four businesses from the start-up phase to over a million dollars in revenue. I've had successes and I've also experienced failures. In this book, I want to reveal how the systems behind a business are really the secret behind their rapid and sustained growth. The system *is* the secret.

Business is a blast, but it can also be extremely challenging. There is nothing like the feeling that comes from being in control and making your goals and dreams happen. Yet, failure is something that every entrepreneur faces. Failures offer us an opportunity to improve the systems in our businesses and in our lives so we can do it better the next time. A successful business can quickly spiral out of control without careful attention to the many facets and critical factors that can make or break you. In this book, I will talk straight with you about the things you may have been ignoring, what you should be paying attention to, and will share with you the systems and the strategies that will help your business grow.

Before we get started, I want to introduce myself briefly so you get to know me as we take this journey together. I don't want you to make the same systems mistakes my wife and I did when we opened our first business in the fall of 2001. I truly want you to be as successful as you want with your business and I sincerely believe that what I share with you in this book will change your life. I know that you may not agree with everything I've written in this book. But I would like you to read with an open mind and seriously consider what I have to say about what it takes to build systems and succeed in business.

You may be wondering, "Who is James Karl Butler and why should I listen to what he has to say?" That's a fair question and one I will try to answer briefly here. (Side note: I most often go by Jim or James, but I use my full name in my books and podcast because there are more than 5,200 Jim Butler's in the United States alone. I use my full name James Karl to differentiate myself from the many other Jim Butler's in the world, but if and when we meet in person, you are welcome to call me Jim or James.) I already consider you a friend since you have made the investment to purchase my book and my hope is that as you learn and apply what is in the pages that follow, that we'll become even better friends. When you have a similar name to so many others, it can be easy to blend in, yet as you'll read in this book, that is the last thing one should do. My goal is to help you stand out from your competitors by building better systems so you can be more profitable and successful.

I was born in upstate New York. My father is a farrier (shoes horses) and educator who taught at several universities and colleges when I was growing up. My mother stayed in the home raising my six siblings and me. I was born third. I have to be honest that I never really saw myself being an entrepreneur when I was growing up. I moved from New York when I was five and grew up primarily in west Texas and northwest Missouri where I graduated from high school.

I graduated from college with a microbiology major and a double minor in chemistry and Spanish. In fact, I put myself through school by teaching Spanish. I always thought I would go to medical school and work on developing vaccines in the field of immunology. While I was in college, I met my wife Heather. When I graduated from college, I couldn't get a job in my field to support my family. I realized I could go back to school and go into debt or I could find a job. I ended up working in construction for a while and absolutely hated it. As I mentioned, I couldn't afford to go back to school. I wound up in sales so I could pay the bills and support our young daughter Madeline who was born thirteen months after we got married.

In a word, I stunk at sales. I was terrible at it. We nearly starved as I spun my wheels trying to figure out what would work. I quickly learned that there were books that had been written on selling. I couldn't afford them, but I went to a local Barnes and Noble and read books with a note pad each night before coming home. I took copious notes of ideas I could try in my next day's sales efforts.

As I started to implement what I was learning and along with the coaching of my sales manager and the top sales people in the office, I started to make improvements. The week before Madeline was born I had one of my best sales weeks ever and beat everyone else at the office in total sales. I even got an award for selling the most that week. I became excited about what I was learning and studied with even more diligence.

I realized that there is a system for selling, a step-by-step process I could use that would help me sell more. I realized that when you outline and follow a proven system, you get results. My first year in selling I read over 60 books. I was on fire and very excited about business and selling. Even though I was new to business, I was excited by what I was learning and found that I enjoyed selling and business much more than the science I had been studying in school.

After Madeline was born, I worked for my father selling his one-on-one farrier training and coaching programs and helped him write many articles for horse industry publications. I also did a lot of research and helped him outline and write two books (one on creative thinking and the other on business). I loved the process of writing and owe a lot to my father for teaching me how to distill a lot of information into a few key ideas.

After working for my father for a year and a half I helped start an interactive marketing agency called Impact Media which grew to be one of the top 100 interactive advertising agencies (#84) in the United States. I was their Director of Business Development (and their top sales person) with millions of dollars in sales with such clients as Fidelity Investments, Hewlett Packard, IBM, Upper Deck and Toyota. I also worked with many of the top advertising agencies in the country including Ogilvy, J. Walter Thompson, Brodeur Worldwide and DNB Media. This company was publicly acquired twice during the .com era.

My wife had a good friend who was in the bridal business and Heather actually worked at her store while we were dating and going through college. We ended up starting our bridal business together in Mesa, Arizona. We grew our business as I mentioned from $0 to over $1,000,000 in sales each year in three years. In July of 2006, I began a consulting and training company to help other bridal retailers learn many of the secrets we had learned as we grew our business. I have since helped many of the most respected and largest bridal stores across the country to grow their sales and shatter their previous sales records. I realized as I consulted with these business owners that the biggest thing they lacked was good systems. When I shared with them what we were doing and they applied our system, their sales exploded. We began and operated a wholesale bridal company, traveling to China and learning the import business. This company did millions of dollars in sales.

Early in the growth of each business, I realized that systems were the key to getting more done. I found holes in our business systems through the mistakes we made. Some mistakes were very costly. With each successive business, I have gotten better at reverse engineering the process required to build the systems that would create predictable results. At one point, I had five concurrent businesses. It was difficult to manage it all, but was much easier because of the systems we set up. In the midst of this rapid growth, I wrote five books, several e-books, and created numerous online training courses. I won the 2010-2011 Retailer of the Year award from Glazer-Kennedy Insider Circle (GKIC). Today, I speak and train other entrepreneurs how to build better systems in their business so they can create predictable, profitable, and exceptional results. In this book, you'll learn how *The System is the Secret.*

Systems don't just happen. They take intensive work and focus to build. Yet, this work is the most profitable work you will do as you focus *on* your business. Rapid growth can expose holes in systems that you thought worked very smoothly and can reveal your weaknesses in ways that can be frightening and humbling. I've written this book to help you assess how well your systems are currently working and to help you patch up the holes before they lose you money and clients.

I've written this book in three sections. The first section, Systems, gives an overview about why systems are so important and will help you begin the process of putting together the systems that will turnaround or transform your business.

When you make mistakes in your business and holes in your systems are revealed to you (especially ones that cost you money), it is easy to get angry with yourself for why you are in the situation you are. It can be difficult to balance reality about where you are with optimism about where you are going in the future. Everyone learns much more from failure than they do from success, but no one wants to have to have difficulties or adversities. Anyone would prefer to skip these lessons all together, yet this is where we learn the most.

In Section 2, I detail sixteen specific systems in thirteen chapters and give you ways to assess your current systems, specific tasks lists to build and improve your systems, and detailed instructions of what you need to do to build these systems on a solid foundation. These assessments will be challenging and thought provoking because if you want to create a road map to where you are going, it is critical to understand your starting point first. At the end of each chapter, these assessments will allow you to come face to face with uncomfortable realities about the state of the systems in your business.

Systems work can often get postponed in the middle of the growth of a business. In Section 3, I detail secrets of implementation so you can do your systems work now, instead of waiting until the opportune moment to do it. Small investments of time now can prevent massive and costly mistakes later. Inaction won't prepare you for the future. After applying what you learn in this book, you'll be able to rescue revenue and profits that were spilling and leaking out of your business.

Today my wife Heather and I have five children (two girls and three boys). A few of our children have already expressed and demonstrated entrepreneurial seizures and my oldest son has already started two companies. As our children get older, I'll continue to teach them how to build systems in their businesses just like we have in ours.

I've made it my mission to study and share the laws of success and the secrets behind systems implementation to assist entrepreneurs in their journey. I'm so happy that you've decided to join me on this quest and look forward to hearing of your successes as you read and put the principles in this book into practice. Please visit my web site at www.SoundLawsofSuccess.com to connect with me and listen to my podcast. I hope that as you apply what you will learn that you'll not only *see* your business more objectively, but you'll *know what to do* so you can make a quantum leap in your business as a result. Let's get started.

CHAPTER 1

CREATE AND USE SYSTEMS TO RUN YOUR BUSINESS

*"Let systems run the business and people run the systems.
People come and go but the systems remain constant."—Michael E. Gerber*

I've written this book to help you as a business owner shift from your business being entirely dependent upon your own personal skills to a business that is dependent upon a systematic process through which these skills can be transferred to anyone to whom you teach your system.

Why is this so important? The reason is that the majority of small business owners feel that they can't take a break or go on vacation or ever leave their business because it is **entirely dependent upon them and their skills.**

If this is how you feel about your business, this chapter will help you start the process of shifting your thinking from skills to systems. This really is the big secret to scaling any business: rapid growth and success happen because of your ability to shift your thinking and your focus from skills to implemented systems.

A system is defined as a set of things, actions, ideas and information that interact with each other, and in so doing, alter other systems. Let me give you an example. You have a system for selling, unless you're winging it, in which case you're not making many sales. **The reality is that if you do not have a system for selling, you are at the mercy of the prospect's system for not buying.** Does this happen at your business? Do you and your sales consultants handle sales situations the same way?

The thing I've realized over the years is that the process of what happens when selling is pretty predictable. You are not going to have prospects come into your business tomorrow giving you objections to concerns you've never heard before. Since this is the case, I have felt that it is best to train your staff is to anticipate objections that may come up and know how to handle them (such as "someone else has to see this before I can buy" and that they have to "think about it").

If you are in any way wondering whether a sales system might be helpful in your business, I invite you to ask yourself this question: "What would happen if all of my sales consultants overcame every objection and had the tools and resources to help them close the sale virtually every time?"

If you can help your staff to overcome the most common objections, think about how much more powerful your sales team could be.

What I have found is that most businesses don't have a systemized way of running their business. They wing it. They do things off the cuff. They react or respond to what happens in their business. They sell and operate their business one way this week and another way two or three weeks from now. The best and most successful businesses have a system for how they operate every aspect of their business. It is scripted, well-thought out, practiced, implemented, and improved on (when needed). In reality, systems are an organized process set up to ensure that the process of running the business happens in the same way and challenges that come up are handled in the same way every single time.

That is the power of an effective system. In business, a system is a way of doing things to produce a specific result such as a way to ensure a number of leads or a system to close sales. The system is the solution to get the results you want. The system is the secret to transforming a business from a simple start-up to a profitable and successful enterprise.

A great system has three characteristics:

1) *It leverages or magnifies people to the point at which they can produce extraordinary results consistently again and again* (like the sales example I just mentioned).
2) *Every possible problem has been thought through and a solution is known and practiced by all who follow the system.* For example, you have thought through, identified and have a solution for every customer service issue that could come up in your business and how you will handle it.
3) *Every part of the system is organized, has order, and every process is defined in detail.* For example, when a prospect buys a product or service, everything that happens in that transaction, how it is ordered, what happens when it arrives, how it is serviced, how you interact with the client when they pick it up, how the client is approached for referrals, etc. is all carefully defined and executed. The goal of a great system is to give each client a consistent experience and value that meets and hopefully exceeds their expectations.

As a business owner, you must constantly ask and think about this question: how can I improve my business so that it is systems dependent rather than people dependent?

When you refine operations to improve how the systems in your business work, you are working *on* your business, not just *in* it.

Order is the basis of having and executing a great system. When prospects come into your business (whether that is online or offline), they can sense how orderly you are by how you act. When they sense that your business is orderly and organized, their sense of risk disappears, and they feel they can trust you.

This allows you to utilize your system of selling to help a prospective client find exactly what he or she is looking for and help them have an incredible experience as they interact with your business.

To succeed in business, you've got to make the mind shifts that will help you shift from being a technician to an entrepreneur and a manager. This is not easy because we each see the world in different ways. We have different paradigms and mind sets that influence the way we think and the way we act. In order to achieve the highest levels of success and achievement, we must make mind shifts that take us from the status quo to new vistas and levels.

Most people who get into business don't have an entrepreneurial background before they start. My wife and I discovered when we went to and graduated from college that our educational training did more to prepare us to be an *employee* than to be an *employer*.

After having built several businesses from the start-up phase to seven figures plus in revenue, I've discovered that the businesses with the best-implemented systems are the ones that have long-term sustainability and success. Some businesses grow rapidly and then fall apart because they can't recover from mistakes made due to inadequate and ineffective systems.

Michael Gerber famously talked about the importance of systems in his excellent book *The E Myth*. The book in its different versions has sold more than a million copies. Gerber has helped re-engineer thousands of small businesses to aid people in gaining control over and get better results from their businesses. He updated his original book with *E-Myth Revisited* in 1995 and *E-Myth Mastery* in 2005. The book contains critical lessons that you as an entrepreneur need to take and apply in your business. This book *The System is the Secret* seeks to build on the key idea of the importance of systems from Gerber's book and give you the tools to help you implement specific systems in *your* business.

The essence of the E-Myth is this: understand that your business is a system rather than a place to go to work—a system designed to give the prospects who come in to your business (online or offline) what they want in a way that successfully differentiates you from your competitors.

Michael Gerber explains the E-Myth as follows: "To understand the E-Myth and the misunderstanding at its core, let's take a closer look at the person who goes into business. Not after he goes into business, but before.

"What were you thinking before you started your business? If you're like 99 percent of the people I've known, you were working for someone else.

"What were you doing? Probably technical work, like almost everybody who goes into business. You were a carpenter, a mechanic, or a machinist. You were a bookkeeper or a poodleclipper; a draftsperson or a hairdresser; a barber or a computer programmer; a doctor or a technical writer; a graphics artist or an accountant; an interior designer or a plumber or a salesperson. But whatever your profession, you were doing technical work. And you were probably [really] good at it. But you were doing it for somebody else.

"Then one day, for no apparent reason, something happened....It could have been anything; it doesn't matter what. But one day, for apparently no reason, you were suddenly stricken with an Entrepreneurial Seizure. And from that day on your life was never to be the same....

"In the throes of your Entrepreneurial Seizure, you fell victim to the most disastrous assumption anyone can make about going into business. It is an assumption made by all technicians who go into business for themselves...That Fatal Assumption is this: *if you understand the technical work of a business, you understand a business that does that technical work.*

"...When the technician falls prey to the Fatal Assumption, the business that was supposed to free him from the limitations of working for somebody else actually enslaves him. Suddenly the job he knew how to do so well becomes one job he knows how to do *plus a dozen others he doesn't know how to do at all.*"--Michael Gerber, *The E-Myth*, pp. 8-11.

The reality is that the technical work of a business and a business that does technical work are two totally different things. Why is this important to understand? The reason is that we all have a split personality in business. We are three people in one: the Entrepreneur, the Manager, and the Technician. To the technician, the business is not a business but a place to go to work.

The problem comes because in Michael Gerber's words: "Each of these personalities wants to *be* the boss, but none of them wants to *have* a boss. So they start a business together in order to *get rid of* the boss."--Michael Gerber, *The E-Myth*, p. 12.

In the book, Gerber gives a great analogy to how our multiple personalities interact with his analogy of the Skinny Guy vs. The Fat Guy. He says: "The Skinny Guy and The Fat Guy are two totally different personalities, with different needs, different interests, and different lifestyles. That's why they don't like each other. They each want totally different things...Anyone who has ever experienced the conflict between The Fat Guy and The Skinny Guy knows what I mean. You can't be both; one of them has to lose. And they both know it. Well, that's the kind of war going on inside the owner of every small business. But it's a three-way battle between the Entrepreneur, The Manager, and The Technician. Unfortunately, it's a battle no one can win." – *The E-Myth*, p. 15.

The three personalities can best be described by describing what each one focuses on.

Entrepreneur: Sets vision, lives in the future, looks for control, thrives on change, sees opportunity, and dreams.

Manager: Plans, lives in the past, looks for order, clings to the status quo, sees problems, and frets.

Technician: Does, lives in the present, does the work, resists change (only wants to do the work), sees the work in front of them, and ruminates.

Each of these personalities sees the work of the business as being different. Since most small business owners tend to view themselves as technicians, they typically gravitate back to this role whenever they feel stress and hope that the other two personalities will sort things out. As Gerber says: "To The Manager, then, The Technician becomes a problem to be managed. To The Technician, The Manager becomes a meddler to be avoided. To both of them, The Entrepreneur is the one who got them into trouble in the first place."--*The E-Myth*, p. 19.

The problem is that technicians never master the skills of the manager or the entrepreneur without focused discipline and work. They hope or assume that things will just sort their way out. The problem is that this assumption leads to the decline and failure of the business.

In *E Myth Mastery* on page 6, Michael Gerber makes this point: "The E-Myth says that all of these technicians, anyone who does technical work of any kind, make the same, fatal assumption: that because they understand how to do the technical work of the business—building a house, cutting hair, practicing law, cooking food—they understand how to build a business that does that work. Untrue, says the E-Myth. Untrue, untrue, untrue. The truth is that knowing how to do the work of a business has nothing to do with building a business that works. Failing to understand and appreciate, deeply, the difference between entrepreneurial perspective and the perspective of a technician suffering from an entrepreneurial seizure is almost sure to be catastrophic for anyone starting her own business....Let's look at the difference between the two. Between the technician's point of view and the entrepreneur's.

"The technician builds a business that depends on him, around his skills, his talent, his interest, and his predispositions. He devotes his time, his energy and his life working for a living, albeit self-employed. In the end, there is a little equity to show for the investment of his time. At the beginning, he bought a job. In the end, if he's lucky, he sells the job to a person who acquires it for little more than break-even, but most often at a net loss. The most a technician can show for the time he spent in his business is the income he earned, the feeling he had of being 'independent,' and whatever few assets he may have acquired with the income he earned over the time he was in business.

"The entrepreneur on the other hand, builds an enterprise that liberates her, creates endless amounts of energy, and increases her financial, emotional, and mental capital exponentially. In the end, there is significant equity to show for her investment. The enterprise runs itself in the hands of professional management. It has real value in the world. The entrepreneur is now free to invest what she's learned in another enterprise, depending on what she wishes to do with the rest of her life. In any event, she has learned how to grow an organization, how to utilize her creativity in the real world, how to expand her reach, and how to add value to many people, all while creating income that she no longer has to 'work' for, not to mention an estate for herself and the people she loves.

"Same amount of time invested, significantly different return on investment. The technician goes to work *in* his business. The entrepreneur goes to work *on* his business."--*E Myth Mastery*, pp. 6-7.

This is such an important concept to understand and why this book is so important and so powerful. When you understand the systems that make up your business and focus on implementing them, you will be so much more successful than you will by just working in your business.

It is so easy to lose focus when you are working in your business. You will always have too much to do and too little time to do it in. It is difficult if not impossible to catch up. There is always more to do. It doesn't stop. Instead, you have to choose what you will focus on. What you need to focus on is doing more *on* your business and less *in* your business.

In the foreword of *The E Myth*, Michael Gerber makes this observation:

"...The people who succeed in business don't do so because of what they know, but because of their insatiable need to know more. Conversely, the problem with most failing businesses is not that the owners don't know enough about finance, about marketing, about management, about operations....the problem is that they think they know enough. And so they spend their time defending what they know, rather than discovering what they don't."--*The E Myth*, p. xiii.

This book will help you face the areas where you personally may not have strengths so you can build systems in your business that will allow your business to be strong. While there initially will be more work involved to set up your business systems, this heavy lifting will pay off with higher profits and more time and energy for you. The system is the secret. The work to create your systems will help you create your future.

It takes courage to actively pursue the actions that will help you get what you want in life. Gerber says: "The difference between great people and everyone else is that great people create their lives actively, while everyone else is created *by* their lives, passively waiting to see where life takes them next."-- Michael E. Gerber, *The E-Myth*, p. 85.

How do you see yourself?
Do you consciously create your life?
Or do events of life create you?

You must be proactive about creating systems in your life and business. Hoping it will get done or waiting until a better time will never help you build the life you really want. With that in mind, let's talk about the three stages of business (Infancy, Adolescence, Maturity) and why you need different systems in each phase to help you grow to the next level:

1. Infancy - The Entrepreneurial Phase

Gerber says: "It's easy to spot a business in Infancy—the owner and the business are one and the same thing. If you removed the owner from an Infancy business, there would be no business left. It would disappear! In Infancy, you are the business....you love it!...but then it changes. Subtly, at first, but gradually it becomes obvious. You're falling behind. There's more work to do than can possibly get done. The customers are relentless. They want you, they need you. You've spoiled them for anyone else. You're working at breakneck speed. And then the inevitable happens. You, the Master Juggler, begin to drop some of the balls!

"...What do you do? You stretch. You work harder. You put in more time, more energy. If you put in twelve hours before you now put in fourteen. If you put in fourteen hours before, you now put in sixteen. If you put in sixteen hours before, you now put in twenty. But the balls keep dropping....There's simply no way in the world you can do all of that work yourself!

"...Infancy ends when the owner realizes that the business cannot continue to run the way it has been; that in order for it to survive, it will have to change. When that happens—when the reality sinks in—most business failures occur. When that happens, most of The Technicians lock their doors behind them and walk away."--*The E-Myth*, pp. 22-24.

Trying to do everything yourself without systems is a recipe for stress, burnout, and collapse. Intention to build systems *someday* doesn't count for much when you're buried, exhausted, and stressed out. As an example, here is a comment I heard from an entrepreneur in this stage:

"I always feel overwhelmed lately as well. I have a new sales person so that means I am here 24/7 with very little relief. Yes, the economy is hurting my business so much that I truly don't think it's worth it for me. My husband keeps topping it up with money that should be going into our retirement. But more importantly, I just don't think I like this business enough to keep it up. I think I'm almost done. I long for my previous job where I worked 4 days a week at home doing _____. I found it very challenging and I didn't go to bed worrying about payroll, marketing, EEs, etc. I'm trying to figure it all out this week. But, I think I want my old life back. One of my biggest problems is I can't find consistent, competent sales people who can fill in the gap. They're very much spoiled down here and don't have to work. The older women as well just want to work here because it may be fun. You mention Saturdays to them and they're out the door. I thought at this point I would have someone I could count on to be a real manager so I could get relief. I'm just more and more exhausted so I think this is not working for me. Sorry, but I just don't love the no paycheck, b----y clients and unstable staff enough to keep me in this business."

Have you ever felt these emotions?

If so, you are not alone. The key is to avoid the temptation to quit and move into the next phase or stage of business.

2. Adolescence (Second Phase)

Gerber explains: "Adolescence begins at the point in the life of your business when you decide to get some help. There's no telling how soon this will happen. But it always happens, precipitated by a crisis in the Infancy stage. Every business that lasts must grow into the Adolescent phase." --*The E-Myth*, p. 25.

This stage is initially a great stage for the overwhelmed and overworked entrepreneur. When you hire help and delegate some things and it goes well, it is a moment of great happiness since you now feel freer to do other things. Now, you feel that you finally have time to work on systems or other aspects of business improvement. Perhaps, you feel ready for a break. As a result, the technician part of you starts to go to sleep (since someone else is now doing the work) and you put on the manager hat. But, as Gerber says, here is where a new challenge begins since you aren't used to being the manager:

"...Unaccustomed as you are to being The Manager—your newfound freedom takes on an all too common form. Management by *abdication* rather than by *delegation*. In short, you give [someone the assignment] and run."

For a while this is great, until you walk by and see someone doing something or you get a call from a customer and you hear that someone wasn't treated exactly like they should be treated. In short, what happens is we immediately shift from being the manager to being the technician because "if you want something done right, you have to do it yourself."

Here is where many make a big mistake. They get back into doing the technical work (like selling, doing the technical work of the business, etc.) instead of training and making sure that it is understood and then done correctly. When you get back into the technician role, you quickly find yourself stressed out, overworked, and frustrated again.

Instead, what usually happens is what Gerber illustrates:

"This is the beginning of a process which occurs in *every* Adolescent business, once the owner's Management by Abdication begins to take its toll. It's the beginning of the process of deterioration, in which the number of balls in the air not only exceeds *your* ability to juggle them effectively, but your *people's* ability as well.

The balls begin to fall, faster and with greater confusion than they ever did when you were doing everything yourself. And as the thud of their landings becomes deafening, you begin to realize that you never should have trusted [the person you hired to help you]. You never should have trusted anyone. You should have known better.

You begin to realize that no one cares about your business the way you do. No one is willing to work as hard as you work. No one has your judgment, or your ability, or your desire, or your interest. If it's going to get done, you're the one who's going to have to do it.

So, you run back into your business to become the Master Juggler again. It's the same old story. One finds the owner of every Adolescent business doing, doing, doing—doing the work of the business—*despite the fact that he [or she] now has people who are supposed to be doing it for him [or her].* And the more he [or she] does, the less *they* do."--The E-Myth, pp. 29-30.

Pretty soon, you are right back where you started except now you're paying others to do the work that you're doing anyway. Business owners who find themselves in this situation feel immense frustration and resentment.

Is this where you are doomed to end up in your business? Thankfully, the answer is no. Instead, you have to learn a new set of skills of being a manager and an entrepreneur. You have to become skilled at setting up and implementing systems.

The problem is that technicians won't typically stop doing the work of the business long enough to learn the skill sets of managers and entrepreneurs. To be a successful business owner, you must get out of your comfort zone and learn how to lead and delegate. If you know how to do the technical skills of the business, you MUST also learn the skills of the manager and entrepreneur or hire and delegate out these tasks to those who do.

To truly grow your business and have it be what you want, you have to get out of your comfort zone and learn a new set of skills. You have got to learn how to lead and to delegate.

Michael Gerber makes this important point:
"Every Adolescent business reaches a point where it pushes beyond its owner's Comfort Zone—the boundary within which he feels secure in his ability to control his environment, and outside of which he begins to lose that control."

Instead of learning the new skill sets required and doing the systems work necessary, most business owners choose to do one of three things:

1. **Get small again (return to infancy) to stay in control.** When this happens, you own a job, not a business.
2. **Quit.**
3. **Hang on for dear life.** The business survives, but eventually you become completely consumed with the business and you do everything you can to save it. Unfortunately, the business doesn't explode, but you do. You may lose your marriage, your health, and your sanity. As Gerber says: "You're like a twelve cylinder engine working on one cylinder, pumping away, trying with everything you have to produce twelve cylinder's worth of results. Finally, there's nothing left. There's simply nothing more you can do, except face the fact that one cylinder can't produce twelve cylinders of results, no matter how hard it tries. Something has to give, and that something is you."--*The E-Myth*, p. 36.

The best thing to do when you find yourself in this situation is learn the truth about what works and do it. Effective systems are what works in business and is what this book *The System is the Secret* is all about. In a nutshell, you can divide these tasks into three steps. They are:

1) Create systems for every aspect of the business.
2) Set up the business to be run by systems.
3) Then have your team (manager, assistants and any other roles in your company) run the system.

This requires discipline, standardization, and order and requires a new set of skills that you may or may not have developed yet. This is the key to having a successful and profitable business.

Let me share with you a great example of how a company has grown through systems.

"In 1961, founder [of Weight Watchers] and New York housewife Jean Nidetch was thirty-eight, weighed 195 pounds, and described herself, her bus-driver husband, her two sons, her poodle, and most of her friends as overweight. A 'When are you due?' question tipped Nidetch over the edge and she decided to do something about her ballooning weight. She began her battle to overcome an addiction to chocolate cookies, which she would eat by the packet, and took herself to the New York City Department of Health obesity clinic for a diet plan.

Months later, Niedetch invited a group of six 'fat friends' around for coffee and announced that she had lost 40 pounds, challenging them to get with her program. The group began meeting regularly: Nidetch would hand out diet sheets and everyone would assess their weekly progress. Two months later, they all chipped in and bought some scales. 'We weren't going to blame our genes, our hormones, or our mothers anymore,' says Nidetch. Demand was huge. Soon there wasn't enough chairs or space in her apartment.

Al Lippert, an overweight buyer for a coat company, and his wife, Felice, heard about Nidetch's meetings and invited her to their home for a meeting. As well as quickly starting to lose weight (one of the Lipperts' sons had described his parents as being 'like two beach balls'), the Lipperts immediately saw the business potential in these meetings.

Nidetch and the Lipperts hatched a plan at the Lipperts' kitchen table for an enterprise they called Weight Watchers. They would run weekly motivational, empathetic meetings and charge a fee.

The first commercial Weight Watchers meeting was held in 1963. The company charged $2 per person, per session, the same price as a movie ticket at the time. After the first meeting, Nidetch recalls stuffing more money than she had ever seen in her life into her bags. Within a year they were selling Weight Watchers franchises. The business expanded through a system where franchisees paid a few thousand dollars for a license and agreed to pay 10 percent of their revenues back to Nidetch and the Lipperts. Within three years, they were generating $160,000 and by 1970, $8 million.

With the combination of Al Lippert's business administration and marketing prowess, Felice's writing and support skills, and Nidetch's natural leadership, motivation, and speaking skills, Weight Watchers was the perfect way to make money at a time when the post-war generations were packing on the pounds. Nidetch was the 'Energizer bunny,' Al was the marketing genius, and Felice the creative force.

In 1978, the Lipperts and Nidetch sold the company to H.J. Heinz for $72 million. Heinz sold the business to European investment firm Artal Luxembourg in 1999, and today the company is worth $4.8 billion.

There are more than 46,000 weekly Weight Watchers meetings in 30 countries around the world, with sixty million people attending meetings in 2004."--*100 Great Businesses and the Minds Behind Them*, pp. 54-56.

"In the 50 years since it's founding, the Company has built its meetings business by helping millions of people around the world lose weight through sensible and sustainable food plans, exercise, behavior modification and group support. Each week, approximately a million members attend over 40,000 Weight Watchers meetings around the world, which are run by more than 10,000 leaders—each of whom has lost weight on the Weight Watchers program.

"In 2013, consumers spent approximately $5 billion on Weight Watchers branded products and services, including meetings conducted by the Company and its franchisees, Internet subscription products sold by WeightWatchers.com, products sold at meetings, licensed products sold in retail channels and magazine subscriptions and other publications. With five decades of weight management experience, expertise and know-how, Weight Watchers has been established as one of the most recognized and trusted brand names among weight-conscious consumers."-- http://www.weightwatchersinternational.com/phoenix.zhtml?c=130178&p=irol-IRHome

The kind of growth Weight Watchers experienced and has sustained is the result of well thought out and executed systems. It never would have grown to the level it has without well thought out and implemented systems. Making the choice to think through and start implementing systems in your business will help you run more efficiently and profitably and will be some of the best work you have ever done on your business.

Before we get into more detail about how to build the systems for your business, let's talk about the third phase of business.

3. **Maturity (Third Phase)**

The third phase of the business is Maturity. This is the stage of growth that is exemplified by the best businesses in the world. The important thing to remember is that these businesses didn't end up as mature companies. They started out that way. The original owners planned the business before it began. The owners saw their job as working *on* the business instead of working *in* it.

Look at great companies like Microsoft, Google, Apple, Starbucks, and IBM. These owners had a model in their minds of a business that was already working. They had vision. They saw and see the business fulfilling the needs of a specific group of customers in an innovative way.

These are the companies that Jim Collins talks about in his books *Good to Great* and *Built to Last*. The people who started these successful businesses started out with the vision of what it would be like.

Tom Watson, the founder of IBM once said: "IBM is what it is for three special reasons. The first reason is that, at the very beginning, I had a very clear picture of what the company would look like when it was finally done. You might say I had a model in my mind of *what it would look like when the dream—my vision—was in place.* The second reason was that once I had that picture, I then asked myself how a company which looked like that would have to act. I then *created a picture of how IBM would act when it was finally done.* The third reason IBM has been so successful was that once I had a picture of how IBM would look when the dream was in place and how such a company would have to act, I then realized that, **unless we began to act that way from the very beginning, we would never get there.**"--*The E-Myth*, p. 39.

That kind of thinking requires a different mindset. The best explanation of this type of mindset can be found in Robert Kiyosaki's excellent book: *The Cashflow Quadrant*. If you haven't read that book, I strongly encourage you to do so. It will change the way you think about your business and more importantly will teach you the skills you need to move from one quadrant to the other.

I love this statement he makes on page 18: "When it comes to money and the emotions attached to money, we all respond differently. And it's how we respond to these emotions that often determines which quadrant we choose to generate our income from [and what type of business owner we will be]."--*The Cashflow Quadrant*, p. 18.

He also makes this observation: "Changing quadrants is often a change at the core of who you are, how you think, and how you look at the world. The change is easier for some people than for others simply because some people welcome change and others fight it. And changing quadrants is most often a life-changing experience."--*The Cashflow Quadrant*, p. 18.

He also asks this question (which really tells you what phase your business is in or as Kiyosaki puts it the difference between being self-employed and owning a big business): "Can you leave your business for a year or more and return to find it more profitable and running better than when you left it?"-- *The Cashflow Quadrant*, p. 46.

Now, that may not be a goal that is desirable or completely achievable in your business the way it is currently set up. If it is your goal, realize that systems are at the heart of making it happen so you can build your business long-term.

A good way to build systems that Michael Gerber points out in the book is to think of your business as a prototype. In other words, what would you pattern your business like if you knew someone was going to replicate 5,000 of them across the country?

Most people who get into business for themselves have no intention of opening another business (and that is totally fine). It is plenty enough work to have one or two. But, regardless of its size, you want to standardize and create a system that can be operated by individuals with a low level of skill. Discipline, standardization and order are the keys.

The franchise model works. Where 80% of all businesses fail in first 5 years, 96% of all business format franchises succeed. Why? Because the prototype suits the technician because all the entrepreneurial and management factors are established by someone else. You can then be a technician and have the other two aspects of the business figured out for you.

Here are six rules for creating systems that are found in *The E Myth*:

- The system will provide consistent value to and exceed expectations of prospects and clients.
- The system will be operated by people with the lowest possible level of skill.
- The system will stand out as a place of impeccable order.
- The work done in the system will be documented in operations manuals.
- The system will provide a uniformly predictable product and/or service to the customer.
- The system will use a uniform color, logo, dress and facilities code.

Building a system and defining the prototype of what your business should look like is a continuous process, but this book is designed to help you identify, build, and implement systems for your business in specific areas and all of the subsets and systems within these systems.

This book will help you with the framework you need to help create checklists and systems within your business that will help you become a world-class organization.

When you have better systems, your business will be more successful and you will be happier. You'll be able to take more time off. You'll make more money and you will be more profitable. You will be able to work *on* your business and not just *in* your business. And that will make all of the difference.

You have likely heard that you should put systems in your business before you started reading this book. Yet, you may not have done it yet for many reasons. My goal is to give you a step-by-step approach so you can do what must be done.

I really like this Chinese proverb which says:
When you hear something, you will forget it.
When you see something, you will remember it.
But not until you do something, will you understand it.

It is time to move past the hearing and seeing about the importance of systems to actually doing the work necessary to have better systems in your business. My hope is that you will take the principles I've described from *The E-Myth* and in this chapter and *do something* about creating systems within your business so you can raise your skills, abilities, and your business to new heights.

## CHAPTER 2

AVOID SURPRISES AND
BLIND SPOTS IN YOUR BUSINESS

"For a business to survive and thrive, 100 percent of all the systems must be functioning and accountable. For example: An airplane is full of systems. If an airplane takes off and the fuel system fails, there is often a crash. The same things happen in business. It's not the systems that you know about that are the problem—it's the systems you are not aware of that cause you to crash."
—Robert Kiyosaki

Anyone can be hit by something on his or her blind side. A blind side is the side on which one's vision, especially the peripheral vision, is limited or obstructed. When you get hit from behind by something without expecting it (because it is in your blind spot), you or your business can get severely hurt. All entrepreneurs face unexpected challenges that can hit them from the blind side. A blind side is also the side *away* from which you are directing your attention. Most entrepreneurs don't think about the systems of their business that need attention until they find themselves blindsided by an unexpected crisis or challenge. Sometimes these issues can even cripple or destroy a business.

To avoid being hit in your blind side, you need to be aware of what is going on around you and also surround yourself with those who can watch your back and protect you. It can be easy to be so completely focused on one thing that you don't realize what is happening around you. In such a situation, it will only be a matter of time before you get hit hard or possibly even knocked out of business by a savvy competitor who wants to take your market share away from you.

Author John Maxwell defines a blind spot as "an area in the lives of people in which they continually do not see themselves or their situation realistically. This unawareness often causes great damage to those around them."

Here are four questions for you to evaluate as you think about the blind spots of your business. Take time to analyze each question and carefully think about what you need to do to fix your systems in these areas and prevent yourself from getting hit there by an aggressive competitor.

1. Are there areas of your business that you don't want to look at?
Just because you don't like what you see is not a good reason to ignore something. An example from the football field is insightful. For example, it takes a lot of courage for a quarterback to keep getting up to face the big, opposing team play after play (especially if he has to spit out dirt and grass when he gets up from being sacked over and over again). He doesn't want to look at the defensive player who wants to crush him; yet trying to run his offense without thinking about what the defense is doing is a sure recipe for being blindsided and losing ground on the play. The only way a quarterback can successfully move the ball down the field and score is to have a well-thought out plan or strategy and a team who works together to follow it. Staying calm and cool under pressure is the mark of a great quarterback on the field and a great leader in business. On the other hand, responding to the opposition with fear and chaos is a sure recipe for disaster and defeat on the football field and in business.

It isn't easy to look at areas of your business where you see deficiencies or weaknesses. It takes undaunted resolution to keep on going everyday when you've had an unexpected challenge arise or because you've lost a sale to a vicious competitor. It takes courage to look at challenges with your cash flow and develop a plan to pay your bills, cover your other expenses, and manage your cash flow, especially when it isn't where you want it to be and your immediate prospects for generating *any* kind of revenue look dismal.

Your response to every adversity and challenge you face will determine how successful you will be now and in the future. Every business across every industry has to look carefully at their expenses, adjust their sales approach and modify their marketing as circumstances and situations change and as their business grows. You can learn a lot by being observant and seeing what other successful entrepreneurs in other industries are doing in such situations.

Successful businesses across every industry must be vigilant and look for new ways to adapt and shift their systems to avoid being blindsided. In many cases, they find new markets they can enter and old markets they can better master. Businesses that are willing to look at the areas they don't like and do something about those issues are the ones that will consistently improve and grow their revenues and profits. The ones that will go out of business or get passed by are those who ignore the fundamentals and avoid looking at what they don't like and are blissfully ignorant of the looming problems that will lead to their downfall.

As I mentioned, many entrepreneurs don't want to look at problems. It is easier to pretend these issues don't exist, try to do everything on their own without asking for help with their challenges, and hope that by simply ignoring their challenges, that they will all go away. They won't.

If this has been a concern for you in your business, I want to address it here because managing your cash flow is critical to the future success of your business. Every business has faced challenges with cash flow at one time or another. The truth is that when you find yourself in a cash crunch you can do one of three things. These are:

1) Borrow money
2) Go out of business
3) Learn the truth about what works in your business and do it

My goal here is to share some things you can do confront this issue head on so you can overcome it and focus your energy on growing your business instead of becoming overcome by fear, not knowing what to do. When you have well thought out and implemented systems, you can be better prepared for the ups and downs in your business.

There are several reasons for lack of cash flow. Most of them stem from poor sales, ineffective marketing, and the inability to take action and cut out all unnecessary costs. Here are seven ways you can create a better cash flow system for your business now.

1) The best way to create cash flow is to learn to sell better.

Every business can improve their ability to sell effectively. If you aren't closing at least 50-60% of the qualified prospects you work with, you need to learn how to do that and learn how to do it quickly. The skills of selling can be learned and you and every member of your team must pull their weight in selling every hour of every day.

In order to sell better, it is important to think about what is going on in the mind of the prospects to whom you are selling. The reality is that it can be a nerve-racking experience for any prospective client entering your business (or that of a competitor) for the first time. If it is a large purchase, they may be particularly fearful and may not even be sure how to go about finding the perfect item they need to solve the challenge that confronts them. They are many reasons why prospects may feel uncomfortable and why they haven't already taken action to address the problems they are facing.

Your job as an entrepreneur is to help your prospective clients neutralize any anxiety so they feel comfortable around *you* and trust you to the point that they choose to do business with you. Customers today are more savvy than ever before. There are more choices than have ever been available in more places and *they know it*. As a result, you have to be much more aware of what happens to your prospects before they ever come in contact with your business and work harder to pre-sell them on why you are the best choice to provide the product or service they are considering.

2) Put your ideas into action.

This book is about systems and implementation. The reality is that all entrepreneurs know more than they do. Every entrepreneur has great ideas or has observed things that could be done to generate more sales and cash flow. The key is to put these ideas into action.

Authors Steve Chandler and Sam Beckford point out why acting on ideas is so important in their book 9 Lies That Are Holding Your Business Back. They say: "The reality is that our businesses should provide the money to make money. What we really need is ideas put into action. Small businesses that succeed do so because of ideas and action, not because they have been well-funded."

They continue: "As a general rule, whenever a person or a business has an infusion of unearned money (from loans or investments), **they stop thinking.** *They stop asking good questions.*"

Instead, you have to think and then act on the answers to questions like these:
- How can we get prospective clients to share their contact information with us?
- What information can we offer them that would encourage them to share their information with us?
- What can cause prospects to be pre-sold on us?
- How can we get prospects to buy sooner rather than later?
- How do we get clients who purchased from us once back to buy from us again?

Ask hard questions and be willing to act on the answers. One of my mentors, Bill Glazer, says that "the difference between an exceptional income and an average income is implementation." You can do this. Put your ideas into action. Don't delay.

3) Practice mindstorming.

I first learned this practice from author and speaker Brian Tracy. The basic concept is to write down a question and then sit still until you come up with 20 answers to the question you're asking. He told me that the first few answers come pretty easily, but the last five are the most difficult of all to come up with and are often the solutions you are looking for.

Here are seven questions you should take the time to write down twenty answers to in the next seven days. Take one question each day and sit still and write down twenty answers to each question. Then, take one of those ideas, circle it, and implement it immediately.

- How can I attract 100 new prospects to my business in the next 7 days?
- If I only had 48 hours to come up with $5,000, $10,000, or any other amount you need, what would I do?
- What can I do to take care of all of my fixed expenses by the first of each month in my business?
- How can we increase our closing percentage to at least 60% and get it to 75-80% over the next 60 days?
- What can I do to bring 200 qualified prospects to our business in the next 90 days?
- What can I do to make $10,000 (or any other amount) this week in sales? When mindstorming to get breakthroughs, stretch for a higher goal that is at least two to three times higher than your usual revenue.
- What can I do to sell 100, 250, or 500 more of our best and most profitable product offerings this year than we did last year?

Don't postpone or ignore this assignment. If you just take one idea and implement it immediately each day, you will find that you will be working on seven ideas to help you increase your sales and get control of your cash flow within the next week. Most importantly, you will be amazed at the results. You will continue getting great ideas since you have been priming the pump and using the creative power of your own brain to come up with solutions to the challenges you've been facing.

I have gotten a ton of great ideas over the years by taking the time to mindstorm. Your best ideas will come from doing what needs to be done with what you have and by creating opportunities around you.

4) *Look for ways that you can create your own money.*
One way that we did this in our bridal business was by selling ads in our bridal catalog. I started doing this the second year we were in business and it created the money we used to put into our prom marketing as well as paid for the printing and distribution of

our bridal catalogs. I created an advertising program by thinking from the perspective of other wedding businesses in our area and generating leads from online and offline methods to get brides into our store and then shared these leads with other wedding businesses for a price. Later, my wife and I wrote a wedding planning book to help couples with the often overwhelming task of planning their big day. We approached wedding vendors in different categories who were all excited about being a part of this book who paid us to be included in it.

Business leaders across a wide variety of industries have figured out how to create their own money. They have literally figured out how to print money through their ideas. You can do the same.

The biggest danger when you are having trouble with cash flow is to go out and get another loan to cover your fixed expenses. Why? Because when you have an infusion of unearned money that is covering your expenses *you don't need to go out and make that sale. And that is the most dangerous situation you can be in.*

I had times where I didn't know how we were going to make payroll the night before it was due and sometimes the day it was due. We got up and sold what we had to in order to get to the next step. That forced efficiency taught me what works and what doesn't when marketing and selling and that formed the system and processes that I teach today. Those who follow these systems are able to sell at a very high closing percentage and run more efficiently so they grow their business.

5) *Know your reasons.*

Brian Tracy once said, "Reasons are the fuel in the furnace of achievement." Write down your reasons for what you want to gain from your business. Post your reasons where you can see them. Keep your reasons in front of you. If you have individuals in your life that are cutting you down, who don't believe in what you are doing and where you are going, *stop allowing this* in your life. Get around people who believe in you and who are committed to help you accomplish your goals and make your reasons happen. If you need to make a move mentally, do it. If you need to have different associations, start associating with those who are where you want to be and stop spending time with those who aren't where you want to be. Remember, your life is the sum total of the top six people you spend the most time around. If you need to make a move from some of these associations, do it. Don't make excuses about this. As Benjamin Franklin once observed: "He that is good for making excuses is seldom good for anything else."

Your reasons can be the motivating force that allow you to get up when you get knocked down. Limits can be overcome and the best way to get where you want is to write down and know your reasons—what you would do, have, and be if there were no limits. Outlining your reasons is the first step to creating the blueprint of your vision for your future. Not knowing your reasons or not taking the time to outline and visualize your reasons is the quickest way to get discouraged and have the desire to quit when things get hard.

6) ***Cut unnecessary expenses and develop creative ways to cover your fixed expenses every month before they are due.***
A big part of managing your cash flow is to simply reduce the cash that is going out. Carefully examine your fixed expenses. Look for ways you can cover your fixed expenses by the first of each month by selling by billing your clients that way.

Then, consider your variable expenses. For example, look at your utility bills and implement a conservation program. I once visited with a very successful factory owner in China. He told me that he instituted a policy where employees simply turn off the lights in their large facility when they are not using that area. He discovered that this saved him over $1,000 a month in utility bills in a large operation with over 2,500 employees. You may not be able to save on that level, but every little bit sure adds up.

Review your insurance premiums to be sure you are not over-insured. I recently was able to save nearly $1,700 in my yearly insurance premium for one of our businesses with exactly the same coverage simply by shopping around for the best coverage I could get.

Analyze other expenses with your accountant or by yourself to determine what needs to go. I cut back over $18,000 in expenses in one area of our business last year by simply reorganizing and cutting back something that wasn't absolutely essential.

7) ***Plan ahead and time your payments carefully.***
Without exception, planning ahead is the most crucial aspect of cash flow management. Develop a game plan that will work best for you based on the expenses and sales you have had over the past six months and year. Review all of your vendor bills to ensure that you are taking advantage of any discounts. Delay all non-discounted bills as long as possible. If you are having trouble making payments, contact and work out a payment plan with your vendors. Keeping them in the dark is not a good idea. They will appreciate your honesty and will work with you if you keep your word and make good progress and let them know what you are doing to take care of your balances.

Hiding from creditors will cause them to worry and more aggressively pursue payment from you.

I hope these seven ideas are helpful to you. As I mentioned earlier, face your challenges head on. Do something about them everyday. Simply ignoring them doesn't make them go away. Instead, the problem can be accelerated until the resulting crash is even greater.

Developing a system for better managing your cash flow is just one example of an read of your business that you may have been ignoring. By choosing to focus on better system implementation, you can be more aware of your situation and make the changes necessary to get back on track.

2. Are there markets you aren't paying attention to?

Just because one area of your business has been profitable in the past, doesn't mean that it will continue that way, especially when aggressive competitors think there is money to be made. Consider this frightening statement by Jeff Bezos, the founder of Amazon.com, who once said: "Your margin is my opportunity." There are aggressive competitors you can't ignore or you will be beat by them.

I've learned this lesson the hard way. I once took a market niche area that we were well known for and that was profitable for granted. Shortly thereafter, I saw an aggressive competitor promoting this specialty niche and I realized that we were losing a lot of sales to them. While I had been taking that market niche for granted, this competitor had grown much more aggressive in marketing that aspect of *their* business. It took a lot of effort to regain ground that had been lost that never should have been lost in the first place. In many cases, when you lose ground in a competitive landscape, it is very likely that you may never regain it again.

When you take any aspect of your business for granted, you are likely opening yourself up to a future crisis. My real problem was that I took this market for granted and forgot to do what I had done in the beginning to attract this market to do business with us. As a result, our prospective customers were going to one of our competitors. If we are honest, I think any entrepreneur is guilty of this mistake at one time or another. My point is this: Don't lose a connection to where you are already good. Build upon your strengths and then look for new opportunities. Don't lose ground in an established niche through neglect on your own part.

3. Are your competitors building better bait so that clients are attracted to do business with them instead of doing business with you? Are you aware of these or will you be blindsided by these down the road?

Several years ago, I had an experience while fishing with my oldest son Mason that taught me an important lesson. When we arrived at our destination to go fishing, we commenced to put worms on the hook of our fishing pole and cast the line into the water. After 10 minutes or so an old fisherman came up and asked us: 'What are you using for bait?' We told him and he said, "None of the fish here will go for that." He then pulled out his tackle box and put his bait on a hook and cast it into the water. Within seconds, he had a bite and reeled in a fish. We asked him what his secret was. He wouldn't tell us what the bait was but said it was a combination of several things that he had tested in that exact spot. After he left, my son and I laughed at the experience, yet I have never forgotten the lesson I learned that day. He had tested several kinds of bait and found out exactly what the fish he was looking for were interested in at that exact spot. Then, he used that bait to nearly immediately catch his fish. There were obviously other fish in the water. He was only concerned with catching the fish he wanted. He also kept his bait a secret so he wouldn't have his competitors (us) copy him and take the fish from his coveted spot.

There is a lot to be learned from this experience. The big lesson is simply this: If you are going trout fishing, you use a different kind of bait than you do if you are going deep-sea fishing. Do you know what kind of bait attracts your prospective clients? Is it a discount offer? Is it a free premium? Is it a choreographed experience they'll never forget that they can't get anywhere else? Is it valuable coupons or offers they can't get from anyone else? Is it a referral program that rewards clients for referring others to your business?

You need to figure out what attracts the prospects in your market niche so they can enter your marketing funnel. Then, you can educate and pre-sell them so they will *want* to do business with you. The bottom line is that if what you are offering is not exciting and doesn't provide prospects with immediate gratification to what they want, it probably isn't appealing enough to get them into your marketing funnel.

This may mean that you have to spend more on the bait to attract the right kinds of prospects to your business. You may have to spend more to maximize your overall value. If you don't, they will probably find more attractive bait at a competing business that is more appealing to them and you will lose the opportunity to sell to them.

One advantage the big box businesses have over smaller businesses is that they have more money to spend on better bait. You don't have to be the richest fisherman, though, to be successful at catching fish as the old fisherman taught my son and I. You just have to know what is most appealing to the type of prospects and clients you are inviting to do business. Then, and only then, will you be able to draw in those who want to do business with you.

4. Are you paying attention to shifting trends in your business?

One big blind spot that can hinder anyone's business is moving with trends in the marketplace. Some businesses have ignored trends that have caused them to lose an advantage or position in the market they once had. Others have shifted with change and have seen their business increase as a result. The marketplace in every industry is shifting and changing. It is no longer the same as it once was. Waiting or deciding to develop a plan at the moment of disaster is really too late. It is much better to develop a response *before* a disaster occurs.

What trends do you see happening in your industry? Do you have a response plan for how you will address a disaster that might happen?

There is a big danger in ignoring trends that can and will likely blindside you later. There are many examples of businesses who ignored trends and where they were moving and as a result their business moved (and they didn't). Here are three examples:

1) Blockbuster and Hollywood Video – it used to be that video stores were on nearly every corner or found within every grocery store. The trend of renting movies has shifted to a new industry player (NetFlix), who saw and acted on a couple of important trends: a) people are busier today and don't want to take the time to go to a video store just to find out that the movie they wanted to watch is no longer available because everyone else has already come in and rented every copy the store had and b) people hated having to pay late fees if they didn't get their videos back in on time. Netflix eliminated both of these problems by allowing people to pick out which video they wanted online and then receive it in the mail the day it came out, or shortly thereafter without the worry of having to pay late fees. Now they offer streaming video of a huge selection of movies and television shows so viewers can watch what want to see immediately without having to wait for a physical copy to arrive at home.

Netflix completely dominated the business by changing the way that they billed for movies—one flat rate per month for as many rentals as you wanted. Blockbuster and Hollywood Video eventually tried to shift to this model too, but in many ways it was too little, too late. Another competitor, Red Box came in and offered more convenient distribution of movies at gas stations and fast food restaurants. What important lesson can you learn from this? There is a danger in waiting too long to act on trends and ignoring complaints that customers in any market segment are looking to have addressed. The same is true about opportunities that could be available with some thought and action.

One important lesson you must think about carefully is how your clients interact with you and how they interact with your competitors. Ask: Do clients have to do more work now to do business with you compared with your competitors? Who is perceived to have the more convenient option? Who seems to cater better to the concerns they have or the solutions they want? Is it possible for a prospect or client to get the same thing (or better) from a competitor for less effort on her part? If so, and you see trends heading in a certain direction, it would be wise to think and act on a solution or strategy that will allow more clients to do business with you (the way they want) instead of find that clients have shifted away from you to one of your competitors (because they feel that they are easier to do business with than you).

2) *Sony and Apple* – It used to be that Sony dominated the music industry. Apple saw the trend with music was heading towards digitized music. They knew that most music listeners didn't want to buy the whole album to get the one or two songs that they liked on it. Apple paid attention to this customer complaint or problem and offered a solution by working out content distribution deals with the record companies. They even created a new platform (iTunes), which could be downloaded for free, and in many cases was available on new computers that were purchased. This software allowed users digitize their existing music libraries from CDs so that they could listen to their music on the go without having to carry around a stack of their favorite CDs everywhere that they went. Then, they offered the opportunity to buy just the one song they wanted on an album instead of the whole thing. Apple dominated the portable music player market. Other competitors tried to catch up (Microsoft and Zune), but they failed because they were too late to the party. This is why it is so important to consider the experience of the customer, what she is looking for, and what's missing as often as possible. Failing to take time to think about where things are heading (and what opportunities are available as a result) can lead to being bypassed by competitors who do.

3) *Amazon's Fire and Apple's iPad* – The jury is still out on this one, but Apple has been quite successful in dominating the e-reader market that Amazon cornered first with their Kindle reader just as they crushed Sony and their Walkman/Discman with

the iPod. Numerous versions of both products have been released. This will continue to be an interesting competitive battle to observe in the months and years to come.

The point I want to make by sharing these three stories is that business today is hypercompetitive and you can't stand still and expect things to remain the same. Blockbuster, Sony, Amazon.com, and even Apple were or are all market leaders, but new, aggressive competitors have come in to meet new customer demands and the needs of a shifting marketplace.

You must do the same thing to succeed in your business. You need to band together with other like-minded entrepreneurs to watch out for one another as a football team. When you have others watching out for you, they can protect your blind side and help you pay attention to trends that could cause you to be blindsided at one time or another. Your blind side may be an area of your business that you aren't particularly comfortable with or very good at. My encouragement to you is to not ignore your blind spots and focus your attention solely on areas of your business where you do have particular strengths.   Then, build and implement systems to make these areas stronger.

In the future, you will be blindsided by an unforeseen problem that wasn't anywhere on your radar screen. Take the time to think and plan your response to potential disasters in your business.

At the end of each chapter on specific systems in Section 2, I have an assessment so you can think about these systems of your business in ways that you may not have thought of before, exposing areas of your business that you may have been ignoring. Be courageous enough to take and act upon what you find from taking these assessments.

Don't ignore potential blind spots of your business. Not paying attention to an area is an almost certain recipe for disaster. Be on the lookout for new opportunities. I'll talk more about a system you can develop in your business to see opportunity in a future chapter.

I love the question Jim Champy poses in his book *Outsmart! How to Do What Your Competitors Can't*. He asks: "Why do some people easily spot opportunities where others see only obstacles, if they see anything? The answer begins with the human penchant for living in a bubble—an airtight cocoon of assumptions, beliefs, or worldviews. The bubble mentality shows itself in a runaway bull market, for example, when speculators who should be thinking about sharply escalating risks are blinded by greed. Convinced that soaring prices will keep going up indefinitely, they keep on buying. And then one day they are blindsided when the bubble bursts."

He continues: "The good thing about business bubbles, however, is that they invite inventive minds to stick pins in them....Bubble bursters come in all cultural shapes and financial sizes, but they share one indispensable trait: They see what others can't, and they act on it by applying solid practices that everyone else agrees are irrelevant to their industry or company. Admittedly, it's a challenge to peer outside the bubble, see problems waiting to be solved, and find solutions in other companies or industries that no one else has thought to apply to your field. But it's not impossible: Open yourself to seeing the bigger picture so you can assess what others are doing that will actually work in your industry and your company." –*Outsmart!*, pp. 40-41.

Here are three ways you can see opportunities better that can help you respond to trends you see:

1) *Become an expert on businesses in your market category.* Study what the good ones are doing. Take notes on what you've seen and learned and share this information with your team.

Stu Taylor said in his book *How to Turn Trends into Fortunes*, "In his autobiography, *Made in America*, [Sam] Walton proudly claims that he visited more retail stores than anyone else ever has. He just as proudly admits that the purpose of those visits was to borrow every good idea, no matter how insignificant, that he observed...Walton analyzed what he had learned and transmitted it to his key executives in Wal-Mart's weekly Saturday morning company meetings. Walton insisted that his employees learn from others, too, and be prepared to share their insights. It's no wonder that Wal-Mart is the number-one retailer in the United States-they've incorporated all the best ideas from all the other top retailers in the country." –pp. 122-123. That is good advice.

2) *Talk to others in a wide variety of industries.* Don't just talk to those in your industry. Seek out great ideas by associating with top businesspeople in other industries. Ask them and learn from them about where things are heading for them. Be a part of a mastermind group or at the very least, set a goal to take one business leader in your community out to lunch once a month where you can share what you've done in your business, but more importantly so that you can learn what they are doing. Have a prepared list of questions you can ask.

3) *Connect the dots.* Look for opportunities that may be hiding in plain sight. Tony Hsieh, the CEO of Zappos.com tells the story about how he met Alfred, who later became the CFO and COO for Zappos.com. He met Alfred because he would come

into his pizza business and order a large pepperoni pizza every night. At first, he thought he just ate a lot of pizza until he came back a few hours later one night to buy another large pepperoni pizza. Instead of asking why, Tony just sold him the pizza. Tony says this in his book *Delivering Happiness*: "I found out several years later that Alfred was taking the pizza upstairs to his roommates, and then selling them off by the slice....We ended up doing the math a few years ago and figured out that, while I made more money from the pizza business than Alfred, he made about ten times more money per hour than me by arbitraging pizza...I didn't know it at the time, but our pizza relationship was the seed that would lead to many million-dollar business opportunities together down the road."—pp. 28-29.

Do you take the time to look for new opportunities that may be hiding in plain sight? Do you connect the dots between what you see and what you do?

Always be on the lookout for new opportunities and surround yourself with those who will watch your back and protect your blind spots. Make the commitment to share what you've learned with others and help them be aware of what may become a blind spot in their business as well. Protect and look out for one another. You will get farther in life and business when you share what is working for you and simultaneously protect your friends from things they may not see coming than you ever could by simply trying to do it all on your own.

CHAPTER 3

FOCUS ON WHAT YOU CAN CONTROL TO PRODUCE RESULTS

"We build our business systems the way we build our cities: over time, without a plan, on top of ruins."—Gene Brown

One of the biggest traps you can fall into as a small business owner is choosing to focus on what happens and external problems in your industry that you don't have a lot of control over. Individually, we don't have a lot of control over what is happening on the stock market or the day-to-day fluctuations in our economy. Instead, do as achievers do—focus on what you want to produce and cause to happen.

Ask yourself: Where is your focus throughout the day?

Do you spend time thinking, talking, and focusing on things you have little to no control over? Or Do you spend time thinking, talking, and focusing on things you can *control*?

Instead of listing and talking about the myriad of things you could focus on that you may not be able to control, spend more time on what you *can* control: If you will take the time to overcome these common mistakes and really take the time to define *why you are unique and different* from your competitors, along with utilizing more effective marketing and sales strategies, you will be able to weather shifts in the economy and successfully compete against your competitors. If you don't, your competitors likely will and you will be defined by default. Look closely at the systems that make up your business and resolve to fix the leaks and weaknesses that may have sprung up or that are exposed. There is a lot of good that can come from fixing these systems while improving your overall sales and profitability as a result.

Here are five things that you *can* control that you can do something about:

1. Productivity

This is everything in your business. The most important areas that you can control are the areas of selling and marketing. In Chapter 1, I discussed making the shift from thinking in terms of skills to systems. Your productivity system will ensure that you are working on the right priorities.

To start off with, I think it is really important to understand what productivity is and what it is not. I think Dan Kennedy's definition of productivity is probably the best one I've seen. He defines productivity this way: "Productivity is the deliberate, strategic, investment of your time, talent, intelligence, energy, resources, and opportunities in a manner calculated to move you measurably closer to meaningful goals."—*No B.S. Time Management for Entrepreneurs*, p. 60.

This is the distinction. To be productive, it has to be moving you towards your goals. If you get a lot done during the day, but it doesn't help you reach your goals, you aren't productive. Passing time in activity doesn't mean that you're closer to accomplishment. If you want to be really productive and move closer to your goals, you have to change the way you look at your time and what you do in each day.

Why aren't you as productive as you know you could be? The problem in large measure lies within you. If you don't clearly define what it is that you want and make sure that every activity you do moves you closer to that goal, you likely don't have enough a big enough or compelling enough reason to be productive. Do you have enough reasons to keep you productive? Or do you allow yourself to get easily distracted from the things that you do that create profit for your business?

What this really means is that you have to control yourself. Most people have never been around someone who is extremely productive. They haven't observed the success habits of those who get more done than others do. The reality is that the most productive individuals are those who have learned to control themselves and what they do day in and day out.

They put themselves in an environment where they can focus and where distractions are eliminated. In many cases, they use their environment to control their behavior. Great writers like David McCullough and Dan Brown have revealed that they work in a secluded environment where there can be no distraction from what they are doing, which in their case is writing. Some writers even have special computers they use to write that do not have a plug in connection for the Internet or wireless connectivity so they can focus on the task at hand.

To help you be more productive, you must learn to eliminate distractions that will prevent you from accomplishing the tasks you need to get done. This may mean working on marketing campaigns or other projects you need to get done out of your business or to start earlier in the morning before anyone else can interrupt you. You have to discipline yourself to unplug the phone, turn off your cell phone, not connect to the Internet, and avoid anything that will distract you from the priority in front of you. Distractions today are incredible. Many are completely consumed by technology and have an automatic tendency to constantly be checking email, text messages, voice mail, Facebook and Twitter updates, phone calls, updates on their favorite web sites, etc.

Even if you are the most productive person on the planet, you will still have productivity issues with those around you who interrupt you or who aren't as focused on the task at hand as they could or should be. You must first learn to control yourself and your environment and then help your team members to do the same.

Everyone has some form of productivity kryptonite—something that interrupts you and prevents you from performing at peak productivity. When you are clear about your priorities, you can and will stay focused on the task at hand. You may need to write down what your rules will be and post them on your wall. We'll talk in an upcoming chapter about specific systems you can put in place to help you be more productive.

Another key productivity area you can focus on is how well you are closing sales. The key is to evaluate both the successful ones and those that didn't happen. Find out the commonalities that are causing the sale to happen and the objections or obstacles to why they aren't. Then, train your team to sell better based on your evaluation. My sales training program and the sales flash cards that I use to train our team were created out of such evaluations. You can't get better at closing if you aren't evaluating why you're not. One of the most important things to focus on and manage is your sales team's performance. Part of this is setting a standard of performance for the job. It is so important to create an expectation and hold sales consultants accountable to reaching their daily goal. As the old saying goes, "If you can't measure it, you can't manage it."

Here are some questions you can use to think through how well your interaction with prospects that come into your marketing funnel or business went. Asking these questions has made a world of difference in improving our closing ratios and will for you as well.

- How long did I work with the prospect? Could I have been more effective?
- Did I deliver the most compelling message about why our business is the best one to buy from that I could? How could I have done this better?
- Did the prospect trust me? Did she feel comfortable enough to tell me what she really thought of the products or services she was considering?
- Would I have bought what I was selling from myself?
- What did the prospect do at the end of our time together? Did I create urgency for him or her to buy now, rather than later?
- If the prospect bought from me, could I have sold her anything else that she needed? What upsells exist in the future?
- What do I think this prospect would say about me, our business, and the time we spent together?

Then, as you evaluate these questions (or your own) give your consultants feedback that helps them improve, especially if they didn't close the sale. I have had our sales consultants fill out a form each day that is titled "What I could have done to make the sale..." This helps me know what we should train on and gives me the chance to offer specific coaching and feedback to help them get better at selling, especially if I wasn't there to help them evaluate how well they did or help them close the sale. Your end goal should always be to help them improve and be the kind of leader they want to follow because they see you succeeding at selling.

The last productivity area I will mention here is your marketing focus. Here are two questions to ask yourself as you think about your marketing focus:

1. Which of my marketing or sales efforts brought in the bulk of my sales? What total percentage of my business comes from this particular effort now?
2. Do I test various aspects of my marketing and selling activities to make sure they're producing the best and most profitable results?

If a marketing approach isn't working, stop doing it and look for productive ones that will bring in prospects. You have to inspect what you expect. Always be looking for ways to get more back for what you spend. Remember, efficiency is doing things right. Effectiveness is doing the right things. Sales and marketing are productivity areas that you should always be focused on.

2. Customer Satisfaction

With all of this talk about what you should be focusing on, sometimes it is easy to forget that the most important thing you do is focus on the experience that prospects coming to your web site or interacting with your employees are having in your business. Remember, nothing good comes out of trying to think or do too many things at once.

Steve Chandler in his book *100 Ways to Motivate People* makes this observation:
"It's important that I don't race around thinking that I've got too much to do. Because I don't have too much to do. The truth is, there is only one thing to do, and that is the one thing I have chosen to do right now."

He adds:
"Doing more than one thing at a time produces fear, adrenaline, and anxiety in the human system and people pick up on that. People are not drawn to that. They keep away from that."

Think about this in context with the prospects coming into your business. The only way you can create a great experience is to focus on the prospect in front of you, not the mountains of work you have waiting for you in your office. Focus on the prospect in front of you. Isn't she the only thing that really matters at the moment you or someone on your team is working with her?

Most of the time when you lose a sale, it is because you are not *really* focusing on the prospect or the client.
Here are three questions to focus on in this area:
1) What are prospects or clients saying about your business?
2) Are they talking about their great experiences at your business?
3) How can you encourage that better?

3. Profitability

One of the biggest mistakes businesses can make during challenging times is to focus more on sales than on profits. This may be a quick short-term solution to cash flow shortages, but long-term it can dramatically affect your long-term staying power in business. You control what you spend in your business and in large degree what you sell. Carefully analyze your P&L statements to help you make decisions about where you can cut back and how you can increase your profitability in future months. Then, focus on selling more of what has been most profitable for you.

Here are three questions to ask yourself as you focus on your profitability:

- What are our most profitable products and services? Which is the most profitable?
- Are we focusing on selling these products or services over other products? How can I sell more of that?
- What are the things that contribute most to our bottom line?

4. Quality of Experience the Your Prospects and Clients Have in Your Business

The goal to delight each of the prospective clients who enter your marketing funnel and begin their experience with you is a noble and a challenging goal. It is something everyone can strive for. It is a choice to be better at going beyond just aiming to satisfy your customers. The first six words of the business classic *Good to Great* state, "The enemy of great is good." Never be satisfied with just *good* customer service. Strive to be *exceptional* throughout your entire interaction with your prospects and clients.

In the end, if you only do what average businesses do, you'll never be better than they are. You have to aim higher. Systems will help every prospect and client leave your business feeling better than when they entered. Give responsive service and personalized advice, be seen as a trusted advisor for your clients, and to be known in your market area as the business that delivers results.

Here are some questions to focus on as you consider the experience your customers are having at your business:

- How does you customer service measure up? Does it beat the pants off your competitors? As the old saying goes: "When there is not much difference between your product and that of your competitors, there had better be a big difference in the way you deal with your customers."
- Do you delight and dazzle those coming into your business, or are they disappointed and discouraged when they leave or when they come to you with legitimate concerns and problems?
- How are your clients treated when they deal with you?
- Where do you rate in the marketplace in terms of quality?

5. Innovation

When you consider any type of innovation, consider the Law of Three. This means that in order to be innovative, you need to be better in at least three areas from any of your competitors and have at least one very compelling reason why you are clearly the best choice. For example, 7-Eleven or Walgreen's main competitive advantage is convenience. They build locations that are close to you so you don't have to drive very far to get medicine or basic needs items. Domino's and McDonald's have built their businesses around the competitive advantage of speed. Domino's became popular by offering free pizzas in 30 minutes or they were free. To sustain and increase growth over time, you must innovate or you will be left behind by those who do.

Here are some questions for you to consider as you focus on being more innovative in your market niche:

- Ask: What is your competitive advantage in your area of specialty? What makes you better? Are there things that you could change to be even better?
- In what ways are you superior to your competition?
- In what way does your business excel? You can't say you give quality and service because everyone says that. When everyone says something, it doesn't mean very much at all. An important part of concentrating on what you do best is to specialize. The natural tendency is to generalize and try to be good at everything. Unfortunately, what happens is that you end up being good at nothing.
- Ask yourself: What products or services do I offer today? What will it be tomorrow the way things are going? What could it be? What should it be? Stay on top of what is going on in the marketplace – ask yourself – What is selling and why?

Ralph Waldo Emerson once said: "Shallow people believe in luck. Wise and strong people believe in cause and effect." Focus on the causes that will create the effects you want. You are in control. You determine what happens. Work on the areas that you can control. Focus on the critical success factors that will lead to the results you desire and you will be successful even in uncertain and complicated times.

## CHAPTER 4

USE SYSTEMS TO TRANSFORM AND TURNAROUND YOUR BUSINESS

"All wealth is based upon systems."—*Dan Kennedy*

Your business is constantly changing. Competitors are becoming more aggressive about how they market and sell to your prospects. Your cost of goods and the expense of running your business are increasing. To succeed in today's competitive marketplace, you must get better at marketing and selling and have efficient systems that ensure that what is sold delivers on its promise. You must get better at lowering costs and increasing revenues. In this chapter, I want to discuss how you can use systems to help you succeed as you deal with the challenges in your business. I hope you will use these ten strategies to transform or turnaround your business with systems.

You'll notice that each system strategy I'll share here is designed to get you thinking differently about your business and to shift the perceptions your prospects and clients have about you as well.

1.   Use systems to turn what you do into something extraordinary.

To begin, I have a homework assignment for you. As you are going through this chapter and this book, I want you to keep a notebook near you at all times (or make notes on your cell phone or tablet). Whatever you use, refer back to it often so you can jot down and implement the best ideas you're learning. As you think about what I will share with you here, split your notebook (or the file you've created on your desktop) into the following categories:

- Implementation list – This is what you are going to work on and do. The first and last page of my notebook contains my implementation list.

- Advertising that works - When watching TV, perusing industry publications, or listening to advertising of any kind (regardless of the industry it is), jot down the words you hear that cause you to feel persuaded (pay attention to how you *feel* and what you *think*)
- Headlines that work - Take note of the headlines used by successful print ads you see
- Powerful stories that move you and that work - When you hear a story that moves or inspires you, take note of where you heard it and the names involved. Collect great stories from clients and team members that can help you inspire the prospects and clients you work with.
- Study the headlines and ad copy that sells products or services to your target market.
- Make a list of businesses to study and pay attention to
- Follow what they are doing (what direction they're moving in)
    - Use Google Alerts to track what they are doing
    - Study qualities of the leaders of these businesses
    - Force yourself to pay attention to industries that you would not normally pay attention to and learn from others
- List of ideas of things you could do for others
- Quotes, pictures, or ideas that inspire you

Ok, now that you've got your notebook organized, let's address the strategy I mentioned. Specifically, how do you use systems to turn something ordinary into something extraordinary? To do this, you must move up what Sally Hogshead calls the "fascination scale" so that prospects and clients in your market niche are attracted to you and what you do. In other words, it doesn't matter if you are the best business in the world if nobody knows.

Here are three assignments for you:

1) List all of the things that prospects or clients might perceive to be ordinary about your business by dividing a page into two sides. Put all of the ordinary things on one side and then write ideas on the right side of the page about how you can romance these ordinary things up and make them more fascinating. This exercise can give you specific ways to shift the perceptions clients have about your business so you can be more fascinating and attractive to do business with.

2) List all of the specific ways why you are different and better than your competitors. Then, gather testimonials from your clients that show how these claims are true.

3) Focus on a key, core message that you can use to identify why you are the best. Craft a story that will help you communicate this message faster and in a way that prospects and clients can share with others they know.

The goal of these assignments is to help you move up the fascination scale in the mind of your prospects and clients by articulating a point of difference in a way that is meaningful for her. What are you doing to increase your fascination so those who need your products or services are compelled to do business with you?

Here are some questions for you to consider:
- Does your business brand provoke a strong and immediate emotional reaction? If you aren't generating a negative reaction from someone you're probably not fascinating *anyone*. What reactions do prospects and clients have when they hear about your business?
- Are your clients actively promoting you to their friends and family as the best place to get what you offer?
  - Can you create ambassadors?
  - How will you reward them, inspire them, and support their communication with you?
  - Do you have customers posting videos of their experience with you and your product? How can you encourage this?
- Does your business incite conversation amongst your competitors and other prospects in your market niche? How are you changing the game so that you are the most fascinating and trusted business in your market niche?

- Does your business force your competitors to realign themselves around you? Do they have to change their business to stay in business?

These questions will help you begin the process of setting up systems in your business that will help you transform from an ordinary experience to an extraordinary one. You will never be in a category of one until you figure this out for you and your business.

2. Defy industry norms. Don't let others tell you how to run your business.

Here are ten common statements that entrepreneurs will say on occasion that limit them to norms within their own industry. These thoughts and beliefs have consequences. What you think and believe determines what you will have. Consider these harsh questions as you consider these statements: Are these the statements of wealthy or broke individuals? Are these the statements of individuals who have high or low profits?

1) "I can't go above the industry standard of pricing my products."
2) "My clients are price shoppers. I have to be lower than other businesses out there or no one will buy from me."
3) "In this economy, everyone is looking for a bargain and if I don't give it to them, they won't buy from me."
4) "I know I should sell items that help me make a higher profit, but I have to have to sell this product that I barely break even on..."
5) "I'll never be able to..."
6) "That may work for you, but it will never work for me because..."
7) "How am I ever going to pay for all of these bills?"
8) "I can't pay myself anything..."
9) "Everything is so expensive..."
10) "I would do _____ if I could just afford _____."

Now, you may think it is kind of harsh for me to point out some of these thoughts and word patterns associated with being broke and having low profits in business. The truth is that you have heard friends of yours make these statements or perhaps even heard yourself say some of these things. I caught myself saying some of these things earlier in my own life before I truly understood that thoughts are powerful things and have consequences. All of our thoughts (whether positive or negative) lead to beliefs and action or inaction.

Here is a question for you to carefully consider: Are you being held captive by thoughts that limit your productivity and profitability? If so, you need to break free from these thoughts by replacing them with new thoughts that can help you change your behaviors and actions.

Just because a lot of people think or say something in an industry doesn't make it right or true. I really like what Kevin Myers says about why you should challenge popular thinking. He says: "The problem with popular thinking is that it doesn't require you to think at all."

John Maxwell makes this observation about popular thinking: "Unfortunately, many people try to live life the easy way. They don't want to do the hard work of thinking or pay the price of success. It's easier to do what other people do and hope that *they* thought it out."--*Thinking for a Change*, p. 195.

To be wildly successful in any business, you have to challenge and defy industry norms. There are countless stories of successful businesses that have been created that have simply tweaked something that others in their same industry accepted and went about doing as an industry norm. These tweaks or defiance of what everybody was "supposed to do" allowed them to gain a competitive advantage and create a much more successful business.

The stock market is a great example of this. By the time so-called "experts" publish their stock picks, most investors who are really going to make money on that stock have already done so. When the general public hears about a "hot tip," and blindly follow a trend, they are often not doing their own thinking.

I really like what John Maxwell says about this in his book *Thinking for a Change*. He says:
"Many people look for safety and security in popular thinking. They figure that if a lot of people are doing something, then it must be right. It must be a good idea. If most people accept it, then it probably represents fairness, equality, compassion, and sensitivity, right? Not necessarily.

"Popular thinking said the earth was the center of the universe, yet Copernicus studied the stars and planets and proved mathematically that the earth and other planets in our solar system revolved around the sun. Popular thinking said surgery didn't require clean instruments, yet Joseph

Lister studied the high death rates in hospitals and introduced antiseptic practices that immediately saved lives. Popular thinking said that women shouldn't have the right to vote, yet people like Emmeline Pankhurst and Susan B. Anthony fought for and won that right. Popular thinking put the Nazis into power in Germany, yet Hitler's regime murdered millions and nearly destroyed Europe. We must always remember that there is a huge difference between acceptance and intelligence. People may say that there's safety in numbers, but that's not always true.

"Sometimes it's painfully obvious that popular thinking isn't good and right. Other times it's less evident. For example, consider the staggering number of people in the United States who have run up large amounts of debt on their credit cards. Anyone who is financially astute will tell you that's a bad idea. Yet millions follow right along with the popular thinking of buy now, pay later. And so they pay, and pay, and pay. Many promises of popular thinking ring hollow. Don't let them fool you."–*Thinking for a Change*, pp 196-197.

What industry norms or popular thinking have you allowed to sway your beliefs about your business?

How has this limited you?

Are you taking time to think and question the acceptance of popular thinking or ideas you hear from others that may be taking you away from where you really want to be in your business?

Donald M. Nelson, former president of the Society of Independent Motion Picture Producers made this great statement:
"We must discard the idea that past routine, past ways of doing things, are probably the best ways. On the contrary, we must assume that there is probably a better way to do almost everything. We must stop assuming that a thing which has never been done before probably cannot be done at all."

The real reason you must question what you have been told about profits and pricing in this business is because as John Maxwell says: "Popular thinking brings mediocre results. Here is popular thinking in a nutshell: Popular = Normal = Average. It's the least of the best and the best of the least. We limit our success when we adopt popular thinking. It represents putting the least energy to just get by. You must reject common thinking if you want to accomplish uncommon results."--*Thinking for a Change*, p. 199.

You didn't get into your business just to be average. You started your business to accomplish great things and make a difference for yourself, your family and your clients. Don't get so caught up in the ways things have always been done that you can't ask questions and look for new ways to do your work. Don't get caught up in the deceptive comfort of following the crowd.

Here are some examples of ways I went against the flow and resisted popular thinking in our first business:

- When we opened our bridal store, we opened to sell off the rack. Most bridal retailers in the industry with the exception of the big box retailers had samples and allowed brides the opportunity to place an order off of these sample gowns. Brides would then have to wait for up to sixteen weeks for the ordered items to arrive. We invested in inventory and sold it right off the rack so clients could enjoy having their wedding dress right away. We asked questions of those who were already selling dresses off the rack successfully and began our business this way.

- Popular thinking said you can only charge the bride 50% at the time of order and 50% when the dress comes in. I rejected that thinking after one bride wouldn't call us back to pay for or pick up her dress when her dress came in. I immediately changed our policy to having all special orders require a 100 percent up front payment. This immensely helped our cash flow and brides paid that way because we required it. It still amazes me that this popular belief is still so prevalent in the bridal industry.

- Popular thinking says you have to carry the popular lines in the bridal magazines. I helped develop a buying group so that we could go directly to the largest factories in China and manufacture our own line of dresses that we wouldn't have to worry about getting shopped on.

- Brides asked us to give out cards with style numbers and prices at the end of their visit. I was determined to learn how to persuade the bride to buy on her first visit and created my own sales methodology and program that many around the country also use to great success.

- When I got into business, popular thinking said that you could only get a certain margin on what we sold. I rejected that thinking and looked for and created ways to create more profit for our business (and helped many bridal stores across the country to do so as well).

- Many wedding related businesses brought in business cards and asked us to display them. Instead of doing that, I created an advertising program where we allowed these businesses to promote themselves to our clients in exchange for an advertising fee. That program brought in thousands of dollars each year, which paid for the bulk of our advertising throughout the year.

I could list a lot more, but I just wanted to share a brief list so you can see that going against popular thinking will help your business be more successful. Here is a question and an assignment that you should think about often: Am I consciously rejecting the limitations of common thinking in order to accomplish uncommon results in my business?

What industry norms have you defied up to this point in your business? Are there any other norms that you could change or tweak these to give you a competitive advantage?

Accomplishments where you successfully go against the flow can do great things for your self-image and confidence. Get around others who think differently and stretch your mind. I am a part of several mastermind groups that help me stretch my thinking and go against popular thinking. As a result, I am able to get more done and think differently about my business. I would encourage you to do the same.

3. **Position your business so you dominate a territory, niche, or market square. Then, be sure you market with the purpose of evoking an emotional response.**

First off, you need to look at what market gaps exist or may exist in your market area. Look for areas where you've already have paying customers tell you: "I'm sure glad you offer that. No one else I went to did or could do what you just did..." or something to that effect. Ask: What unmet needs or desires do your prospects have? How could you meet those? How could this set you apart from your competitors?

Once you identify these niches, you need to evoke emotion as you market them. Without emotion, your message will fall on deaf ears. P.T. Barnum once wrote: "The great secret of success in anything is to get a hearing. Half the object is gained when the audience is assembled."

What are you doing to create excitement and build drama for your prospects and clients through your pre-sales efforts?

Are you persuading them that you are worth the time and effort to see so you can position your competitors in a way that highlights your best differentiating point and that is most favorable to you?

If not, you are missing the entire essence of the magic of marketing. Let me give you an example of a French entrepreneur and showman named Monsieur Mangin who sold pencils that Barnum learned this principle from. Listen to how this marketer created an experience that got attention and got people emotionally involved.

"Mangin would appear on a street corner dressed in unusual royal garb, riding a team of large horses. He would park, open his wagon with a great deal of pomp and circumstance, and slowly begin to put on a theatrical performance. A crowd would always form, wondering what was happening. The French entrepreneur would then demonstrate his pencils, involve members of the audience, and end by selling his product to nearly everyone present.

"Years later, Barnum met Mangin and complimented him on '...your manner of attracting the public. Your costume is elegant, your chariot is superb, and your valet and music are sure to draw.'

'Aha! You never saw better pencils,' Mangin replied. 'You know I could never maintain my reputation if I sold poor pencils. But, my miserable would-be imitators do not know our grand secret. First, attract the public by din and tinsel, by brilliant sky rockets and Bengola lights, then give them as much as possible for their money.'"—Joe Vitale, *There's a Customer Born Every Minute*, p. 45.

What are you doing to stand out and be unique to grab attention? Focus on finding what your prospects and clients are looking for and then help them to find it.

4. **Improve and change your processes so they consistently deliver results.**

As an assignment, evaluate the interaction you have with prospects in the following six areas:
•   The Pre-Sale

- Your Interaction with the Prospect and How You Schedule Appointments
- Your Approach
- The Presentation of Your Product or Service
- The Offer and Your Close (Do members of your sales team know at least five ways to ask for the sale? This is necessary because most prospects today buy the third or fourth time they are asked)
- Follow Up Sequences to Get Prospects Back into Your Marketing Funnel

Ask yourself the following questions about each area:
- Are you effectively communicating your difference?
- Where are you dropping the ball?
- Are you getting the results you really want? If not, where are you dropping the ball?

Here are several processes that you could improve in your business through systems:
- How is the phone answered?
- How are orders processed?
- What do prospects experience during the first 30 seconds after they visit you on your web site, interact with you online, on the phone, or in person?
- What do prospects experience on their first visit to your business (or their first interaction with you online)?
- How can you better target prospects who don't buy from you on the first visit? What bait will entice prospects to come back in?

Pay attention to your processes. Create fun experiences by connecting the experience of shopping with you to something that will get your clients and their friends talking about you. As an example, I often see comments posted by clients who have had an amazing experience shopping online at Zappos.com or at an Apple store. They are talking about that experience because it amazed them. You should engineer your experiences so that this happens for you as well. Once you figure out what works best, duplicate it as often as you can without diluting the experience the prospect or client will have.

The most successful business owners I know are constantly tweaking their processes and systems to improve their customer experience and to plug leaks that may appear as a result of holes in their processes. You should do the same.

5. Raise your price and your margin on products for which you have exclusivity and a truly unique position.

This is pretty self-explanatory. Look at what is selling best in your business. Could you offer even more value and raise your price accordingly? When you deliver great value, your clients will pay for it at a higher price if it continues to deliver the results they want. Figure out the most profitable area of your business. What could you do to enhance your value and the experience you provide?

6. Put systems in place in your business that can function perfectly if you're not there.

As I've mentioned, a system is a way of doing things to produce a marketing and a sales result in your business. The system is the solution to get the results you want. Remember, when you refine operations to improve how the systems in your business work, you are working *on* your business, not just *in* it.

Here are specific areas of systems you should have in your business and some questions to think about for each one. We'll talk more about the specifics of these and other systems in Part 2 of this book:
1. Strategic Objective Systems (your goals: how you set them and how you will reward yourself for their accomplishment) – I'll discuss this system in Chapter 6.
   * Do you and every member of your team know your minimum, target, and optimal goals for each area of your business?
2. Advertising and Marketing Systems – I'll discuss these systems in Chapters 7 and 8.
   * Do you have a marketing flow chart that shows what should happen to each prospect coming into your business? It is best to have both inbound and outbound marketing systems.
   * Do you have a marketing calendar for next year in place and are you following it?

3. Sales Systems – I'll discuss these systems in Chapter 9.
   - Are you training and rehearsing the information that will help you sell more now?
   - Do you have systems in place to help you review performance and replace those who aren't selling?
4. Organizational and Internal Business Process Systems – I'll discuss these systems in Chapters 10 and 11.
   - When a prospect or client buys something, do you have an organized system that shows how the paper and the product flow through your business?
5. Management and Leadership Systems – I'll discuss these systems in Chapters 13 and 14.
   - Do you have systems in place to help you develop leaders around you?
6. People (Employee) Systems and Training Systems – I'll discuss these systems in Chapter 12.
   - Do you have mandatory training meetings that effectively train each employee how to implement the systems you've put into place in your business?
   - What are you doing to ensure that these meetings are effective and help increase performance?
7. Financial and Inventory Systems – I'll discuss these systems in Chapter 15.
   - Do you have systems in place to monitor what is selling on a weekly or monthly basis?
   - Are you using this information to make sure your future product offerings are informed, profitable, and sellable?
8. Customer Service Systems – I'll discuss these systems in Chapter 11.
   - Do you have a written plan for any and all customer service situations that come up that your team members can refer to in case you aren't available?
9. Productivity Systems – I'll discuss these systems in Chapter 16.
   - Do you measure what you are doing on a daily and weekly basis to ensure that you are being as effective as you could with your time?
10. Creativity and Business Renewal Systems – I'll discuss these systems in Chapters 17 and 18.
    - Are you planning and actually taking breaks that help you rejuvenate yourself?

7. **Little hinges open big doors. Look for the small and big changes that can yield powerful dividends in your business.**

Little hinges can open big doors. For example, one question or a series of questions and sales sequences can be the difference between persuading a prospect to buy from you and become your client and her deciding to wait and buy from you later. Always be asking questions that can help you improve. Be willing to ask the questions others won't.

Luke Williams talks about three questions in his book *Disrupt: Think the Unthinkable to Spark Transformation in Your Business* that every business owner should ask as they think about creating their own disruptive hypothesis to shake things up in their market area. According to him, these are:

1. *What do you want to disrupt?*

To successfully think about this question, it is a good idea to 'hover above your world' and think about the realities that face prospects today and how you could change these. Williams says: "One of the major hurdles facing today's executives and business leaders is how to meaningfully differentiate themselves from everyone else who's operating in the same space. To do that requires that you define the situation in the industry, segment, or category that you want to challenge. And by 'situation,' I mean the broad view from 10,000 feet.

Here's what this might look like:
- "This is an area in which everyone seems to be stuck in the same predicament and nothing has changed in a very long time.
- "This is an area where profit performance is average—it really should be more successful than it is.
- "This is a category where growth is slow and everything seems the same.

Williams continues:
"Once you have a situation to focus on, describe it in one sentence: 'How can we disrupt the competitive landscape of [*insert your situation*] by delivering an unexpected solution?' –pp. 20-21.

The goal here is to start thinking in terms of specific problems that your prospects and clients have that you can come up with a way to solve. When you can solve the problem that a lot of people have, you have a much more persuasive marketing message and you stand out head and shoulders above your competition.

As an example, when Netflix originally began, they asked the question: What would it be like if you didn't have to pay late fees when renting movies? This question caused them to figure out a solution to a problem that was a big hassle for many individuals. Netflix built a very big business out of offering their solution in a way that sidestepped a problem that many people had with an unexpected solution.

Are you thinking hard enough about the problems prospects and clients are facing and how you can solve them?

2. *What are the clichés?*

Williams says:
"Now that you've defined your situation, the next step is to identify the assumptions that seem to influence the way insiders (and often outsiders) think about an industry, segment, or category. In other words, what are the clichés—the widespread, hackneyed beliefs that govern the way people think about and do business in a particular space. If you pay attention, you'll notice that clichés are everywhere."

The best example of a business that went against clichés in their marketing was that of Nintendo in its battle with Sony with its Playstation and Microsoft with its Xbox. Williams says: "Both were driven by several clichés. First, that the world is split into 'gamers' and 'nongamers.' Second, that gamers mostly care about faster chips and more realistic graphics. Third, game consoles are expensive. And, fourth, that people play video games sitting down, barely moving anything but their fingers.

"Then, along comes Nintendo, a distant third player, which turned the gaming industry's clichés on their head. Nintendo's Wii is relatively cheap, has no hard drive, no DVD, has weak connectivity, and comparatively low processor speed. But, within weeks of its launch, Wii became a hit with consumers, thanks to its innovative motion controller, which integrates players' movements directly into the game.

"With the Wii, you can play tennis, baseball, golf, and even bowling. You can sword fight and box, too. Nintendo opened up the console world to a huge demographic of people who never considered themselves gamers." –p. 23.

Today, the battle between Microsoft and Nintendo continues with Kinect, X-Box One and WiiU. The story has yet to be written about who will ultimately be victorious, but there is no question that Nintendo has achieved the success it has because it thought about how to remove the clichés in their marketing approach. They also dominated the landscape of the video game consoles through a carefully crafted scarcity strategy that helped propel the desire for these devices into the stratosphere.

My question for you is: How carefully are you dissecting the clichés that your prospects have about your industry? How are you looking to capitalize on your growth by how you market your business to avoid the clichés that prospects and clients are tired of and that no longer work for them?

Your careful analysis of these clichés can give you some opportunities from which to attack with your marketing collateral and showcase your true differences. Take the time to think as a team in your business about the numerous clichés that prospects see when they come into you and your competitors. Your willingness to list and attack these clichés can help you overcome the status quo and rise in importance to the prospects and clients in your market niche.

3. *What are your destructive hypothesis?*

Williams says:
"Now that you have a list of the clichés that are influencing the business situation you're focused on, your next goal is to start provoking the status quo. To do that, you'll take those clichés and twist them like a Rubik's cube and look at them from the inside out, upside down, backward, and forward. You're trying to find a way to rearrange the pieces, which in turn will provoke a different way of looking at the situation. Specifically, you're looking for something (or things) that you could scale up or scale down, move in the opposite direction, or completely do without." –p. 27.

In other words, by looking at things in a new way (and through the eyes of your prospect), you can resist what most of your competitors are already doing and truly break out. Most entrepreneurs don't do this because the resistance is too great and they aren't willing to do the work necessary to break free from the self-imposed limitations that they put on themselves.

Williams suggests that you can take action and create your 'What if?" hypothesis through three methods:

1) *Inversion* – prospects usually receive some information from your web site or from their sales rep after an appointment; inverting this idea would involve giving a gift to the prospect when she shows up on your web site or in your business and completely changing the dynamics of the relationship and the expectations that might go with it.

   One way to look at inversion is to ask: *Is there something that is successful and big that could be successful and small or vice versa?*

   You can better visualize this and how it will apply for your business if you think about it with other industries. Think about how White Castle and Burger King on both extremes of size of hamburgers or how compact cars are now overtaking SUVs in overall sales.

   A great question you should ask is: *Are there any attributes of your business that you could minimize in your prospect's mind?*

   Or: *Are there any attributes of your business that you could maximize in the prospect's mind?*

   Could you offer a special bonus to prospects who actually buy the product or service they are considering in advance? Or a bonus if they purchase on their first visit? Or if they purchase a secondary item with the first product or service they are considering?

   Inversion can help you look at a common situation from a completely different perspective and often will give you answers to how you can position and market your business in ways that others may not have considered or thought about.

2) *Denial* – One way to look at denial is to ask: *Is there something that other businesses in my niche don't give to prospects that you could?* For example, the first time advantage incentive we offered at our bridal store was an answer to this question. We knew that if a prospect didn't buy on her first visit, the likelihood that she would return with all of the competition we have would be much less. So, we decided to factor a bonus into the price of what we sold so that there would be an added incentive for her to act on her first visit to our store. Then, we structured the entire marketing and sales system around this benefit or bonus. Questions like these can transform your business and increase your sales. Another question you could ask: *Is there something that prospects need to have replaced each month? Is there something that your business can replace for them?*

3) *Scale* – this is looking at one thing someone offers and looking to see if you can scale it up or down on one side of the equation or the other.

Good examples of this in other industries include: shifting small TVs to big screen TVs and then scaling them back again on mobile phone devices as well as McDonald's successful campaign of super sizing their meals and changing the process of how they took orders at drive through windows by asking an upsell question. Today, you also see many infomercials offering "double your money back guarantees" to ramp up the stakes with scale.

How can you use scale to let your prospects know that you do more than any of your competitors?

Here are some other examples of "what if" questions that you could answer to help you stand out:
- What would happen if prospects knew there was a specific experience they could have that would help them find their the solution to the problem they are facing easily and without stress?
- What would happen if prospects could be involved in the design and creation of the product they will buy?

- What would happen if prospects didn't have to wait to get what they wanted (they could have immediate gratification and receive it immediately)?
- What would happen if prospects could find products at our business that they couldn't find at any other business around your region, state or country?

Williams offers a really interesting example of El Bulli (a restaurant that was rated the best restaurant in the world a record five times) and how this process allowed them to create a completely different experience than they would have anywhere else. The restaurant closed in 2011 so the head chef could focus on creating a culinary museum experience (which opened in 2014) and because it had become challenging to keep the restaurant profitable. However, the idea is an interesting one. Customers only received a menu when they left that detailed what they had eaten in the 30 courses that were provided. The menu was signed by the chef and it was a five hour experience to eat there. According to several sources, they were only open from April through September and in recent years had been booked solid years in advance and between 800,000 and 2 million people each year requested a table. It cost about 250 euros (close to $320 U.S.) to eat there. You can see from this example that they shifted the way people thought about eating at this restaurant by only giving people a signed customized menu at the end and they offered a thirty course meal when many restaurants only offer three.

The El Bulli restaurant used creativity and the sequence of the questions I just shared with you to create a very unique experience that probably was unsurpassed by anyone who ever had the opportunity to eat there. You should think about how you can shift the perceptions of what your clients expect when they do business with you in a way that is both profitable and unique. By doing this, you can stand out from your competitors. It will also help you get out of your comfort zone and do something unique that clients will never forget.

In challenging times, it is much easier to hold on to what you have than to make changes that can get you back on track. It is easier to cower and hide than it is to face the music and do what needs to be done. Remember, getting out of your comfort zone keeps you on the edge of your fear which can help you channel that energy into growth and excitement that can set you apart from those around you who are content to just remain with the status quo. Look for the little hinges that can open big doors in your business and build systems around them.

8. Focus on the little things that will have the biggest results. Don't get caught up in activities that don't reward you with accomplishment.

To succeed at turning around or transforming any business, you've got to give up your excuses and focus your efforts and priorities only on what really matters.

Most unsuccessful entrepreneurs get caught up in activities that make them feel busy, but in reality are doing little to nothing to help them prosper and succeed. Another way to look at this: It is easier to make an excuse than it is to do what really works. If you want to succeed in your business, you must find a way when others see a wall.

Thomas Carlyle, an English writer and philosopher once said: "The block of granite which was an obstacle in the pathway of the weak, became a stepping-stone in the pathway of the strong."

Tony Robbins once said:
"The truth of the matter is that there's nothing you can't accomplish if
(1) you clearly decide what you're absolutely committed to achieving
(2) you're willing to take massive action
(3) you notice what's working or not, and
(4) you continue to change your approach until you achieve what you want, using whatever life gives you along the way."
This statement really gets to the heart of this principle. You've got to focus on the little things. A decision to focus on the priorities in your business that really matter, that only you can do, may seem like a little decision, but what a difference it makes!

The decision to pay attention to what's working and eliminate what's not could be viewed as a little thing, but it's not! Most importantly, the decision to implement and to take massive action is absolutely critical to turning around or transforming any business.

When Lee Iacocca took over Chrysler he simultaneously began doing multiple things to turnaround the company. He didn't sequentially do one thing and then another thing. He began massive action in numerous areas of the company that needed to be fixed. This all gets to the big question: What little changes can you make at your business that will have a big effect?

As an example, consider the power of a new concept or idea on how someone perceives why they need what you sell (and that you are the only one they can get it from). What is new and unique grabs the attention of the brain, especially when what you are offering to prospects and clients speaks to how you will solve a specific challenge or problem he or she is facing.

Apple is a great example of a company that does this very well. According to Dr. Pradeep: "Apple made an innately strategic decision a long time ago to help the brain do what it loves to do: identify and categorize. Apple focused on consumer ease of use, inherent fear/distrust of complicated and, therefore, intimidating technology, and designed beautiful products and packaging, which in turn gave the Apple brand enhanced meaning and an even stronger consistent, and lasting identity. Apple also strictly controlled distribution, giving their product an identity that was separate from other computer brands. And they adhered to price points above the category norms, imbuing the brand and the products under that umbrella with the aura of desirability." –p. 130.

In other words, Apple positions their products into a category of one with unique packaging, price, and new technology. If you watch any of their product launches, you'll see how they masterfully present their new product releases in this format and most importantly into a category of one (so there is no need to compare) because their product is perceived to be the very best.

Dr. Pradeep continues:
"Context has a huge impact on how the brain processes an experience. Apple understands this, especially in their retail operations. If you shop a store aisle, where everything is piled up or kept in bins, your takeaway is a perception that all is cheap. Implicitly, if it's of value it won't be piled up in the corner. On the other hand, this can also work to some brands' advantage; a bargain retailer deliberately stacks things up to give

you the view that you are getting a deal. For luxury brands, of course, the opposite is the case. When you go to a Rolex store, your watch is displayed in a locked case. And when they bring it to you, they polish it and present it on an elegant padded case. The unspoken but clearly communicated message is that this brand is inherently precious, highly valued, and valuable, and therefore, worth the price. The feeling of desire is actually heightened by this air of exclusivity, reinforcing the individual elements of Rolex's Brand Essence Framework." –pp. 130-131.

Is the way that you are presenting what you sell in your business allowing you to present yourself in the context of being truly unique and in a category of one (as a new idea)? If not, you should carefully think about what it is that you are actually selling.

You must be the one who controls the message about your business. Perception is the reality for your prospects. If you don't believe this is true, go to YouTube.com and type in the name: Joshua Bell and violin experiment. What you will see is a short video that shows nearly 1,000 people walking by him in the corner of a Washington DC Metro station where he played for about 45 minutes. Every few minutes, someone might stop by and listen or toss a dollar into his open case. In that short performance, he made $32, yet he is one of the world's most famous musicians. He was playing on his $3.5 million Stradivarius violin (one of the most rare and expensive violins in existence). Yet, very few of those who walked by had any idea who he was or paid attention to the amazing music he played. The previous night, he played to a sold out concert in Boston where the average seat averaged $100. In other words, because of context, Joshua Bell's performance at the Metro station made him $32 where his performance at Boston's Symphony Hall was worth approximately $220,000.

Create the perceptions you want clients to have about you and your business. There is no excuse for letting someone else brand you for you or being like Bell in the Metro station where prospects are walking by your business and have no idea who you are or why you are so important to them. Be unique. Stand out. Present yourself and your business in a category of one. When you do that, you'll truly stand out and the financial rewards will be much greater to you and your business as well.

9. Implement quickly.

I love this statement from author and business improvement speaker Warren Greshes:

"You have 24 hours to act on a good idea. If you do nothing about a good idea within 24 hours, rest assured, it's dead. Now, I'm not saying you have to do everything about a good idea within 24 hours, but you have to take at least one action step, if for nothing else than to keep the excitement going.

"You know as well as I do that we're most excited about our good ideas when we first get them. The longer we wait to do something about an idea, the less excited we get. In fact, we probably spend more time talking ourselves out of it or letting other people tell us why it's a lousy idea." –*The Best D--- Sales Book Ever, p. 94.*

He continues with his seven-step action plan:
"1. First, make a copy of the page where you wrote down all your goals and make a copy of the three forms where you created action plans for your three most important goals.

2. Take these pages and post them someplace where you can see them every day. If you don't want anyone else to see them, a good place is the inside of your closet door at home....Posting [your goals] up where you can see them every days keeps the goals fresh in your mind and makes them dominant in your thoughts. Napoleon Hill, author of *Think and Grow Rich*, stated, 'We are what we think about all day long,' and 'We move toward our most dominant thoughts.'

3. I believe in posting goals up where anyone can see them because 'you never know.' In fact, if you want to get to your goals even faster, tell everyone you know, even people who you would never expect to be able to help you, because you never know, help can come from some of the most unexpected places.

4. Once you have your plan posted up, it's important to review it on a regular basis. I suggest you review your plan every quarter, if for no other reason than to make sure the goals you set for yourself are still important to you. Let's face it, people change and priorities change. What's important to you today might not be important a year from now. If that should happen, what do you do about the goal? Change it, of course, or get rid of it. Remember, this plan is yours; it can change. It

was written in pen or pencil on a sheet of paper. It wasn't carved into a block of stone with a chisel. It can change.

I think it is important to review your goals much more often than this. It is a good idea to at least look at them weekly and prioritize what you will work on at your business. You can change your goals, but I believe it is best to be solidly committed to the achievement of a few goals than have a lot of ambiguous goals that aren't really your priority or your focus.

5. What do you do if you get to reach your deadline and you haven't yet reached your goal? Kill yourself, of course! No, of course not—just move back the deadline! Remember, it's yours! It can change. Believe me, the goal setting police are not going to bash in your door, grab you by the neck and say, 'Okay pal, you're coming with us.' That's not going to happen....The deadline is there to give you a frame of reference and to give you the incentive to get started. It's not there as a punishment, something to flog yourself with should you not achieve your goal in time.

6. What do you do if you happen to achieve all the goals you set for yourself? Stop right there, your life is now over. No! Set some more goals! Create an action plan for each one. Do the same thing to set the new goals that you did to set these.

7. Here's a guarantee for you: I guarantee that if you shove this plan into a drawer and never look at it again, it will never work." –Warren Greshes, *The Best D--- Sales Book Ever*, pp. 94-96.

I think the key to successful goal setting and their achievement is that you've got to stay hungry. You've got to stay motivated and understand what it is that you really want. Then, and only then will you do what it takes to succeed.

T. Harv Ecker makes this point in his book, *Secrets of the Millionaire Mind*: "During the 2004 Olympic Games, Perdita Felicien, a Canadian and the reigning world champion in the hundred meter hurdles, was heavily favored to win the gold medal. In the final race, she hit the first hurdle and fell hard. She wasn't able to complete the race. Extremely upset, she had tears in her eyes as she lay there in bewilderment. She had prepared for this moment six hours a day, every day of the week, for the past four years. The next morning, I saw her news conference. I wish I had taped it. It was amazing to listen to her perspective. She said something to the effect of 'I don't know why it happened but it did, and I'm going to use it. I'm going to focus even more and work even harder for the next four years. Who knows what my path would have been had I won? Maybe it would have dulled my desire. I don't know, but I do know that now I'm hungrier than ever. I'll be back even stronger." –p. 99.

That attitude is impressive. It is what it takes to do the work necessary to put systems into any sized business. To be and stay successful, you've got to stay hungry. You've got to know what you want and what you will do to make it happen. This means massive action and implementation. Garrison Wynn makes this statement in his book *The Real Truth About Success*:

"Willingness to use an advantage is just as important as discovering it. Cross that line from knowledge to implementation, and be willing to act! Not everybody is. Many need to be coaxed into utilizing their distinctive edge to their advantage. Most people tend to draw a line in the sand or create a boundary they're unwilling (or afraid) to cross. Many of these are not based on ethical or legal bounds; they're rooted in personal fears of how others will perceive us. Can you step back and look beyond the conventional business culture? Are you willing to take a chance? Can you create a plan for yourself? Can you adapt your beliefs in order to utilize your advantage?

"Creating that willingness to actually utilize your edge is how you achieve greater success. The funny thing about willingness is that it's like opening a door. If you just crack it a little, you'll find it's relatively easy to move forward from there. But you first have to turn the knob and push. If you start with a little willingness to change or improve in certain areas, you'll soon find it easier to tackle other areas of your life or business relationships. But if you aren't willing to look at all or if you try to avoid delving into some particular area, you'll wind up getting stalled. Any advantage that gets you noticed is worth pursuing. Opening a door just a little bit is much easier than worrying about all the closed doors in life you'll have to go through to become successful. Knowing something and doing it have very little in common!" –p. 206.

Here are two assignments for you:

1. Ask the following questions.
   - Who do I need to *be* in order to get what I want?
   - What are the behaviors that I actually *do* day in and day out at my business?
   - What are the behaviors that *others do* that I would like to do?
   - What are the behaviors that I do that *I don't have to do*?

2. Determine your most important priority and start working on it today. Have a beginning and end time. We'll talk more about systems to help you get more done in Part 3 of this book.

10. Focus on doing only things that cause money to flow towards you and your business.

According to Dan Kennedy, there are four big factors that cause money to move. These are:
1) Decision and clarity about what you want.
2) Subconscious programming, which attracts money to you.
3) Asking for the sale.
4) Being a celebrity and promoting what's new.

Are you doing what's necessary to have money move towards you and your life? Are you clear about what you want?

Are you writing down your goals?

Are you asking others for help to get what you want?

Are you building your celebrity?
Are you constantly focusing on what's new so that prospects and clients are attracted to you and your business?

Kenneth Foster makes this observation in his book *Ask and You Will Succeed*:
"I am amazed by the number of times I meet with clients and we're discussing what they think is holding them back from really creating success in their lives and they tell me it is because they are overwhelmed. But once we dig in, there is often one common denominator at the root of what is holding them back: Clutter!

"Clutter in the workspace, clutter on the kitchen table, in the closets, clutter underneath the bed, in the car, clutter in the basement...clutter everywhere! Do you know where clutter starts? In your mind. It is a symptom of an unruly mind. What is showing up in your environment starts first in your mind. And it starts many times with the questions you ask and choices you make.

"Many people keep clutter in their lives because they ask poor questions. Questions like 'Should I save or keep this magazine, file folder, picture, discount coupon, and so forth, or not? Remember, the answer is in the question you ask. So, if you ask a poor question like the one just asked, you will get answers like 'Maybe, I don't know, or let me think about it,' or the most classic answer of all, 'You never know, I might need this some day.'

"These answers lead to confusion and indecision, which is the main reason people can't get rid of their clutter. They don't have a clear understanding of what to do with it. So, to clean up a messy environment, you will have to take back control of your thinking by asking questions that will direct the focus of your mind to come up with an empowering answer.

"Try asking questions like 'What is the system I can come up with to always have a clutter-free environment?' Or 'What has to happen for me to live clutter-free?' Or 'What three steps can I take daily to live clutter-free?' By asking these types of questions you will be getting answers that will solve your problem rather than increase the clutter.

"Consider this: If you haven't used something in a very long time, if you haven't worn that shirt, opened that book, or spent that coupon, chances are it has outlived its usefulness to you. You no longer need it. It's time to let it go.

"The social scientists tell us that the subconscious mind keeps track of every piece of paper and every object in your environment. Have you ever had an uneasy feeling or maybe the feeling of being overwhelmed when you looked at a messy office or house? If so, then you have experienced the results of clutter.

"It's so easy to let clutter pile up. In fact, in the short-term, it seems easier to just let it build, rather than taking the time and energy to do something about it. Did you know that the number one reason that clutter builds up is from the inability to make a quick decision? That's right. When you are consistently uncertain or doubtful, the result will be clutter. So clutter is actually a mirror of the places in your mind where you are struggling with doubt. Instead of tossing one more magazine onto the pile, start by asking yourself, 'Where in my life am I feeling uncertainty, and what has to happen to move past it?'

"Think about it. Have you ever sorted through the mail and couldn't make a choice of whether to throw out a piece or save it, so you set it aside for later? Or you come back from a meeting with a folder full of notes but don't have a good place to file it, so it sits? Or you hold on to old items that no longer serve any purpose, but you are afraid to let them go because you think you will need them someday in the future? And then all the stuff seems to somehow multiply, until you've got yourself...a pile of clutter!

"While just letting things pile up might seem like the easy way in the moment, in the end, you will need a lot of energy to get rid of the junk. It has been said that our environment is more powerful than our willpower. If you don't believe this, then try to be upbeat and filled with positive energy on a consistent basis in a cluttered room.

"Set your intention to create a clutter-free environment and watch your creativity and energy soar. Clutter needs to be dealt with right from the start—before it takes over. It's important to be in charge of clutter, rather than it being in charge of you! Holding on to the clutter is like carrying around a 50-pound weight. Is this the way you want to go through life?
"Remember that whatever clutter you might have in your life didn't build up overnight, so it will take some time to deal with it once you decide to roll up your sleeves and dig in. You may want to try using this acronym: F.A.D. When a new piece of mail or information comes in, 'File it,' 'Act on it,' or 'Discard it.'" –Kenneth D. Foster, *Ask and You Will Succeed*, pp. 54-55.

Now, that I've given you these ten tips to help you create systems in your business, I'd like you to think through the following questions:

Current Reality:

1. Where in your business do you feel you need a big breakthrough?
2. In what areas of your business are you feeling stuck?
3. What is it that you want to achieve, but feel like isn't happening for you?
4. What drives you to persist and strive to get what you really want?

Your Future:
1. What would your life and business look like if you released all of your self-doubt?
2. Where can you find the answers you need to get what you want?
3. What goals will you set to make a quantum leap in your business this next year?
4. What goals are the most important ones?
5. What priorities will you act on everyday to help you get what you want?

Your Limiting Beliefs:
1. What limiting beliefs do you believe about yourself that cause you to doubt your ability to succeed?
2. What one belief could you change right now that would change your daily reality and help you get what you want?
3. What story have you been telling about yourself that you need to change?

Your Actions:
1. What actions do you need to take right now to create more create more abundance in your life and in your business?
2. What areas of your business do you intend to change forever in the next two weeks?
3. What is one thing you can do right now that will help you move a big door and create a profound long-term positive result?

Pay attention to these ten tips. Be working on them daily. Pick the one that you feel will have the biggest impact and start working on implementing that one first.

<u>Chapter 5</u>

Adopt the Systems and Behaviors of Top Business Owners

"I have never known a really successful man who deep in his heart did not understand the grind, the discipline it takes to win."—Vince Lombardi

In Jim Collins' book *Great by Choice*, he makes the following statement: "We cannot predict the future. But we can create it. Think back to 15 years ago, and consider what's happened since, the destabilizing events—in the world, in your country, in the markets, in your work, in your life—that defied all expectations. We can be astonished, confounded, shocked, stunned, delighted, or terrified, but rarely prescient. None of us can predict with certainty the twists and turns our lives will take. Life is uncertain, the future unknown. This is neither good nor bad. It just is, like gravity. Yet the task remains: how to master our own fate, even so."—*Great by Choice*, p. 1.

Anthony Robbins once said: "Success leaves clues." You can choose to be great in your business and create what you want by the habits and systems you employ.

In this chapter, I want to outline the ten habits and systems I've observed that top entrepreneurs have so you can have utilize them in your life and your business:

1. They are highly ambitious and extremely resistant to the status quo.
Most business owners are committed to preserving a status quo as long as possible. They want to set up a system or a series of systems in their business and then leave it alone and keep taking money from it for years. This is done without looking for ways to expand, improve, or change what is already working. Why fix what isn't broke, right? The problem with this philosophy is that it is not really possible anymore. Change is happening too fast. If you want to multiply and expand your business, you have to force

yourself and your business to change for the better. You can't be reactive to the changes around you. We'll talk about some specific exercises and systems you can use to stay on the cutting edge and reinvent your business in Section 2 of this book.

The top professionals in any industry that I know never permit themselves a moment of mental rest. They are always simultaneously working on implementing what is working now and working on a replacement for it when it is no longer working. This requires that you become resistant to anything that would cause you to be happy with the status quo.

Charles Darwin once observed: "It is not the strongest of the species that survive. It is those most responsive to change."

The biggest way you can diversify your knowledge and your action so you can get more done and beat the resistance of complacency is to continually educate yourself. Choose to read voraciously and study other successful business individuals. If you read one book/week, in ten years you will have read 520 books. In twenty years, you will have read more than 1,000 books. You can learn so much by associating with other individuals and business owners in other industries through mastermind groups.

When you associate with others who are where you want to be, you'll work hard to not only understand the marketing methods and business systems they're using to get the best results, but you'll also implement these systems into your life as well. Your goal should be to become familiar with marketing methods and media beyond what you are currently familiar with and use. Look for new ways to attract and bring prospects into your business.

This can't be something you'll get around to someday, it must be something you are constantly working on, testing, and implementing. In today's marketplace, you must diversify your lead sources. Being reliant on any one single method to bring in business is a recipe for disaster. This is true because if the media stops working or is no longer available you don't want to discover this and have no alternative plan for your business. As I mentioned, great systems not only allow you to employ best practices, they are also ensuring that you have a secondary option in case your best method that used to work no longer does. As I mentioned earlier, you need to have a back up system that you can deploy when it is necessary or you discover that what used to work no longer does.

2. They think with big, bold ideas. The biggest players in any business are the biggest thinkers.

Some businesses hope to be bigger and more successful someday. They aren't really serious or committed to what it takes to achieve greater success. If you've read Walter Isaacson's book on Steve Jobs, you'll remember that in the introduction to the book, Isaacson talks about how Jobs revolutionized seven industries. In other words, he spent a lot of time thinking about where the market was heading.

Isaacon says:
"[Steve Jobs] and his colleagues at Apple were able to think differently. They developed not merely modest product advances based on focus groups, but whole new devices and services that consumers did not yet know they needed." –*Steve Jobs*, p. xxi.

It takes commitment and focus to think big. It takes courage to act on these bold ideas. I believe that Apple is one of the most valuable companies in the world today because of the big thinking that went into it first. Your business will only become as big as you think it can.

You have to be 100% committed to whatever you set out to accomplish. Ken Blanchard once observed, "There is a difference between interest and commitment. When you're interested in doing something, you do it only when it's convenient. When you're committed to something, you accept no excuses, only results."

Stephen King, best-selling author with over 40 books in print, many of which have been made into movies said:
"Talent is cheaper than table salt. What separates the talented individual from the successful one is a lot of hard work."

Here are some big, bold ideas that can help you achieve more in your business:
- Become a celebrity and brand your own business.
- Make more and better follow up calls than your competitors
- Have a bigger and better referral program that enables your best clients to become your biggest sales team
- Have a sales system in place that ensures that each member of your staff is well trained and can close at a 75% or higher close rate with qualified prospects

- Specialize and be unique so prospects and clients can't get what you offer anywhere else except from you
- Sell experiences and stretch what you do so you can sell to more affluent clientele

These are big, bold ideas that can transform your business. Such big ideas become reality by thinking big. Many aren't able to think big, bold ideas because their own negative and limiting self-beliefs prevent them from doing so.

Werner Erhard once observed, ""If you want to be successful in life and in business, you have to give up *your* story and change it to a *different* story." If you are to succeed at thinking bigger, you must change the story that you are telling to yourself and oftentimes that discussion revolves around your beliefs about money and wealth.

Kevin Hogan in his book *The 12 Factors of Business Success* makes this statement:
"Wealth is not wired into anyone's genes. Your unconscious motives actually move you toward comfort and away from building wealth. And unconscious motives are very powerful drivers of most behavior. It takes great effort for conscious thought to become an even more powerful driver of behavior."--p. 136.

He continues:
"To override the unconscious mind, you cannot let your guard down until you have altered your dominant drives. It is that simple. The unconscious drives are so strong that it takes a planned, determined, and driven desire at the conscious level to overcome your unconscious feelings and emotions. Once the drives are altered, then they become the drivers toward the desired behaviors. People are not unconsciously predisposed to wealth. People are predisposed to consume...now.
To eat now.
To drink now.
To feel good now.
To want to be calm now.
To want to be out of pain now.
To want to be secure now.
To want to relax and be comfortable now.
There is very little genetic predisposition toward anything that would lead you to wealth.

There is no 'save for a rainy day' gene.
There is no 'men be a responsible dad' gene.
There is no 'money consciousness' gene.
Wealth building is about conscious decisions overcoming hardwired programming, programming that only a small percentage of people ever conquer....

"Wealth begins with a mind-set. It is what you choose to think and act upon that produces the wealth you want. When you stop acting to produce wealth then you stop building wealth. What you think will be...pretty much will be. Research shows that wealthy people tend to get wealthy using similar thinking processes (and so do poor people). To create wealth, you need to think like a wealthy person and then put your thinking into action."--*The 12 Factors of Business Success*, pp. 136-137.

Unfortunately, many people have been raised to think thoughts and words of poverty instead of thoughts and words of wealth. No matter your background, you can accept responsibility and learn how to think differently, to think bigger, and to believe that you can have what you want in life.

I really like what Suze Orman says about this:
"It is not enough to push away thoughts and words of poverty. You must also use words of wealth, bounty, and abundance. Any words, repeated often enough, become true. Begin your process of change with thoughts and words that encompass richness, possibilities, dreams, openness, and hope....Here is an exercise I always practiced with my clients and still practice myself. It's a simple, one-step exercise to make sure your thoughts and words are in agreement. Before you say anything with respect to your money—your prospects, your goals, your financial worries—I want you to ask yourself the following question: Are your words stating what you wish to be true? For example, if you are about to say, 'I will never get out of debt,' I want you to first ask yourself: Is this what I want to be true? Of course it isn't, so don't say it. Rephrase what you're trying to express until it passes this test. In this case, 'One day I will be out of debt' is likely what you want to say.'

"Every time you're about to speak about your money, ask yourself this essential question—Do I want this to be true?—and speak only when the answer is yes." –*The Courage to Be Rich*, pp. 31-32.

What a great statement. When you catch yourself thinking or saying something that you don't want, ask: "Do I want this to be true?" When you change your language, you will shift the way you think about money and profits. Those big, bold thoughts will help you get your business to where you want it to be. Remember, your thoughts lead to your words which then lead to your actions. You'll never be able to put systems in place to raise your prices and your profits until you believe in your thoughts that you can, which will lead you to actually put the pieces in place to help you make this happen.

Here are some language patterns you may have caught yourself saying that I have heard from other entrepreneurs and what you should start saying instead:

"I'll never be able to take a salary from my business."
Do you want this to be true?
Say instead, "I am finally beginning to take a salary from my business."

"I'm so busy but I can't afford to hire anyone."
Do you want this to be true?
Are you clear about what type of person you need to hire, how often they should be there and what you will do with the time you will free up from having some help? If not, this attitude won't help you change. Instead, you should say, "I'm so busy and hiring someone will help me take care of all of our prospects so we can close more sales."

"I just know prospects and clients aren't going to come into our business and buy now. The economy is down...unemployment is high...etc."
Do you want this to be true?
Stop making excuses for why you can't be successful. Put the parameters and systems in place to help you make better profits..

"I'll never get out of the mountain of debt I and my business have."
Do you want this to be true?
Say instead, "Slowly, but surely I am putting my business finances in order. I'm cutting costs and increasing profits every day and in every way."

"I can't control myself when I'm spending money. I always end up spending too much."
Do you want this to be true?

Say instead, "I spend only what I can afford to spend. I focus on making the profits that will help me get out of debt and on my way to achieve my goals."

"I just can't save money."
Do you want this to be true?
Say instead, "I am beginning to save a little from every sale I make."

"I'll never get back the money I invested into this business."
Do you want this to be true?
Say instead, "I have a monthly and yearly plan for paying back what I've invested into this business over the next five years."

Orman says this:
"After you start to think you can, your thoughts become more powerful; after you start to use only words that say you can, you start to feel more powerful. When you feel more powerful you have the energy to propel you toward the actions that create a life of real wealth. That's the cycle: from your thoughts and your words to your actions." – *The Courage to Be Rich*, p. 33.

Thoughts are powerful things. Author Napoleon Hill wrote in his book *Think and Grow Rich*:
"Our brains become magnetized with the dominating thoughts which we hold in our minds, and, by means with which no man is familiar, these 'magnets' attract to us the forces, the people, the circumstances of life which harmonize with the nature of our dominating thoughts."

It is not enough to just think bigger and better thoughts. You also have to take action that will change these beliefs as well. The problem is that many people never think differently about their business because they have mental hangups about money, profits, and wealth. They know they should do something different, but they don't. They never get around to taking action. Ideas are a dime a dozen. Ideas that are acted on are rare.

Dan Kennedy says it best:
"There is no wealth to be found in an idea. There is only wealth from acting on an idea." – *Wealth Attraction for Entrepreneurs*, p. 80.

The question you have to ask yourself is this: How much longer do you want to go in your business before you are making what you want to make?

How many more years will you let pass by continuing selling what doesn't allow you to make money or the same kinds of profits that you could shifting what you offer?

Have you created systems and processes in your business that will allow you to make maximum profits? If not, when are *you* going to change that?

It is *your* business. *You* have to decide to take control and run it in such a way that you can make money.

Here are several specific limiting beliefs that can hold you back in your business:
1. Thinking your business is different.
2. Allowing yourself to be controlled by the opinions and beliefs of others.
3. Allowing yourself to be controlled by past experience ("I tried that and it didn't work...")
4. Being a slave to industry norms ("I can only get x amount of markup on what I sell because...")
5. Fear
6. Indecision
7. Lack of clarity and focus – continually distracted by new, shiny objects instead of focusing on the areas that will bring you success.
8. Having a strategy that is incongruent with your goals (Goal: "I want to sell $1,000,000 this year." Strategy: "I'm going to sell 3 products/day at an average of $1,000 and in order to do that I have to bring in 6 new prospects/day and sell at least 50% of them."
9. Small thinking
10. Incorrect thinking about money, profits, and margins
11. Thinking that you have to sell what you do for the same or lower price as your competitors in order to get the sale.

Which of these limiting beliefs have you thought about your business that are preventing you from thinking with boldness? Get over the stories, excuses, or beliefs you have been telling yourself. Start thinking bigger and develop the habit of big, bold thinking.

3. They are extremely self-confident. They believe in what they do.
Look at the most successful individuals in any business or industry and you will see that they are extremely confident in themselves and what they are doing.

They believe they can make things happen, conquer any difficulties that come in their path, and do what others can't or won't. This attitude and belief comes from confidence in what they know and what they have already done or accomplished.

Unsuccessful individuals never launch ideas or projects or fully commit to implementing ideas because deep down, they lack confidence in their own ability to follow-through with what they start.

Here are ten ways you can develop extreme self-confidence:
1) Change your associations (what you read and who you associate with).
2) Do something well.
3) Be and act better than your competition. When your clients notice the difference, your confidence skyrockets.
4) Develop new skills and competencies.
5) Surround yourself with A players who you have confidence in and who you know will hit the goals you need to hit every day.
6) Do what you say you will do.
7) Expect and anticipate great things in your business and live into the picture or vision you have for yourself.
8) Reward yourself and your team when you accomplish extraordinary things.
9) Be immune to criticism.
10) Take the responsibility to create your own story. Don't listen to what others have said about you in the past.

You have greatness within you. There is no reason why you can't go out there and make it happen in your business now. If you haven't been confident in yourself up to this point, that's okay. You can change today by changing the way you talk to yourself.

Eric Lofholm teaches this powerful concept in his excellent book *The System*. He tells the story of one of his star clients, Joey Aszterbaum, a loan officer. "While attending one of my one-day sales seminars, Joey said: 'I am not good at time management.' [Eric] responded: 'I believe you. If you say you're not good, then you're not good.' Change begins in language. Speak as if what you are saying is truth. Speak into existence what it is that you want. I said, 'Joey, if you want to become good at time management, then speak that. If you want to become a time management master, then speak that. The Law

of Belief is simply that whatever you tell yourself over and over again, you
will eventually believe.'

"Well, Joey started affirming that he is a time management master. I taught
him to affirm it three ways:

"I am a time management master. He is a time management master. And
then your name: Joey is a time management master."

"I told Joey to tell himself this over and over and over again. In doing this,
he literally reprogrammed his subconscious mind for success. Napoleon Hill
in his book *Think and Grow Rich*, calls this autosuggestion. I call it repeated
affirmation....[Joey] says his affirmations over and over. And wouldn't you
know it, he starts to get really good at time management. One day he was
meeting with a real estate agent, who said, 'Joey, you're so good at time
management. How are you able to do all that you do?' And Joey simply said,
'It's easy. I am a time management master.' That's what came to Joey's mind.
He literally reprogrammed his subconscious mind for success."—pp. 5-6.

You can gain confidence in any skill by working at it and by reprogramming
your thoughts with big, bold thinking. Remember, change begins with
language. Choose to say, believe, and act in accordance with what you want.

4. They protect profit margins at all costs.
It doesn't take much imagination to cut prices, discount and discount more
so that you have a slim to non-existent profit margin. To succeed, you must
go to work on protecting your profits, not sacrificing them. If you can't
figure out a way to sell what you sell profitably, you won't be in business long.

With the increased cost of running your business on almost every front
(shipping, health care, salaries, etc.) and with clients expecting more today
than they ever have, you must be profitable if you are to stay in business.
Prospects and clients today feel entitled to a lot because that is what they've
seen and what they've gotten from other businesses. This means that you
have to get better at building more and more value into what you sell in ways
that don't increase your expenses. If you don't do this and your sales
revenues remain flat, you will fall behind very quickly with the rising cost of
everything.

There are five ways to protect your profit margin:
1.   Know and pay attention to the financial numbers in your business.
     Alter your systems to sell more of what is profitable.
2.   Change your lead flow systems so you attract better and less price
     sensitive customers.

3. Offer new and different products and services that have high profitability. When you find something that works, scale up.
4. Force a higher transaction size by bundling products and services that aren't easily compared.
5. Elevate the value of what you sell so you won't be commoditized.

The problem with the quick and easy fix of jumpstarting your sales with substantially discounted prices and offers is that it leads downhill. When your competitors offer discounted products and you choose to match them or offer something similar for less, you have to trade away more and more profit to succeed, especially if you selling what everyone else is selling.

When you have decreased profits, you have less money to spend in your advertising efforts to get more prospects into your marketing funnel. When you have fewer prospects entering your business, you make fewer sales. Fewer sales means that you have less ability to pay others and yourself well which will lead to an inability to bring in new, profitable items to sell and for you to be innovative in the future.

Here are six questions for you to think about so that you can ensure this doesn't happen to you:

1) What is the most profitable product offering I have?

2) What would happen to my profitability if I invested more of my resources into selling more of my most profitable products (instead of diluting it with less profitable offerings)?

3) How much money am I really making from what I am selling the most of?

4) What profitability am I giving up by what I continue to sell in my business?

5) Does the product turnover of what I am selling justify its continued presence in my business?

6) Will increased costs allow me to continue to be profitable with what I am selling?

Take responsibility for the profitability of your business. Only you can control this. Dan Kennedy once observed: "Control equals responsibility and responsibility equals control; and anybody adept at making excuses is usually inept at making money." Are you in control or are you making excuses?

5. They continually work at improving their ability to persuade and look for new opportunities to sell more and better.
Any prosperous business revolves around solid salesmanship. If you aren't able to sell and persuade others to do business with you, you will fail. As an entrepreneur, you may have mastered the skills of selling. To succeed on a larger scale, you've got to train those on your team to sell as well or better than you do. Most people generally resist salespeople. Your prospective customers may resist you initially because of their fear that you are like all other salespeople that he or she has dealt with. By providing more value and by sincerely discovering what it is that your prospects are looking for, you'll be able to overcome this perception and serve those who need what it is that you offer.

In today's competitive environment, if you aren't creating an environment where we are creating meaningful experiences for your prospective clients, showcasing why you are the best choice (through your own celebrity and expertise), and then having the skills necessary to persuasively talk individuals through their decisions so that they want to buy now as opposed to waiting, you shouldn't be surprised by mediocre or lackluster results. You've got to spend more time helping prospects experience the difference of working with a world-class trained sales organization.

When you're ask a prospect to take time to take time to visit with you about their needs and your offer (and this is true when you are promoting the appointment online, on the phone, or in person), you need to show her that the experience you provide will offer her more value than her perception of what her time is worth. You've got to help her *see* the benefits of spending that time with you and take away her fears.

For example, if I say, "let's meet for lunch and I'm buying....", there is a stand-alone benefit to the exchange of time the individual will give up. When scheduling an appointment with your prospect, you've got to help her see that the exchange of time will be more than worth it to her.

You can do this by explaining the benefits of coming into your business and by using the principle of ingratiation which is how you make others feel important and how you gain favor by your deliberate efforts.

Kurt Mortensen makes this statement in his book *Maximum Influence*: "Ingratiation is gaining favor by deliberate effort. Ingratiation techniques can include compliments, flattery, and agreeableness. Ingratiation can also involve a special recognition of someone such as, 'We don't usually do this, but in your case I'm going to make an exception,' or 'I am personally going to take care of this matter and see that you get what you want.' Many people consider ingratiation sucking up or brown-nosing, but it is an effective technique for making others more persuadable. The reason this strategy works is because The Law of Esteem increases likeability and promotes an increase in ego."

He continues:
"Research has demonstrated these conclusions about using ingratiation. In one study, 'ingratiators' were perceived as being more competent, motivated, and qualified for leadership positions by their supervisors. In another study, subordinates who used ingratiation developed an increased job satisfaction for themselves, their coworkers, and their supervisor. In yet another study, ingratiators enjoyed a 5 percent edge in earning more favorable job evaluations. Ingratiation works even when it is perceived as a deliberate effort to win someone over. Our esteem is so starved that we accept any flattery or praise we can get." –p. 164.

What are the benefits a prospect has by agreeing to watch a video you post or to take the time to talk with you on the phone or in person at an appointment? Do you have a list of benefits that you can clearly articulate? Do you explain what a prospect gets when she buys from you and becomes your client?

When you explain the true benefit in a compelling way, you are in a much better position to persuade the individual you are talking to at the end of the appointment because of how you've promoted your benefits list for buying now as opposed to waiting.

As I've mentioned before, prospects coming into businesses or web sites today have extreme resistance to wanting to buy anything now. Rapport reduces resistance. Prospects have resistance because they view you as a salesperson. If you are going to change this, you've got to provide evidence to the contrary. You've got to show that you are there to help them BEFORE the resistance will be dropped.

What do most prospects think of when they think of a salesperson? When you understand this, you understand what causes their resistance.

The answer is that most prospects see salespeople as someone who will twist their arm, use high pressure, be manipulative, have a used car salesman approach where they will lie and talk fast to get the sale. If a prospect perceives that you are any of these things, you are guilty until proven innocent.

In order to be innocent, you've got to view sales as service and sell from a point of honesty, integrity and compassion. Selling is about leading and moving people to action.

In order to beat this increased resistance, you need to have more rapport with your prospects and clients. Rapport is a state of harmony. On a conscious level, you notice differences. On a subconscious level, you notice similarities. What you need to do in order to be more successful in getting a prospect to drop resistance, he has got to see that you are similar to him. You've got to help her see subconsciously that you are there to help her and that you have her best interests at heart. You can't be seen as someone who is just there to sell her something.

When you are selling, it is not about you. It is about the prospect. Everybody would rather talk about themselves because we all have a selfish tendency to look at things ONLY from our own perspective.

To break through this barrier, you must ask prospects questions about themselves. You've got to begin the process of looking at what you're offering with trust and rapport. The easiest way to persuade or influence someone is to find out what they want and give it to them. In order to find out what a prospect is looking for, you've got to ask questions.

Are your questions prepared in advance or are you winging it? If you are winging it, you will get wing it results, which means that your sales results will be much lower than you really want them to be. With a selling system, you are able to get predictable results because human beings make buying decisions in patterns. The questions you ask should help you determine a prospect's buying fingerprint. When you understand a prospect's buying pattern, you can help him or her lower their resistance and be excited about the decision to own what it is that you are offering.

The first time a prospect buys from you is because there is a tangible benefit that she sees that outweighs the cost. The second time someone buys from you is because he or she likes you and your business. The better your relationship, the more likely the client will buy from you again and again.

To sell more, you need to help prospects see all of the benefits of choosing to buying now as well as all of the consequences that will happen if he or she chooses not to take action. If you haven't been selling as well as you would like (and especially if you don't have a sales system in your business), it is easy to make excuses instead of focusing on what needs to be done to get results.

Author Robert Johnson says: "I can imagine a cave-salesperson somewhere selling a whole lot more wheels and fire than the competition, while the underperformer was blaming his poor sales record on dinosaur attacks, evolution, floods, fires, and meteor strikes."—*This is Harder Than it Looks*, p. 22.

He continues:
"Sales success doesn't just come simply from the execution of sales skills. Rather, it's an amazing journey wherein you develop the ability to manage the will, the skill, and drill of selling."
He defines these as:
"The *will* is the required mental preparedness: the drive to persevere and to face and overcome fear, procrastination, constant adversity, and rejection. Your will sets you in motion, and can also stop your momentum. This quality is the toughest to diagnose and handle since so much of our internal struggle is masked by excuses and our positive external voice.
"The *skill* is rooted in a vast foundation of knowledge of product, industry, competition, and selling skills. It is the mastery of these four basic areas that enables you to successfully guide prospects through a sales process.

"The *drill* is the process of setting goals, creating strategic and tactical plans, planning territory, and executing the key leading indicator activities that create sustained superior results on a daily basis. The 'drill to sell' is possible only by engaging the 'will to sell.' *– This is Harder Than It Looks*, p. 28.

You prepare for success by hiring those who already have the will to sell. You ensure success by training your sales team the skills of selling. And you maximize success by practicing the skills again and again through focused and effective training systems.

Tony Little, who is the one who popularized the Gazelle Free Style Glider elliptical trainer has an inspiring story about the will, skill and drill of selling. He almost wasn't known for that though because of a car accident that nearly claimed his life on Halloween night a few weeks before he was to shoot the Gazelle Glider infomercial. I want to share his story with you and then make some parallels for you to consider about sales in your business.

When he woke up following the accident in the emergency room, he had a concussion and a horribly cut up face. A plastic surgeon was called in and Tony spent five hours in surgery and received 200 stitches that crisscrossed his face. It didn't look promising that he'd be able to shoot the infomercial as planned. In fact, the executive of Fitness Quest (who was marketing the device) told Tony, "We love you, but you can't shoot an exercise video looking like this. We'll have to get someone to stand in for you this time."

Tony said:
"I really needed this job to stay on top in TV sales. I really believed in the Gazelle. Most important, I knew that if I could get on the air and pitch this thing, it would take off like a rocket ship. But only if I sold it! It was my baby! I wanted it, I needed it, and I refused to quit! Tony went to Canton, Ohio and persuaded the executives to go ahead and shoot the infomercial. Tony said, "The American public loves tales of adversity to victory," I explained. "I'll go on the air and say to them, look, I shouldn't be here in front of you today. I was in a bad car accident just a few days ago. It tore up my face pretty badly, as you can see. But I'm not going to let this stop me. I don't go backward. I've learned to go forward in life no matter what happens to me. That's a major lesson that fitness has taught me. And it can teach you the same.

So let me show you this amaaaaazing piece of exercise equipment that you're going to love, and that's going to make you feel better, look better, work better—my new Gazelle Free Style Glider."

The executive, Bob Schnabel, was skeptical. He didn't believe that Tony could sell the 250,000 Gazelles needed to make money. So, Little made a deal with him. He said, "Here's the deal. If I make this infomercial and I sell less than 250,000 machines, I'll go out and buy you a new 1997 Porsche Carrera. Okay? If I do sell 250,000 machines, you'll come down to Florida and buy me the same car. Wanna shake on it?"

Tony ended up getting the go ahead to shoot the commercial. He said: "I shot the infomercial live. In the first 30 seconds of the show I announced to the audience that by all rights I shouldn't be on this stage today. Because I'd just gotten out of the hospital from a terrible car accident. As you can see, I told them, my face is pretty messed up. I then flashed visuals on the screen showing me backstage an hour before showtime having makeup applied. The photos showed my face before the makeup had disguised the lacerations and stitches. There was a big audience for the show and they responded sympathetically with applause and lots of 'oh's' and 'ah's.' I then turned to the audience and said, 'Look, it's not what happens to you in this life that matters. It's how you respond to it.'

He continues:
"It was the first time I'd ever made this statement on TV. But it was definitely not the last. That slogan remained my theme in business and in life from that time on. I then launched into my sales pitch for the Gazelle. Not too long after this, Bob Schnabel, always true to his word, was on a jet down to Tampa Bay, Florida, to buy me a new white 1997 Porsche. The infomercial went on to gross $66 million. The last time I checked we'd sold more than seven million Gazelle Gliders around the world for over $1 billion. Perseverance will always overcome." – *There's Always a Way*, pp. 120-125.

I think there is a big lesson hidden in Tony's story. And it is found in Adam Grant's book *Give and Take*. It is simply that being more vulnerable allows you to get prospects to drop their resistance much faster and be much more open to your attempts at persuasion.

Adam says:

"Research suggests that there are two fundamental paths to influence: dominance and prestige. When we establish dominance, we gain influence because others see us as strong, powerful, and authoritative. When we earn prestige, we become influential because others respect and admire us. These two paths to influence are closely tied to our reciprocity styles. Takers are attracted to, and excel in, gaining dominance. In an effort to claim as much value as possible, they strive to be superior to others. To establish dominance, takers specialize in powerful communication: they speak forcefully, raise their voices to assert their authority, express certainty to project confidence, promote their accomplishments, and sell with conviction and pride. They display their strength by spreading their arms in dominant poses, raising their eyebrows in challenge, commanding as much physical space as possible, and conveying anger and issuing threats when necessary. In the quest for influence, takers set the tone and control the conversation by sending powerful verbal and nonverbal signals. As a result, takers tend to be much more effective than givers in gaining dominance. But is that the most sustainable path to influence?

He continues:

"When our audiences are skeptical, the more we try to dominate them, the more they resist. Even with a receptive audience, dominance is a zero sum game: the more power and authority I have, the less you have. When takers come across someone more dominant, they're at risk of losing their influence." –p. 130.

He concludes:

"Takers tend to worry that revealing weaknesses will compromise their dominance and authority. Givers are much more comfortable expressing vulnerability: they're interested in helping others, not gaining power over them, so they're not afraid of exposing chinks in their armor. By making themselves vulnerable, givers can actually build prestige.

"But there's a twist: expressing vulnerability is only effective if the audience receives other signals establishing the speaker's competence. In a class experiment led by the psychologist Elliot Aronson, students listened to one of four tapes of a candidate auditioning for a Quiz Bowl team. Half of the time, the candidate was an expert, getting 92 percent of questions right. The other half of the time, the candidate had only average knowledge, getting 30 percent right.

"As expected, audiences favored the expert. But an interesting wrinkle emerged when the tape included a clumsy behavior by the candidate. Dishes crashed, and the candidate said, 'Oh, my goodness—I've spilled coffee all over my new suit."

"When the average candidate was clumsy, audiences liked him even less. But when the expert was clumsy, audiences liked him even more. Psychologists call this the pratfall effect. Spilling a cup of coffee hurt the image of the average candidate: it was just another reason for the audience to dislike him. But the same blunder helped the expert appear human and approachable—instead of superior and distant." –pp. 133-134.

Isn't that interesting? One reason why I believe Tony sold so many of the Gazelle glider was because he was approachable and vulnerable. You and I will sell more as well if we adopt this approach as well and come across as real and authentic to the prospects and clients we serve everyday. When you combine a servant heart and attitude in your sales approach, you will come across as approachable and resistance will drop so you can make the sale. Be sure that this important element is a part of your sales system.

Finally, I want to talk with you briefly about what you will do to ensure that your sales team is actually following your system and reaching your company's goals. Here are eight questions you can answer that can help you evaluate how effective your sales system is on achieving the results you desire:

1) What are the closing percentages of your current sales consultants? If it is down from what you want it to be, what specific things will you do to help those consultants improve? By what date will improvement happen?

2) What are you doing to move those who are under 50% to be above 50%?

3) By what date will you eliminate those who are at 30% and under?

4) What are you doing to get your team to 70-75% close ratios?

5) Ask: 1) Who should you continue investing in, 2) who should you replace with someone else who can help me get where you want to go?

6) What selling processes do you need to focus on training more in your business?

7) What impact will that have for you and your business?

8) What one area of your sales system do you need to spend more time training and focusing on that will help you achieve the greatest increase in results?

The most effective business owners have mastered a sales system that allows them to become more valuable in the eyes of the prospects in their market niche. Give your prospects a reason to believe that your business is the best choice and accelerate the process of building and earning trust. When you do this effectively, you can develop a relationship and help each prospect become a client now.

6. They have an unrelenting focus on the setting & achievement of goals.
Jim Collins calls this habit or behavior "fanatic discipline" or the 20-mile march in his book *Great by Choice*.

He says:

"The 20 Mile March is more than a philosophy. It's about having concrete, clear, intelligent, and rigorously pursued performance mechanisms that keep you on track. The 20 Mile March creates two types of self-imposed discomfort: (1) the discomfort of unwavering commitment to high performance in difficult conditions, and (2) the discomfort of holding back in good conditions." –p. 45.

Collins lists seven major components of these types of goals:

- You must have performance markers. *I think these should be your minimum, target, and optimal goals.*
- You must have self-imposed constraints. You have to decide what goals you will march towards every day and do so consistently.
- You must tailor your goals to your business and its environment.
- You must set goals that are largely within your control to achieve. In other words, work on the critical success factors that lead to success instead of shooting blanks in the dark. You've got to aim and focus on your target.
- The goal should be just right for you and your team. He calls this a Goldilocks time frame (where the goal is not too long or too short, but just right).
- Your goals should be designed and self-imposed by you, not set by someone who doesn't understand your business.
- Your goals must be achieved with great consistency."-*Great by Choice*, pp. 48-49.

You've got to be responsible for your goals. You've got to sit down and be clear about what you're after in your business. If you don't, you'll settle for less than you should. I'll talk more about your system of setting goals and how it relates to your vision in Section 2 of this book. For now, I just want to stress how important it is to decide to do something and be fanatically disciplined about choosing to do what's *right* over what's *comfortable*. This discipline or habit is critically important because even though it is easier to avoid the conflict that inevitably comes when you confront your obstacles by letting things slide instead of addressing them head on, it will never help you get closer to the achievement of your goals. There will always be conflict or resistance from moving from a lower level to a higher level as Steven Pressfield talks about in his book *The War of Art*.

I really like what Tony Hartl of Planet Tan (a chain of tanning salons) says about this in his book *Selling Sunshine*: "No one likes conflict, and most people will go to great lengths to avoid it. But running a successful business requires making tough decisions, and that's often uncomfortable. Our philosophy at Planet Tan was that you can be comfortable, or you can be right. In other words, you can either do what is comfortable at that moment—knowing deep inside—that you're going to pay for that decision later—or you can do the right thing from the start. Doing the right thing creates energy and momentum."

He continues:
"In certain situations, you've got to make a conscious decision to do the right thing, even though that's more than likely *not* the path of least resistance. This is where the 'comfortable versus right' choice must be made. The popular decision or the easy decision is not necessarily the right decision." We adopted this philosophy from our COO, Nick, who had used a decision-making process when he had been COO at a major restaurant chain. Nick further distinguishes between comfortable decisions and right decisions: 'Comfortable decisions create incremental degradation that kills an organization in small, seemingly unnoticeable chunks, until one day it is too late. It's much like taking a tiny drop of arsenic each morning, which in itself would be uneventful, but will eventually kill a human being. Right decisions create a firm foundation of trust, deep belief in core values, and loyalty for all the correct reasons. Simply making the right decisions consistently raises the bar for everyone, because it becomes expected and indeed demanded, weeding out the imposters.' –pp. *Selling Sunshine*, 117-118.

Conflicts where you must do the right thing instead of the comfortable thing in your business will likely be:
- Letting someone go who isn't hitting sales goals.

- Letting a team member consistently show up late and not doing anything about it (because he or she is a good salesperson)

- Letting an employee conduct personal business while working in yours or doing personal business when they are on the clock (social media, email, texting, etc.)

- Failing to eliminate advertising mediums that are no longer working

Are you willing to do the right thing instead of the comfortable thing? My hope is that you will make the tough calls in your business and do what needs to be done *now*, not later.

Let me share with you an example of the power of doing the right thing and making adjustments to hit goals told by Steven Schussler, a serial restaurant entrepreneur, who made this observation about his restaurant Yak & Yeti, which he opened at Disney's Animal Kingdom in his book, *It's a Jungle In Here*:

"In 2006, we opened the Yak & Yeti Restaurant...A family-friendly, Asian-inspired restaurant, it was divided into two parts: a sit down indoor area and an outdoor walk-up window. One of the advertised benefits of the walk-up window was the opportunity to get faster service.

"Several months after Yak & Yeti opened, I stopped by to see how things were going. I took a seat outside, near the 'quick service' outdoor section of the restaurant, and noticed people having to wait in line for up to fifteen minutes to place their food orders. In my mind, this was a substantial problem, and what made things even worse was the realization that an obvious solution to the problem existed, yet none of the staff had either seen the problem or had chosen to correct it in the eight months the restaurant had been in operation.

"The problem involved the placement of the menu boards customers used to make their food selections. They were on signs behind the serving counter, so that the patrons had to get close to the line before they could see what items were on the menu. This gave them precious little time to make their choices, meaning that when they reached the employee taking their orders, they weren't ready to announce their selections. This, of course, delayed everything as the employee waited patiently for the customers to make their decisions. The way to fix the problem was simple enough: additional menu boards had to be posted farther back along the sidewalk where the customers were lined up. That way, people positioned at the back of the line would have more time to make their decisions and, when they got to the front of the line, would be ready to place their order without further delay, speeding everything up significantly.

He concludes:
"How can a restaurant advertising quick service expect to make significant money when people have to wait two or three times as long as necessary to get their meals? It can't, and that is why it is important to monitor what services or products you have provided: to make sure things are going smoothly, and, if not, to make the necessary improvements to ensure that they do." –pp. 82-83.

Are there issues at your business that you need to face up to? Are you thinking like a customer and looking for ways to improve your customer experience? If there are areas that need improvement, take action and do what needs to be done. Choose what's right for your business over what's comfortable. Set goals, take action, and do it now.

7. They have the habit of choosing and prioritizing opportunities and manage their daily schedule around them.
Robert Kiyosaki defines focus as: Follow One Course Until Successful. He says:
"My favorite two words of that acronym are these: until successful. Focus...is power measured over time. For example, it is easy for me to stay on my diet from breakfast to lunch. But to stay focused for years on the diet is the true power of focus. I have gone on diets, lost weight, gained it back, and had to lose the weight again. That is the lack of focus over time."—*The Midas Touch*, p. 51.

Here are some questions for you to reflect on:
1) What are your most important priorities?

2) Are you focused on them? Does your daily schedule reflect those priorities?

3) What are the things that you do well that you and only you can do at your business?

4) How is what you are presently doing, helping you build the future you desire for yourself?

5) List three areas where you are most productive. In what area of your business are you currently best using your time? Is this the right area of focus?

6) Are you using your time in your business in a way that allows you to work on your greatest opportunities *or* do you find yourself bogged down dealing with your greatest challenges?

7) What opportunities do you see now that you didn't see last year that you could focus on (and that are really worth developing)?

8) What can you do daily to stay focused on new opportunities?

We'll talk more about productivity systems in Chapter 16 in Section 2 of *The System is the Secret*. Follow one course until success. Your daily schedule is yours. Schedule it to focus on your most important priorities or someone else will.

8. The habit of utilizing leverage points and multipliers in your business to maximize productivity and results.
Every business has leverage points and multipliers that are responsible for its success. To grow your business, you need to better leverage the assets you have. Your own individual assets aren't enough. You are looking for multipliers that will give you a big crowbar and even more leverage and that you can build systems around.

To help you evaluate how well you are utilizing leverage points and multipliers in your business, consider the following twenty-two questions:
1. How have you better leveraged unused capacity in your business (times when you're not usually busy)?

2. Is your pre-sales process more effective than your competition? What are you providing to prospects before they enter your marketing funnel?

3. Are prospects commenting on the experiences they're having in your business? What specifically is driving your focus on selling experiences, not just products at your business?

4. What game changing elements have you introduced in your business (different payment offers, incentives, fractional ownership, all-inclusive packages)?

5. Do prospects perceive that you have additional value above and beyond just a place to purchase what you sell as they search for a solution to a challenge they've been having?

6. Are your clients loyal to you once they've purchased from you (or are other competitors more persuasive in their marketing to pull these clients into their businesses)? How do you know?

7. What recurring problem do you solve that prospects and clients have been talking about today? How specifically are you solving it?

8. Do clients feel that what you do is extraordinary or ordinary? What have clients told you that you are doing that is new? How could you better leverage this?

9. Do you feel that you've re-invented the experience that prospects and clients have in your business? How specifically have you re-invigorated your processes, systems, and staff?

10. What industry norms has your business defied? What are you doing to stand out and be different? How could you better leverage this to your advantage?

11. What territory, niche, or market square are you now dominating? Are there market gaps that no one is really addressing in our area?

12. What unmet needs or desires do prospects or clients have? How could you meet those better than your competitors?

13. In what ways have you stretched the price pyramid in your business (are you selling high margin, lower price products or selling to more affluent clientele)?

14. Do you have relationships with individuals in specific niche channels that your competitors don't have that you are able to monetize?

15. What processes are you leveraging in your business to have more success (how the phone is answered, how orders are processed, what prospects experience in first 30 seconds and during their entire experience in your business?

16. What have you done to increase your margin on the products you are carrying in your business? What leverage points or advantages has this given to you?

17. How much time are you spending thinking about where you want to be in the future? What leverage does this give you?

18. Are you copying your competitors or are they copying you? Are your competitors aggressively pursuing your clients? How do you know? What will you do about it?

19. How does your web site compare with that of your competitors? Does your web site leverage your business and help prospects and clients see why you are the best choice?

20. How do your sales closing percentages compare with those of your competitors? Do you have a sales training system and regimen that you use to keep your consultant's sales skills sharp?

21. How well are you implementing what you are learning? Are you where you want to be? What are you doing to ensure that you'll be in a different place six months from now than you are today?

22. What is extraordinary about your business as compared with your competitors? Do prospects and clients perceive this difference?

To grow your business, you need to better leverage the assets you have. Your own individual assets aren't enough. These questions can help you use them better.

9. They plan and stick to systems. A big part of this is evaluating what's working and continually looking for better ways to improve them.
For example, let's say that you wrote down three of your most successful marketing promotions that were generating the most leads and helping you get the most new business right now. As part of this exercise, you could list

each campaign or promotion. Then, you could identify what it is that you feel is causing those promotions to work so well. To improve them, you could run your marketing copy through a system like the one below in six areas to see how effective your overall marketing funnel sequence and promotion is and then look for ways to improve it.

This system includes six specific areas of focus and can be used to identify where you may be dropping the ball before you send out a direct mail piece or send out an email inviting prospects to enter your marketing funnel. As you'll see the system is designed to remind you about what has worked in the past and ensure that you aren't forgetting what will work going forward. I would invite you to use this system to get better results.

Use of Headline

Select One	Elements of Your Advertising / Marketing Promotion
	No headline is evident.
	Headline present, but no big, bold, or exciting promise to the prospect.
	Headline is vague and contains no meaningful specifics (could apply to any competitor in your business niche).
	Fails to grab interest of the prospect and keep her reading.
	Headline is effective in grabbing attention, creating interest, and engaging the prospect so she wants to keep reading and find out what your offer is all about.

Testimonials

Select One	Elements of Your Advertising / Marketing Promotion
	No testimonials are present.
	Testimonial present, but it is vague and offers no specifics.
	Testimonial is unemotional and impersonal.
	Testimonial doesn't identify your business by name.
	Testimonials all say the same thing, they aren't categorized by how they can answer specific concerns that prospects may have.
	Testimonial is effective, but would be even better with pictures or videos.
	Outstanding use of emotional, specific testimonials that can eliminate fears in prospects.

Use of Reason Why to Overcome Doubts and Explaining Your Specific Offer

Select One	Elements of Your Advertising / Marketing Promotion
	No use of reason why trigger (no explanation about why you're having the promotion).
	Use of reason why is vague and unemotional. Little excitement is created for the prospect.
	Reason why doesn't make sense and prospect has to guess about why you're doing what you are.
	Reason why is insufficient. It isn't written in a persuasive way.
	Reason why offers solid reasoning and is very persuasive.

Organization and Layout/ How the Prospect Will Scan Your Offer

Select One	Elements of Your Advertising / Marketing Promotion
	Layout is confusing and not well thought out.
	Layout is confusing and seemingly has contradictions or many disclaimers.
	Layout isn't summarized visually so it is difficult to see what is going on when it is scanned.
	Layout is clear, but should be summarized.
	Layout is clear, visually summarized and is crystal clear to the prospect. The layout allows the prospect to see clearly what it is that he or she should do next.

Uniqueness of Offer

Select One	Elements of Your Advertising / Marketing Promotion
	Offer is same as everything else the prospect sees.
	Offer is interesting, but it is vague and offers no specifics.
	Offer is unemotional and impersonal.
	Offer doesn't identify your business by name.
	Outstanding offer with emotional pull that incites prospect to take action and interact with you.

Call to Action

Select One	Elements of Your Advertising / Marketing Promotion
	No call to action.
	It is ordinary and unexciting. Prospects aren't going to be excited to respond.
	Offer is unclear and confusing. Confused prospects don't take action.
	Offer doesn't clearly tell the prospect what to do next.
	Complete lack of urgency and deadline.
	Insufficient reward, incentive or bonus for the prospect to act quickly.
	Insufficient loss, penalty, or fear of loss for the prospect if she doesn't act quickly.
	Great call to action. It is clear, concise, and speaks to both reward and loss to the prospect and has urgency so she wants to take action now.

What one thing will you to better market your business as a result of this systematic approach to evaluating a marketing piece?

10. They are implementers. They get things done and insist on things getting done.
Section 3 of *The System is the Secret* is all about getting your systems in place and getting things done. I've also written an E-book entitled *Secrets of Implementation* that you can buy from Amazon.com to help you implement better in your life and business.

You don't stay at the top for long by being easy on yourself. The leaders in any field are those who expect superior, on-time, on-target results from themselves in every setting. This can cause stress and unhappiness because you are always working to implement and know you must continually do more than you are.

Jim Collins calls this habit "productive paranoia" or being obsessed on implementation. One of the interesting observations he makes in *Great by Choice* is: "...Leaders remain obsessively focused on their objectives *and* hypervigilant about changes in their environment; they push for perfect execution *and* adjust to changing conditions..."—p. 114.

Implementers know what they need to do and get busy doing it and doing it consistently. Don't procrastinate or make excuses. As an implementer, just get your most important priorities done, period. Be one who implements quickly. Remember, the top earners in your business or any other are those who have adopted the habit of implementation.

I hope this discussion of the systems and behaviors of top entrepreneurs has been helpful for you.

I'm reminded of something Robert Kiyosaki said in his book *The Midas Touch*. He says: "Leaders have vision, which is nothing more than the ability to see into the future. Entrepreneurs are different. They need more than vision. Entrepreneurs must have vision plus the power of focus."—*The Midas Touch*, p. 65.

My hope is that you will take these ten habits seriously and adopt each and every one of them into your life. You can choose to be great by what you focus on. I would encourage you to pick four of these habits I've discussed in this chapter and decide to adopt them and have them be a major part of your life by this time next year. Which of the ten I've discussed will be the habits you will master in the coming year?

If you will work on one habit every quarter (3 months or 13 weeks) – if you will work on that habit at least 20 minutes a day for the next 13 weeks, it will be yours for life.

Put up signs around your home or your business to remind yourself of the habits employed by the world's most successful entrepreneurs that you are going to develop and make a part of your life. Then, you will employ the behaviors and skills necessary to build a great business with systems that will propel your business to new heights.

Section 2:
Mapping Out the Specifics

CHAPTER 6

GOALS / MISSION / VISION SYSTEMS

"The problem is never how to get new, innovative thoughts into your mind, but how to get old ones out."—Dee Hock, Founder of Visa

In Section 1 of *The System is The Secret*, I taught you about the importance of systems and why you will need them as your business grows to not only adapt to changes occurring in your market but also to ensure that what *must* be done in your business is *actually* getting done. This requires you to search out *what works now* and *actively implement* it in your business. In this section, I'm going to cover the most important systems you need to implement in your business starting with your goals, mission, and vision. A lot has been written and said about goals. You need to be absolutely clear about what you want. Remember, the rewards of the future won't come to those who wait or those who are content to keep doing what they've always been doing.

To help you gain more clarity about what you are working towards, here are five fundamental areas of your business that you must pay attention to:

1. Where you are really going.
When things are challenging in business, many entrepreneurs try to hang on to what they've got. When this happens over a long period of time, it is easy to forget about *where* you are heading. Every business challenge is different, but one constant truth remains. If in the midst of all of the turmoil around you, you forget where you are going, you *will* end up somewhere else.

Taking the time to determine where you are really going is a scary task for many. It is especially difficult to set goals or have a vision for the future when there are too many unknown variables. Some settle for just getting by and inadvertently put off their goals and dreams because they forget to take the time to plan where they are really going.

A great story that really explores this idea is found in two-time heavyweight champion George Foreman's book entitled *Knockout Entrepreneur*. There are many great lessons in this book, but one I want to highlight here has everything to do with knowing where you are really going and wanting it bad enough to do what it takes to get there.

On October 29, 1974 in Kinshasa, Zaire, George faced Muhammad Ali in a fight that was called "The Rumble in the Jungle". During the fight, Foreman got knocked down by Muhammad Ali. Laying flat on the mat, he looked over to his manager Dick Sadler who had told him previously, "If you ever get knocked down, don't try to get up too quickly. Look around the ring. Find me, and let me do the counting."

Foreman said, "Rather than bounce back to my feet, I did just as we had always planned. I stayed on the mat for a few seconds, allowing my head to clear as I looked for Dick. I caught his eye and watched for his signal that it was time to get up. But something went horribly wrong. I was on the floor, but I was not listening to the count. I was watching Dick. By the time Dick signaled me to get up, the ref had rattled off a quick, 'Eight, nine, ten!' The fight was over and I had lost! I had been technically knocked out, even though I had the strength, the ability, and the will to get back up."–*Knockout Entrepreneur*, p. 186.

Foreman continues: "I was embarrassed and angry; angry at Dick for not getting me up in time, and most of all, angry at myself for not listening to the count. I hurt inside, not from physical pain, but from the embarrassment and revulsion I felt at losing that way. I was lower than low. The knowledge that I had not been beaten—but that I had actually beaten myself by not getting up in time—lurked constantly in the back of my mind. I said, "I will never allow that to happen to me again."–p. 186.

Have you been knocked down by a competitor? By a client who attacked you or your business personally online? Has the up and down roller coaster ride of the economy beaten you down? I love Foreman's commitment and conviction in that last sentence: "I will never allow that to happen to me again."

Once a commitment is made, it will be tested. George Foreman's was tested 15 months later in a fight with Ron Lyle on January 28, 1976. Foreman was knocked down in the 4th round. He said: "I knew that getting up meant that I was going to get clobbered again; I knew I couldn't stop him from coming at me, and this man's punches packed some wallop!"

He continues:
"Then I remembered how I felt that night in Africa when I should have gotten up, could have gotten up, but didn't. I said to myself, Today, I may die, but I must get up. I couldn't see very well, and I knew that Lyle would come at me with full force again, but I said to myself in those moments on the floor, I never again want to live with the knowledge that I could have gotten up and didn't. I don't want to look myself in the mirror and hear me saying, 'You didn't get back up.' Foreman got up and hit Lyle "so hard that the blow dislodged his mouthpiece". When Lyle got back up, he came at Foreman even harder and stronger and knocked Foreman down again and the 4th round ended.

When Foreman went to his corner, his cornerman Gil Clancy said "George, the one that's gonna win is the one who wants it most."

Then Clancy asked him, "Do you want it most?"

Foreman came back out and knocked Lyle out in the 5th round. This story is a great example of what you should be thinking about as you think about the future in your business. What do you really want? How badly do you want it? What are you willing to do to make it happen? Who will you get around to get back on track? What will you do to keep your vision in front of you as you struggle through difficulties to get there?

If you have stopped dreaming, now is the time to start again. Don't let the nightmares in your business closet stop you from getting out into the sun and thinking about what you want to accomplish. There was a reason you got in business for yourself. Adversity, heartbreak, despair, and discouragement have been holding you back from dreaming. Get out of the darkness and go towards the light – go toward what you want, not what you don't.

2. Your most important priority or what matters most.

Former Lufthansa jet pilot Dieter Uchtdorf recently told this story about the importance of not losing sight of what matters most. He said: "On a dark December night 36 years ago, a Lockheed 1011 jumbo jet crashed into the Florida Everglades, killing over 100 people. This terrible accident was one of the deadliest crashes in the history of the United States. A curious thing about this accident is that all vital parts and systems of the airplane were functioning perfectly—the plane could have easily landed safely at its destination in Miami, only 20 miles (32 km) away. During the final approach, however, the crew noticed that one green light had failed to illuminate—a light that indicates whether or not the nose landing gear has extended successfully. The pilots discontinued the approach, set the aircraft into a circling holding pattern over the pitch-black Everglades, and turned their attention toward investigating the problem. They became so preoccupied with their search that they failed to realize the plane was gradually descending closer and closer toward the dark swamp below. By the time someone noticed what was happening, it was too late to avoid the disaster.

After the accident, investigators tried to determine the cause. The landing gear had indeed lowered properly. The plane was in perfect mechanical condition. Everything was working properly—all except one thing: a single burned-out lightbulb. That tiny bulb—worth about 20 cents—started the chain of events that ultimately led to the tragic deaths of over 100 people. Of course, the malfunctioning lightbulb didn't cause the accident; it happened because the crew placed its focus on something that seemed to matter at the moment while losing sight of what mattered most."

Has this happened to you in your business? Have you gotten caught up in the heat of the moment and lost sight of the fundamentals of your business? It is so easy to get distracted by the new, shiny object. Unfortunately, like the pilots of the disaster just mentioned, it is easy to lose your bearings when you focus on what seems to matter now at the exclusion of your business fundamentals.

Will what you are considering offering in the marketplace help your business be profitable? Spending your profits on bringing a new product to market without also eliminating unprofitable areas of your business is an example of focusing on what seems to matter at the moment with what matters most (your overall profitability and long-term plan). What is happening in someone else's business isn't nearly as important as what is happening in *your* business. Be sure you focus on what matters most *to you* now. John Maxwell makes this point: "I read a study of thirty-nine midsized companies stating that the characteristic that differentiated the successful companies from the unsuccessful was simplicity. The companies that sold fewer products to fewer customers, and who worked with fewer suppliers than other companies in the same industry were more profitable. Simple, focused operations brought greater results. As Warren Buffet observes, 'The business schools reward difficult, complex behavior more than simple behavior, but simple behavior is more effective.' By striving for simplicity, I [keep] my mind on the main thing."-*Leadership Gold*, pp. 97-98.

As an entrepreneur, it is very easy to get caught up doing so many things that you end up doing the wrong things. Find and focus on the main thing that will help your business be successful. The bottom line is that the things that matter most (getting new paying clients into your marketing funnel and learning how to sell more effectively once they are there) should never be at the mercy of what matters least.

3. The limiting factors that are holding you back.
What are your limiting factors? A limiting factor is an area of your business that holds you back from accomplishing all that you could if it weren't present. For example, an inability to close sales is the limiting factor that holds you back from hitting your weekly and monthly sales goals.

There are parts of your business that you may be ignoring or forgetting about that are the limiting step in why your business isn't growing like it could or should. You have to determine what these areas are and face them head on instead of pretending that they don't exist simply because you're not confident or competent in them.

In addition to these limiting factors, you may also be guilty of being afraid to make mistakes. In other words, you don't want to take on these areas of your business because you may make a mistake in them. Ignoring them doesn't make them go away. You may have seen the sign in a high-pressure sales office that says, "Do you like to travel? Do you want to meet friends? Do you want to free up your future? All this can be yours if you make one more mistake."

Are you or members of your team consumed with fear of making a mistake? Do members of your team feel intimidated by you so that they are afraid to bring up warning signs because of how you might react? This fear of intimidation may be a limiting factor that prevents those around you from speaking up and telling you what you need to know.

Michael Abrashoff talks about this issue in his book, *It's Your Ship*. He says: "The moment I heard about it [the tragic sinking of a Japanese fishing boat off Honolulu by the submarine USS Greeneville], I was reminded that, as is often the case with accidents, someone senses possible danger but doesn't necessarily speak up. As the Greenville investigation unfolded, I read in a *New York Times* article that the submarine's crew 'respected the commanding officer too much to question his judgment.' If that's respect, then I want none of it. You need to have people in your organization that can tap you on the shoulder and say, 'Is this the best way?' or 'Slow down,' or 'Think about this,'....History records countless incidents in which ship captains or organization managers permitted a climate of intimidation to pervade the workplace, silencing subordinates whose warnings could have prevented disaster. Even when the reluctance to speak up stems from admiration for the commanding officer's skill and experience, a climate to question decisions must be created in order to foster double-checking." –p. 33.

Be approachable. Let others know that you value their input and feedback on your team. Meet often to discuss the challenges and problems that are going on in your business. When you ask members of your team for help with issues that are going on, they will share wonderful ideas with you that can help you take your business to the next level.

Identify your limitations and surround yourself with others who can help you do what needs to be done in all of the areas of your business. Don't let your limitations hold you back from accomplishing more.

4. What your competition is doing.
One of the most frightening things that you may have been ignoring about your business is what your competition is doing. In challenging economic situations, competitors often become much more aggressive

about their pricing and their marketing approach.

If business has been slower for you lately, it isn't just the "economy" that is the problem. It is that your competitors are being much more aggressive about luring away your clients or prospective clients with nearly unbelievable offers designed to get them to buy from them instead of from you.

When marketing your offer, focus on the total value clients get at your business, your reason to choose you over your competitors. Having a distinct difference helps you build contrast in the eyes of the prospects, and if the contrast is great enough, they will buy from you, since you have the best overall value. Also, pre-empt your competitors with a great pre-sales strategy and lots of testimonials from clients who have already purchased from you.

Here are six suggestions to help you stay on top of what your competition is doing:
1) Do a SWOT analysis.
Analyze your competitors in four areas:
- Strengths: What are their strengths in your market?
- Weaknesses: What are their weaknesses in your market?
- Opportunities: What major opportunities exist to outsell them?
- Threats: What major threats do they pose to our survival?

Evaluating your competitor's game plan is a good way to evaluate how to take on your competitors.

2) Watch what your competitors are doing with their social networking sites and advertising.
Watch your competitors closely to see how they are marketing now. Study what they are doing on Facebook and Twitter. This will give you a good indication of what prospects in your market niche are hearing and can give you some good ideas for how to counteract what they are doing and have a competitive advantage.

3) Visit their web site often.
When was the last time you went to the websites of all of your competitors? If they update their sites often, go back frequently. Pay attention to what they're doing to attract prospects into their business.

4) Build a contrast diagram for what you offer in comparison with other competitors who offer a similar product or service.

Contrast is a powerful psychological trigger that helps people make the decision to buy. It is a good idea to put together a contrast diagram for how you are different from your competitors. If you haven't done this, I would strongly encourage you to take the time to do so. You don't have to show this to the prospects who come into your business (either online or offline), but it can be a helpful way to build contrast in their minds if you do. It is a great exercise that will allow you to discuss the benefits of buying at your business with other members of your team.

5) Listen carefully to what clients say about your competitors.

Ask them for the differences they experienced between your business and theirs. If a client says something negative about one of your competitors, don't pass that negative information on to others. It will only make you look bad. Instead, use the information to more effectively position your business in the marketplace. Another important thing to do is to ask those who buy from you to share how your experience, your offer, and your business compared with others she may have visited as she was making her decision via a written or video testimonial that you can post on your web site or social media.

6) Develop friendships with your competitors.

It is amazing what can happen when you get to know your competitors. Now, you may have some competitors that you could never envision being friends with in a million years because of some past experience. Don't let that negative experience prevent you from getting to know your other competitors. As an example, when my wife and I opened our first store, I introduced myself to the managers of one of our competitors at a trade show. I told her what we specialized in and where our business was. We got a lot of referrals from them because she told prospects to come to our business when they didn't have exactly what the individual was looking for. Get to know your competitors. They are good people too. They may end up being a great source of referrals.

Here are ten questions you can use to evaluate your competitive advantage:

1. Is what you sell in your business perceived by clients to be unique enough to ask a premium price and get it?
2. Can clients get the same products or services you sell from a local or Internet competitor for less? Or are you perceived to be the only

provider of what you offer (seen as specialist)?

3. Do prospects and clients perceive you to be an authority figure in your market? Do they look to you for advice and follow it?

4. Do prospects and clients perceive you to be a better value overall than what your competitors offer? What do they perceive is the most valuable aspect of what you are offering?

5. Do prospects perceive you to be a lower risk provider of what you offer than your competitors as they deal with their dream or nightmare?

6. Are your clients loyal to you once they've purchased a product or service from you (or are other competitors more persuasive in their marketing to pull them into their businesses)?

7. Are you perceived to be a generalist or a specialist by prospects in your area?

8. Do prospects perceive your marketing materials to build your brand or the brand of the category of what you offer in your business?

9. Do clients feel assured by their peers that your business is the best place to shop for what you sell? Are your video and written testimonials persuasive?

10. What reputation does your business have online and how do you respond to negative reviews?

Here are twelve questions to help you evaluate your overall strength as compared with your biggest competitors:

1. Do you have any economy of scale advantage in how you purchase what you sell? (example: you buy your product lines for less allowing you to maximize your profitability)

2. Do you occasionally or regularly cut your prices and lower your profit margin to match or beat a competitor's price to get the sale? If so, select 1-5 (depending on how often it occurs)?

3. Do you have operations advantages (better fixed costs) that help you have an advantage over your competitors?

4. Do you have relationships with individuals in specific niche channels that your competitors don't have that you are able to monetize?

5. Do you have territory protection with certain vendors to give you exclusivity to stand out from your competitors? (If so, rate your strength 1-10 based on what percentage of the total vendors you carry that give you this advantage)

6. Do you have a better follow up sequence than your competitors to get sales from those who have purchased (or haven't purchased) than your competitors?

7. What advantages do you have over competitors at trade shows (bigger booth space, more sales consultants, better offers, etc.)?

8. How does your social networking presence compare with that of your competitors (Facebook, Twitter, blogging, etc.)?

9. How does your web site compare with that of your competitors?

10. How do your sales closing percentages compare with those of your competitors? Do you have a sales training system that you use to keep your consultant's sales skills sharp?

11. How well do you ask for and get referrals from the clients you sell to as compared with your competition?

12. What is extraordinary about your business as compared with your competitors? Do prospects perceive this difference?

Hopefully these questions have helped you realize that ignoring what your competition is doing is not a good idea. While you don't want this to dictate your long-term strategy, it is very important to not only be aware of what is going on, but also to look for ways that you can pre-empt your competition and get prospects to your business first.

5. What you do to stay up when you are down.
In today's marketplace, it is easy to allow yourself and your thinking to be swayed by the constant barrage of breaking news and the changing buying patterns of prospects coming into your business. If you don't learn to overcome the resistance you are experiencing in your business, your life, and from the prospects who come into your business, your sales numbers will go up and down and cause you great anxiety and stress.

A great analogy that really helps me understand what it takes to stay up when you are down is found in the difference between a thermometer and a thermostat. Consider this statement from John C. Maxwell in his book *Developing the Leaders Around You*: "At first glance, a person could confuse these instruments. Both are capable of measuring heat. However, they are really quite different. A thermometer is passive. It records the temperature of its environment but can do nothing to change that environment. A thermostat is an active instrument. It determines what the environment will be. It effects change in order to create a climate."—pp. 17-18.

Great leaders are able to set the temperature and create an environment where growth and results continue even in difficult and challenging circumstances. Difficult moments reveal our true character. Are we easily swayed by the swirling winds around us or do we hold a steady course and do what it takes to persist in the face of tremendous adversity and difficulty? What type of leader are you in your business?

Do you simply record the sales that are made at the end of each day or do you create the environment necessary to have your sales rise? Having the courage to remain persistent and exerting the effort it takes to create consistent accomplishment and results is what generates momentum. It takes a lot of work and discipline to stay steady while continually analyzing performance in order to increase closing percentages and increase sales month after month.

Persistence and steadiness are what keep the thermostat leader up when things are down. There is a big distinction in the results that come from being a thermostat leader versus a thermometer one. Make the commitment and choose to be a thermostat leader.

With these five areas in mind, let's talk more specifically about your business systems, your goals, and how you should set them up for your business.

First, let me share with you a brilliant strategy I learned from Cameron Herold. Cameron has more than twenty years of experience operating some of the biggest business success stories in North America. He was the former COO of 1-800-GOT-JUNK? and was instrumental in growing the company from $2 million to $105 million in revenue in six years. In his book *Double, Double*, he explains that one way they were able to fix systems was through a seven minute stand up huddle meeting that started everyday at 10:55 and ended at 11:02.

The huddle was broken down into six areas. These were good news, numbers, what does it mean?, departmental update, missing systems/frustrations, and the cheer.

Here is how you can use a huddle meeting for your business:
1) **Good news** – report on what's working well

2) **Numbers** – review what happened the previous day (Are you on track or off track for your monthly goal? If you are off goal, what needs to be done to make up what you're missing?)

3) **What does it all mean?** - Show everyone on your team where you are at in reaching your weekly and monthly goals. Talk about what the achievement of that goal will mean for every member of the team.

4) **Departmental update** – Herold explains that they had eight areas of their company and one person was in charge of each area. They would rotate through these (one per day) and then repeat them again. You could do this by dividing up each area or department of your business and then take 60 seconds to report on what is being done in their area of responsibility. The most important thing is that each of the individuals always bring their discussion back to the top three projects that you are working on each quarter (or one big goal per area of your business per month). You may want to break these up into the your specific systems we'll discuss in Section 2 of *The System is the Secret*. If you have a smaller team, you can divide out the responsibilities depending on who would do best in each area and then have them report on what is happening in these meetings daily. If you are a smaller business and you will be doing the majority of these tasks, then update yourself daily in what you are doing in each of your system areas. Focus on one area per day and think about what you are doing to help accomplish this goal.

5) **Missing Systems / Frustrations** - Herold says that this was key in how they improved their business. He said: "We'd then share any missing systems we'd found or things that were frustrating us in some area of the business. Anyone could share these, and it was always done in a no-blame environment. After each frustration was shared, someone else would raise their hand and simply say, 'I'll take it,' meaning that they would take ownership and see to it that the problem got fixed. No debate or discussion happened during a Huddle: issues were simply raised and then someone offered to resolve them." –p. 103.

You may find this a great opportunity to discuss an area where a system has broken down. For example, let's say that someone dropped the ball with a client. Just say: "As you are probably aware, yesterday the following situation occurred. We want to make sure that this doesn't happen again. Who will help us plug the holes in our system and report back on what has been done to resolve this problem going forward? (Then, ask the individual who says: "I'll take it" to report back on what has been done in the next huddle.)

6) Cheer

Herold says: "We'd then finish Huddle with what we called the "High Gloss Cheer," named after Christopher 'High Gloss' Bennett, who was always a huge culture booster for the company. The cheer was something based on the good news we'd heard that day at Huddle. And yes, it was dorky at first, but everyone grew to love it, and it always ended Huddle on a high note.

Use this section of the book to learn how to break down the tasks and responsibilities within each system to make your own list of what areas within your system that you need to improve. Then, delegate and assign these tasks as assignments when you meet with individual staff members or as part of your own Huddle type meeting.

I would highly recommend that you follow this approach especially as it relates to systems improvement. There are always things that you can do to improve and get better at what needs to be done.

If you choose to use the first five, six, or seven minutes of your day in a huddle type meeting, you will need to spend a little bit more time preparing what you will discuss by coming in a little earlier or by preparing what will be on your huddle form the day before. Such planning and preparation time will be invaluable to help you start each day off right.

One of the challenges with implementing effective systems is knowing whether you have set it up correctly. While some systems work has to be perfected with experience and time, I've created evaluation charts for you to consider where you are starting from (or where you're currently at) with each of the systems we'll talk about in *The System is the Secret.*

This will help you see obvious areas for improvement and can help you evaluate your preparedness in other areas you may not have considered.

Here is an example of what your huddle form could look like:

HUDDLE MEETING

Date: _____

GOOD NEWS / WHAT'S WORKING	NUMBERS FROM YESTERDAY
	Daily Sales
	_____
	Close Ratios
	_____
	On Track for Month:
	_____
	What Do We Need to Make Up:
	_____
TO GO TO REACH GOAL: Target:	**DEPARTMENTAL UPDATE**
Optimal:	
MISSING SYSTEMS/FRUSTRATIONS:	**CHEER**

Notes / Delegated Assignments:

To help you evaluate your systems overall, complete the exercise as it appears in this section. There will be an assessment for each system.

We'll start with an assessment of your systems overall. Rate yourself from 1-10 (with 10 being the best) based on your current business behaviors. The statements on either side of the 1-10 numbers show opposite ends of the spectrum with what is being done. You may find that you excel with certain systems and need improvement in others. You can go back and re-take the assessments from time to time to evaluate how you are doing.

#	Rank yourself from 1-10 based on your current business behaviors.	1	2	3	4	5	6	7	8	9	10	Rank yourself from 1-10 based on your current business behaviors.
1	We don't have any systems.											Our systems are right for our business.
2	We have processes we follow at our business, but if the owner wasn't there to oversee it, it wouldn't happen correctly and mistakes would be made.											Our systems are well documented and updated regularly.
3	If the owner is gone from the business, no one else knows how to pull reports or analyze business performance information.											Important business performance information from all of our systems is readily available and easy to retrieve.
4	The same customer service issues seem to plague us over and over. The processes in our business don't seem to prevent problems from happening on a regular basis.											Our systems are reliable and there are minimal customer service issues as a result.
5	I am not able to make good decisions about our business because I am unable to retrieve the information I need.											Our systems give me the information I need to make important decisions about our business.
6	Our critical computer data is not properly backed up and safe and it would be a disaster if we could not access it.											Our critical computer data is properly backed up and safe and can be recovered quickly in the event of a disaster.
7	We have systems but few, if anyone (other than the owner), pay attention to them.											Our systems are in place and each member of our team adheres to them.
8	We hope that things show up on time and don't really have a mechanism to check to ensure that things are on track.											We have an ongoing system to regular communicate our orders with our suppliers.

To improve systems and operations, you need to follow the Jack Welch rule. Jack Welch believed in dumping the under-performing 20% of everything (at least) once a year. Taking these actions allows you to prune back what is no longer working for you. Welch used four standards to make pruning decisions in his business. These were:

1. If a GE business could not be number one or number two in its market, it would be cut.
2. Any business that was struggling (sick) would be 'fixed, closed, or sold.'
3. Every year, GE would fire the bottom 10 percent of the work force.
4. Welch would get rid of the layers of bureaucracy in the company that slowed down communication, productivity and ideas." – *Necessary Endings*, pp. 24-25.

As a result of having this pruning approach, "GE grew from $26 billion in revenues to $130 billion and from around $14 billion in market value to over $410 billion, making it the most valuable company in the world at the time."

In his book, *Necessary Endings*, Dr. Henry Cloud says:
"Are you only achieving average results in relation to where you or your business or team is supposed to be? In other words, given your abilities, resources, opportunities, etc. are you reaching your full potential, or are you drifting toward a middle that is lower than where you should be if you were getting the most from who you are and what you have? When pruning is not happening, average or worse will happen? –*Necessary Endings*, p. 19.

He continues:
"Sometimes people equate the concept of pruning with cutting expenses or 'reducing head count.' They say things like, 'You're right. We have got some fat around here and need to cut some costs.' But cutting costs is not what pruning is about, and when someone says that, they are thinking more like a manager than a leader....The kind of pruning I'm talking about has to do with focus, mission, purpose, structure, and strategic execution. A mere expense cut might have enabled GE to keep all of the two hundred or so businesses it got rid of, if it has just followed a mantra to cut all expenses by 10 percent. As a result, the 'average roses' would then become even less than average, and we would not still be talking about GE's accomplishments. So what we are talking about here is not just 'cutting fat,' as the phrase goes. We are talking about defining what the bush is going to look like and pruning everything that is

keeping it from realizing that vision—be it good, bad, or dead."– Dr. Henry Cloud, *Necessary Endings*, p. 29-30.

What do you need to prune out of your business? What is in the bottom 20% of:

- Your product offerings?
- Your customers / clients?
- Parts of business that no longer are producing?
- Sales consultants?
- Friends?
- Vendors?
- Investments?

You should rank the underperforming areas of your business because it forces you to evaluate, assess, and rank things based on what's working and what's not. It also allows you to make room and space to *attract* better and higher value items into your business. The biggest reason is that it prevents complacency (which is the killer of all progress). Systems allow you to set up standards by which everything that you run in your business can be enforced.

For example:

- How many rings before the phone is answered in your business?
- Is the script adhered to?
- How is a prospect educated on your unique advantages in the marketplace on your web site?
- How well do you follow up with each prospect who registers on your web site and enters your marketing funnel?
- Do prospects and clients go through the three steps of every sale (approach, presentation, close)? If not, where are they dropping out of your sales process?
- Do you have a pre-sales system that prepares your prospect to buy? How could you better implement this type of system in your business?

Let's take a minute to talk more specifically about your goals. I hope you've taken the time to figure out your goals so that you are absolutely clear about what you want. If not, you need to do that within the next week and determine what targets you are going to strive for and hit in the weeks, months, and year ahead. If you don't, you'll be stuck with what you've always been doing.

For example, you could set goals for a specific month and then looking at growth targets based on your minimum, target and optimal goals. I've found it helpful to have a minimum goal (which should be at least a 3-5% increase over the previous year just to keep up with inflation). You can set your target and optimal goals at whatever percentage increase you desire. This chart gives an example of a 6-9 percent increase for target goals and a 10-15% increase for optimal goals.

Once you've set your own goals, you can actually track how well you've performed in the last column. The worksheet also allows you to see on paper how you will be able to reach your goal based on the numbers you'll actually need to be able to hit to reach the goal.

Thinking in specifics like this will help you be much more effective than just setting a goal. You've got to have a thought out process that allows you to determine exactly what must be done to reach your goals. Here is an example of a chart you could use as a system to think and plan out how you will increase your performance goals as they relate to sales.

Month:	Example	Sales This Month Last Year (or Historical Best Month)	Your Minimum Goal (should be 3-5% increase over last year)	Your Target Goal (should be 6-9% increase over last year)	Your Optimal Goal (should be 10-15% increase over last year)	Actual Results This Month
1. What are your monthly sales?	$100,000					
2. What is your percent targeted increase?	5%					
3. What increase in your gross sales is actually needed to accomplish this goal?	$5,000					

Month:	Example	Sales This Month Last Year (or Historical Best Month)	Your Minimum Goal (should be 3-5% increase over last year)	Your Target Goal (should be 6-9% increase over last year)	Your Optimal Goal (should be 10-15% increase over last year)	Actual Results This Month
4. What is your average sale per transaction?	$1,000					
5. What is your conversion / closing ratio?	50%					
6. How many new prospects are needed to reach your goal?	You need to bring in 10 prospects to sell 5					

With these numbers in place, you can figure exactly what you must do in revenue by month, week, day, and hour to reach your goals:

1) Total # of _____ Products Sold / Month: _____

2) Total # of _____ Products Sold / Week: _____

3) Total # of _____ Products Sold / Day: _____

4) Total # of _____ Products Sold / Hour: _____

Clarity is the key. When you are clear about your hourly, daily, weekly, and monthly targets, you can evaluate what you are doing at any moment to see whether it is moving you towards or away from your goal. In this way, your goals system will keep you on track towards the accomplishment of your goals and you can make adjustments when necessary.

If you have set goals in the past, but haven't achieved them, let me offer you three suggestions.

1) Don't emotionally throw in the towel.

Virtually all people who have accomplished anything have thought about quitting when they've been discouraged. The difference between those who succeed and those who end up failing is that the successful ones don't act on those thoughts.

I once read an interesting statement about former Green Bay Packers coach Vince Lombardi. He was widely recognized as one of the greatest motivational and optimistic coaches in the history of the game. Yet privately, he once considered quitting coaching and becoming a bank teller. Think about how many would have never benefited from his tremendous wisdom if he had decided to throw in the towel and give up. You have greatness within you as well. You have a mission you are here to fulfill. Don't let discouragement prevent you from making your goals happen.

I suppose that there will always be those willing to promote their attitudes of pessimism and doom and gloom. You may have thought these thoughts before. However, I've found that even when you have discouraging days in business, a shift in perspective can help you start **thinking differently** and **acting decisively** towards putting together marketing promotions and sales training that will help you get better results. Choose to focus on what you do want and be absolutely clear about it.

There is an interesting statement in Napoleon Hill's classic *Think and Grow Rich* that addresses this. He said: "Fears are nothing more than states of mind. One's state of mind is subject to control and direction. Man [or woman] can create nothing which he [or she] does not first conceive in the form of an impulse or thought.

He continues: "Face the facts squarely. Ask yourself definite questions and demand direct replies. When the examination is over, you will know more about yourself. If you do not feel that you can be an impartial judge in this self-examination, call upon someone who knows you well to serve as judge while you cross-examine yourself. You are after the truth. Get it, no matter at what cost even though it may temporarily embarrass you." –p. 225-226.

He then lists six symptoms of fear. These are:

1) *Indifference*. Commonly expressed through lack of ambition; willingness to tolerate poverty; acceptance of whatever compensation life may offer without protest; mental and physical laziness; lack of initiative, imagination, enthusiasm and self-control.

2) *Indecision*. The habit of permitting others to do one's thinking. Staying 'on the fence.'

3) *Doubt*. Generally expressed through alibis and excuses designed to cover up, explain away, or apologize for one's failures, sometimes expressed in the form of envy of those who are successful, or by criticizing them.

4) *Worry*. Usually expressed by finding fault with others, a tendency to spend beyond one's income, neglect of personal appearance, scowling and frowning; intemperance in the use of alcoholic drink, sometimes through the use of narcotics; nervousness, lack of poise and self-consciousness.

5) *Over-caution*. The habit of looking for the negative side of every circumstance, thinking and talking of possible failure instead of concentrating upon the means of succeeding. Knowing all of the roads to disaster, but never searching for the plans to avoid failure. Waiting for 'the right time' to begin putting ideas and plans into action, until the waiting becomes a permanent habit. Remembering those who have failed, and forgetting those who have succeeded. Seeing the hole in the doughnut, but overlooking the doughnut."

6) *Procrastination*. The habit of putting off until tomorrow that which should have been done last year. Spending enough time in creating alibis and excuses to have done the job. This systems is closely related to overcaution, doubt and worry. Refusal to accept responsibility when it can be avoided. Willing to compromise rather than put up a stiff fight...." –pp. 226-227.

Fear can mean different things to different people. It can mean *F*alse *E*vidence *A*ppearing *R*eal, *F*orget *E*verything *A*nd *R*un or it can mean *F*ace *E*verything *A*nd *R*ise. Fears can be controlled through your decision to manage them. As Ralph Waldo Emerson said: "Do the thing you fear and the death of fear is certain."

2) Pay attention to the critical numbers. Focus on the fundamentals. Don't let yesterday's successes or failures prevent you from doing what must be done today.

Tennis champion Chris Evert once said: "If I win several tournaments in a row, I get so confident I'm in a cloud. A loss gets me eager again." That is great perspective for how you should react to both the day's successes and failures. Sometimes you win. Sometimes you lose. When you win, briefly celebrate your victory. When you lose, focus on what you will do differently the next time. Celebrating too long can cause you to be complacent. Beating yourself up for too long will cause you to become despondent. Either behavior causes you to take your eye off of the fundamentals. Don't let this happen to you. Focus on the now and increase your sales with the prospects and clients in front of you.

What are the critical numbers you should pay attention to? Here are eight important financial indicators and numbers you should be looking at:

1. **Customer count and number of transactions.** Is your appointment schedule completely full (and you don't have any more available appointments to accommodate prospects who come in more than 50% of the time)?
   If you are losing sales because you don't have enough help to take care of all of the prospects coming into your business, then you need to figure out how to solve this problem quickly.

2. **Weekly sales by category.** Sometimes you are busier during different weeks of the year. How can you plan better? A great lesson about systems planning is found in a story told about Walt Disney and how he planned the opening of Disneyland. Walt anticipated times when he feared attendance would slacken and then created promotions to boost his business during those times. You should do the same. Splitting up your weekly sales by category can help you see where you have slower times so you can prepare and plan to promote yourself accordingly. You may also choose to add additional revenue generating activities that will help you get through slower times if it is justified.

3. **Weekly sales by salesperson and sales per hour of each sales person.** Sometimes you think you need more employees to increase your sales volume, but it may come down to the fact that what you *really* need is more exceptional salespeople. When you can visually see how each salesperson on your team is contributing to the overall goals of your business, you will make better decisions. Better sales training systems can also help you improve your results.

4. **Year over year by week.** How are you doing compared to the same week of the previous year? When you can visually see exciting upward or disappointing downward trends, you can make better decisions. Such analysis can help you determine whether you should sell your current product offering to new vertical markets or have better offerings for your current and best customers.

5. **Year over year to date.** What direction is your business heading? The more you can watch these trends and anticipate which product categories are doing best, the quicker you'll be able to act on what you're seeing.

6. **Number of units per transaction.** How many add on sales are being added to each ticket? Where is there room for improvement? How well is your staff upselling? The more upsells you have, the more opportunity for profit there will be.

7. **Number of voided or missing transactions.** This is particularly important to watch in any point of sales environment where there may be the temptation for someone to steal cash sales from you (by voiding them out after the sale is completed and pocketing the cash). If you see something that concerns you, you must watch it much more closely and catch the person in the act to prevent theft.

8. **Top and bottom 3 to 5 categories.** What are your top 3 categories? These are your opportunities. What are your bottom three categories that continually seem to decline from quarter to quarter and year to year? These are your liabilities and weaknesses and you should seek to drastically improve them or get rid of them.

3) Intensify your marketing.

One of the biggest mistakes entrepreneurs make during periods of economic slowdown is to cut back on their marketing. Intensifying and focusing on better marketing will help you be busier when other businesses in your industry may be slower.

In our retail businesses, I had our marketing calendar marked out a year in advance. This way I knew I had a specific strategy or promotion coming up in the next week or two to help to get more prospects into our business. If you don't have an effective marketing system and plan, it is easy to stop promoting yourself and get into a mindset where your behavior shows little to no action that is not healthy.

Looking for new ways to improve is so critical and important. Ask questions of others to find out what is working. Don't be content with how things are. Constantly seek to be learning and improving your marketing. There is one constant with today's buyers: **The expectations of what prospects and clients expect when they go into a business of any kind are changing.** Clients are experiencing new and exciting opportunities and offers everyday. Simply standing still will ensure that you get left behind in a hurry.

At the end of each specific systems area, I am going to give you several questions and tasks to complete that will help you implement what has been discussed.

First, here are seven questions to help you evaluate your Goal Systems:
1. What is the biggest challenge you are facing right now in your business?
2. What is exciting about your business?
3. What are the five most important goals you want to accomplish this year with your business?
4. What might stop you from achieving those goals?
5. What are you committed to doing that will get everyone else on your team on board with your goals?
6. What are you tolerating in your business?
7. What is taking you off track or preventing you from having the business you really want?

Set productivity goals as part of your goals. We'll talk more specifically about how to do this in Chapter 16. Be sure you use time blocking and get control of your time so you can ensure that you are clear about what you should be focusing on and doing every day.

Here is an assessment of your goals / vision / mission systems:

#	Rank yourself from 1-10 based on your current in-store behaviors.	1	2	3	4	5	6	7	8	9	10	Rank yourself from 1-10 based on your current in-store behaviors.
1	We don't really have any idea why we are selling what we are selling in our chosen market niche(s) at all times.											We have our finger on the pulse of our chosen market niche(s) at all times. We anticipate what these customers need and want and offer it.
2	We aren't moving in a clear direction. We make decisions haphazardly and as the need arises.											We are moving in a clear direction and every strategic decision supports that direction.
3	We don't follow our competition and really have no idea what they are doing.											We have a good knowledge of our competition and their practices and how we stand out from them.
4	Our business isn't going in the direction that we originally intended and/or in a direction we are really happy with.											Our business is going in the direction that we originally intended and/or in a direction we are happy with.
5	Vision, mission, goals, and strategies are well known by all.											We have clarity and consistency for our goals.
6	I'm often frustrated with myself as a business owner. I feel overwhelmed with problems and don't think about my long-term vision.											I am proud of myself as both a business owner and as a human being and feel confident with our vision.
7	I am not happy with the amount of money I am making.											I am happy with the amount of money I make.
8	No one on our team is really clear about what needs to be done daily, weekly, and monthly to make it happen.											Everyone on our team has clarity and consistency for our goals. They know what daily, weekly, and monthly targets we need to hit to make it happen.
9	I stay awake at night worrying about my business.											I do not stay awake at night worrying about my business.
10	The prospects coming into our business have no idea what we stand for and support.											The prospects coming into our business have a positive perception about our mission and purpose. They know what cause(s) we stand for and support.

Here are six tasks for you to complete as part of improving this system area in your business:

1. Set goals for each area of your business.
2. Extrapolate these goals to set overall revenue targets for your business.
3. Set goals for how you will use and be productive with your time.
4. Begin having Huddle Meetings daily with key members of your staff that are no longer than ten minutes.
5. Have each member of your team who is over a specific department submit to you their top five suggestions for how they will hit the targets you've set as a business and their recommendation of what the reward should be if the goal is achieved.
6. Meet with key team members weekly to discuss how these goals are being met and to give you a department update. If you do this as part of your Huddle meeting, be sure that you are only taking one minute as part of this meeting and rotate through each of the department areas so that you can cover each area two to three times each month. This will also ensure that those responsible for helping you achieve the business goals are held accountable for helping you reach those goal targets.

Remember, systems are the processes you put in place to automate tasks and keep your business on autopilot. In the remaining chapters in this section, I'll focus on each system and give you specific questions and tasks for you to work on next.

In Chapter 1, I explained that a great system has three characteristics:

- *It leverages or magnifies people to the point at which they can produce extraordinary results consistently again and again.*
- *Every possible problem has been thought through and a solution is known and practiced by all who follow the system.*
- *Every part of the system is organized, has order, and every process is defined in detail.*

Your goal as you complete each chapter in Section 2 of *The System is the Secret* is to set up and implement the systems you need in your business to consistently deliver value and results.

## Chapter 7

Monitoring Your Inbound/Outbound Lead Flow Systems

"The most dangerous kind of waste is the waste we do not recognize."—Shigeo Shingo

In this chapter, I'd like to discuss how you can better monitor and improve your in-bound flow of leads and how you can better prepare these leads to buy when they enter your marketing funnel and go through your sales process.

Don't let the time and money you spend in gathering leads go to waste by not having good systems in this area. This is what drives it all. Carrie Wilkerson says, "Systems are not sexy-but they really DO drive everything we do." This is especially true when it comes to lead flow systems. Without leads, you have no appointments and no sales. Without sales and cash flow, any business is on shaky ground.

Your inbound/outbound lead flow system is designed with three chief purposes:
1) Generate leads
2) Inform and educate about limited time offers (LTO)
3) Sell products

Most web sites only focus on informing and educating about what products are sold by a business. They rarely talk about LTOs and they don't have very good systems for how they generate leads on their web sites.

Clate Mask and Scott Martineau make this statement in their book *Conquer the Chaos* about the importance of a good lead generation system. They say:

"Don't you wish you had so many new customers coming in that you could pick and choose who you wanted to work with and then turn away the rest?

"Wouldn't it be great to know you'd never again have to stress about whether you'll reach your sales goal for the month? No more pulling your hair out and biting your nails in front of the spreadsheet, trying to make your numbers work, no more lying awake at night staring up into the dark, trying not to give in to that tight knot of tension in your stomach, hoping and wishing for it all to be somehow okay when you wake up?

"Imagine not having to worry about making your payroll or paying that pile of invoices on your desk. Wouldn't it be just incredible to know you have plenty of new business and money coming in, day-in, day-out, as regular and predictable as the tides?

They continue:
"Well, the truth is, you can do this in your business. It's not snake oil, it's not fantasy or fiction, and it's not hype. It's about knowing a few simple statistics about follow-up marketing.

"Consider this: Most sales do not close on the first point of contact. In fact:
Only 2 percent of sales close on the first contact
3 percent close on the second contact
4 percent close on the third contact
10 percent close on the fourth contact
81 percent of sales that close, close on or after the fifth contact! (Source: Sales and Marketing Executives Club of Los Angeles)

"So, according to this statistic, keeping in touch with your prospects is critical to closing more deals. Thus it would make sense for a business owner (who wants more than just a 2-3 percent close rate) to stay in contact with their prospects past the fifth point of contact, right?
"Well, even if it makes perfect sense to stay in touch, that's not what's happening.

"48 percent of businesses quit following up after the first call
24 percent quit following up after the second call
12 percent quit following up after the third call

6 percent quit following up after the fourth call
10 percent quit following up after the fifth call" (Source: Dartnell Corporation)

"If 81 percent of prospects buy on or after the fifth contact with a business and only 10 percent of businesses are following up past the fifth contact, guess who's getting all the business? The 10 percent who keep following up!

"Do you see the disconnect? When businesses fail to follow up, they fail to capitalize on the opportunity staring them in the face. Instead, they succumb to the chaos of the standard sales cycle. Let's talk about the sales cycle for just a minute. Though each business offers different products or services, the sales cycle is about the same for each one, in a very general sense. Before you can have a business, you've got to have customers. And in order to get customers, you've got to generate a few leads. This can be done by advertising, buying lists, setting up a website, referrals, and so on. Really, the ways of generating leads are nearly limitless.

But what happens next? Once you have your leads, what do you do with them?

"Every time you bring in new leads, the leads you get can be divided into three categories:
1. Leads ready now (Hot)
2. Leads not ready now but will be ready some day (Warm – these leads are critical to your success)
3. Leads that may never be ready (Cold or Bad Leads)" –pp. 143-145.

So, let's translate this to your business:
1. Hot Leads - Leads ready now would be prospects who have predetermined need and who who have requested information from your web sites (catalog request, special reports, etc.) about a specific product and who have scheduled an appointment or want to talk now about how they can utilize your products or services.

2. Warm Leads – leads at trade shows or leads generated by those who come to your web site and who aren't currently needing your product or service, but will soon

3. Cold (Bad) Leads – leads of those who have just purchased something else who may or may not realize that they *could* buy something from you someday.

Mask and Martineau continue:
"The problem is, you can't divide the leads into categories because you don't know which leads go into which categories. In most cases, small business owners make a few phone calls, write a few emails, and complete a quick 'temperature check' on the leads they've just received.

"Sorting out the most interested candidates, business owners and sales reps tend to chase after hot leads, trying to close the deal. But in doing so, they use up most of their available time and tend to neglect all their other customers and prospects.

"Now don't think we're criticizing. This behavior is completely understandable. In order to keep a business running, the business owner needs to bring in money. To bring in money, they've got to make sales. So of course the focus is going to be on the prospects most likely to buy, or customers who look as though they might buy again. This is called cherry picking.

"This is the stage most small businesses are in right now. And it's the same stage most of them will stay. Because once those hot prospects have either purchased or walked away, the cycle starts all over again. The small business owner needs more sales, so he finds more leads, chases after the hot prospects, closes a few deals, then fulfills the orders and starts back at the beginning.

"As long as this cycle continues, the treadmill will continue to speed up. You can almost hear the panicked thoughts of the business owner as they close a sale. Rather than rejoice in their success, they're thinking, 'Deal closed. Where will I find my next one?' As long as the small business owner is forced to hunt for new, hot leads, they will be unable to free themselves from the chains on their business. They will be running on the treadmill faster and faster, eventually falling flat on their face." –p. 145.

I think that is a very good description of why so many entrepreneurs are so frustrated. There is so much to do and so much focus on making the next sale that not enough focus is given to managing one of the most important systems of all—that of your lead flow acquisition and management.

This is why I want you to spend some time thinking about what you can do to improve this critical system in your business. You've got to know which method is bringing in leads and then what actions you can take to warm up the cold leads, and excite the warm leads so they are ready to buy now (which is essentially what the pre-sale is all about). The problem comes if you aren't converting the leads that you're spending money on so they are prepared to buy from you now.

There are twelve main ways to generate leads for your business. I'd like to explore each of them briefly and then give you an assignment to determine how many leads you are generating from each category. In fact, you may realize that you don't even really know where your leads are coming from and which methods are the most effective and productive for you.

Let's discuss each area briefly:

1. **Direct Marketing**

Within this category, here are twelve ways this can be done:

1) *Direct mail* – mailing a LTO directly into the home of a prospect
2) *Radio* – targeting a specific demographic with your LTO and with an invitation to act on it
3) *Business Card with Offer* – putting a specific offer on the back of the business card that you and every one of your sales consultants have. For example, your business card could have a special offer on your service on the back of it. You could give this out and invite friends to use it when they buy something from you.
4) *Telephone Invitation / Follow-up* – Making phone call to prospects to invite them to schedule a phone or in-person appointment or to come in and redeem a coupon with you:
   a. Your sample script could say (if you talk to the prospect live):
   "This is _____*name*_____ with _____*name of business*_____ and I'm calling to let you know that you just won a drawing in our business for a FREE ___*premium offer*__. You've been selected for this prize since you registered on our web site and you can redeem it by scheduling a phone or in-person appointment at our

business and by purchasing _____ on your first visit. Is there a time this week when you can schedule your appointment so you can redeem your prize?

b. If you are leaving a message, I think you should put more intrigue into the message so the prospect *wants* to call you back. For example:
Your sample script could say (if you leave a message):
"This is _____*name*_____ with _____*name of business*_____ and I'm calling to let _____*premium offer*_____. You've been selected for this prize since you registered on our web site and you can redeem it by calling me back at __*phone number*_____ and scheduling an appointment (by phone or in person). The prize is void if I don't hear back from you in the next 24 hours so please call me at __*phone number*___ right away so I can schedule your appointment and help you redeem your prize. I look forward to hearing from you soon.

5) *Movie ads* – placing an offer in front of where your audience is (many businesses have found this a great way to get exposure, but many don't have any kind of offer or code that could be captured by having someone take a picture of the offer on the screen that they can show you when they phone or visit you. Another effective way to use this type of lead generator is to link the ad to another medium such as inviting viewers to join your text message club or to enter their email on your web site so they can be entered in a drawing for a free gift of some kind that will be of value to your prospects.

6) *Ads in shopper's mailers (local publications mailed into homes).* These can be Val-Pak or other local shoppers.

7) *Ambassador cards* – these are cards that you invite your existing customers to give out to their friends to invite them into your business. Referral cards are one example of this being used well. You can also invite prospects or clients to hand these out to their friends in order to have a chance to win. You could also utilize ambassador cards digitally through social media channels and tie sharing the promotion with the opportunity to get a discount on a product you offer. For example, anyone who shares the card with their network and has 25 likes can get $25 off a product or if they get 50 likes, they can get $50 off a product. They have to show you their Facebook page and show that the ad has been shared to their network as well as the number of likes to the promotion in order to

redeem the offer.

8) *Catalog* – this can be a great way of generating leads on your web site and can help you consistently get numerous leads a day from prospects requesting catalogs or magalogs from your web site.

9) *Newsletter* – this lead acquisition strategy can help you convert cold or warm leads into warmer or hot leads. It allows you to stay in touch with your lead list in a non-threatening and informative way.

10) *LTOs (Limited Time Offers)* – these are specific offers that are given to prospects or customers when they buy. You could also offer something specific to your prospect or client if they bring in a copy of a testimonial that they've posted online about your business.

11) *Upsell in business* – inviting the prospect to buy an additional item at the time of checkout for an additional savings can help you boost sales and profits.

12) *Bounce back coupon* – a series of coupons designed to get the prospect to return for additional purchases or to invite other acquaintances to return to buy something else from you as well.

Now, I want you and each of your sales consultants to look at how many leads they are generating monthly. Here is a very important reason why you should do this according to Dan Kennedy: "People read your ad, call your place of business, ask a question, the receptionist answers it, and that's it—no capture of the caller's name, address, email, etc. and no offer to immediately send a free report, gift, coupons. That is criminal waste. It cost money to get that call. Doing nothing with it is exactly the same as flushing money down the toilet. Please go and do so, right now, so you internalize the feeling. Take the largest bill you have in your wallet (or purse)—a $10, a $20, preferably a $100—go to your toilet, tear it into hunks, let them flutter into the toilet, and flush. You probably won't like it. Good. Remember how much you don't like it every time you fail to follow-up (a lot) on a lead or customer....From now on, nothing you do will just be one thing. There will be a planned sequence of things completed. Any contact by you with a prospect or any contact with you by a prospect will trigger a series of follow-up steps."—No. B.S. *Direct Marketing*, pp. 16-17.

For each of these categories, you should determine if you could use the lead generation strategy. If you are already using the lead generation system, determine how many leads you are currently generating / month and how much money you're generating per month from these lead sources. This will help you determine what is working and where you can improve the number of leads and the amount sold per lead.

2. Print Ads

Within this category, there are five specific ways this can be done:

1) *Industry Specific Magazine Ads* – running print ads in magazines that aren't seen by a large number of your prospective customers are generally a waste of money. However, industry specific magazines can be effective if they have a good distribution channel. If you use print ads, be sure that you are educating and informing your prospective clients of something of interest to them, inviting them to receive a lead magnet that is designed to get prospects to share their contact information with you. Your print ad should invite the prospect to do something so they can enter your lead funnel.

2) *Billboards* – generally these are quite expensive, but there can be ways to do these during certain times of the year or on public transportation such as buses depending on your product, your demographics, and how they typically best respond. If you choose this option, be sure that your ad has a specific offer and invitation to enter your lead funnel by receiving something of value from you.

3) *Local PR with your story (paid)* –You can pay someone to print your own story or article or you can put together your own marketing pieces. The goal is to educate, inform and inspire prospects to want to share their contact information with you because there is a sense of connection and they feel that you could help them with a challenge or solution they are seeking.

4) *Ads in niche publications* – these could be in publications specific to your industry niche.

5) *Pre-sale collateral* - What to Expect At Your First Appointment with First Time Advantage program offer

If you are already using this lead generation system, determine how many leads you are currently generating / month and how much money you're generating per month from print ad lead sources. This will help you determine what is working and where you can improve the number of leads and the amount sold per lead.

3. Internet (Google, Google Ad Words, any other site other than your web site)

Within this category, there are fifteen main ways this can be done:

1) Personalized emails

2) Email signature invitations
3) Google Places
4) Domain names that fit key word search terms
5) Auto-responder emails
6) RSS Feeds to your articles
7) Blogs
8) Social media
9) Your own podcast
10) Ezine publications
11) Articles submitted to other web sites
12) Webinar
13) Viral marketing with memes
14) Pay per click ads (Facebook, Google Ad Words, etc.)
15) Reciprocal link exchanges

If you are already using this lead generation system, determine how many leads you are currently generating / month and how much money you're generating per month from each or all of these lead sources on the Internet. This will help you determine what is working and where you can improve the number of leads and the amount sold per lead.

4. Your Web Site
Within this category, there are eight main ways this can be done:

1) Capturing leads from your site
2) Special Reports, chapter from book or ebook which prospects can download and read
3) Videos explaining next step of sequence
4) "Schedule an appointment" button
5) Upcoming Events
6) Countdown Clock for LTOs
7) About Us Story
8) Lead generation site tied to key words that appears as though it is from a third party source (For example, you could create a web site using these key words in your web site name like this example that illustrates what will generate traffic: www.bestproductorserviceinyourstateorcity.com)

If you are already using this lead generation system, determine how many leads you are currently generating / month and how much money you're generating per month from each or all of these lead sources on the your web site. This will help you determine what is working and where you can improve the number of leads and the amount sold per lead. You can also discover where you can make improvements.

5. Other Media (television, newsletter, local wedding publications, etc.)

Within this category, there are eight main ways this can be done:
1) Television
2) Newsletter
3) Write in local industry publications
4) Local PR with your story (unpaid)
5) On hold phone marketing
6) Guest on local TV show
7) Online TV show
8) Moving billboard (truck)

If you are already using this lead generation system, determine how many leads you are currently generating / month and how much money you're generating per month from each or all of these lead sources using other media. This will help you determine what is working and where you can improve the number of leads and the amount sold per lead.

6. Events

Within this category, there are six main types of events you can conduct to help you generate leads:
1) Planned marketing calendar events
   • Monthly Promotions
   • Events
   • Client customer appreciation events
2) Trade shows
3) Membership Meetings specifically geared to allow existing clients to bring their friends or acquaintances to get to know you and your business
4) Buying leads from trade shows you don't attend
5) On location events (at the prospect's home or business)
6) Product showcase events (demonstrations in high traffic areas where your prospects are or will be)

If you are already using this lead generation system, determine how many leads you are currently generating / month and how much money you're generating per month from each or all of these lead sources using events. This will help you determine what is working and where you can improve the number of leads and the amount sold per lead.

7. On Site Advertising

Within this category, there are nine main ways you can generate additional sales or leads for additional sales:

1) Indoor signage
2) Outside signage
3) Window displays
4) Posters
5) Published Star/Story profile (Ebook, published magazine, etc.)
6) Letters from happy clients online or in lobby
7) Employee attire
8) Upsell in business
9) Promote book or the articles you've written

If you are already using this lead generation system, determine how many leads you are currently generating / month and how much money you're generating per month from each or all of these lead sources using on site advertising. This will help you determine what is working and where you can improve the number of leads and the amount sold per lead.

8. Community Advertising

There are four main ways you can promote events within your community to generate leads:

1) Local fundraisers
2) Free or paid seminars or speeches to local groups (Chamber of Commerce promotions, other events where your prospects congregate)
3) Community outreach programs
4) Scholarship offers

If you are already using this lead generation system, determine how many leads you are currently generating / month and how much money you're generating per month from each or all of these lead sources using community advertising. This will help you determine what is working and where you can improve the number of leads and the amount sold per lead.

9. Industry Web Sites

There are seven main ways you can generate leads from industry web sites and Pinterest:

1) Forums
2) Pictures
3) Testimonials
4) Offers / Promotions
5) Contests
6) Ads on other industry web sites
7) Creating memes that can be posted on your Pinterest page to generate interest and leads to your web site

If you are already using this lead generation system, determine how many leads you are currently generating / month and how much money you're generating per month from each or all of these lead sources using other industry web sites. This will help you determine what is working and where you can improve the number of leads and the amount sold per lead.

10. Referrals

There are five main ways you can generate new leads through referrals:

1) Referrals from current clients
2) Referrals from employees
3) Referrals from past clients
4) Gift certificates
5) Video testimonials where current or past clients promote you on your web site that are captured at the point of sale

If you are already using this lead generation system, determine how many leads you are currently generating / month and how much money you're generating per month from each or all of these lead sources using referrals. This will help you determine what is working and where you can improve the number of leads and the amount sold per lead.

11. Vendors and Affiliates

There are three main ways you can utilize vendors and affiliates to generate leads:

1) Cross marketing promotions
2) Networking events
3) Gifts or bonuses to add value to your sale

If you are already using this lead generation system, determine how many leads you are currently generating / month and how much money you're generating per month from each or all of these lead sources using vendors and affiliates. This will help you determine what is working and where you can improve the number of leads and the amount sold per lead.

12. Employees
There are three main ways you can have your employees generate leads every day:
1) Have every employee making a minimum of 2 outbound phone calls/day or scheduling 2 appointments/day
2) Social Networking (promoting LTOs and interacting with others with whom they have with once a week or once a month posts regarding specific promotions or offers-if applicable)
3) Word of mouth buzz (have them write blog posts or share Facebook posts with their friends)

If you are already using this lead generation system, determine how many leads you are currently generating / month and how much money you're generating per month from each or all of these lead sources using employees in your business. Set the example of what you want to have happen. This will help you determine what is working and where you can improve the number of leads and the amount sold per lead.

Here is an important chart for you to study and use to help you manage your lead flow.

Managing Your Lead Flow

Department	Number of Leads Needed to Enter Funnel Daily to Achieve Goals	Who Is in Charge of Managing These Leads?	Are Back Up Systems in Place?	Best Three Ways to Generate Quick Lead Flow	Best Three Ways to Generate Consistent Steady Lead Flow
Product Category #1					
Product Category #2					
Product Category #3					
Product Category #4					
Product Category #5					

Regardless of your lead generation system, you can better prevent leads from escaping out of your marketing funnel. Understanding what funnels or systems to have underneath each marketing funnel is the advanced work that can be done to improve this area of your business.

Unfortunately, most don't even have the lead flow systems set up in the first place. Get this area of your business mastered and put into place quickly.

Here is an assessment to see how well you are doing this:

#	Rank yourself from 1-10 based on your current business behaviors.	1	2	3	4	5	6	7	8	9	10	Rank yourself from 1-10 based on your current business behaviors.
1	We are not capturing accurate leads from arriving prospects or clients (ensuring accurate spelling, no email, etc.)											We are capturing accurate leads from every arriving prospects or clients (ensuring accurate spelling, no email, etc.)
2	Leads enter our marketing funnel, but immediately flow out because: • We're too busy to handle them • We have no plan for follow-up • We have disorganized follow-up • We have insufficient follow-up											We properly handle every lead flowing into our marketing funnel.
3	We have a plan on paper, but are disorganized and inconsistent in implementation.											We have a plan on paper and we implement it with every lead coming into our business.
4	We lose prospects because we don't have back up systems to prevent leaks in our marketing funnel.											We have backup systems to prevent leaks in our marketing funnel. We have a process that everyone in our business understands so that leads can flow from one funnel to another.
5	We are lucky to get the referrals we do. We don't have any type of system to get referrals from clients exiting our marketing funnel.											We capture referrals from every customer so that customers coming out of the bottom of the funnel refill the funnel.

#	Rank yourself from 1-10 based on your current business behaviors.	1	2	3	4	5	6	7	8	9	10	Rank yourself from 1-10 based on your current business behaviors.
6	Our consultants rarely ask for upsells for the next item in our marketing sequence.											Every consultant asks for the upsell for the next item in our marketing sequence consistently every time.
7	We know there are leaks but we haven't put a system in place to prevent them from recurring.											If there are leaks in our marketing funnel sequence, we determine the place of escape and patch the holes.
8	You don't know what you next offer will be so you don't offer it.											You know what your next offer will be so you can offer it to a prospect as soon as possible (if she doesn't want __x___, does she want __y__?)
9	You don't plan for slower times and jump into action when you realize that your business is slow.											You anticipate slower times and plan accordingly so you are continually filling the top of the funnel (especially in slower times).
10	You rarely, if ever monitor your processes to see where there may be holes and where prospects are falling through the cracks.											You are continuously monitoring your process so you can better determine how your leads can flow from one funnel to another.

Here is a task list to help you implement better systems for managing your inbound and outbound lead flow:

1. Study the twelve lead flow systems that operate within your business. What are three things you can do this week from what was discussed in this chapter to help you more effectively utilize these systems to keep prospects coming into your business?

2. Assess your best three ways to generate lead flow quickly when you are slow in your business and you need to generate sales immediately and your best three long-term steady drip lead flow systems. What can you do to enhance or improve these three areas for each category?

3. Assign someone in your business to manage the lead flow of each category of your business. If you are the only one who can do this in your business, divide out each category into different days of the week and work on that category for at least 60 minutes each day on

lead flow systems for the next 30 days. Once you've done this, then work the next 30 days on improving lead flow in these systems.

4. Set the goal that you will FOCUS on at least one of the 12 lead flow systems at your business each month for the next year. Devote yourself to studying and learning everything you can about the marketing funnels within those lead flow systems to improve what you are doing to generate interest and excitement so that prospects flow into your business are already interested and ready to do business with you.

5. Ensure that you are following up properly with every lead that is coming into your business. Put systems in place to ensure that your sales consultants are following up with your prospects that you are spending so much money to acquire.

Let me share with you a final thought from Clate Mask and Scott Martineau: "Over 99 percent of small businesses don't properly follow up. Why? Because they don't have a centralized database, they don't have time, they don't realize how valuable it is, and the truth is, they don't know how to follow up!"

They continue:
"First, you need to understand that a couple of random follow-up phone calls to each lead will help you close more deals, but it's not going to produce big numbers. Plus, it's time consuming, tedious, and discouraging.

"Second, you need to realize that the purpose of your follow up is to endear you to your prospects and customers so that they trust you, like you, and want to do business with you. *What you need to do is shift from being a vendor to becoming an expert.*

"To accomplish this shift from vendor to expert, your follow up must take a combined approach that incorporates these five elements:

1. *Segmentation* – Not every contact you have is exactly the same. Though many of them have similar characteristics, your contact lists cannot be lumped into one group. As the business owner, you need to make sure you're sending the right message to the right people at the right time. In other words, the messages you send to your customers should be targeted to their specific needs and wants. Far too many business owners throw all their prospects and customer

email addresses together and send out a mass, generic message to everyone on their list. If you want your follow-up to be effective, you've got to craft messages that work for individuals, not entire databases.

2. *Education* – Your follow-up needs to provide valuable information to your prospects and customers. If you're showing up with no value, you'll wear out your welcome fast. You need to communicate that you are an expert on their side and you deserve to be trusted. You'll accomplish this if you provide them with accurate, insightful information. Truth be told, the sales process is confusing and intimidating for your customers. They want to trust you. Give them the information they need and you'll earn their trust. Help them. Serve them. Provide them expert guidance and they'll appreciate you for it.

3. *Repetition* – It's a proven fact that human beings have to hear the same thing over and over before it sinks in. Follow-up is no different. You know your products and services like the back of your hand, but your customers don't 'get it' the first time they hear the message. Don't make the mistake of thinking that if a prospect heard your message once, he understood it. Chances are he either didn't hear it or didn't understand it. Tell him again and again and again.

4. *Variety* – This doesn't mean you vary your message! You need to consistently tell your message, but your follow-up delivery needs variety. To maximize your sales, you must use multi-step sequences that incorporate and orchestrate direct mail, phone, email, fax, voice and other media. Some prospects will respond to your phone call, others to your email or letters, and others to your fax or voice messages. Serious results come when you contact your prospects using multiple methods.

5. *Automation* – The biggest challenge with follow-up is time. Reconnecting with your prospects and customers could take weeks. That's why no one does it. They're trying to do it on their own and failing miserably. Fortunately, follow-up doesn't have to be difficult or time consuming. All you need is the right software program to make follow-up an automated masterpiece." --*Conquer the Chaos*, pp. 152-153.

These five steps are critical for your long-term lead flow strategy. You need to segment your leads into the right category, educate them, repeat your message often through multiple media sources in a variety of ways and once the system has been all thought out and put into place, you need a great way to automate your system so that you have a consistent flow of leads day in and day out. When you start managing your lead flow closely, you'll start seeing more consistency in your daily, weekly, and monthly sales numbers and you'll be able to have confidence in the achievement of your goals.

<u>CHAPTER 8</u>

YOUR PRE-SALES AND MARKETING SYSTEMS

"Most companies leave far too much of the sales process up to the individual sales people. Yet to create the Ultimate Sales Machine, you must work as a team, utilizing everyone's brainpower to drill down, perfect, and procedurize each aspect of the sales process."
—*Chet Holmes*

In this chapter, I'd like to discuss your pre-sales and marketing systems to ensure that your leads are being developed and best utilized in your active marketing campaigns. Marketing for your business is like gasoline is to an automobile. It is the fuel that helps it run. If you aren't putting anything in the tank, it is no surprise if you aren't able to go where you want to go.

Scott Stratten tells a story in his book *Unmarketing* that I think really illustrates the challenge with marketing for entrepreneurs. He says: "[There is] an event called *Art by the Lake* in my hometown. Artists gather down by our shoreline and set up in tents, displaying their paintings, sculptures, and photographs. It's well attended and looks like a great success but I noticed a problem. The problem was not with the attendees. They were great—enjoying themselves walking into each artist's tent, admiring the work, making comments, and giving compliments. The artists, unfortunately, were not nearly as engaging. Most were sitting in lawn chairs, halfheartedly thanking people for their kindness, but you could just tell they were secretly saying to themselves, 'If you like it, why don't you buy it?!?'

"The ratio of lookers to buyers was at least 100 to 1. The artists were doing the old-school method of sales, which I like to call 'push and pray' marketing.' Push something out there and pray people buy it. People are there to look at great art pieces; they were even saying to the artists that they might be interested in buying from them eventually. The most I saw any of the artists do was to hand them a card and say 'Let me know!'

and then, nothing. With that, the crowd of potential customers would move on to the next tent.

"What were the artists hoping these people were going to do? Go home, realize they had a perfect spot in their living room for one of their paintings or sculptures, and try to remember who the artist was? Here every vendor had a prime opportunity for engagement. Crowds of people were raising their hands expressing interest in the artists' products, but they were just being allowed to walk away.
"Let's take the artists' situation and use the pull-and-stay method instead. You pull customer information and stay in front of them. Let's imagine that you are one of the artists at Art in the Park. Someone comes into your tent and mentions how wonderful the work is, especially your landscape photography. Instead of just saying thanks, you could say, 'I appreciate it. I regularly take landscapes, and it's amazing how well they're received. I know it's tough to decide on art, especially when there are so many great artists here today. Would you like to sign up? No charge." Now you control the contact. After potential customers visit 50 other booths this day at the show, they will remember that you are the only one who stood out after the event is long over. Now you can start to build a relationship.

"Take it another step. That night, after taking the visitors' email addresses, write to them to say thank you for coming by the booth. Send them a few shots and ask what they thought about the event. Start a conversation. Engage with them, get to know your marketplace. You'll be amazed at the responses you receive...."

Then, he makes this great statement:
"Remember, marketing is not one department of your business; it is every point of engagement, including sales. The mistake made by too many businesspeople is that if shoppers do not want to buy immediately, they just let them walk away when they should be Unmarketing and pulling in these potential customers."—pp. 22-24.

What would you do if you were a vendor at this art show? The reason I ask this question is that it is often easier to think about marketing when looking at another industry or business because you are usually a little more open minded to new ideas.

Here are a few suggestions of what you could do to market your art business. Notice how each of these ideas are systematic ways to move a prospect into a greater state of excitement about going ahead and purchasing while simultaneously building authority and expertise for the artist.

1. Have a way to capture names, email addresses and phone numbers. Give away a free gift or the chance to win a free painting for registering.

2. Offer a small 3x5 print of your most popular picture for free with a description of your story (how you got into painting, why you are respected by art professionals and art aficionados, etc and why your work is in demand). Every person who registers for the free drawing gets a copy of this print to take with them. You could even make this a more special experience by signing the small print when you give it to each potential art customer.

3. Announce the winner of the free drawing on your social media pages, and then call or email each other person who registered and tell them that they were the runner up and that you have a special offer for them of 10% or $100 off one of three in-stock paintings (or any from your catalog) if it is purchased by the end of the week. Give a specific offer.

4. Invite people who came by your booth to an exclusive "wine and cheese" tasting art appreciation party at your studio where those who met you at your booth can bring one friend who also appreciates art. You give free refreshments to those who attend and give a brief 5-minute talk at the beginning where you teach those in attendance the 5 Ways to Appreciate Great Art. The talk is education-based. In addition, you could invite someone from a local winery to bring some of their wine so those at my studio could learn something new and try something or have an experience that they wouldn't otherwise be able to. You could also invite those who bring a friend that they will get an extra entry in a drawing for a free original painting that I will do following the art show. Then, I would capture the contact information of all of the friends and repeat the process over and over again with a weekly or monthly event.

5. You could also put together a "Date Night" event with a local bridal salon. You could offer these tickets to couples at the local university or church groups. The tickets would include entrance to the art show at a local restaurant that you could work with. The restaurant could offer 2, 3 or 4 tables of their business to these new prospects

who might not otherwise know about the restaurant, the three of you could split the costs (bridal store owner, art gallery owner and the restaurant owner) and all three of you would have access to the leads. As a gift to the couple at the end of the dinner, you could present dessert that has been paid for by the bridal store owner in exchange for their email contact information to receive a free email brochure about their business.

I could go on and on with promotional ideas like these, but you see the principle. If you want to generate leads and sell more today, you've got to have an effective system that allows you to capture leads from each of these groups.

What did you learn from that exercise?

First, think about what it is that your prospect wants. What can you provide to her (an art experience, a restaurant experience with a free dessert, etc.) that would help her warm to the idea of doing business with your company?

Dan Kennedy says it this way:
"You need a direct marketing system. What is such a thing? As its name implies, it directly reaches out to, connects with, and brings the desired prospective customer, client, or patient to you. All systems use bait to lure the desired creature into the trap." –*No B.S. Marketing to the Affluent*, p. 240.

He continues:
"The trap is a place where the creature's name, address, email address, fax number, and phone number are captured and, of utmost importance, permission to use this information is secured."—p. 241.

Now that is kind of a crude way to explain what marketing is, but I think you get the point. Your lead generation system which we discussed in the last chapter is one part of your marketing system. This system is designed to help you capture the contact information of your prospect. The next part is how you build a relationship with and extend an offer to your prospect so he or she wants to buy from you and become your client.

Second, put together an offer that is compelling to your prospects. This may not just be the product that you sell. This could include other offerings joined together with other professionals in your area that can accompany your product and service and make it easier to use or enjoy.

Third, you need a system to ensure that there is adequate follow up and that a relationship is built with every prospect you work with.

Now, since a marketing system is so critically important, why don't more entrepreneurs build one? Kennedy has a very concise explanation. He says:

"There are three chief reasons that, frankly, the vast majority of marketers shown this systematic approach fail to develop it for their own businesses....
Problem 1. It's work, to get it built, tested and working for you successfully. Sadly and stupidly, most people would rather spend every day of their entire lives chopping wood manually with a dull axe, complaining all the while, than turn off the TV and put in a few extra hours a night for a few months building an axe-sharpening device or, better yet, an electric, power wood-cutting machine.

"*Problem 2.* It's complicated. Most people desperately want a magic pill, not a diet regimen incorporating food choices, portion control, nutritional supplementation, and exercise. That, incidentally, is why 99% of the fat folk stay fat. In business, it's the same thing. There's rarely a single, simple magic pill-like solution to any problem or exploitation of any opportunity. There's even virtue in possessing a complicated process, as most competitors will be too lazy and simple-minded to copy it, even if it is successful and shown to them.

"*Problem 3.* Specific to the marketing to the affluent—the higher up in affluence you go, the more protected are the prospects. Gatekeepers screen the communications you try to send to them. There are obstacles in your way. It is not necessarily easy to reach out to them and attract them. Also specific to the affluent—the higher up in affluence you go, the less responsive to advertising and more responsive to peer recommendations and referrals people are."—pp. 250-251.

Then he adds several solutions that can be very helpful to you as you build your systems:

"Now, for what it's worth, the solutions...For Problem 1, work. What we are talking about here is nothing less than the transformation of your business from random acts of marketing that produce erratic and unpredictable results to a machine that runs dependably and efficiently, day in and day out, much of it automatically. Ownership of such a machine is a wonderful thing. But you can't expect to build such an enormously valuable thing for yourself with nominal effort or investment. You will need to, first, thoroughly understand it, and then experiment with specific application to your business.
For Problem 2, embrace the complexity! It's a source of power. But, to be fair, the actual mechanics of managing the prospects (databases) and the multi-step, multi-media follow up with color coded file folders and Post-It notes or ordinary contact management software can be messy. Problem 3 requires two things. One, appearing in the places where your affluent prospects pay the most attention. This will lead to different media choices, than, say, your regular daily newspaper, mass-circulation magazines, or run-of-day TV or radio advertising. Two, direct mail to carefully selected lists, using more elaborate pieces and delivery means than ordinary mail." –pp. 251-252.

Be sure you are building up the lead systems in your business that will help you get more prospects in your marketing funnel.

In particular, pay more attention to the affluent. Most marketers in general give up on marketing to the affluent and don't really build much of a referral system, which is a big mistake.

What really makes any promotion you do powerful enough to flood your business with prospects and clients who are ready to buy is to **have a comprehensive strategy** *and* a **well-thought out system to help you implement it**.

Your system should include the following eight things to accelerate the efficiency of your marketing:
1. A specific call to action.
2. A unique difference between you and everyone else.
3. A way for your prospect to contact you with the invitation of what to do next after she sees your marketing campaign or promotion.

4. A strong headline that grabs your prospects by the eyes or ears so that they feel compelled to pay attention to what you are offering.
5. An irresistible offer (especially when compared to anyone else).
6. An amazing experience that is nothing short of amazing (so that when prospects do enter your marketing funnel), they are completely blown away.
7. Specific follow up offers that educate and provide additional experiences and referral systems for prospects that your competitors would never even consider (but that will inevitably persuade them to buy from you).
8. A great story that is easy for prospects and clients to tell others about.

In addition to these eight things, the big secret to getting prospects into your marketing funnel who are ready to buy now is all hidden in how you *plan* and *execute* great promotions and promotional events.

One of the reasons why marketing is so challenging today is because people are constantly bombarded by ads everywhere. Everyone has their own protection mechanisms to avoid marketing promotions. So, you've got to stand out. On top of that, everyone is very busy and has a long list of things they have to do. In order to be successful, your offer must stand out and invite them to consider your offer without the prospect *feeling* like you are trying to sell them something (because that will cause a prospect's resistance to be even higher). Without an effective system to ensure that your marketing promotions are implemented, it is likely that they won't be, which means that you won't have the traffic you need in your business.

A relationship, not an ad campaign (no matter how clever or creative it might be), is what wins the marketing battle. Businesses today are spending more money than ever on advertising, but they are getting fewer results. Why? Simply put, entrepreneurs have become impatient. They plant a tomato seed in the morning and expect to harvest tomatoes to enjoy for their lunch or for dinner *that* same day. That's not how the law of the harvest works. The sales process may occur much more quickly, and occasionally you may make a sale that quickly without any preliminary pre-sales work. However, this is more due to the needs of the prospect and their timeline and is usually the exception.

Instead, your pre-sales sequence and your positioning will do more to cause you to make the sale ahead of time than any sales judo strategies you may use in the heat of the sales process. Don't get me wrong. What happens in the sales process works by a system too and there are definitely things that can be done to create urgency and persuade prospects to become buyers. However, the nature of buying has changed. Solid, sustainable client relationships are built over a period of time using a systematic process. Never get so caught up in big picture thinking that you forget the close relationship that your marketing needs to foster in order to build trust and confidence *before* a sale can be made.

Your biggest competitors may have the ability to spend more money on advertising than you can. As a result, you have to think differently so that you can position your business effectively. An effective marketing strategy and system will work in your favor if you do the simple, affordable, and effective marketing tactics I'm describing here. Your competitors may ignore the systems work required here simply because they don't know how or because they don't think they need to market themselves any more. This book is teaching you how and will give you the tools to build your systems to build relationships and make sales in this way.

To help you start building your pre-sales and marketing systems, here are five specific suggestions:

1. Plan for slower times so you will be ready when they come.
Here are five examples of ways you can do this:
1) *Anticipate your slower times and develop a marketing plan to prevent them.* If you wait until you are slow, it will take too long to create the momentum to be busy. Start marketing and promotions before a slower season begins and it won't be a challenge for you. As part of your system, establish a marketing calendar for the entire year paying particular attention to times when you are slower and what you will do to reverse that trend.
2) *Increase value of your premium offer or referral bonus during slower times to incentivize action.*
3) *Promote a contest that has something prospects would really want to win and have a system to capture and follow-up with the leads generated.*
4) *Have a follow up offer or a series of follow-up offers that you use to*

invite prospects to return to your marketing funnel. Have each member of your sales team reach out and make at least two of these follow up calls every day. Why two? Well, it is better than zero or one, but more importantly it will start a habit. The important point is that when this habit is multiplied out over your sales force, it will add up in appointments and revenue generated. For example, if you have a sales team of ten and each person makes two follow up phone calls, you'll be making 20 follow up phone calls per day and when you multiply that over a five or six-day work week, you will have 100 to 120 phone outbound phone calls that can help you generate appointments and sales. Let's say 25% of those actually end up buying a $1000 product. That means 25 clients x $1000 will equal an additional $25,000 in sales each week. Over a month, you will have generated $100,000 in sales and over a year, an additional $1.2 million in sales. Small actions can produce big results.

5) *Pick a faltering or soon to be discontinued product that you have stock of in your business and offer an ascending discount sale for one week.* Offer 25-50 specific clients the opportunity to be part of an exclusive buying event held over the period of one week. You'll notify your clients that a product will be priced 10-70% off over the next week (unless it is all sold first). Start on a Monday at 10% off, Tuesday at 20% off, Wednesday at 30% off so that by the next Monday you are at 70% off. Have a promotion like this a couple of times a year in slower seasons to move through inventory that is no longer moving through your business.

2. Reward your sales consultants when they help promote your business. A great way to do this is to have a daily set of goals and responsibilities for each of your sales team and tie specific rewards to the achievement of these goals.

For example, here are ideas of five daily goals that you could modify and offer to your sales consultants:
- Schedule two appointments everyday (Reward: the first sales consultant to schedule 12 appointments a week (2/day x 6 days per week we are open) gets lunch on you
- Invite all clients who have bought something in the last 90 days to come in and get a specific offer towards their next purchase.

The sales consultant who has the most of these total sales over five will get a gift card to a local restaurant.

- Invite clients who didn't purchase a specific add on for a product they've already purchased to get a special offer on that item for a limited time.
- Invite clients who haven't purchased anything from you in the past six to twelve months to receive a new offer and the option to be put in a drawing for one of two prizes when they do.
- Invite clients to invite their friends to a customer appreciation event where you will create an amazing experience they can enjoy together. For example, I have a friend who owns a swimming pool business who hosts a pool party at the house for all of the friends to celebrate its completion. He puts $500 into the price of every pool he sells to cover the food and the prizes he offers to those who come. It is a great way for him to get another pool construction job in the same neighborhood in a low-key way where the current client introduces him to their happy and amazed friends. How could you modify this idea for your business?

You can change the rewards for each category or you can have one contest with a reward for the sales consultant who does the best job converting leads into sales within your business within a month or specific quarter. Reward those on your staff who do an exceptional job of promoting your business to their friends and family as well as to your existing clients and prospects.

3. Develop a great cross-promotional program. If you don't have good cross-promotional programs in place, you need to put these into your marketing system. Here are four cross-promotional ideas you could use and to get you thinking about how to put together your own systems with cross-promotions:

1) *Contact clergy, religious leaders, or leaders of other community groups in your area and write a letter like this on your letterhead, included with coupons and your business card:*

Dear Reverend/Father/Rabbi/Bishop/Community Leader:
As a member of our community who appreciates the important role you play, I would like to offer you a simple, cost-free way to raise money for your building fund, your youth group, your foreign ministry, or any other program you may need money for. Here's

how it works:

We'll furnish you with coupons that can be given to your congregation. The coupons state that ___ percent of any purchase made with the coupon at our business will be donated to your organization for your unrestricted use.

It's that simple. There's nothing else for you to do. We will tabulate and distribute funds to you on a weekly basis for four weeks, beginning as soon as you like.

After you've had a chance to think about the idea, I'll call you to answer any questions and to discuss the idea in more detail.

I look forward to working with you and helping you meet your fundraising goals.

Warmest regards,

(Your name)

2) *Have a group event at your business once a month or once a quarter on a night when you are typically slower.* This event can be used to introduce yourself to prospects in the community who could use your products or services. For example, at our bridal store, we invited youth groups at local churches to come into our store to try on prom dresses on a Tuesday or Wednesday night (which was typically slower for us). We then gave them a coupon they could use within 24-48 hours of being in the store. These events are a lot of fun for those who attend, generate sales and most importantly, we now have youth leaders call us to schedule their own appointments for these kinds of events in our business.

3) *Contact local jewelers* –contact local jewelers in your area and send them a $20+ bonus for every referral they send to your business that also buys from you. You could also buy necklaces or jewelry from them to use as part of a specific promotion that you could give to prospects when they become clients.

4) *Contact local restaurants* - Work up a promotion with a restaurant to help prospects or clients celebrate their birthday. The restaurant can provide a free dessert to your client when it is her birthday – they will also get the meal sale plus the opportunity to wow them so they want to return to eat dinner at their restaurant again and again. This is great for you because you have a 'wow' experience you can offer to your client on his or her birthday. You can mail her a birthday card with a coupon at the restaurant for a free dessert on you. Your cost on this would be printing up the coupons for the free dessert and the birthday card (mailer). The restaurant would have

the expense of the free dessert (or you can offer to pay for it), but would gain new customers for rehearsal dinners and the price of the meal will likely cover the other costs.

4. Send out a VIP invitation letter to every client who purchased something from you a few days to a week after her purchase from the owner of the business.
The letter could say:

Dear _____ :
Just a short note to thank you for purchasing _____ from our business. I'm the owner and I wanted to personally thank you for trusting us for such an important decision.

I wanted to invite you to a special event that we are extending to our favorite clients. We will be hosting _____whatever the event is_____ on (day of the week), (date), (time). We would be very pleased if you would attend. A "Be Our Guest" card is enclosed which you only need to present at the door (or wherever you are having the event). We encourage you to bring a friend or family member with you to this party. I've included three additional invitations that I would like you to give to your friends who would enjoy coming to this event as well. When you do, we will enter each of your names in a drawing to win _____*a $1000 coupon off an anniversary travel package or whatever your prize is*_____. Please RSVP and let me know how many will be attending from your group. I look forward to meeting your friends and family and seeing you again soon.

Sincerely,
Your Name
Title

5. Have a systematized approach for each offer or promotion you do.
A big part of your pre-sales and marketing system is to ensure that you are aware of each aspect of what makes a successful promotion work. It isn't just about mailing out a postcard or making a single phone call and expecting that prospects will come beating down your door to buy from you. Here are ten specific things you should do to make sure that your marketing system and marketing campaign works effectively.

1. **Determine your objectives for the promotion.** Be specific and be realistic. Know what results you need before you begin.

2. **Think about your strategy and create a plan.** In particular, you need to pay attention to events that are happening at the same time of your event, how frequently you'll need your message seen by prospects to take action, and how your promotion will compete with that of your competitors.

3. **Focus on your target market.**

    a. Who is the promotion targeted to?

    b. Where is my list coming from? How many people do I need to have on the list? Do I have multiple ways of contacting each prospect (address and email are best followed by phone number)?

    c. How can you zero in on making sure they hear about the promotion?

    d. Have you used persuasive sales copy in your promotions to create interest, excitement and a need for the prospects or clients you are targeting to be at the event?

4. **Review your promotion expenses and calculate your costs.** Remember, every promotion should increase sales and produce a profit or you shouldn't do it.

    In order to help you evaluate this, ask:

    a. How many sales do you need to cover the cost of the promotion (hard numbers)?

    b. How many prospective clients must you convert to new clients to consider the promotion a success?

    c. Go back to your objectives. Are they realistic?

    d. What adjustments need to be made?

    e. Do we need to hire or train new individuals to help this promotion be successful? (factor in the costs of doing this)

5. **Check the calendar and determine drop dates for your marketing sequence.** If you are having an event on a Thursday, Friday, or Saturday, at the very latest, you will want to send out your mail piece on the Friday or Saturday before the event (depending on

how far the fulfillment house is from your business).

6. **Refine your offer so that it is right for the prospect you are targeting.**

   a. Go back over your offer and see if there are other persuasive elements you can add in to make the event more successful. Have your sequencing plan in place to get the word out.

   b. Are you utilizing psychological triggers to help you build desire and cause action?

   c. Get feedback from other successful marketers (if you can) that can enhance the offer and the marketing.

7. **Improve the aesthetics of your business or the location where you'll be having the event.**

   Make sure that your selling and event areas are attractive and that your business is clean and tidy. Everything in your business sells.

8. **Execute the marketing plan.**

9. **Check the logistics.**

   a. Does everyone on your team understand the offer? When the phone rings with questions, will everyone who can answer the phone understand any questions that may come up? Have they been trained to help the prospect get to the next step (appointment to meet with a consultant or to follow up with helpful information and the opportunity to get a gift for taking immediate action)?

   b. Do they understand their role in helping the promotion to be successful?

10. **Train your team and sell like crazy.**

    Help them understand the objectives, the rationale, the implementation and the fun of your upcoming promotion. Let sales consultants know what is expected of them, what is in it for them personally (have special bonuses and spiffs), and how much you care about their feedback so you can find out what is working, what isn't, and why.

Finally, evaluate how any marketing promotion you've conducted actually worked for you.

- How many new and existing prospects did your event attract?
- How much in sales did you ring up?
- What is the big lesson to remember about this marketing campaign that you want to remember for next time?

Most entrepreneurs find themselves so consumed by all there is to do in running their businesses that they really struggle to find the time to plan out their marketing campaigns in advance much less do all of the work required to have a successful promotion.

Since the goal of this chapter is to help you monitor and improve your pre-sales and marketing systems, I want you to look at the twelve categories of marketing promotions I discussed in the last chapter and think about what you are doing with your marketing campaigns now. Previously we discussed how many leads you are generating from each category. Now, let's discuss which categories are most effective for generating new business.

While this will take time and may initially be a little discouraging, you've got to prioritize your time and block out the time to make these successful campaigns happen for you.

This is some of the most important and productive work you will do in your business. If you don't already have time scheduled to work on this, block out at least an hour next Monday and start having Monday Morning Marketing meetings where you can work on these systems in your business. When I have this meeting, I think about what our business just did the previous week, what we have coming up and start implementing the things on the list to help get in more prospects to enter our marketing funnel with the promotional strategies we have in place. Even though most people will never see all of the planning effort it takes to put on a successful event or put together a successful marketing promotion, you will know that when you block out the time and do this well that nothing could be more important and worthwhile to your business and to your success.

As I mentioned, there are twelve main categories of marketing campaigns you can use.

Use the charts on pages 177-189 to determine which ones you have used in the past 90 to 180 days and which ones you've used previously that have had great results for you.

In the last chapter, I had you analyze this for the number of leads each system was generating for you. If you had zero for your response in the last 30 days, evaluate it for the past 6 months or 12 months and determine whether you should zero in on such a promotion again.

Now, look at the following for each category:
- Whether or not that area has been used in the past 5 months or 6-12 months
- Whether you should use the strategy again
- Whether your systems are in place to generate leads for each category
- Ideas for implementation to generate more leads in the next 60 days

1. Direct Marketing

Marketing Campaign Category	Used in the Past 5 Months (Yes or No)	Used in the Past 6-12 Months (Yes or No)	If it Worked, Could/ Should You Be Using it Again Now?	System in Place to Generate Leads through this Category? (Yes or No)	Ideas for Implementation (Which marketing campaigns will you use in the next 30-60 days to bring in new prospects?)
Direct mail (postcards)					
Radio					
Business Card with Offer					
Telephone Call Follow-up					
Movie ads					
Ads in shopper's guides					
Ambassador cards					
Catalog					
Newsletter					
LTOs					
Upsell					

Marketing Campaign Category	Used in the Past 5 Months (Yes or No)	Used in the Past 6-12 Months (Yes or No)	If it Worked, Could/ Should You Be Using it Again Now?	System in Place to Generate Leads through this Category? (Yes or No)	Ideas for Implementation (Which marketing campaigns will you use in the next 30-60 days to bring in new prospects?)
Bounce back offers					

Ideas for Implementation:

2. Print Ads

Marketing Campaign Category	Used in the Past 5 Months (Yes or No)	Used in the Past 6-12 Months (Yes or No)	If it Worked, Could/ Should You Be Using it Again Now?	System in Place to Generate Leads through this Category? (Yes or No)	Ideas for Implementation (Which marketing campaigns will you use in the next 30-60 days to bring in new prospects?)
Magazine Ads					
Billboards					
Local PR with your story (paid)					
Ads in niche publications					
Pre-sale collateral					

Ideas for Implementation:

3. **Internet** (Google Ad Words, any other web site other than yours, etc.)

Marketing Campaign Category	Used in the Past 5 Months (Yes or No)	Used in the Past 6-12 Months (Yes or No)	If it Worked, Could/ Should You Be Using it Again Now?	System in Place to Generate Leads through this Category? (Yes or No)	Ideas for Implementation (Which marketing campaigns will you use in the next 30-60 days to bring in new prospects?)
Personalized emails					
Email signature invitations					
Google Places					
Domain names that fit key word search terms					
Auto-responder emails					
RSS Feeds to your articles					
Blogs					
Social media					
Your own podcast					
Ezine publications					

Marketing Campaign Category	Used in the Past 5 Months (Yes or No)	Used in the Past 6-12 Months (Yes or No)	If it Worked, Could/ Should You Be Using it Again Now?	System in Place to Generate Leads through this Category? (Yes or No)	Ideas for Implementation (Which marketing campaigns will you use in the next 30-60 days to bring in new prospects?)
Articles submitted to other web sites					
Webinar					
Viral marketing					
Pay per click ads (Facebook, etc.)					
Reciprocal link exchange					

Ideas for Implementation:

4. Your Web Site

Marketing Campaign Category	Used in the Past 5 Months (Yes or No)	Used in the Past 6-12 Months (Yes or No)	If it Worked, Could/ Should You Be Using it Again Now?	System in Place to Generate Leads through this Category? (Yes or No)	Ideas for Implementation (Which marketing campaigns will you use in the next 30-60 days to bring in new prospects?)
Capturing leads from site					
Special Reports, Book Chapter, or Ebook					
Videos explaining next step of sequence					
"Schedule an appointment" button					
Upcoming Events					
Countdown Clock for LTOs					
About Us Story					
Lead generation site tied to key words					

Ideas for Implementation:

5. Other Media (television, newsletter, local publications, etc.)

Marketing Campaign Category	Used in the Past 5 Months (Yes or No)	Used in the Past 6-12 Months (Yes or No)	If it Worked, Could/ Should You Be Using it Again Now?	System in Place to Generate Leads through this Category? (Yes or No)	Ideas for Implementation (Which marketing campaigns will you use in the next 30-60 days to bring in new prospects?)
Television					
Newsletter					
Write in local publications					
Local PR with your story (unpaid)					
On hold phone marketing					
Guest on local TV show					
Online TV show					
Moving billboard (truck)					

Ideas for Implementation:

6. Events

Marketing Campaign Category	Used in the Past 5 Months (Yes or No)	Used in the Past 6-12 Months (Yes or No)	If it Worked, Could/ Should You Be Using it Again Now?	System in Place to Generate Leads through this Category? (Yes or No)	Ideas for Implementation (Which marketing campaigns will you use in the next 30-60 days to bring in new prospects?)
Planned marketing calendar events					
Monthly Promotions Tied into Event					
VIP Events					
Customer appreciation events					
Trade shows					
Membership Meetings					
Buying leads from events you don't attend					
Other business events					

Ideas for Implementation:

7. On-Site or In-Business Advertising

Marketing Campaign Category	Used in the Past 5 Months (Yes or No)	Used in the Past 6-12 Months (Yes or No)	If it Worked, Could/ Should You Be Using it Again Now?	System in Place to Generate Leads through this Category? (Yes or No)	Ideas for Implementation (Which marketing campaigns will you use in the next 30-60 days to bring in new prospects?)
Inside Signage					
Outside Signage					
Window displays					
Posters					
Published Star/Story profile					
Testimonial Letters from clients					
Employee attire					
Upsell in business					
Promote book or the articles you've written					

Ideas for Implementation:

8. Community Advertising

Marketing Campaign Category	Used in the Past 5 Months (Yes or No)	Used in the Past 6-12 Months (Yes or No)	If it Worked, Could/ Should You Be Using it Again Now?	System in Place to Generate Leads through this Category? (Yes or No)	Ideas for Implementation (Which marketing campaigns will you use in the next 30-60 days to bring in new prospects?)
Local fundraisers					
Free or paid seminars or speeches to local groups (Chamber of Commerce promotions, other events where your prospects congregate)					
Community Outreach Programs					
Scholarship offers					

Ideas for Implementation:

9. Industry Web Sites

Marketing Campaign Category	Used in the Past 5 Months (Yes or No)	Used in the Past 6-12 Months (Yes or No)	If it Worked, Could/ Should You Be Using it Again Now?	System in Place to Generate Leads through this Category? (Yes or No)	Ideas for Implementation (Which marketing campaigns will you use in the next 30-60 days to bring in new prospects?)
Forums					
Pictures					
Testimonials					
Offers / Promotions					
Contests					
Ads on other industry web sites					
Creating memes that can be posted on your Pinterest page					

Ideas for Implementation:

10. Referrals

Marketing Campaign Category	Used in the Past 5 Months (Yes or No)	Used in the Past 6-12 Months (Yes or No)	If it Worked, Could/ Should You Be Using it Again Now?	System in Place to Generate Leads through this Category? (Yes or No)	Ideas for Implementation (Which marketing campaigns will you use in the next 30-60 days to bring in new prospects?)
Referrals from current and past clients (Asking)					
Referrals from employees					
Referrals via party or event Ex: Dinner Wine and cheese tasting Chocolate tasting Cooking class Sporting event Golf outing or lesson Date Night Campaign					
Gift certificates (Predetermined reward or optional reward)					
Video testimonials					
Making a connection everyday to someone who could refer you					
Web site or forum where clients can go and promote you					
Networking group with other industry professionals					
Process or system that gets others talking about you					

Marketing Campaign Category	Used in the Past 5 Months (Yes or No)	Used in the Past 6-12 Months (Yes or No)	If it Worked, Could/ Should You Be Using it Again Now?	System in Place to Generate Leads through this Category? (Yes or No)	Ideas for Implementation (Which marketing campaigns will you use in the next 30-60 days to bring in new prospects?)
Thanking referrals in newsletters to promote referral culture					
Sharing introductory email with clients for referrals					
Host or sponsor affinity group events where prospects congregate					
Implied Referrals					

Ideas for Implementation:

11.   Industry Vendors and Affiliates

Marketing Campaign Category	Used in the Past 5 Months (Yes or No)	Used in the Past 6-12 Months (Yes or No)	If it Worked, Could/ Should You Be Using it Again Now?	System in Place to Generate Leads through this Category? (Yes or No)	Ideas for Implementation (Which marketing campaigns will you use in the next 30-60 days to bring in new prospects?)
Cross marketing promotions					
Networking at trade shows, events					
Coupons to add value to your sale					

Ideas for Implementation:

12.   Employees

Marketing Campaign Category	Used in the Past 5 Months (Yes or No)	Used in the Past 6-12 Months (Yes or No)	If it Worked, Could/ Should You Be Using it Again Now?	System in Place to Generate Leads through this Category? (Yes or No)	Ideas for Implementation (Which marketing campaigns will you use in the next 30-60 days to bring in new prospects?)
Outbound phone calls/day or appointments					
Networking (handing out business cards)					
Word of mouth buzz					

Ideas for Implementation:

Here is an important chart for you to study and use to help you manage your marketing campaigns.

Managing Your Marketing Campaigns

Area of Business	Best Three Ways You've Brought in Customers by Category	Is this Marketing Campaign Systematized So It Continuously Generates Results?	If Not, What Must You Do to Systematize This Marketing Campaign Strategy?
Product Category #1			
Product Category #2			
Product Category #3			
Product Category #4			
Product Category #5			

Every entrepreneur can better systematize his or her marketing campaigns (especially the best ones that consistently work). Unfortunately, most don't even have effective lead flow systems set up in the first place within each category. Knowing how to campaign to and get these prospects and clients to act on your marketing campaigns is the next step that will yield powerful results for your business. If you don't know and act on what's working and better implement what has worked in the past, you are leaving huge opportunities for business on the table. Study your marketing campaign systems and take action to ensure that they will work for you.

Here is an assessment of your marketing systems:

#	Rank yourself from 1-10 based on your current business behaviors.	1	2	3	4	5	6	7	8	9	10	Rank yourself from 1-10 based on your current business behaviors.
1	I wing it and hope that what I've done in the way of marketing will bring in prospects.											I have a complete marketing plan for the year.
2	I throw together something to market our business when it gets slow.											I adhere to the marketing plan throughout the year (with some adjustments).
3	I don't get the input on our marketing from anyone else on my team or from others who have had successful promotions.											Our marketing plan is a result of input and involvement from key managers and team members.
4	We don't have a marketing plan or sequential way that our staff can follow up with prospects.											Our marketing plan guides the actions of our staff to achieve our financial goals and objectives.
5	I'm not really aware of what our competitors are doing to market their businesses and how I should market in comparison with what they are doing.											We have a contingency plan to adjust for external changes that can affect our business (what our competitors do, how prospects are reacting to other promotions, etc.)
6	We don't have specific and measurable objectives for the promotions we do at our business.											Our marketing plan contains specific and measurable objectives for each sales event.

#	Rank yourself from 1-10 based on your current business behaviors.	1	2	3	4	5	6	7	8	9	10	Rank yourself from 1-10 based on your current business behaviors.
7	We don't track how well our promotions work and so we do things that probably aren't working.											We track the effectiveness of our marketing collateral and promotions to ensure that advertising expenditures are wisely made.
8	I spend money on advertising because someone shows up to sell it to me.											We only advertise when we can test and measure the results.
9	I don't go through any checklists to ensure that things are in order before I release my ads/promotions.											Our marketing pieces are evaluated carefully before they are sent out to ensure that they will grab and hold the attention of our prospects and cause them to act.
10	If our marketing plans don't get implemented, there are no consequences.											There is accountability for implementation of our marketing plan.
11	We rely upon the branding of the manufacturers of the products we carry.											We have quality marketing materials that build our brand, not a specific manufacturer's brand.
12	We seek to spend as little as possible in attracting prospects and clients customers to our marketing funnels.											We seek to spend more than our competitor in attracting high quality, qualified prospects into our business.

Here is a task list to help you implement better systems for managing your pre-sales and marketing campaigns:

1. If you haven't already done so, put together your marketing calendar for the next 90 days. Study the twelve categories of marketing campaigns that operate within your business. What are three things you can do this week from what was discussed to help you more effectively utilize these systems to accelerate the number of prospects entering your marketing funnel in the next 90 days?

2. Assess your best marketing campaigns you've used in your business that consistently produce results. What can you do to enhance or improve these three marketing systems? What areas of opportunity do you see?

3. Assign someone in your business to manage the marketing campaigns of each category of your business. If you are the only one who can do this in your business (and you haven't already done so), divide out each category into different days of the week and work on developing 3 marketing campaigns from any of the twelve categories for at least 90 minutes each week for the next 30 days. This will give you 6 hours of marketing campaign work within your business in the next 90 days. Then, if you haven't already done so, work on improving the lead flow that is yielded from each of your marketing campaign systems.

4. Set the goal that you will have a FOCUS on at least one of the 12 marketing campaign categories at your business each month for the next year.

5. Ensure that you are following up properly with every prospect that is entering your marketing funnel from your three most successful marketing campaigns. Work at improving your follow up systems for these three methods so you ensure that you are capitalizing on your marketing campaign dollars.

6. Think about your pre-sales marketing collateral. What can you do specifically to increase your authority and credibility in the marketplace so that prospects realize that you are the most qualified individual and business to help them with their challenges? Put these elements on your web site and into the flow of your marketing campaigns.

When you start better monitoring your most effective marketing campaigns, you can make tweaks in them to improve the number of leads you get from each one.

One of the biggest mistakes you can make in your business is to think that you act in a vacuum so you don't anticipate and plan for what your competitors will do in a competitive market. I really like this statement that Bob Rice makes in his book *Three Moves Ahead* where he compares business to the game of chess. He says:

"Always, always expect your opponent to make his best move. One of the silliest things beginners do is make moves that are fundamentally unsound in the hope that their opponents won't see something. Hey, this is the information age: Everybody sees everything. You absolutely must make decisions based on the market, your competitors, and your customers seeing the consequence of your move and being very smart and self-interested in the way they react."--p. 180.

He also says that this is one of the challenges with business books today:

"Readers of recipe-for-success books often fail to produce a cake for a simple reason. In the kitchen, there are rarely opponents who fight you tooth and nail for access to the springform pan. Most business advice books do not account for this fact. Instead, they preach that internal factors are primarily responsible for an entity's success. But in real life, someone's over there playing the Black pieces, and she gets just as many moves as you do."--p. 12.

That's a great point. This book outlines why you need systems and what you must do to create them in your business. However, never forget that you must plan your strategy and execute your systems in a competitive marketplace. Those who do the best planning *and* execute great systems will win the game in the end.

As the business leader, you may have the greatest skills, but you can't expect to win consistently if everyone on your team is flying by the seat of their pants solely with their skills instead of with well-thought out and executed systems. Systems works ensures that not only are you setting up the game board for success but that you're in the game to win consistently and at a high level.

One last thought. Don't spend so much time planning and working on systems that you don't get out there and play the game. You can't win if you don't get into the game. Remember, a lot of systems work is done in the trenches as you go. Yet, once you figure out what is working, you want to systematize it and duplicate it again and again to get even better results so that your business is relying more on systems than just skills. The flow of prospects into your business is a key marketing system and one that you must figure out and implement in your business. Get out there and make it happen.

CHAPTER 9

SALES & PERSUASION SYSTEMS / SALES SCRIPTING SYSTEMS

"If you can't describe what you are doing as a process,
you don't know what you are doing."—W. Edwards Deming

In this chapter, I'd like to discuss sales & persuasion and the sales scripts you use. Developing and mastering this system will help you sell more as prospects and clients move and flow through your business. Many businesses have very detailed and organized systems around how they track and control the flow of products that move through their supply chain. Yet, they don't have the best systems in place to ensure that the upsell or the next sale will happen every single time. This chapter will help you put these sales systems in place.

When businesses first get started and as they grow, it is easy to make a lot of mistakes around product flow and control. This can result from bugs in your software or from inefficient systems that delay ordering and production. Regardless of the mistake (which the customer doesn't care about), it can result in a lot of frustration and unhappy customers. If those clients are frustrated enough, they will leave your business and never return. We'll talk more about how to set up the right customer service systems in the next chapter.

Once you have things flowing smoothly within your business, you will want to add better and more effective sales scripting strategies into your processes to ensure that you get more add on sales.

Most people have an improper perception of sales scripting. They believe it is canned, rehearsed, mechanical, inauthentic, robotic, or like someone reading something from a page talking as fast as they can. This is NOT what I am talking about. In reality, sales scripting is words and questions in sequence that have meaning.

If you or any member of your sales team goes through your next sales appointment and just wings it, you are actually following a script. By definition, a script is words in sequence that have meaning. Therefore, if you are talking and making sense, you are following a script. It may not be a very good script.

Michael Gerber in his book *The E-Myth* says: "Things need to be sold. And it's usually people who have to sell them. Everyone in business has heard of the old saw: 80 percent of our sales are produced by 20 percent of the people. Unfortunately, few seem to know what the 20 percent are doing that the eighty percent aren't. Well, let me tell you. The 20 percent are using a system, and the 80 percent aren't."—p. 145.

Gerber talks about how a selling system is comprised of two parts: "Structure and Substance. Structure is *what* you do. Substance is *how* you do it. The Structure of the System includes exactly what you say, the materials you use when you say it, and what you wear. The Substance of the System includes how you say it, how you use it when you say it, and how you *are* when you say it."—p. 146.

What you want to do (as I talk about sales scripting strategies in this chapter) is think about the scripts you are using that are helping you make or lose sales.

With that in mind, here are eight sales scripting strategies so you can help your sales consultants sell within every situation.

1. Educate prospects by connecting what they already know with what they don't yet know (until they talk with you).
A big part of your sales system should be education based. Your prospects are very savvy. They have looked online and seen a wide variety of ideas of what they think they need from your web site, your competitor's site, You Tube, Pinterest, Facebook, or any other social media sites and have seen a wide variety of product ideas that may solve their unique challenge or problem before they ever call you, email you, or enter your marketing funnel in any way. Sometimes, what they think they want isn't realistic for the budget they have and this is where your education can come in and be very helpful to them.

In order to make that education connection, it is best to connect something they do know to something they may not yet know. In your business, you should devise your own sales script for your introductory interview with a prospect to find out what they've already considered so you know exactly where you stand when you begin the sales process. Look for ways to discover where they are at in the sales process, what other options they are considering, and what potential obstacles there may be to the sale.

When you are clear on this information and have a great sales script including questions and potential responses, you are much better prepared to help the prospect and stand out as a helpful resource, not a scary salesperson.

2. Help prospects project how they will feel in the future with the purchase of your product or if they choose not to buy how they'll anticipate the feeling of regret.
Most prospects aren't very good at predicting what emotions they will feel when they make a choice that doesn't work out for the best for them.

As a professional persuader, your job is to help your prospect overcome his or her initial resistance by experiencing what the emotion of regret will *feel* like. The better you can do this, the more successful you will be at the art of persuasion.

The key to improving your business systems here is that you want to always be asking this question: How can you set up your sales script so that your prospect is buying at the end of her appointment or after you've completed making your offer?

To improve your closing ratio, you've got to do something different or better than what you're doing now. In other words, you've got to rise above your baseline performance. You've got to improve your sales script. Scripting is critical. It helps you learn how to be persuasive. Remember, sales is a language of persuasion and influence. Anyone can learn it with the right teacher.

It has never been more important to follow scripts and anticipate what will happen in your sales conversation than it is right now. Everything that happens in the sales conversation with a prospect flows from the process and the script that details what questions you should ask, and how you persuade prospects to actually take action.

3. Use contrast when selling.

Contrast is a power psychological trigger. It is one of the most persuasive ways to help prospects make a decision.

A Tesla sports car is sold using the persuasive trigger of contrast. The script says:

"Yes, it is more expensive, but you will never have to buy gas again. You'll be savings hundreds of dollars in fuel costs a year and you'll feel good knowing you are making a difference for the environment."

Or, here is an example of how a Honda is sold in comparison with a BMW using contrast: "The Honda Accord is similar to the BMW sedan except you don't have to put more expensive high-octane fuel in the tank and it is 1/3 of the price."

If you are selling a higher priced product, then you build value by pointing out the benefits and features that outweigh the price. In this case, prestige, quality, and experience will trump the lower price for the discerning buyer.

In each case, the seller uses scripting to explain the advantage of buying one product over another using contrast. Consider this statement to a prospect:

"This product is similar to the one you showed me you like at another business except you don't have to do _____ here or here (which will save you $____) and with our first visit advantage program, our referral program and our additional coupons, you'll not only save money on this item you love, you'll save nearly $____ in other aspects of your purchase."

Think about your most challenging objection or a competitor that you have lost a sale to recently.

How could you use contrast to help build a more persuasive reason why a prospect should buy from you?

When you take the time to think through this question, you'll be much more successful in persuading your prospects to buy from you because you'll point out the REASONS why your offer is the better value overall (even if it is priced higher).

At the end of an appointment when your offer has been extended, a prospect may say that she has got to go to another business because she has another appointment already scheduled. When this happens, you can use the combination of an analogy and contrast to explain why she can get what she wants now and not postpone her decision any longer.

Here is how you can do this when a prospect says: "I've got to go to my other appointments. I can't cancel them."

I'm glad you brought that up. I can appreciate your sincere desire to keep your appointment. Can I tell you a secret I've discovered after working in this industry for the past ____ years? On occasion, individuals have called to cancel an appointment when they've already found what they were looking for. I don't consider it rude. If they've found what they needed, there is no need to keep looking. They've already found the perfect solution.

It would be like going to a doctor, getting medicine and feeling better and deciding to still go see the other doctor when you've already been cured. It isn't about being rude. It is about already having a solution. You've already found what you are looking for...so another appointment really isn't necessary, is it? (softly)

Let me ask you another question: What are you hoping to see at your next appointment that you haven't seen here?

Or:
What happens if you keep your appointment, come back and find out the exact product you love has already been sold? How would you feel? What would be worse: the brief, temporary fleeting experience of canceling an appointment OR the heavy weight that would come from feeling of a lifetime of regret by wishing you could have had what you you really loved now?

Work harder on your sales scripts to build contrast. It is very persuasive and powerful.

4. Use words in effective and powerful ways.
Words are powerful things especially when you use them in one of the following ways:

- Define words that you use (especially when explaining what you do and the service you provide) – this helps prospects feel comfortable around you since you teach her things she may not know and she feels that she can rely on you to help her find out what she needs to do next
- Compliment or flatter a prospect's previous choices
- Give direct invitations or commands. Here are a few great examples:
  o   Here's what you need to do next...
  o   I need your help...
  o   Can you help me out? Can you do me a favor? (when asking prospect to fill out a testimonial form)
  o   Imagine what it will be like when you're at home (or wherever) enjoying this product for the first time
- Share stories: you should tell your story, listen to the prospect's story about what they've been up to, their search for the perfect product or service. You can also talk about recent stories of clients who have made great choices or who lost out on money by not making a choice, etc. Stories are powerful because they create rapport, influence on a subconscious level, bring the benefits you offer to life, can be used very effectively to overcome objections and in subtle ways can suspend time because the listener enters into a trancelike state when the story is really compelling. Here are a few examples of ways you can transition into a great story.
  o   You can do this by saying: "That reminds me of a client I recently worked with. She had the same concern you did...."
  o   "Maybe you can relate with this....One of our clients recently told me..."

5. Ask better questions to find out how each prospect you work with makes decisions.

You can do this by asking questions or making a statement such as, "Tell me more about that." You can also discuss a little bit about the process by which decisions are typically made by asking: In the past, when you've found a solution to a challenge you were looking at, what was the process you went through to find the right solution? For example, when we would talk with a bride who came to an appointment to shop for wedding dresses, we would often say and ask: "I love your ring. How did you ever know which ring would be the right one?" The answer to that question helped us understand the process by which the prospective client would make a decision when she found what she was looking for. It was done in a non-threatening and positive way that allowed us to get into her mindset so we could understand her process for making decisions.

To improve your sales systems and have better scripts, you should ask questions like this as well. For example, if they don't have all of the decision makers present, you can ask: "Is there anyone else that can't be here today for your appointment that will be helping you make your decision? If we do find what you're looking for today, how will you go about getting his or her input? This works particularly well if you have a first visit advantage package that incentivizes the prospect who takes action on what she is looking for.

Build a sales script to help you overcome each objection that you may face in this process. For example, you could ask: "Do you have any other appointments scheduled today at other businesses like ours? If yes, say: "The reason I asked is that I was curious if you would you like to know how *our* offer compares to the other places you've said you're going to be visiting?" When she responds in the affirmative, you can ask: "Who else are you going to be going to see today?" This allows you to find out *who* else they're going to see. Then you can build contrast to show why your overall value is the best by comparison.

Never underestimate the power of questions in great sales scripts to get to the bottom of any objection a prospect may have.

6. Better explain the benefits the prospect will get from doing business with you.

There are five main ways you can explain benefits:

1) List the tangible benefits a prospect gets with your offer such as a beautiful product, you'll save money and save time.

2) Discuss the intangible benefits such as happiness, peace of mind, not being embarrassed, not having to worry about any hassle because you'll take care of all of the details, etc.

3) Discuss the benefits for taking action on the first visit (If you utilize our First Visit Advantage Program, you can save $_____ by taking action today and getting exactly what you're looking for...)

4) Discuss the consequences of not taking action. What exactly will your prospect lose out on if she doesn't take action? What regrets might he or she feel if they return and can no longer get what you are offering?

5) *Discuss the benefit within the benefit.* You could do this by asking: "How else could you use the $_____ you'll save on your ___product or service_____ when you go ahead and get what you love today?" A great way to explain the benefit within a benefit is to add the phrase "so that" to the end of every statement you make.

7. Use more effective closing statements.

Here are nine examples of ways you can finalize the transaction:

o   Take away: This is where you offer the prospect a deal and then take the deal away. If she wants the deal she has to take action now.
  o   "This offer is only good until we close tonight. If you choose to wait to get it, I'll need you to initial this waiver form that indicates you are forfeiting your right to get these great savings today...so when you come back you won't be mad at me because you won't be able to get these great savings...
  o   Or, you can just go ahead and lock in the savings now by putting this product on hold or layaway. Which would be best for you?
o   Give the prospect two or more choices (where both choices are a yes):
  o   Would you like this product with this _____ or this one?
  o   You can pay with VISA or Mastercard. Which would work best for you?
  o   We can bring this to you on Thursday at 5pm or Friday at 6pm. Which would you prefer?
o   Ask for the sale
  o   What if anything would prevent you from going ahead and getting what you love now?
o   How do you feel?
  o   How do you feel about getting _____ now?
  o   How will you feel if you go to three other businesses and don't find anything you like better only to return and find out that what you love has already been sold?
o   Assumption
  o   When would you like to pick up or take delivery on _____?
  o   What day would you like to have us go ahead and prepare _____ for you?
  o   Let's go ahead and get you your _____...

- o When would you like to schedule your next appointment, etc.?
- o Bonus for Taking Action Now
  - o By taking advantage of this offer today, you'll also get...(then list the benefits)
  - o Here is your homework Assignment: What will persuade *your* prospects to take action now?
- o Would you be comfortable?
  - o What would have to happen so you would feel comfortable going ahead and getting what you love today? Then be quiet. Let her share with you her last objection (if there is one). Then, go ahead with the sale.
- o Reduce it to the ridiculous
  - o "The price difference between this product and the one you like at one of our competitors is $300. This makes your investment less than $25 a month or less than $1 per day. You'll have the memories of enjoying _____ for the rest of your life. Is it worth less than the cost of a soda everyday to have exactly what you love here for such a great value....Ten years from now, you'll look back on your decision here today with fondness knowing that for less than $30 a year or $2.50 a month, you got exactly what you wanted and didn't have to settle for anything else.
- o Ask for the sale, then be quiet

In this chapter, I've covered seven specific script strategies you can use to successfully implement your sales systems. To successfully implement these systems in your business, you need to make a list of the scripts you need.

There are at least eight specific scripts that should be a part of your sales systems. These are:

1) Appointment Setting Script – this is a system and a process that helps you persuade prospects to be ready to come into your business ready to buy (as we discussed in the previous chapter)

2) Pre-Sales Script – what is on your web site (your script that excites prospects with your special reports, videos, text, etc.)

3) Approach Script – how you approach the prospect who has expressed interest in what you offer through education and value

4) Interview Script – the questions you ask and what you say is choreographed to create a specific result starting with "I'd like to outline what we hope to help you achieve today during your appointment..."

5) Product Presentation Script

6) Overcoming Objection Scripts

7) Closing Scripts

8) First Visit Advantage Script or Decisive Action Bonus Script– In the beginning of the sales process, you can explain how you the prospect will be able to get the best possible deal when she utilizes the bonuses and benefits that she'll get when you buys from you on her first visit.

In my advanced systems course, I can teach you the exact wording you can use to create results and actually implement these scripts in your business. Having and utilizing these scripts everyday according to each of these scenarios will help you either make or lose sales every single day.

Don't leave money on the table. Know what works to get prospects to take action now and make sure your sales scripts reflect that.

Keep a folder on your desktop entitled "Sales Scripts." When you do something that works well, write it down, train everyone on your team how to use it, and then utilize it to overcome objections and successfully close sales.

For example, in a sales situation, sometimes a prospect will offer you the objection that he or she needs to go to lunch before a decision can be made. As an example, here are three scripts that can be used to overcome this objection.

1) That's a good idea. Let's say you're at lunch. Based on what you know now, what would be the reason you should go ahead and get this?

2) That a good idea. Tell me, what are you hoping you'll realize about this product at lunch that you don't know now? In other words, are you leaning one way, but are feeling a little nervous

to tell me because you are leaning towards another solution? If so, tell me more about it....It's okay....You can tell me what you're thinking.

3) I'm glad you brought that up. Let's say lunch has passed. How will you know what you should do?

Each of these scenarios allows you to continue the dialogue and the conversation so you can get to the sale. Without a script, such an objection will likely stall you. You may not even know what to say in such a situation and you will likely lose the momentum and the sale. You've got to practice your sales scripts. You and your sales consultants should work each day on training to overcome the objections that you face. When a sale isn't made, stop and then analyze what you could have done better and practice what you will say the next time.

When you are practicing a script, practice it word for word. Then, when you are in front of your prospect, don't worry about trying to do it word for word. Just do the best you can and try to remember as much of the script as you can. As you continue to practice, you'll find that the script will work better for you and you'll remember more and more of it each time.

Sales scripting systems are powerful because they allow you to visualize what you will say in different situations. Since the subconscious mind doesn't know the difference between a real or an imaginary event, your practice will help you know *what* to say *when* you need to say it.

A script allows you to set up the sale so only certain things can happen. The prospect can say 'yes'. She can say 'no' or she can put up resistance to giving you an answer now. A script helps you get to a definitive answer while lowering resistance so you can help him or her make a decision to buy now. Scripts help you achieve a predictable result.

When you have better selling scripts and systems, your sales consultants will be more successful and you will be happier. You'll make more sales. You'll make more money and you will be more profitable. You will be able to work *on* your business and not just *in* your business. And that will make all of the difference.

Here is an assessment for your sales and sales scripting systems:

#	Rank yourself from 1-10 based on your current business behaviors.	1	2	3	4	5	6	7	8	9	10	Rank yourself from 1-10 based on your current business behaviors.
1	We don't analyze our mistakes and rarely practice improving our skills.											We analyze our mistakes when sales don't happen and learn from them.
2	Sales reports are rarely posted and individual team members don't know how they are doing.											Sales information is readily available and closely monitored.
3	We don't track our prospects, our close ratios and the number of transactions per client continuously. If our consultants aren't where they need to be (closing percentages), it is tolerated and accepted.											We track our prospects, our close ratios and the number of transactions per client continuously. If our consultants aren't where they need to be (closing percentages), we help them become better or replace them quickly.
4	If sales per hour, week, and month aren't achieved, there is little to no consequence if sales consultants don't hit their targets.											Every sales consultant knows and achieves their sales goals per hour, week, and month.
5	Every member of the team is unaware of what their contribution needs to be each day, week and month to help make goals happen.											Every member of the team recognizes and works to help achieve daily, weekly, and monthly sales goals.
6	Our sales consultants don't follow a system that allows them to stay in touch with prospects and clients in the marketing funnel.											Our sales consultants follow a system that allows them to stay in touch with prospects and clients in the marketing funnel.
7	Irregular sales training occurs and bad sales habits are regularly found when observing sales consultants at work.											Regular sales training is offered to every member of our staff and it is implemented.
8	Our sales consultants don't have a system in place to prioritize the prospects and clients they are working with.											Our sales consultants have a system in place to prioritize the prospects and clients they are working with.

#	Rank yourself from 1-10 based on your current business behaviors.	1	2	3	4	5	6	7	8	9	1 0	Rank yourself from 1-10 based on your current business behaviors.
9	Our sales consultants don't always act professionally and they don't have the experience necessary to excel at selling.											Our sales consultants are professional and have the experience necessary to excel at selling.
1 0	Our methods for selling haven't changed with what is happening in the marketplace.											We evaluate and make changes to our sales training based on changes in the marketplace.

Here is a task list to help you implement better selling systems for you and your team:

1. Look at how well you are using sales scripts in the following eight areas and consider these two questions: 1) What are you already doing well? 2) Where is there room for improvement?

Go through each script and document what you are saying that is working well. Use this in your training system to ensure that new hires are properly prepared to sell your products and services.

1) Appointment Setting Script – this is a system and a process that helps you persuade prospects to be ready to come into your marketing funnel ready to buy

2) Pre-Sales Script – what is on your web site (your script that excites prospects with your special reports, videos, text, etc.

3) Approach Script

4) Interview Script – the questions you ask and what you say is choreographed to create a specific result. "I'd like to outline what we hope to help you achieve today during your appointment..."

5) Product Presentation Script

6) Overcoming Objection Scripts

7) Closing Scripts

8) First Visit Advantage Script or Decisive Action Bonus Script

2. Have each of your consultants make a list of their most challenging objections. Have them write out the questions they will ask to get more clarity on what the prospect is feeling and thinking while overcoming the objection. Have them reverse engineer the objection so they can see how they can overcome it more persuasively. In particular, have them

write, study, and practice better questions to successfully overcome stalls, smokescreens and any other objection that stops the sale. Create and study flashcards or sales training specifically designed to help members of your team with the objections they struggle with the most.

Most objections will fall into one of these categories:

o   I need to think about it.
o   I don't have any money with me.
o   I need to get the approval of someone else who didn't come with me today.
o   The price is higher than I wanted to spend.
o   I like a product or offer at another business.
o   I've got lots of time.
o   Delay of any kind: I've got to go to lunch...; I'll come back by the end of the day, etc.

Do you have your scripts memorized to handle each and every objection you will face?

3. When you present products to your prospects, use the following formula:

o   Explain the price of what you're selling
o   Explain what they'll get at your business with their purchase
o   Explain what bonuses they'll get at your business by buying today
o   Ask questions about how they feel once they've solved the challenge their facing or gotten the results they're after by implementing the solution you're offering
o   Ask questions to create urgency and uncover feeling of regret for waiting
o   Have a call to action

When evaluating your sales scripts, look at how well you are following this formula. Where applicable, make changes to be more effective here.

4. Study the nine scripts I discussed in this chapter to be more effective at closing. Incentivize your sales consultants who use at least four to five of these in each interaction they have with their prospects this week.

5. Write your own benefit within the benefit statements for your business. Be clear about what a client gets from you that she really can't get anywhere else. The more specificity you have here, the more successful you'll be in being persuasive.

CHAPTER 10

FOLLOW-UP SYSTEMS

"The only thing keeping you from going out and trying one more time is you."
—Dave Lakhani

Tom Hopkins in his book *Selling in Tough Times* quotes Dan Kennedy about the lack of follow-up in businesses today. He said:

"I don't believe in a poor economy as much as I believe in poor follow-up. In the past year, I've not heard from the salesman or dealer I bought my most recent automobile from, the real estate agent I bought properties from, the clothing stores and their salespeople in two different cities of residence I've patronized in the past, the restaurant I used to visit frequently but haven't been to in six months. But I have bought a car, real estate, clothes and gone out to eat. And it's a safe bet a bunch of those business owners and salespeople guilty of zero or poor follow-up are poor-mouthing about the poor economy." –Tom Hopkins, *Selling in Tough Times*, p. 91.

I wholeheartedly agree with what Dan Kennedy says in Tom's book. Most people really struggle in their businesses because they don't have a good system and method of implementing good follow-up with their customers. I recently shared much of what I'm going to share with you in this chapter with a close friend of mine who isn't in our business. He was surprised by how much thought and effort went into the follow-up sequences we use to get clients back into our business if they already purchased from us and also all of the follow-up sequences if they don't. In his business, he didn't have any follow-up sequences for those who didn't buy and they also don't do much of anything for those who already purchased from them.

If you only have 10 to 20% of your prospects that return to your business from your follow-up efforts, you'll be so much farther ahead than competitors who don't do anything at all. But, if you can have a coordinated approach to get qualified clients who've already purchased from you and a concurrent process for those prospects who don't buy from you, you'll be leaps and bounds ahead of competitors who are barely paying attention to the prospects who come into their marketing funnel that do buy. I've found that the key to good follow-up is to have a planned sequence for what will happen next based on what the prospect or client does. The purpose of this chapter is to pull back the curtain and show you the power of specific follow-up sequences you can use to get prospects back into your business whether they've bought something from you or not.

To be successful at follow-up there are several things you need to keep in mind. The first is the importance of being flexible. In this chapter, I'm going to share with you several ways to follow up with prospects via phone, direct mail, or email and how you can respond to objections that your prospects bring up. I'll also talk about how you can set up your own follow-up system for your clients who buy (to get additional sales) and those who don't buy.

Garrison Wynn in his book *The Real Truth About Success* makes this observation:
"Business, like life, is similar to landing an airplane on an aircraft carrier. It's a moving target. Success has plenty to do with knowing where that target is and using the skills you have developed to get there. But skills will get you only so far. The rest is determined by how you come in and feel it out as you go. You need to be acutely aware of your surroundings and flexible when necessary. You almost never hear someone say, 'The key to success is rigidity.' That's how your plane ends up in the water. Life and business, like those jets, move and shift, and things snap if they're too rigid—whether it's a bridge, your emotions, or your sanity."

He continues:
"Don't get me wrong: You cannot fly that plane without qualifications, and you must follow a basic process to land. There is value in processes—the way they help us stack things in neat little piles and set up systems for the flow of information and production. A process is a guarantee: Everybody can follow its rules and know on a certain level what he or she must do. There's a lot more to success than just process. In the long term, when facing moving targets, we must adapt." – *The Real Truth About Success*, pp. 190-191.

This is so important when following up with clients or prospects. In this chapter, I'm going to cover several very specific processes about how you can follow up with your clients and prospects. The success of your follow-up sequences will really depend on how well you get into the world of those you are talking to. Remember that the purpose of the follow up is to re-engage the prospect or the client and show them how you can offer more value and help them get what they really want. Be flexible about how you get to the result but never forget that the result is the most important thing—otherwise, why make the call, send out the mail piece, or send the follow-up email?

Here are three questions you should have in mind when thinking about your process of follow-up and how you relate to a prospect and the challenge they have:

1. **Are you really clear about what she is looking for?** Does she sense that? The clearer you are about what the prospect wants and the more that she senses that you really want to help, the more successful you'll be in your follow up calls and sequence. You'll be viewed as a welcome guest instead of an annoying pest. Here are several good questions for you to ask so she senses your commitment to her and her challenge (and which will unveil opportunities for you to help her):
   - What is it that keeps you up at night?
   - What is your biggest concern right now?
   - What is the one thing you would fix if you could change anything?

2. **Does the prospect sense that you are as concerned or more concerned than he is about his concerns with resolving the challenge he has?**

3. **If you can't solve his or her problem, can you direct her to someone who can?** If that person does a great job solving her problem and he or she wouldn't have met them without your help, what does that do for your reputation? It builds a stronger bond of trust and it will position you to be of service in the future (when you follow up).

Tom Hopkins makes this point in his book *Selling in Tough Times*:

"We should all learn a lesson from the movie *Miracle on 34th Street*. The Macy's Santa tells a child they'll get a certain toy for Christmas. When the mother hears what Santa said she's upset because Macy's is out of the toy. Santa tells her that Santa's competitor, Gimbels, has it. At first the managers of Macy's want to fire Santa for sending their clients to the competition, but when they realize the goodwill Santa has generated and see the increase in loyalty from their customers, the story changes." –p. 95.

He then asks:
"Are you finding that your prospects have needs you can't serve? If so, be the hero and help them find a quality source for those needs."–*Selling in Tough Times*, p. 95.

A good question you should always ask at the end of every interaction you have with prospects in your business is: "Is there anything else I can do for you?"

A second thing that is absolutely critical to success in follow-up is understanding how what you are doing in that step fits into the overall sequence of what happens next (when your prospect buys from you or doesn't buy from you).

A good way to do this is to create a flow chart where you look at what typically happens when a prospect buys your product or doesn't buy your product and how you interact with him or her based on those decisions (and most importantly what happens next).

For example, at our bridal store, we set up six follow-up sequences if a bride bought a dress and three follow-up sequences if the bride didn't buy a dress that were designed for her to return to the store) so she would buy a dress or something else from us.

Amongst other things, there is a thank you sequence, a bounce back sequence inviting brides to come back into the store, a referral sequence, a vendor sequence inviting brides to do business with the other wedding businesses we refer them to, a sequence to gather pictures we can use for testimonials and a sequence to sell items after their wedding (wedding gown preservation kit, etc.). We then have a completely different set of sequences if the bride doesn't buy.

The reality is that most entrepreneurs don't think about their follow-up sequences very much. They have one response if the prospect buys and then do little to nothing to get them back in if they don't buy. This lack of planning prevents the prospective client from having any kind of meaningful experience with your business.

To help you think through this process, take the time to list all of the things you sell in your business. Then, list *when* a prospect typically buys them, and *how* you invite a prospect to do business with you (from the first moment he or she enters your marketing funnel). Then, outline this process in a flow chart and look for ways to anticipate and prepare marketing pieces to surprise and delight your prospects and clients and get them back into your business to do more business with you.

Don't ignore the sequence of what should be done next and just assume it will happen. Instead, anticipate what your prospect will do (and you can do this even better when you've gathered information from them when they arrive in your marketing funnel) and then choreograph your response accordingly.

The third aspect of follow up that is critical is how sold you are personally on taking the daily initiative to follow up. If you are not sold on the importance of making follow up phone calls or sending out follow up postcards or emails, your prospects won't be able to respond. The reality is that it takes a tremendous amount of commitment to consistently make follow up phone calls or follow a sequence that will yield results. Yet, it is this consistency that will propel your business even higher.

So, with those three things in mind, let's discuss three phone follow up sequences you can use:

1. Follow Up to Invite Prospect Back into Your Business Who Has Already Purchased Something From You:
Hi. This is _____ with _____ (name of your business).
Did I catch you at a bad time?
Two potential responses:
Yes, I'm busy right now.
No...no, this is fine. What are you calling about?

I'm calling to thank you for your recent visit to our (web site, business…) and to ask you a couple of quick questions about your experience with us. If you can take a couple of minutes to answer these four to five quick survey questions, I have a special offer I've been authorized to extend to you when we've finished that you're absolutely going to love. How does that sound?
Great!

How was your experience on our web site (or in our business)?

How did you feel about our selection?

What other options are you still looking at to help you with the reason you visited us in the first place?

Have you been able to find a solution for _____ (your next product or service offering)?

What could we do to improve our experience for other clients who come to our web site?

Thanks for taking the time to answer those questions for me. As I mentioned, I've been authorized to offer a special incentive to you as a way to express our thanks to you for giving us your valuable feedback. You mentioned that you were still looking for _____.

If you can come in before this Friday afternoon, I can offer you:
- A $_____ coupon off on _____*the next product or service in your marketing sequence*_____. When do you think you would be available for a special appointment with me this week? What time would work best?
- A 25% savings off _____*another product or service in your marketing sequence*_____. What time would work best for you to come in and redeem this coupon?

2. Follow Up to Invite Prospect Back If You Have Something New to Offer:
Hi. This is _____ with _____ (name of your business).
Did I catch you at a bad time?

I'm calling because as a client who recently purchased _____ from us, we really value your opinion. We get new shipments of _____ each week and I wanted to find out if you would be interested in knowing about these when they come in?

If yes,

We just received in a brand new shipment of _____ (your product or service) that perfectly complements what you purchased from us. I have a couple of options picked out I really want you to see that I know you'll really like. Is there a time this week before Friday afternoon when you can come in to see them?

If you offer a service option for what you've sold you can say: We have found that some clients forget to utilize the great service plan we offer for _____*the product they just bought*_____. What would you think of a service where you receive a reminder email or postcard to come in and get ____*a service tune-up or follow up visit to see how your product is working for you*____ six months to a year from now?

A furnace company utilizes this type of follow up strategy and is very successful in converting customers to a new service (upsell):

Here is what they say:

"We have found that many of our clients fail to change their furnace filters as often as recommended by the manufacturers. What would you think of a service where you receive new furnace filters delivered to your doorstep during the week you should be changing them?

This is a soft approach and works well with existing customers who are already happy. It continues to build a relationship with them and helps them take care of something they would normally forget about or not pay attention to because they are busy.

How could you adapt this idea for your business?

If they say no to your offer, say:

Thank you. I completely respect that. Thanks again for purchasing _____ from us. We greatly appreciate your business. If you have any questions that come up, please feel free to contact me at.....

3. Follow Up to Invite Prospect into a New Marketing Funnel for a New Special Event / Sale:

Hi. This is _____ with _____ (name of your business).

Did I catch you at a bad time?

Two potential responses:

Yes, I'm busy right now.

No...no, this is fine. What are you calling about?

I'm calling to follow up on a postcard you should have just received from our business in the mail. We are offering _____ right now (with a special offer of _____ *your incentive* _____ and I'm calling to see if we can schedule an appointment for you to come back in to take advantage of this special savings event.

Two potential responses:

1. I already have what I was looking for.

If this is the case, then ask a follow up question that allows you to get to the next offer you have in your marketing funnel.

Do you already have _____?

Or

Do you have all of your _____?

2. Sure, I'd like to set up an appointment.

Find out what time works best for them to come into your business for an appointment.

Thanks for your time. We look forward to seeing you soon!

These three follow up sequences can work wonders for you in your business and start you on the path to increased sales as you let your prospects and clients know what a great resource you can be for them.

Don't delay in creating your own follow-up sequences into your business. Be sure your follow-up sequences have an educational component to them so you are always offering more value to their lives. For example, your marketing sequence should persuasively sell the need for an appointment and pre-sells each prospect on that appointment through very specific steps before she even meets or talks with one of your sales consultants. Your goal is very simply to help each prospect see exactly why her experience at your business will be different from any other business she may visit and covertly persuade her why she should buy from you the first time she meets with your sales consultant or when the offer is extended. You can do this through a series of emails and articles specifically designed to build a relationship of trust with the prospect and by giving her helpful information she isn't getting anywhere else to help her gain the solution she desires.

Your articles should educate the prospect, take away her biggest objections or fears about the process of getting what you offer, and clearly articulate why you are the best place to buy what you sell backed up by dozens of her peers who all rave about the amazing experience they've already had working with you. Your system should also include a very brief questionnaire which will help the prospect prepare for her appointment before she arrives and give her important details about exactly what will happen when your sales consultant sits down with her or whatever your sales process involves.

An important question for you to carefully think about is simply this: **How can you create a memorable experience for your prospects if you haven't planned in advance what is going to happen?**

The unfortunate reality is that you can't and *this is why* it is so important for you to plan and choreograph what happens to prospects even before they enter your marketing funnel. Think about a recent memorable experience you had at an amazing retail store or the last time you visited Disneyland or Disneyworld. If your experience was memorable, how much thought, planning, and rehearsal do you think went into making it extraordinary instead of just mediocre? The answer, especially in the case of Disney, is that nothing is left to chance. Every experience you have is carefully choreographed to appear spontaneous but in reality has happened hundreds and thousands of times before with other delighted guests. How can you apply this lesson to your business? To do so, carefully think through each interaction you have with prospects (HINT: In your business, there are **at least** eleven different interaction points throughout the process of selling your products where you can offer more value and an enhanced experience).

I have two questions for you about this:
1) Do you know how many interactions there are in what you are selling to your prospects and clients?

2) What other things are you doing to enhance the experience your customers have in your business so they're excited when they receive your follow-up notifications from you?

Serious reflection on these questions can help you see what you ought to be doing more of with your follow-up sequences in your business. When you know the answers, you can plan how you can integrate better experiences and surprises into those experiences to make them more memorable and fun for clients to share with their friends. A very big part of building your value in the eyes of your clients is by paying particular detail to the intangible, personal, and unique aspects of what you do.

The second part of this secret involves a concept called "Flipping the Funnel" as outlined by author Joseph Jaffe in his book *Flip the Funnel: How to Use Existing Customers to Gain New Ones*. I would highly encourage you to read and study this very important book. The basic premise of the book is that most prospective customers are invited into a business relationship through the AIDA sales funnel model. This model (which stands for Attention, Interest, Desire, and Action) was developed by sales and advertising pioneer E. St. Elmo Lewis in 1898. Most marketers use one of these four steps to bring customers into their doors, but unfortunately, that is where they stop. They don't continually market and mine the new customer relationship for maximum value over a lifetime of business interaction.

The unfortunate reality is that many entrepreneurs don't execute these four steps correctly in their marketing and as a result they aren't successful in persuading prospects to do business with them. The genius of what Joseph Jaffe has done in his book *Flip the Funnel* is point out the next four step sequence of exactly what you should be doing to get your newly acquired customers promoting your business to all of their friends and family. Following this sequence can literally turn your marketing funnel into a huge megaphone.

Jaffe's *Flip the Funnel* model (ADIA) stands for Acknowledgement, Dialogue, Incentivization, and Activation. I want to go through each one of these points and share with you specific ideas of how you can use them in your business.

The first step is **acknowledgement**, which is basically an interaction of some type with your recently acquired client that acknowledges her and lets her know how grateful you are to have met her and your appreciation for the opportunity to do business with her.

Jaffe points out ten ways you and I can confirm acknowledgement to every client who buys from you. These ten ways of confirming acknowledgement are:

"1. A thank-you from an actual manager or salesperson.

2. A personal, handwritten note.

3. A gift. Why not? The bigger the purchase, the bigger the gift; this is just common sense.

4. Enrollment in a club or community with some kind of status involved.

5. A subtle mention at the next point of purchase. *Aaah, Mr. Jaffe, good to have you back at the Four Seasons. I see it's been three weeks since your last stay at our resort.*

6. Gratitude without benefits: pulling the heartstrings with no strings attached.

7. Gratitude with benefits: A reward at the next point of purchase. Technology has an even better memory than human beings (at least those who work for corporations).

8. A tacit yet effective reminder of tenure. American Express's 'Member since' on their credit cards reminds both customers and merchants how long they've been aboard. Many companies, including several primary credit card competitors, have since followed this lead.

9. Integrating appointments into personal Outlook or Entourage calendars using simple Web-based functionality.

10. Extending these ideas to the social web using widgets, feeds, and other applications."-- *Flip the Funnel*, p. 64

The second step is **dialogue**. Jaffe explains this concept with this statement:

"We need to encourage and engage in dialogue by providing our customers with multiple ways to contact us at will, whether they have a purpose or not. We need to get them talking about the little things, the big things, and everything else in between. We also need to come to terms with the fact that they'll talk, whether we want them to or not; and the only thing worse than our customers talking negatively is not talking at all."

He continues:
"The choice is therefore twofold: Do we want them to talk about us to our faces or behind our backs? Do we want to be masters of our own fate or victims to it?" *–Flip the Funnel*, p. 70.

Here are five things you can do to activate dialogue in your business based on the italicized points Jaffe makes on pages 70 and 71 of *Flip the Funnel* which are followed by my comments.

1. *Establish clubs, forums, communities, groups, or hubs where clients can connect with each other, ask questions, provide answers, and socialize.* The question for you to consider is: Can you create a forum within your own site with your blog where your clients can interact? You may resist doing something like this, but think about the power and influence you will have with prospects and clients in your area if you are the first to build an online community or club like this (not to mention the advertising revenue you could gain from selling ads to such a targeted niche market).

2. *Make the first move.* Do clients hear from you after they buy from you? If not, you are missing out on big opportunities to build even more trust and a valuable long-term relationship. Don't wait for clients to contact you. Make the first move instead. You may want to take a picture of every client who buys a product from you (with her sales consultant and her together) and then mail a customized Thank You card to them with this picture via a service like Send Out cards.

3. *Listen.* Is there a way for clients to reach you on your web site or via your social media platforms? Do you promote these links from the home page of your web site? Could you invite clients to upload videos of their experience at your business for a chance to win some prize each month? This way you could listen to what they have to say and create a contest where the most creative clients have a chance to win. You can make it even more interesting (and get other clients to listen to what they have to say) by making an interactive contest where clients can actually vote on the winner after they watch the videos.

4. *Have a system to provide timely and relevant information to ongoing comments that clients have.* Do you have a system in place to monitor what clients are saying on social networking sites or in their interactions with you? Are there other resources or vendors you can put the client in touch with as she plans other details for utilizing the product or service she just purchased (since she already trusts you)? Can you create a podcast or an online television channel where you can interview other vendors to provide more information to clients that will allow you to interact with and have more dialogue with other clients (and create an additional advertising revenue source for your business)?

5. *Blend technology and human resources.* Once you have created content in any of the ways detailed above, can you offer replays of this helpful information and dialogue to future clients? If you do this well, you can

also leverage your staff well (you could even have different sales consultants responsible for different segments of the podcast and then be the one who promotes this segment to clients who come into your business—this can also create mini-celebrities out of your sales consultants). Your clients can also recommend or pass this valuable content on to their network of friends by sharing links to this valuable information on their Facebook page.

The third step is **incentivization**. Jaffe defines this step as the point at which: "Our customers are feeling the love, satisfied that their purchase counts and that they're not just another statistic. Their problems are being met proactively and comprehensively. They're also sharing their experiences with personal contacts—and even selling product for you. At this point of the funnel, customers are essentially recognized and rewarded both for their repeat purchase(s) and for their ability to influence other consumers' purchases—*typically via positive sentiment, word-of-mouth, and specifically recommendations and referrals.*"—*Flip the Funnel*, p. 71.

People really only listen to one radio station: WIIFM (What's In It for Me?). Are you offering your clients incentives if they refer their friends and family to you? Having a great referral program in place is a great way to do this. Jaffe asks this pertinent question:

"Do you know what percentage of your total number of purchases come from the same—in other words, returning—customers? If it's higher than two-thirds of your total sales—and more often than not, it will be—ask yourself: 'What am I doing to address the people who come back to buy again and again and again?' On the flipside when we take repeat customers for granted, at some point, they're going to ask, 'What have you done for me lately?' They're going to feel unappreciated, taken advantage of, and essentially abused. And we hasten this process by heaping endless discounts and perks on new customers, thereby, basically slapping our existing loyal customers in the face....One obvious way to avoid this is to reward our customers. Loyalty programs have long been the expression of this kind of best practice."

Here are two examples you have likely seen at other businesses and some questions for you to consider regarding your own incentivization program for you to consider:

- Southwest Airlines – I fly a lot with Southwest and receive free flights with so many flight purchases (last year I received five free flights). My favorite thing they offer is an early check-in process that automatically puts me at the front of the line when checking in – no matter when I arrive at airport or print out my boarding pass – this status is confirmed to me via email every year when I hit their milestone of a certain number of trips flown. Could you offer a frequent purchase club or special incentive to clients at other vendors that they only get by purchasing a product or service from you? What benefits could you include in this service that would make purchasing from anyone else a big let down (and encourage them to buy from you even more)?
- Restaurants – Several restaurants that my family and I frequently dine at offer an 11th meal free when 10 meals are purchased. Since I have five children you can see why dining at these locations pays off rather quickly ☺ and as an added bonus, we all really enjoy the food.

Here are other examples of incentives that you could offer clients:
- Decisive First Visit Rewards – clients who make the decision to buy on their first visit qualify for an exclusive package with additional bonuses which goes away if they don't buy the product they are considering on the first visit
- Gift on Arrival –give a gift to every prospect coming into your business who meets with a sales consultant (whether she buys or not)
- Coupons from other vendors that compliment what you offer in your business
- To encourage testimonials, give clients who provide a testimonial letter or video a free premium or gift. You can also incentivize your team with $1 for every written testimonial they collect and $3 for every video testimonial they receive.

The three biggest benefits to incentives as outlined by Jaffe are that you will get an increased number of recommendations, your business will really be set apart from any other experience the prospect will have and you'll get increased loyalty and increased purchases as a result. What incentives are you offering to clients at your business to encourage them to refer their friends?

Don't ignore the powerful step of incentivization. It can help your business grow exponentially.

The fourth step Jaffe points out in *Flip the Funnel* is **activation.** This is the step where you essentially flip the switch of community or social networking on and watch in wonder as hundreds and thousands of other individuals find out about your business through this coordinated approach. If you do this well, your funnel becomes a marketing megaphone for your new fans to spread the word about you.

Jaffe explains this step as follows:
"The final part of the flipped funnel is about flipping the switch of community or social networking. Up until now, our efforts have been focused on individuals or one-to-one interaction. Now it's time to connect the dots and activate the collective potential of the wise crowds. This explodes the number of potential connections and subsequent transactions, based on formalizing some kind of structure around which all customers—including current employees—are connected." –p. 75.

He continues:
"Whereas the first three stages of the funnel are more commonplace, this final stage is decidedly *not*. In fact, as the flipped funnel widens, we notice an inverse relationship in terms of adoption, incidence, and usage. That's not coincidence, given the fact that every step away from the A of Action is one more step removed from the norm or the status quo." –p. 75

Don't be one who ignores this critically important step in the new economy. If you can be the first business in your market niche to successfully flip the funnel and activate your clients to promote you and your business, you will crush your competitors. The wave after wave of clients who will be promoting you and your business will turn the tide in your favor and it will be difficult if not impossible for your competitors to catch up.

Will you beat your competitors to the punch? Will you create a powerful network of clients in your community that you can leverage to exponentially grow your brand? Will you have the vision and the foresight to create and activate this network now so you can start monetizing it *before* your competitors even figure out that they need to be doing this?

To help you better flip your marketing funnel and create a better follow-up system, I'm going to share two big breakthroughs you can use to propel your business forward.

1. **Create your own media.**

A key component of any kind of lasting success you'll have in flipping the funnel is to create a place where your prospective clients have a chance to get to know and interact with you. Then, once you've positioned yourself and your business as an authority and a celebrity, you can activate your clients by giving them the tools to successfully promote you. In both cases, you'll need your own media to promote what you are doing. In the first place, having your own media will help you position yourself as an expert, an authority, and a celebrity.

Here are five types of media you should seriously consider implementing at your business to help you create your authority first and a place of community to activate your clients in second.

- *Ezines or newsletters* – create your own online or print newsletter which you can send clients each month (you could give a print version of this to clients as part of your gift package when they buy from you and email them subsequent issues. Each issue could contain tips each month to help them with issues they may be dealing with, a profile of a vendor which may want to consider, a profile of one of your sales consultants, and informative and fun news about you and your business (including some of the places you've recently traveled to bring clients the very best products and services in the world).

- *Podcast* – Setting up a podcast is easier today than ever before. You can interview and profile others each month by phone, record the conversation, and then deliver the audio file on your web site through sites like Libsyn or SoundCloud. You can even create your own content with tips to help your clients and charge vendors to be on your program. There is no need to wait for someone else to give you permission. You can create your own show and your own valuable content. I invite you to listen to my podcast which you can find links to on my web site (www.soundlawsofsuccess.com).

- *TV Show (online/offline)* – A domain with the extension .tv can be created and you can host a weekly TV show here which you record in your business with your smart phone video camera or which you host in conjunction with a local videographer. You can then invite clients to link to these special episodes online from your own web site.
- *Magazine* – In our bridal business, we created a magazine at our store that I created and started in 2002. In it, I featured pictures of private dresses we sell in our store, ads (which I've sold to local advertising vendors) and articles I've written which establish my wife as an expert and which feature a personalized note from her to each bride who comes into our store. You could do the same as a positioning strategy and to create a valuable follow-up piece for you.
- *Special Reports on Your Site or a Specialized Blog Addressing Issues Your Clients Have* – This web site will allows clients to learn valuable information and be reminded about how you are the thought leader in your industry and continue to provide additional value to the client (even after they made their purchase).

Create your own media. In today's day and age, there are no limits to what you can do here with your imagination and a little work. Remember, the race is on. The business professionals who do this best will literally dominate every other business in their market niche.

2. Automatically put yourself in front of your clients for the next scheduled visit. Then, put surprises in place to enhance the experience at each step along the way.
The key to making this breakthrough work well for you can be explained by thinking about how you are treated by other businesses that see you repeatedly throughout the year.

A good example of this is when you get your hair cut and styled. Have you ever been to a hair dresser who didn't schedule your next appointment while you were there? If so, think about how much opportunity they missed out on. You will get your hair cut again at some point in the future. If you didn't have a good experience or if they didn't automatically schedule another visit with you, have you ever gone to another place? If so, you can see the value of what I am describing and encouraging you to do.

On the other hand, if you've ever gone to a good dentist or doctor, they always automatically schedule a follow up visit with you while you are still there at their office. You should do the same. You should automatically schedule the client's next appointment with you at your business when he or she is there.

You can embody this principle at your business by embracing the motto: The purpose of an appointment is to schedule another appointment. And, I don't mean another appointment of the same kind unless it is absolutely necessary (you should do your best to close the sale on the first visit and then schedule a follow-up appointment for the next purchase as you are finalizing the transaction of the first one).

I first saw this modeled for me when I was growing up watching my dad book repeat appointments with his horseshoeing clientele. After every appointment when he was collecting the money for the visit, he would schedule another appointment 4-6 weeks out. He did this with every client he worked with. He guaranteed his future success by ensuring that he had the appointment scheduled before he left. Then, he followed up to ensure that the appointment time was still on and had a penalty in place for those who tried to cancel or reschedule appointments (since he was so busy and couldn't easily reschedule appointments).

My insurance agent is another great example of follow up appointments. Every year, he calls and schedules an appointment to come by our home and visit with my wife and I. During this appointment, he gives a yearly performance of what has happened with our insurance to date, checks to make sure that the insurance is still sufficient and looks to add more if necessary. He also always asks for referrals on these visits and gets their name and phone number from me. I've discovered from talking with him about this that this is the real reason for the visit. On his last visit, he got four referrals from me. He does a great job and I am happy to refer him. He could do a better job with incentives (I'll have to give him a copy of my book). ☺

The questions you should be asking are:
- What is your follow-up appointment sequence?
- Are you scheduling the follow up appointment right when each prospects buys from you?

- Could you schedule a 6-month or 3-month out schedule with your prospect to see how everything is going with what they've purchased and then help them with the next step?

Take the time to figure out your sequence of appointments. When you know the sequence of what you would like each client to do who buys from you and you create structure and systems around each appointment and offer incentives, surprises and rewards to those who buy after each appointment, you will be well on the way to ensuring that every client who does business with you once does business with you multiple times.

There is tremendous value in understanding the power of follow up and flipping the funnel in your business. Your follow-up system should detail exactly what you expect each of your sales consultants to do in order to get more prospects and clients to return and do business with you. Outline your marketing funnel and decide exactly what you will do to market to clients who buy (to get them back for repeat purchases) and prospects who don't buy (to get them back into another marketing funnel). If you have already put this system together, train each of your team members on their individual responsibilities and what should be done at each step of your marketing sequence. Make sure everyone knows what role they have and what they are responsible for. If you aren't marketing to those who almost bought, didn't buy, or to get additional purchases from those who did buy, you are leaving large piles of cash on the table. Systematize your follow-up and marketing and you will be amazed at the results you'll see.

Here is an assessment for your follow-up systems:

#	Rank yourself from 1-10 based on your current business behaviors.	1	2	3	4	5	6	7	8	9	10	Rank yourself from 1-10 based on your current business behaviors.
1	We are not capturing accurate leads from our marketing funnel (ensuring accurate spelling, no email, etc.)											We are capturing accurate leads from our marketing funnel (ensuring accurate spelling, emails, etc.)
2	Leads enter our marketing funnel, but immediately flow out because: a) We're too busy to handle them b) We have no plan for follow-up c) We have disorganized follow-up d) We have insufficient follow-up											We properly handle every lead flowing into our marketing funnel.
3	We have a plan on paper, but are disorganized and inconsistent in implementation.											We have a plan on paper and we implement it with every lead coming into our business.
4	We lose clients because we don't have back up systems to prevent leaks in our marketing funnel.											We have backup systems to prevent leaks in our marketing funnel. We have a process that everyone understands so that leads can flow from one funnel to another.
5	We are lucky to get the referrals we do. We don't have any type of system to get referrals from prospects exiting our marketing funnel.											We capture referrals from every client so that clients coming out of the bottom of the funnel refill the funnel.
6	Our consultants rarely ask for upsells for the next item in our marketing sequence.											Every consultant asks for the upsell for the next item in our marketing sequence consistently every time.
7	We know there are leaks but we haven't put a system in place to prevent them from recurring.											If there are leaks in our marketing funnel sequence, we determine the place of escape and patch the holes.

#	Rank yourself from 1-10 based on your current business behaviors.	1	2	3	4	5	6	7	8	9	10	Rank yourself from 1-10 based on your current business behaviors.
8	You don't know what you next offer will be so you don't offer it.											You know what your next offer will be so you can offer it to a client as soon as possible (if she doesn't want __x___, does she want __y__?)
9	You don't plan for slower times and jump into action when you realize that lead flow into your business is slow.											You anticipate slower times and plan accordingly so you continually fill the top of your funnel (especially in slower times).
10	You rarely, if ever monitor your processes to see where there may be holes and where clients are falling through the cracks.											You are continuously monitoring your processes so you can better determine how leads can flow from one funnel to another.

CHAPTER 11

CUSTOMER SERVICE SYSTEMS

"It's the little things that make the big things possible. Only close attention to the fine details of any operation makes the operation first class."
—*J. Willard Marriott, Sr.*

In this chapter, I'd like to discuss how you deal with recurring customer service challenges and issues that continually come up in your business and how you can build systems to deliver exceptional experiences every time.

One of the important things about a system is that everyone on your staff would do something in your business exactly how you would do it (even if you aren't there). This is a challenge for three main reasons:

1) If you experience a high level of turnover and you have new employees who haven't been trained on what to do in specific situations, mistakes can be made because you aren't taking the time to explain it until it becomes an issue.

2) Good employees forget what to do if the issue hasn't come up in such a long time and solutions aren't documented.

3) Well meaning employees assume you would do something that you might not really approve of.

Dr. Atul Gawande, a surgeon, wrote a book entitled *The Checklist Manifesto,* which details the premise that costly human error in everything would plummet if checklists were forced on everybody, for everything. This is all really part of having good systems for your business. This is especially true for customer service issues which can cost you money and more importantly cost you with bad word of mouth on social media or disappointment with a prospect or client's friends and family. This chapter will discuss how you should plan and think through all of the things that should be done with your customer service so you don't have costly mistakes happen again.

Dr. Gawande tells a great story in the book about the systematic detail musical rock group Van Halen included in its contract to ensure that promoters of their concerts paid attention and went through every item on their checklist. Their contract contained a clause specifying that a bowl of M&Ms had to be provided in the group's dressing room, but every single brown candy had to be removed from the bowl.

David Lee Roth (the group's lead singer) explained, "Van Halen was the first band to take huge productions into tertiary, third-level markets. We'd pull up with nine 18-wheeler trucks full of gear....there were many technical errors, girders couldn't support the weight, doors weren't big enough...the contract ready like the Chinese Yellow Pages because there was so much equipment and so many human beings required to make it function. So, just as a little test, buried in the middle...Article 126, the no brown M&M clause. When I would walk backstage, if I saw a brown M&M in that bowl, well, we'd line-check the entire production. Guaranteed there'd be problems." In fact, the mistakes could be life threatening. Once the band found that the local promoters had failed to read the weight requirements in the contract and that the staging would have fallen through the arena floor.

Do you have a customer service checklist to ensure that you don't forget any of the details as a client moves through your business? If not, you should use one to ensure that you don't miss critical thing that may cost you *before* you send out new sales consultants to deal with prospects entering your marketing funnel and buying from you.

Before, we get into the specifics of some of the categories of customer service issues that you can deal with, let's talk about how to evaluate how the customer service in your business measures up.

Does it beat the pants off the competition? As the old saying goes: "When there is not much difference between your product and that of your competitors, there had better be a big difference in the way you deal with your customers."

Do you delight and dazzle the prospects and clients coming into your marketing funnel and throughout their experience in dealing with you, or are they disappointed and discouraged when they leave when they come to you with a legitimate concern?

Every business needs a way to assess how they are doing with customer service. Here are 9 ways to evaluate how well you are doing in meeting the needs of your customers. You can rate yourself on a scale of 1-10 with 10 being the highest and look for ways you can improve your systems in these areas.

1. Vision and Philosophy

Do you have an ambitious and inspiring customer service statement or philosophy that makes a bold declaration about how much you value the prospects and clients coming into your business?
Do your employees know what that vision and philosophy is?
Have they embraced it?
Do you see this vision in their actions with customers each day?

One way to evaluate your vision is in your overall approach. Do you have a caring or a conquering approach? Providing solutions requires caring. In the end, every customer wants to feel important, appreciated and valued. When your customer service systems fail, the problem usually originates because you have forgotten others are thinking only of yourself. When building your customer service systems, help your team think of others first and really care about the concerns that your prospects and clients bring up.

2. Example

Do you live up to your customer service motto?
Do your employees catch you offering great customer service? Or do they catch you grumbling about how mad it makes you when something happens in your business?

Jim Cathcart says, "We judge ourselves by our intentions, but others judge us by our actions." Your clients will care much more about what they *see* you do than what they think you *intended* to do. Does your walk match your talk about customer service issues? Is it consistent with the vision or philosophy you have in your business? Do you support employees who go out of their way to take care of problems that come up or do you lash out in frustration or anger? Do you give your staff the resources they need to excel at delivering an exceptional customer experience?

3. Selection of Employees

Are the members of your staff that you've hired emotionally, culturally, and intellectually prepared to provide the quality of service that your clients expect and deserve?

Do you treat your employees well?

I really like this statement from Herb Kelleher, former CEO of Southwest Airlines. He said: "If you don't treat your own people well, they won't treat other people well."

Staff members who are treated with thoughtfulness, respect and compassion are more likely to treat your customers with the same type of respect that those who aren't. Stephen Covey in his book *The Seven Habits of Highly Effective People* uses the analogy of the Emotional Bank Account to really emphasize this point. He says: "The Emotional Bank Account represents the quality of the relationship you have with others. It's like a financial bank account in that you can make 'deposits,' by proactively doing things that build trust in the relationship, or you can make 'withdrawls,' by reactively doing things that decrease the level of trust. And at any given time the balance of trust in the account determines how well you can communicate and solve problems with another person."--p. 46.

Strive to help your team members take emotional ownership for the service goals you have for your business. You can best do this by hiring the right kinds of people to work with you. Hire people who have the insatiable desire to serve people. If you see a mistake being made by one of your employees, take them aside and privately teach them how it should have been done. Former NFL coach Dick Vermeil observed, **"To not confront poor execution and behaviors is to *endorse* it."**

On the other hand, if you observe one of your employees doing a fantastic job, let her and *everyone* on the team know it. Because if you don't, that behavior will stop. Dick Vermeil also observed: **"To not reinforce good execution and behavior is to *extinguish* it."**

If the people you hire aren't excited about serving the prospects who come into your marketing funnel, you've made a hiring mistake. If there are no systems to properly handle the flow of clients in your business, you have made a systems mistake. Systems should be thought through, written down, and followed.

Have you ever noticed how clean Disneyland is? It's not an accident. Rather, it's a subtle way of building employee morale and telling the customer, 'We take pride in our work.'

It is obvious that they value cleanliness. But, they also work very hard to hire and train people who delight in cleaning and creating an amazing experience for their guests at their resorts and parks. Take more time to look at your business through your *client's eyes*. Be sure to hire those who are motivated to serve. Remember, it is much easier to hire customer service oriented professionals than it is to train professionals how to focus on the skill of customer service.

Customer service training can have a big impact on the way your team members view their work in your business. I really like how Mark Sanborn explains this in his book, *The Fred Factor*. He says: "There are no unimportant jobs, just people who feel unimportant doing their jobs."

What are you doing every day to let your team members know that they are important to you and the success of your business?

Mark Sanborn says: "The difference [in organizations is] in the people. Uninspired people rarely do inspired work. Passionate people in an organization are different. They do ordinary things extraordinarily well....Customers don't have relationships with organizations; they form relationships with individuals. "--*The Fred Factor*, p. 74.

Add meaning to the lives of your team members everyday. If your team doesn't see much *meaning* in what they do, they won't bring much *value* to what they do.

4. Performance Expectations
Do your team members know exactly how you expect them to behave in the various customer service situations they encounter (ex.: answering the telephone, greeting people at the door, helping them experience your product or service, answering questions, creating realistic expectations, etc.)?

• Answering the Telephone – When clients email or call your business, how are they treated? Remember, they are thinking, 'Is this the kind of operation where they would like to spend their hard earned dollars or can they think of some other place that would treat them better?'

- Remember, you have to inspect what you expect. Train your front line staff on your expectation for how the phone should be answered, how a prospect and client should be properly greeted, etc. You create the expectation. If you don't create any expectation, don't be surprised when the result you want doesn't happen.
- Perceptions are realities. What perceptions do prospects in your market niche form when:
  - o They call your business? If they are put on hold, how long are they on hold?
  - o They receive an email, letter, or other marketing invitation from you?
  - o They ask a question?
  - o They see your business?
  - o They see your employees?
  - o They do business with you? Do they receive a thank you card or a personal call thanking them for their business?

The reality about our world today is that *an hour of brilliant service* that you personally offer **can be undone** *by a minute of indifference* by you or one of your team members. What systems do you have in place to ensure that proper training is continuously happening to prevent bad behaviors and attitudes from surfacing in your business?

5. Overcoming and recovering from customer complaints.
Complaints point out things that need improvement. As part of your system, you should make a list of the most common customer complaints that you are experiencing. I'll give you ten categories you can start with later in this chapter. Most don't consider complaints to be good things, but if you use them to identify weak spots in your systems and take corrective action they can be a great help to you.

Most complaints happen because the expectations of our customers are being violated in some way since frustration is the result of violated expectations.

Do you train your team members on what to do in certain customer service situations?

Is each member of your staff trained on what the rest of your team does or cannot do? Big picture systems integration eliminates problems when everyone understands how everything works and how it all works together.

B.C. Forbes, the founder of *Forbes* magazine once said: "Complaints offer opportunities to make friends or to make enemies...Isn't it worthwhile to exert every effort to turn complainers into boosters?"

Sometimes prospects or clients can be downright rude, demanding or wrong...but, the customer is always one thing...the customer. They pay your salary, they pay the salaries of your employees and they keep your business open.

Even the best businesses can make mistakes, especially when it gets really busy. The difference in average businesses and great businesses is how they *recover*. Remember, it's rarely ever too late to save an account if you recover remarkably. The best way to do that is to satisfy the two things that every customer wants: *solutions to their problem and good feelings.*

A sincere apology is the first step in dealing with a customer complaint. Then explain why something may or may not have happened and explain how you are going to take care of it. Don't make excuses. Do your best to take on the problem head on. Don't evade it. *People today want action, not excuses.*

The best problem solving approach to moving clients from mad, sad, or scared to glad is to ask two questions calmly: 1) What is the situation now? and 2) What would you like it to be? Once you know the answers to these two questions, you can decide how to solve a problem. Even if you can't solve everything stemming from a problem, letting the client express it and taking the time to listen will make him or her feel better. Just knowing that you cared enough to listen and tried to help will leave her with a much better impression than if you had taken a 'that's not my problem' attitude.

6. Under-promise and over-deliver.
Customer service issues that come up in your business usually come from one individual overpromising something that created an

unrealistic expectation. When that violated expectation meets reality, sparks can fly.

Don't overpromise and create unrealistic expectations. You may make a sale by promising something, but you may also create a nightmare situation later on. Don't let your mouth write a check your business can't cash. The higher you build customer expectation, the harder it becomes to meet and exceed them.

There is an old saying that the most important rule in customer service is to under-promise and over-deliver. In other words, if you think you can finish the job in three weeks, you should promise it in 4 to six weeks. The problem is that clients have so many options now that if you can't deliver it when they want it, they may be off to your competitor and you will likely lose the sale. However, you've got to be realistic. You will frustrate and annoy your clients if you stretch the truth and overpromise and under-deliver. The cost in these cases may be much more than just the cost of the sale when your reputation is trashed online.

Do you or members of your team under-promise and over-deliver?
Do you exceed customer expectations at every opportunity by doing the little things that mean a lot?
Do you personalize and customize your service?
Do your clients believe that you meet their unique needs?

Keep in touch with clients and keep them informed. If you fail to keep in touch with your customers, they won't be aware of the great service you are giving them until something goes wrong and they choose to leave. Stay in touch and let them know that their satisfaction is our priority in word and deed.

7. Add value to every transaction.
Author Guy Kawasaki and early McIntosh evangelist for Apple Computers tells this story:
"A young girl bought gumdrops from a small shop even though a more convenient supermarket opened nearby. Asked why, the girl said, "Nick [the store owner] always gives me more candy. The girl in the other store takes some away."

"Apparently, salesclerks in the supermarket put more than the weight, and then the clerks subtracted a few gumdrops to get the right amount.

Nick, the owner of the small shop, put in too little and then added more. The children were convinced they got the better deal from Nick."--*How to Drive Your Competition Crazy*, pp. 125-126.

What things can you do to create more value for the prospects and clients entering your marketing funnel and your business?

8. Nurture your clients.

Remember that many clients may have never made the type of purchase you're asking them to make. They may feel anxiety and fear. Help them to know the next steps. Help her feel confident and secure that you will be able to take care of her needs and make the experience of finding what she is looking for an extremely enjoyable and wonderful event.

Help the client know that you are genuinely concerned about his or her well-being by helping make his or her search for what you offer to solve the challenge they are facing easy and fun.

Think about how you appear to others. Coaches and consultants project a supportive, nonthreatening demeanor. They put the client at ease. Inquisitors and prosecutors on the other hand, project superiority and arrogance. Their goal is to make the person answering questions feel uncomfortable and inferior. Be sure that you are projecting a positive, supportive, non-threatening disposition to your clients.

Do your best to treat your clients warmly, friendly, sympathetically, courteously, attentively, sensitively, responsively, thoughtfully, and appreciatively. Let them know that you treasure them by how you treat them.

Author Jim Cathcart says: "When the relationship is right, the details are negotiable. When tension is high, the details become the obstacles." Be sure you are nurturing the relationship so you can negotiate out the details if you make a mistake so you can save face and earn back the trust of those you've disappointed.

9. Soliciting and responding to customer feedback.

Do you make it easy for customers to get in touch with you?
Do you listen to your customers in every way possible in order to understand what they expect from you and how well you're providing it?

Do you act on what you've heard to improve the experiences that clients have in your business?

One way you ensure that you are staying on top of your customer service issues is to offer a customer survey to clients when they've been through the entire process of doing business with you. This questionnaire could include variations of these questions:

1. How do you feel about the selection and offerings we provide?
2. How was the service you received in our business?
3. What made the difference between our business and other offers you may have been considering?
4. What can we do to improve?

Most businesses don't take the time to evaluate past mistakes thinking that once they've dealt with something that it probably won't happen again. However, over time, new employees who aren't aware of those experiences and the lessons you've already learned (and the money that was lost) can be repeated if you don't plan and have a checklist or a reminder about what should be done in various situations.

Put together your own system for how you will deal with the recurring challenges and customer service situations that come up in your business. Failing to do this will literally guarantee that something will go wrong and mistakes can be very costly.

Dr. Gawande says: "Under conditions of complexity, not only are checklists a help, they are required for success. There must always be room for judgment, but judgment aided—and even enhanced by procedure." –p. 79.

You should break down each of the areas in which customer service issues arise in your business, discuss the issues that come up within that category (so you can determine your own way of handling it and your system to back it up) and finally develop a failsafe method or checklist to fix a problem before it comes up.

Here are ten specific classifications of customer service issues that likely have come up or will come up in your business from time to time.

1) Issues revolving around using your product or service

2) Bought another product from another business after they bought from you and now they want a refund

3) Bought product from you and then saw price cheaper somewhere else (wants you to match price)

4) Problem with existing product or service

5) Delivery problem – stressed out as their personal deadline approaches

6) Buyer's remorse

7) Issues where someone has overpromised / under-delivered - Promised something by sales consultant that doesn't happen the way they feel it should

8) Any other issue where expectations are not met

9) Personal needs change – now worried what they purchased your product or service for no longer applies

10) Unusual problems with the use of your product or service

To build your customer service systems, break down what you expect will or should happen in each category and then discuss what you can do to improve these with your team. Writing down the specific ways you've handled each of these categorical issues in the past and stories you've had that have formed your policies are particularly helpful. Share these with your team and detail them in your customer service system manual.

First, briefly describe the category, the specific situation, what happened, and what you did to resolve it. Then, detail what you would expect another member of your team to do if a situation like that came up again.

The big question that really gets to the heart of having solutions to recurring challenges and customer service situations that you should be asking yourself is: What are you doing to eliminate frustrations and problems that could come up _before_ they do?

When evaluating your customer service issues, you have to determine what caused the problem and what you can do to eliminate it in the future. If something continually causes problems and you don't have any control over it, you may have to consider eliminating that area of your business or fixing it (or that problem with consume you).

Seek answers to these questions in your business:
1. How can we do the work better?

2. How can we do it with fewer errors?

3. How can we do it faster?

4. How can we do it for less?

When prospects get upset it is usually due to their frustration about something. Remember, "Frustration is the result of violated expectations."

All customer service issues can be solved through training so that you don't have to deal with the same issues from week to week. It is your job to ensure that everyone on your team knows what to do in certain customer service situations. When everyone knows how the big picture works and how to work on it, you can be much more successful than just being the single focal point of trying to do everything yourself.

When someone comes in and demands attention, it must be taken care of. If you are in the midst of working with another customer, remember that prospect is watching how you will take care of the situation too. She is watching to see how you might treat her if and when she becomes your customer.

As you are putting together your customer service systems, you must remember the principle that "People Do What People See."

Here are some questions to help you think about your customer service systems and the ways in which you and your team members are implementing them.

- Do you lean toward developing systems or doing things yourself (because you feel that you are the only one who can do it right)?
- Do your customer service systems bring fulfillment or frustration to you?
- Would others in your business consider your customer service systems effective and widely understood in your business (in other words, will everyone handle every situation the same way)?
- Can you list the customer service situations that come up in your business and what you or anyone at your staff will do to handle them?

Here is a helpful chart and worksheet you can work through to determine how you will fix your failings when they come up in each of these categories:

Your Top 10 Customer Service Categories & Issues You Continually Face at Your Business	Example of Most Recent Failure	Who Dropped the Ball and the Consequence	What Will Be Done Differently Going Forward?
1) Issues revolving around using your product or service			
2) Bought another product from another business after they bought from you and now they want a refund			
3) Bought product from you and then saw price cheaper somewhere else (wants you to match price)			
4) Problem with existing product or service			
5) Delivery problem – stressed out as their personal deadline approaches			
6) Buyer's remorse			

Your Top 10 Customer Service Categories & Issues You Continually Face at Your Business	Example of Most Recent Failure	Who Dropped the Ball and the Consequence	What Will Be Done Differently Going Forward?
7) Issues where someone has overpromised / under-delivered - Promised something by sales consultant that doesn't happen the way they feel it should			
8) Any other issue where expectations are not met			
9) Personal needs change – now worried what they purchased your product or service for no longer applies			
10) Unusual problems with the use of your product or service			

Here are seven qualities, characteristics, and skills of someone who can develop systems for recurring problems:

1. You must be genuinely interested in your clients and preventing grief and stress in their lives.

2. You must maintain a consistent pattern of quick response to customer service situations that come up. Be willing to step up and take care of these issues yourself.

3. If something goes wrong, begin with assessment. Where did the problem originate? Working backwards, where are the holes? How can you prevent this problem from happening again?

4. Be more observant than others and look for clues indicating where problems may get started.

5. When talking with prospects about the customer service issues they've faced, be an excellent listener and act quickly and decisively to resolve the problem.

6. Be patient and caring toward your prospects who are going through the challenge. They didn't expect for this to happen. They don't want to hear excuses. They want results.

7. Act like you would want to be treated. You are having this experience for a reason. Are you learning the lesson you're supposed to learn?

Here is an assessment for your customer service systems:

#	Rank yourself from 1-10 based on your current business behaviors.	1	2	3	4	5	6	7	8	9	10	Rank yourself from 1-10 based on your current business behaviors.
1	We don't create loyal clients who refer us to their friends. Clients have little to no incentive to refer anyone to us.											We create loyal clients who refer us to their friends. They are motivated to refer clients to us because of how they have been treated by us.
2	Clients are lucky to get a return call or return email from us within 48 hours after they send it. If a customer complains, it could be days before the issue is solved.											We evaluate the timeliness and efficiency with which we handle customer complaints and make adjustments.
3	We rarely if ever stay in touch with our clients once they have purchased and do little to encourage additional business with us.											We have a system by which we stay in touch with our clients once they have purchased and continually encourage those who have not yet purchased from us to do so.

#	Rank yourself from 1-10 based on your current business behaviors.	1	2	3	4	5	6	7	8	9	10	Rank yourself from 1-10 based on your current business behaviors.
4	We rarely ask or remember to ask our clients for referrals.											We always ask every client for referrals.
5	We rarely act on the feedback we receive from our prospects and clients to make improvements. Things now are pretty much the way they've always been.											We act on the feedback we receive from our prospects and clients to make improvements.
6	We never measure our customer satisfaction and train our sales consultants to make improvements based on what is learned.											We measure our customer satisfaction and train our sales consultants to make improvements based on what is learned.
7	We don't have a training system in place for handling customer service issues and complaints.											We have a training system in place for handling customer service issues and complaints.
8	We don't provide rewards or incentives for providing superior customer service to those on our staff who do.											We provide rewards or incentives for providing superior customer service to those on our staff who do.
9	We have an ongoing program to regularly communicate with our prospects and clients (newsletter, Facebook, Twitter, etc.)											We have an ongoing program to regularly communicate with our prospects and clients (newsletter, Facebook, Twitter, etc.)
10	When someone commits do something for a client, things fall through the cracks and I often have to fix something later on with a client.											When someone commits do something for a client, there are systems in place to ensure that it happens as the client expects it will.
11	We rarely remember to send written notes of appreciation to every client who buys from us.											We send written notes of appreciation to every client who buys from us.
12	We never survey those prospects who don't buy from us in order to improve our offerings and service.											We survey those prospects who don't buy from us in order to improve our offerings and service.

This assessment may have shown you some holes in your existing customer service systems. When working with team members who have made mistakes:

1. Take a guiding and shaping role. Be clear. Look for ways to prevent the problem from happening again.

2. Teach consultants to think for themselves. Help them to think the way you would think to handle a difficult challenge or problem.

3. If a mistake has been made, make the sales consultant think, reflect and examine the cause of the problem and what they think should be done to prevent the situation from happening again.

4. Coach the development of the behaviors and essential habits you want followed by all of your team members. If an issue has happened multiple times, what can you do to prevent it in the future? Make up a checklist so the behaviors and habits you want ingrained are easy to follow. Be clear about the consequences of mistakes in the future. Here is the big question you should ask about customer service: If each member of your team copied everything you do, would you be pleased with the results? **The answer to this question will help you identify areas where you could make improvements with your customer service systems.**

Here are some tasks that you should work on to improve your business systems with recurring challenges and customer service situations:
1. List the three to five things you wish members of your team did better at your business. Now, grade your own performance in each of these areas. If your own scores are low, you can't be surprised if your sales consultants are the same or worse. You must raise your own performance and be the example of what you want your team members to be. If your own scores are low, then you need to make your example more visible to your team. Model the behavior and customer service situations you want to see in your business.
2. Identify your ten top recurring challenges and customer service situations. What will you do to prevent these from happening again?
3. Of your categories of recurring challenges and customer service situations, which ones seem to be most common? Meet with your

team in a daily Huddle meeting or in your weekly sales training meeting to discuss what can be done to prevent these issues from coming up again.

4. Have some gift cards on hand that you can use to diffuse serious customer service lapses and turn a bad or unfortunate situation into one where the client feels that you care and are taking care of her frustrations.

5. When a mistake is made, ask the individual who dropped the ball to submit to you their top five suggestions for how this situation could be prevented in the future and what they've learned from the situation that will help them be a better team member going forward.

6. Take the ten categories of recurring challenges and break down the subcategories that I've identified with other leaders on your team. Divide up the list and look for ways you could incorporate checklists to prevent situations from happening again. A great system is really just a checklist of what to do to avoid situations that could come up again.

Finally, I would like you to score yourself on the following report card. Read the statement and then determine what grade you would give yourself.

Scoring Your Performance with Recurring Challenges and Customer Service Situations	Your Grade
When was the last time you or someone on your team did something extraordinary for a client? Who was it and what was the situation? How did you recognize or reward this behavior? *A = last week; B = two weeks ago; C = 3 weeks ago; D = a month or longer; F = I can't remember*	
Do you have a daily conscious intention to make a positive difference? *A = always; B = most of the time; C = occasionally; D = rarely; F = never*	
Do you feel you have the skills to make a positive difference? *A = always; B = most of the time; C = occasionally; D = rarely; F = never*	
Have you or any member of your team recently received feedback (from a prospect, client, colleague, or other) that what you did made a difference in solving a difficult customer service challenge? *A = yes; B = for most situations; C = no, everyone just does what they feel (it has worked out okay so far); D = no, and it has caused big problems; F = No, what's a system?*	

Scoring Your Performance with Recurring Challenges and Customer Service Situations	Your Grade
Do you know the names of your best and most frequent clients (those who buy multiple items from you)? *A = yes; B = yes, but we rarely invite them to buy more from us; C = no, we're just glad when they come in and buy and we take care of them when they do); D = no, we try to take care of everyone the same; F = no, and it has caused big problems.*	
Do you regularly express an interest in them and their lives? When is the last time you wrote a thank you note to them? *A = last week; B = two weeks ago; C = 3 weeks ago; D = a month or longer; F = I can't remember*	
Do your prospects ask you for help with challenges they are facing revolving around what you offer in your business? If so, are the solutions you're providing helping them (or are you just expressing empathy)? *A = always; B = most of the time; C = occasionally; D = rarely; F = never*	
Do you feel you know how to create value in your work? *A = always; B = most of the time; C = occasionally; D = rarely; F = never*	
Do you know what your prospects value? Your clients? What is a recent example where this has been evident? *A = always; B = most of the time; C = occasionally; D = rarely; F = never*	
When was the last time you feel you personally added value to the life of a client? *A = last week; B = two weeks ago; C = 3 weeks ago; D = a month or longer; F = I can't remember*	

It would be a great idea to have each member of your team take this quiz and report back to you on their own grades for their report card and how you can improve.

My final question for you to help you evaluate how you are doing: Do you delight and amaze the prospects and clients coming into your business, or are they disappointed and frustrated when they leave without finding solutions to their legitimate concerns and problems?

Chapter 12

Hiring and Staffing Systems

"If each of us hires people who are smaller than we are, we shall become a company of dwarfs. But if each of us hires people who are bigger than we are, we shall become a company of giants."—David Ogilvy

Having systems in the interview and hiring process will help you make better decisions around whether or not you should bring people onto your team and what will drive that choice. You must have a solid process that is designed to gather data and information and help you objectively evaluate a candidate. By its very nature, the hiring process is stacked against the employer.

Here are eight reasons why hiring has become more challenging today:

- *Résumés are not always accurate* - Studies conducted by The Society for Human Resource Management indicate that 51% of candidates lie on their résumés. On top of that startling statistic, consider that many are also paying career coaches to dress up and critique their résumés.
- *You aren't a behavioral psychologist so you don't really know whether they will do the work until after you've hired them* – your goal is just to hire someone to do the work, and if you make a mistake you will have invested time and training resources into that individual
- *It is very difficult to read the inner world of the individual you are considering* – you don't really know if they will do the job for you at an exceptional level
- *You may project what you want onto a person with your own bias* (because they may look like someone you hired in the past who did a good job)
- *There are changes in generational thinking that affect how someone feels about what their employer deserves to give versus what they feel is the minimum they can get away with and still stay employed* – difficult to build a team with this attitude

- *Those who are applying are those who aren't currently employed* (A players are typically already working for someone else) so you may not be looking at the *best* candidates for the job
- *People have been coached how to behave and act in interviews and it is challenging to see the real picture of what they will do when hired with one sit down interview.* They've likely been reading *How to Answer Job Interview Questions Like a Pro* before they come in to interview with you.
- *Too many bosses leave themselves open to be sold.* They're looking for someone good to fill a position on their team and so they're now open to be sold. Enthusiasm does the trick for a lot of people because anybody can be good for an hour during an interview.

According to the *Harvard Business Review*, the number one reason for high turnover in small business is bad hiring decisions. The costs of making a bad hire are extraordinary and this is why having a system for how you interview and hire is so important.

What does it cost you to hire the wrong person? The numbers are all over the place depending on the role and the industry. Some studies estimate this cost at being up to 10x the cost of a person's salary and others only estimate it to being 2 to 3x a person's salary. Brad Smart in his book *TopGrading* says that this cost can be up to 23x someone's yearly salary. Some industries may *appear* to have a lower cost for hiring mistakes, but even the low costs are stunning when you think about the impact these can have for you over time in the life of your business.

There are 6 particular things that affect this number for you and your industry. These are:

1) **The Cost of Recruiting** – costs here include advertisement, time cost for person who is reviewing résumés, conducting interviews, drug screening and background checks, and various pre-employment assessment tests. You may not have these costs with every person you hire, but these costs can be extensive depending on how much you spend on background checks and if you actually use a recruiting firm to help you find your employees which can really blow these seemingly smaller costs into the strategy.

2) **The Cost of Training** – once you hire someone, you've got to provide adequate training so the person hired can actually do the work and produce work of value for you. Training can be

particularly expensive if you end up hiring someone and then you discover that they aren't the right person for the job. Then, you have to go through the process again and start all over. According to *Training* magazine, companies today spend an average of $1200 annually per employee on training and employees nationwide spent an average of 32 hour per year on training related activities. If you include the cost of orientation, training materials, and initial on-the-job training that you offer, you can see how this can number can grow exponentially if you have high turnover. It's best if you are the boss or manager to directly train people.

3) *The Cost of Salary + Benefits* – this is the obvious cost you are paying out to the employee for the hours they work or their salary. This cost will go up depending on the benefits that you offer as an employer.

4) *The Cost of Integrating a New Employee into Your Workplace* – these costs can include a new computer, software or licenses for the computer, workspace, cell phone, travel, special equipment, etc. This cost can add up quickly, yet one of the biggest costs you will have in integrating anyone you hire into your workforce is the low morale that will result if other employees feel like they have to pick up and carry the load of someone who isn't performing. Even worse, is an employee who steals sales or steals credit for the work of another employee.

5) *Lost Opportunities* – these costs can escalate quickly if the person hired doesn't perform at the expected level or worse if the person does a poor job that costs you existing clients or new business accounts. This can be especially traumatic for your business and cost you an extraordinary amount of money if the new hire does something that causes one of your clients or potential clients to go out and spread negativity about you on the Internet. It doesn't do a whole lot of good to spend all of your time and effort hiring your front line staff at a hotel and then have someone in the hotel gift shop, annoy, upset or say something silly to upset a customer over a small thing. You may never be aware of the damage of what someone can cause for your business. This is one of the most expensive areas of your business and it is even more damaging because it can be nearly invisible to you as the business owner or manager.

6) *The Emotional Cost and Time Cost for the Hiring Manager (or person on your team responsible for hiring)* - The emotional energy

that gets sucked out of a manager when they go through a bad hire is hard to measure, but it is a definite cost. Not only do bad hires cause a manager to worry about behaviors or ineffective results of people who haven't performed, the stress of having to go out and hire a new person, doing the work or making up for their mistakes, etc. can put an added strain on good employees who may question and resent their work over time. When a new hire isn't sharp, isn't clear about what they're supposed to do, when their judgment's not good, they go out and make mistakes, which can be very costly for your company. If a manager is constantly spending their time with the squeaky wheels, they don't have time to spend with their best employees. If your best people are constantly fixing the problems created by others, they'll never be able to reach their full potential or help your company reach its full potential either. Jim Collins warns of this mistake in his book *Good to Great*: "The only way to deliver to the people who are achieving is to not burden them with the people who are not achieving."--p. 53. One of the best things you can do for your high performing people is surround them by other high performing people. When you spend more time repairing than preparing, you have made a bad hire and you'll be spending the majority of your time going back to fix what happened yesterday when you should be focused on the opportunities ahead of you for your organization.

When you factor in the costs above, you could be paying up to ten times the cost of a base salary because of a hiring mistake. In other words, if you pay someone $20,000 a year that could translate into a $200,000 loss for your company. Now your specific number depends on your industry, the position of the employee, and what they do at your company and how you account for the cost of your time. However, to lose one year's salary is significant and is a lost that you can't afford.

Whether your cost for hiring the wrong person is *actually* ten times the cost of their salary depends on a combination of these six factors I just mentioned. While you could spend a lot of time actually calculating what the actual multiple is for you and your business, it is important to remember that *any* cost that prevents you from operating at peak performance levels in your company is *too* much.

Virtually all entrepreneurs have made a hiring mistake. Such a mistake happens because employers are swayed by someone's enthusiasm instead of being clear whether they have the skills to do the job they're being hired for, whether they will do the job (in other words, whether they're self-motivated) and whether they will do the job *for you*.

Once you've made a hiring mistake, it is easy to become hesitant to hire someone again. It is easy to doubt yourself. This is why having a system around how you will interview people, how you will test their ability to do the job you are hiring for, and gaining an accurate assessment is so important. It is beyond the scope of this book to detail all of the different ways you can set up your hiring and training systems. I've co-authored another book with Jay Henderson entitled *The Real Talent Advantage: Proven Ways to Hire Better and Get Super Star Performance from Each Member of Your Team*. This resource can help you better set up the specifics for your interviewing process, your skill assessment, and the very best hiring profile assessment you can use today to determine whether the candidate you are considering is the right one for you.

The bottom line is that it is in your control to set up the right hiring systems. Don't settle for any candidate, nor lower your standards and hire sub-par candidates. Keep looking. Selling someone on your company before you really know *if they will do* what you need them to do *for you* is a big mistake. If you are selling them on why they should come to work for you, you are doing the talking. They're going to be in agreement in the interview, but you won't find out if they are really qualified to do what you need them to do for you if you're solely focused on selling the position to them.

By having your candidates go through your hiring system, you actually weed out marginal candidates. Your system should be a process. Raise your standards. If you don't raise your standards, you'll end up settling for what you don't want. To avoid this, you've consistently got to work on your systems. You've got to inspect what you expect.

Remember, if you don't stand for something, you'll fall for anything. When you give people expectations and guidelines, you've got to have accountability; you have to follow through to ensure that what you expect is actually getting done. Dick Vermeil, former coach of the Kansas City Chiefs, once observed: "To not confront poor execution and behavior is to endorse it. To not reinforce good execution and behavior is to extinguish it." What a great statement! Your choice to settle for poor performance means that you approve or endorse that kind of performance. That's not what you really want. So, stick to your standards.

If you choose to settle for what you *don't* want, you will experience tremendous frustration and exasperation with someone *until* there is a breaking point. I have had many conversations with entrepreneurs who waited too long to let an employee go and then finally have done what needed to be done because they had no choice. It is better to have the courage to act before you have to. Only you can control what happens in your business with your employees and staff. Of course, it is better not to make mistakes in the first place. However, when a mistake has been made, you've got to act.

Fred Smith makes this observation in his book *Learning to Lead*: "No one wants a reputation as a hatchet man. But as a last resort, you must be willing to fire people or relieve them of a particular responsibility. It is more important for the staff to know that you will than that you do. It shows you are committed to your mission and are willing to prune those who will not contribute to it....Whenever I am tempted not to act in a difficult personnel situation, I ask myself, 'Am I holding back for my personal comfort or for the good of the organization?' If I am doing what makes me comfortable, I am embezzling. If doing what is good for the organization also happens to make me comfortable, that's wonderful. But if I am treating irresponsibility irresponsibly, I must remember that two wrongs do not make a right." –pp. 103-104.

Are you doing what makes you comfortable or are you doing what needs to be done for the good of your business? That is a good question to reflect on when you are struggling with a difficult decision about whether to keep someone or let them go.

Holding onto someone for too long who is burned out will cause you to burn out faster than anything else. You will worry, feel stress, and watch your results decline (which will cause even more stress and worry). Have the courage to recognize burnout for what it is and replace those who are no longer contributing to your organization.

There are different skills required to be an excellent manager and to lead your team to accomplish great goals. If you want superstar performance from each member of your team, you need to understand why people leave companies in the first place and what you can do about it.

A study in the *Harvard Business Review* listed the number one reason people leave a business is their direct boss. John Maxwell also makes this point in his book *Leadership Gold*: "As leaders, we'd like to think that when people leave, it has little to do with us. But the reality is that we are often the reason. Some sources estimate that as many as 65 percent of people leaving companies do so because of their managers. We may say that people quit their job or their company, but the reality is that they usually quit their leaders. The company doesn't do anything negative to them. People do. Sometimes coworkers cause the problems that prompt people to leave. But often the people who alienate employees are their direct supervisors."--*Leadership Gold*, p. 145.

When you make a mistake in hiring or when someone quits, it's a real downer for entrepreneurs because you've got to stop everything, start the hiring process again and that takes time and costs money. It can be a real downer. However, there can be good things when people quit. You can take the time at this point to look at the position again and say: *What are the behaviors that have been successful in the past? Does this role need to change? What could be better? How could it be different?*

Let's discuss some of the mechanics of the questions you should ask and your approach to interviewing. Many questions that are asked in an interview setting are very superficial and the responses you get don't really help you see or understand how a candidate will behave when they actually have the job and you realize that you've already made a mistake.

THE BIG RULE: Never hire anyone the first time you talk with him or her. They will always look the best, sound the best and act the best in the first interview. Get the additional perspective of another interview. When hiring, it is best to have others help you make the decision. Never make the decision by yourself. Instead, follow what Brian Tracy calls The Law of Three when hiring.

Here is the law of three:
1. Interview at least 3 people before you hire one.
2. Interview a person 3 times.
3. Have 3 different people in your business interview them.

Let's go through the three types of interviews you should have and what you should ask. First, have a 10-minute phone interview process. Don't waste your time sitting down with everyone because your time is too valuable. Take ten minutes, listen for attitude, listen for tone of voice, ask some basic questions about why they're looking for the position. What is it that they need? Are they still working? What's going on? What is their perfect position? Again, you're listening mostly for tone of voice and for attitude.

Here are a few of the questions that you could ask in this interview:
- How would you describe yourself?
- Why did you leave your last job? Or why are you considering leaving your present employer?
- What would your last boss say about your work performance?
- What qualifications do you have that will help you succeed in the tasks we're looking for at our company?
- How well do you work under pressure? Give me an example.
- What can you tell us about our business?

After you have done this, if you like the candidate, you should invite them in for a 30-45 minute live interview, face-to-face. It's even better to have multiple people interview that person. Have everyone have a scoring page that is based on the job profile.

I've learned a great deal about the types of questions you should ask in an interview from Martin Yate in his book *Hiring the Best*. One of the best parts of the book is the part where he discusses the art and science of interviewing and the hidden psychology behind the types of questions. He even lists eleven types of questions that are typically asked in interviews. I've categorized these questions and then have detailed the questions I typically ask in interviews as part of my hiring system. These eleven types of questions are:

1) Closed-Ended Questions - don't usually give you a whole lot of information
Examples:
- On a scale of 1-10, how well do you deal with conflict?
- Can you work under pressure?

These types of questions allow the candidate to judge themselves which will rarely give you an objective picture of the reality. It is best not to ask questions to which there is a yes/no answer. It really doesn't give you any really good information to know how to find out whether there is a good fit or not.

2) **The Open-Ended Question** – questions that allow the candidate to express themselves in detail

You can start these types of probing questions with softening statements such as:
- I'm interested in hearing about....what you did at your last job....
- I'm curious about....[what you mentioned in your résumé]...
- How do you respond when...?

3) **Questions about Past Performance or Behavior**

These types of questions allow you to look at past performance or behaviors as windows into what they may do in the future. These types of questions are great to ask during the interview. Mix a few of them at the beginning and throwing in a question or two like this at the end of the interview to see if the answers are congruent.

You can start these types of questions with:
- Tell me about a time when...you had a customer who was upset about something...What did you do?
- Can you share with me an experience where...
- What are a couple of things you've accomplished in your life that have given you a great deal of satisfaction?

4) **Questions that balance the positive things they'll share in the interview and allow you to see the other side in a non-threatening way.**

Most individuals you interview will share positive details about their previous employment or actions. These types of questions allow you to get a balanced view of an individual in the interview.

Examples:
- [Following a great story or accolade], that's very impressive. Was there ever an occasion when things didn't work out so well for you? What happened specifically?
  OR
- Now, can you give me an example of something (in this area about which you are talking) of which you aren't so proud?

5) Questions that help you clarify something to be sure that what they've just told you or what you've just learned about them isn't a pattern.

Sometimes a potential hire will say something that causes you to wonder if what they've just told you is a pattern of behavior. A good way to find out if the bad experience they just shared that concerns you is a trend or just a fluke is to ask:

- You know that's interesting. Let's talk about another time when you had to...
- What did you learn from that experience?

Then, you can ask a subsequent question that will help you find out if your suspicions are warranted or if the negative situation they just shared was a one-time occurrence.

6) Control questions – questions that allow you to regain control when the candidate starts to ramble on about something

Example:

- With time so short, I think it would be valuable to move onto another area, don't you? *(Candidate will agree and you can regain control)*

7) Clarifying / Expansion statements – allows you to get the candidate to expand on what they just said that you would like to get more clarity on

Examples:

- Tell me more...
- Then, what happened....
- How do you mean?
- *Mirrored statement* (So, when you have dealt with demanding customers before, you typically refer them to your manager?) – then you listen to what he or she says

8) Judgment questions – questions that require a candidate to decide between options that are tough, and sometimes impossible (allows you to determine how they make judgments)

Examples:

- I'm curious to know how you would handle a situation where _____*list a difficult situation you've had recently in your business*_____ and we have a policy where we expect _____...

• What would be your approach to a situation in which...

9) **Leading questions** – can be used to lead the candidate toward a specific type of answer in order to gain agreement or to begin a series of questions on a specific topic

Examples:
1) During your work here, it is absolutely imperative that
_____*list one of your standards that you expect each employee will do at a high level*_____. Share with me two or three ways in which you would specifically fulfill that role?
2) I'm curious to know how you would handle a situation where
_____*list a challenge or a problem that someone in the role you are hiring for has to deal with frequently*_____. What would be your approach?

You have to be careful with leading questions since the candidate is going to answer it in a positive light based on how you've asked the question. It is best to use them as in the examples I've just mentioned where you are trying to verify information or to get commitment of some kind.

10) Layered questions

Many interviewers ask questions like: How do you work under pressure? (which doesn't give you a whole lot of information). A better way is to have a layered question approach so you can get much more detail into what they've said and to get a better sense of how they would actually behave if hired.

Example of Layered Questions (each subsequent question gives you more information):
• Can you work under pressure to deliver results?
• Tell me about a time when you had to work under pressure to deliver results.
• So, it was challenging to consistently close sales?
• How did this pressure situation arise?
• How would you handle this situation in the future?
• Who was responsible?
• What did you do?
• What have you learned from the experience?
• Why do you think these situations occur?

- Where did the problem originate?
- Where do you go for advice in these situations?

11) Questions that draw out additional information
Examples:
- Give me some more detail on that.
- Can you give me another example?
- What did you learn from that experience?

One of the best ways to get additional information is through the use of silence. Most candidates you interview won't like the lull caused by your silence and will expand on what they've been saying.

Once you have selected a candidate, it is your responsibility to train them and make them even better than they are and remember Peter Drucker's advice that the most important responsibility you have as a leader is deciding "Who Does What" or getting the right person into the right job.

The third type of interview is an on-the-job performance interview. The goal here is to see if they can actually do the job you're hiring them for and how they interact with other members of your team they'll actually be working with. One great way to do this is to score the candidate in one of five areas on a scale of 1-5 (and have others on your staff do the same to get a sense for how well he or she does).

The five areas are:
- Attitude / Personality / Motivation
- Responding to and following directions
- Ability to do the task
- Dress and demeanor
- Interaction with other team members

After the candidate has left, you can ask questions of your current team as part of your evaluation system. For example, you could ask your current team members the following five questions:
1) How did you feel this candidate would do as a member on our team?
2) Do you feel like their current skills would enable him or her to learn the job quickly?

3) What is one specific reason why I should hire this candidate over any other candidates we might be considering?
4) How would you rate this candidate overall? Why or why wouldn't she be an "A" player on our team in your opinion?
5) Any other thoughts or observations?

In the final interview after the on the job trial interview, you could ask:

1) During your work here, it is absolutely imperative that _____*list one of your standards that you expect each employee will do at a high level*_____. Share with me two or three ways in which you would specifically fulfill that role.
2) I'm curious to know how you would handle a situation where _____*list a challenge or a problem that someone in the role you are hiring for has to deal with frequently*_____. What would be your approach?
3) What did you learn from your experience in working at our business here today?

These questions can be a great starting point for your hiring system (if you don't already have one in place). If you do, consider the process and the sequence of the questions I've covered to see if there may be ways you could improve your hiring sequence and process as part of your system.

I don't think there is an entrepreneur who hasn't experienced numerous issues around the topic of hiring and firing. It takes commitment to learn and master the skills required to succeed in these areas so you aren't duped by the factors you've just talked about. Issues around hiring and firing are exactly the same way.

Daniel Pink explains why mastery is elusive in his book *Drive*. He says:

"The path to mastery—become ever better at something you care about—is not lined with daisies and spanned by a rainbow. If it were, more of us would take the trip. Mastery hurts. Sometimes—many times—it's not much fun. That is one lesson of the work of psychologist Anders Ericsson, whose groundbreaking research on expert performance has provided a new theory of what fosters mastery. As he puts it, 'Many characteristics once believed to reflect innate talent are actually the results of intense practice for a minimum of 10 years.' Mastery—of sports, music, business—requires effort (difficult, painful, excruciating, all-consuming effort) over a long time (not a week or a month, but a decade). Sociologist Daniel Chambliss has referred to this as 'the mundanity of excellence.' Like Ericsson, Chambliss found—in a three-year study of Olympic swimmers—that those who did the best typically spent the most time and effort on the mundane activities that readied them for races. It's the same reason that, in another study, the West Point grit researchers found that grittiness—rather than IQ or standardized test scores—is the most accurate predictor of college grades. As they explained, 'Whereas the importance of working harder is easily apprehended, the importance of working longer without switching objectives may be less perceptible...in every field, grit may be as essential as talent to high accomplishment."—pp. 124-125.

It's really about heart. Some people don't have the tenacity to master the skills required to succeed at a particular job. Sticking to a process and getting better as you go is the challenge and you must discover whether the candidate in front of you qualifies to do what you want with this perspective.

Unfortunately, many entrepreneurs don't really like the hiring process. They hire because of necessity—they *need* the help—but the process of hiring and training employees can be frustrating and discouraging, especially when you've worked hard to train someone and they leave. It is your job to train your team members to do the work they've been asked to do. Don't leave something this important to chance or get too busy to make sure it is done right. Part of your hiring system ensures that people are trained correctly and started off right once they have been hired.

Here are twelve ways to ensure that you are starting new team members off correctly once they've formally been hired.
1. Start them off right with training specific to what they will be doing. Make sure they have good direction. Once you hire them, you are responsible for making sure they have the proper knowledge and tools to sell successfully.
2. Assign each new hire to an experienced team member who will work with them for at least a month and who can answer their questions.
3. Make sure you are clear about your expectations on the first day. Being lax on the first day will ensure that the trend gets worse over time. Be specific about what you want done. This will impact her

confidence. They know they can sell because they've already made a sale.

4. Show each team member that you care by taking time to ask how things are going and see if they have any specific questions. Offer encouragement in the areas where they've done well. Invite them to study specifics that will help them succeed in their next day's work.

5. Require daily and weekly productivity reports. You must inspect what you expect.

6. Give team members flexibility to do their work within your current system, but be open to suggestions on how things can improve. When you notice something that needs to be done, be specific in the recommendations you give.

7. Recognize a team member's successes in public in front of other team members. Tell others, "_____ just made a great sale. She did such a great job!" If there is something that needs to be corrected, do so in private.

8. Include a written description of what you expect each team member to do and show them what to do each day. If the expectation hasn't been met, find out why. Be firm but be fair.

9. Invite exceptional performers to train others on your team what they are doing to get such great results.

10. Lead by example. People believe what you *do* far more than what you *say*. Show them your work ethic. Start earlier, work harder.

11. Dedicate yourself to continuous learning. Make sure you are improving your skills just as you expect your team to improve theirs.

12. Spend individual time with your high performers. Spend group time with lower performers. Allocate your time carefully. You can't be everywhere so put your time where it will make the biggest difference.

The essence of getting better results in your business can be summed up in this one sentence by Michael LeBoeuf in his book, *The Greatest Management Principle in the World*: "The things that get rewarded get done."

Here are eleven ways you can get the most out of those you've hired for specific positions on your team:

1. *Set goals and expectations.* Clarity is key. Make sure everyone understands exactly what is to be done. The #1 motivator for

people is to know exactly what is expected and the rewards they will get if they accomplish those expectations at a high level. Your team members need and want to know what is expected of them.

2. *Make detailed plans to achieve your sales or department goals.* Action plans are written down and spell out everything that needs to be done to achieve the goal. Think on paper.

3. *Organize, delegate and divide the work according to experience and skills of staff.* Manage and motivate by numbers.

4. *Communicate clearly.* To successfully communicate expectations, outline what you expect, ask questions, listen carefully to the answers, offer encouragement and ideas, and follow up. Make sure you communicate effectively and interact with each member of our staff.

5. *Measure results against projections and forecasts.* You must inspect what you expect.

6. *Post productivity expectations and exceptional results where others can see them.* Identify your critical success factors and encourage others to consistently hit them. Talk about your best performers in team meetings. Reward what you want to see happen in your business.

7. *Develop and train your team members.* Always be developing and managing people. Invest in your inner circle's training and development. Be sure that your system is set up to ensure that everyone gets the training and development that they need.

8. *Share the credit and rewards.* When your business does well, share the rewards generously. Offer bonuses or food rewards if you hit certain sales goals. Have fun parties or trips if you hit a certain objective. If you share the credit and rewards with your inner circle, when lean times come, they are much more likely to stick by your side. Remember, there is no limit to how much good you can do if you don't care who gets the credit.

9. *Cultivate a positive and growth oriented environment.* Create an environment that is conducive to growth and positive in nature. Consider this research as outlined in *The Invisible Employee*:

"Research supporting the effectiveness of praise over criticism goes back almost a century to 1925 when Dr. Elizabeth Hurlock measured the impact of types of feedback on fourth and sixth grade students in a math class. In the test, one control group was praised, another was criticized, and the third was ignored. The number of math problems solved by each group was measured on days 2 through 5. As early as day 2, students in the "praised" group were performing at a dramatically higher level than the "criticized" or "ignored" students, increasing the number of solved math problems by 71 percent during the study. In contrast, the "criticized" group increased by just 19 percent and the "ignored" group by just 5 percent."--p. 31.

Bottom line: We seem to get a lot more done when there is a positive reinforcement than when there is negative reinforcement. One of the important ingredients to the right environment is your presence. You cannot be gone all the time and expect the organization to reflect your values and standards. Your system should ensure that things are done the way you would do them if you were there.

10. *Create opportunities for their growth and advancement.* Great people do not like to become stagnant in their personal growth. They get restless when there is no room to advance. Do whatever it takes to make sure you do not lose any of your best people because they got bored or stuck in a rut. If it will take some time before the next opportunity, approach them and talk about it. It is also wise for you to share the load. Give others on your team the opportunity to create some of their own opportunities for advancement.

11. *Compensate based on individual contribution.* Pay your inner circle the highest salary you can. Compensation should be tied to results. Look for ways you can help team members make more as they excel and make greater contributions to your business.

Thinking about all that could go wrong when you hire someone and what it takes to train them correctly could keep anyone up worrying and wondering about what to do. But, if you're going to overcome the fear of being paralyzed and grow your business right, you've got to feed your mind the right kinds of things and be focused on the positive. Consider this statement by Darren Hardy in his book *The Compound Effect*. He says: "If you want your body to run at peak performance, you've got to be vigilant about consuming the highest-quality nutrients and avoiding tempting junk food. If you want your brain to perform at its peak, you've got to be even more vigilant about what you feed it....Controlling the input has a direct and measurable impact on your productivity and outcomes.

"Controlling what our brains consume is especially difficult because so much of what we take in is unconscious. Although it's true that that we can eat without thinking, it's easier to pay attention to what we put in our bodies because food doesn't leap into our mouths. We need an extra level of vigilance to prevent our brains from absorbing irrelevant, counterproductive or downright destructive input. It's a never-ending battle to be selective and to stand guard against any information that can derail your creative potential....Left to its own devices, your mind will traffic in the negative, worrisome, and fearful all day and night. We can't change our DNA, but we can change our behavior. We can teach our minds to look beyond 'lack and attack.' How? We can protect and feed our mind. We can be disciplined and proactive about what we allow in." *–The Compound Effect*, pp. 120-121.

If you would like more information on how to create the right hiring systems for your business, I encourage you to read and study *The Real Talent Advantage* written by Jay Henderson and I. It will help you understand why you've made mistakes in the hiring process, what you can do to overcome them, and lay out a specific plan that will help you maximize the productivity you get from those you hire to be a part of your team.

Score yourself on the following report card. Read the statement and then determine what grade you would give yourself.

Scoring Your Performance with Hiring In Your Business	Your Grade
1) Do you conduct three interviews with each candidate before you offer them a job and hire them in your business? *A = always; B = most of the time; C = occasionally; D = rarely; F = Never*	
2) Do you have a written description of your each ideal category of employee at your business? *A = yes; B = for most positions; C = yes, but I don't enforce the expectations; D = I just know what I want people to do in my head; F = No*	
3) Do you feel your employees know exactly what to do in specific situations? Do they revert back to their own ideas or do they follow your system for doing their work? *A = yes; B = for most situations; C = no, everyone just does what they feel (it has worked out okay so far); D = no, and it has caused big problems; F = No, what's a system?*	
4) How well do you follow up with the references and do you have a systematized process to ensure that who you are hiring is going to be the right person for you? *A = always; B = most of the time; C = occasionally; D = rarely; F = Never*	
5) Do you follow a systematic process with specific actions to ensure that a brand new hire is being started off correctly? *A = always; B = most of the time; C = occasionally; D = rarely; F = Never*	
6) When was the last time you feel you personally added value to the life of one of your new hires or existing employees? *A = last week; B = two weeks ago; C = 3 weeks ago; D = a month or longer; F = I can't remember*	
7) When you or any members of your team had a disappointing day, do you talk with them about actions they can take the next day to help them succeed and get back on track? *A = always; B = most of the time; C = occasionally; D = rarely; F = Never*	
8) How often do you delight and dazzle the members of your team when they perform exceptionally well? *A = always; B = most of the time; C = occasionally; D = rarely; F = Never*	

Hopefully this quiz and the assessment below will help you see how you are doing with your hiring and training systems. Jim Collins says in his book *Good to Great* "If you have the right people on the bus, the problem of how to motivate and manage people largely goes away. If you have the wrong people, it doesn't matter whether you have the right direction, you still won't have a great company. Great vision without great people is irrelevant." That is great advice regarding this important system.

Here are tasks to complete to help you build or improve this system:

1. Outline the questions you will ask in your interview from now on into three categories. Set up your own system for how you will evaluate and grade performance in each stage of the interview. Get input from staff members before you make an offer to an employee.

2. Identify your top recurring challenges around hiring. Where are the holes in your systems? What will you do to prevent these from happening again?

3. Detail what you learned from a recent hire / firing situation in your business. What did that process reveal to you about holes in your hiring or firing process?

4. When you make a mistake around hiring, detail five things you learned from the experience and five improvements to your system that you will as a result that will help you better hire in your business in the future.

5. Divide up the three interviews and look for ways you could have different individuals on your team responsible for different areas. A great system is really just a checklist of what to do to avoid situations that could come up again. Come up with your own checklist that will help you do even better.

Here is an assessment for your hiring and training systems:

#	Rank yourself from 1-10 based on your current business behaviors.	1	2	3	4	5	6	7	8	9	10	Rank yourself from 1-10 based on your current business behaviors.
1	Everyone on our team is in it for themselves and doesn't care about our team goals.											There is a synergy among all the members of our team.
2	Sales consultants and team members rarely make recommendations and don't feel like any suggestions they have are listened to.											Everyone is listened to and encouraged to speak up and make recommendations.
3	There is negativity and gossip amongst our team members.											The team always remains positive and does not tolerate negativism or gossiping among its members.
4	The team wants things to stay the same and doesn't like new challenges.											The team sees changes as positive and is always ready for new challenges.
5	Team members make excuses for why they aren't successful at reaching team goals.											Team members are accountable and never make excuses for performance.
6	Important tasks are put off and rarely accomplished on time.											Deadlines are taken seriously and managed by the team leaders. Projects that are delegated are completed on time and at least 75% as well as you could do them yourself.
7	Some members of the team pull others down with negativity and poor performance.											Members of our team enjoy their work.
8	Mistakes are often made that cost the business money and some daily tasks are left undone.											Every member of the team does complete work, nothing is redone or substandard.
9	There is a lack of communication and sometimes duplication of unnecessary activity occurs.											Team communication is effective and duplication of work does not occur.
10	We haven't spelled out what each person in each position is supposed to do.											We have clarity about what we expect new hires to do. They understand and perform to our expectations.

## CHAPTER 13

LEADERSHIP DEVELOPMENT SYSTEMS

"The time, money, and effort required to develop team members don't change the team overnight, but developing them always pays off."
—John C. Maxwell

In this chapter, I'd like to discuss how to work better with those around you as you develop your leadership systems. When I consult with entrepreneurs around the country, it is amazing how many of the issues that we discuss come down to issues with personnel who aren't doing what the owners would like to have done. As a result, there is tremendous frustration and disappointment in overall results.

A big part of having better systems around leadership development is ensuring that you have the right mindset about whom you choose to work with, develop, and grow into a better leader.

The dictionary defines mindset as "a habitual or characteristic mental attitude that determines how you will interpret and respond to situations." Your habitual way of interpreting and responding to situations that come up in your business is a big indicator on the rate at which you will grow and how successful you will be.

Roger Schwartz in his book, *Smart Leaders, Smarter Teams* says: "Your mindset is like your computer's operating system. Every computer needs one to run. Without an operating system any computer is an expensive paperweight. A computer's operating system organizes and controls all the computer's hardware and software so that the computer acts in a flexible but predictable way. Your mindset does the same thing. You use your mindset to act and get results. Your mindset controls the decisions you make, the statements you make, and the questions you ask. Like any good operating system, your mindset enables you to take action quickly, effortlessly and skillfully. It does this by using your core values and assumptions to design your behavior....If your mindset is like an operating system, then your behavior is like application software....This arrangement poses limitations as well, including the fact that the version of the operating system you're running affects how well your application software runs. You know this if you've ever tried to run a new program, like a video game, only to discover that your operating system won't support it. If you're trying to run the most current versions of Google Earth, iTunes, or your favorite video game and you're using the current version of your operating system, your application will probably run happily. But try to run a [new] program on an out-of-date operating system like Windows 95 and you'll be out of luck." –pp. 19-20.

He continues:
"It's the same with people's mindsets and behaviors. Sometimes you want to change your behavior to get better results. You get excited by something you learn or experience, maybe even in a leadership or team development program. You hope you can install the program and run it like new software, and that you and your team will be able to accomplish more, better, and faster. Unfortunately, most of the time it doesn't work. Just as you can't successfully run a new computer application without a compatible operating system, you can't successfully implement a new set of behaviors without also changing the mindset that makes it run."–p. 20.

Now, why is this important in the context of leadership development systems? The reason is that most people try to accomplish results and their goals by controlling everything. Schwartz calls this attitude of "unilateral control" the limiting mindset that prevents you from accomplishing what you could and should in your business.

In other words, according to Schwartz:
"This means trying to get others to do what you want them to do while keeping yourself minimally influenced by others. You view leadership as *power over* others, so it's important to hold on to it. With a unilateral control mindset, you think if you were to share power with others, you'd lose power.....Unilateral control leads to unilateral leadership. Sometimes it's blatant, but often it's subtle. You think of yourself as the sole leader in your team and that makes your team members followers. Consequently, you alone become responsible and accountable for the

team's leadership. This means you guide discussion, challenge team members' thinking, and deal with issues that arise in the team and between team members. When members of your team have different points of view, you see yourself as the person who has the information, experience, and expertise to figure out what the team needs to do. Continuing with the computer analogy, 98 percent of leaders have the unilateral control mindset preinstalled. For almost everyone around the world, it's the default operating system when faced with challenging situations. When the stakes are high, when you feel strongly about the situation or solution, or when others have very different views from yours—chances are you automatically run on this mindset."–p. 22.

This is a very interesting assertion. Schwartz says that in order to be successful today, you've got to be open to being influenced by others and also be influenced by others at the same time, which he calls a mutual learning mindset.

In other words:
"You see each member of your team having a piece of the puzzle. Your job, along with the other team members, is to jointly put the puzzle together. You view leadership as power *with others*, not *over others*."

The problem arises when you think you're working as a team, but in reality you're still working with the unilateral control mindset. Schwartz explains:
"It's easy to think you're using a mutual learning mindset when you're really using a unilateral control mindset. Mutual learning is often what forward-thinking leaders and organizations espouse and their fond beliefs are often touted in the press....[However], in my decades of working with leaders, observing thousands of behaviors, I've found that nearly all leaders who epouse mutual learning seem in fact to be operating from a unilateral control mindset. As a result, they undermine the very results they are trying to create."–pp. 23-24.

Don't be the type of leader who says you believe in teamwork and team-building, but in reality you don't really empower others to become great leaders on your team by taking the responsibility to develop them. The reality is that you can control your mindset. You don't have to let how you feel and think be controlled by someone or something else. You are an adult. You can change your mindset (no matter how set it may have been in the past) simply by changing how you think, who you associate with, and what you actually spend your time doing and implementing in your business. If you want to improve the performance of those who work with you on your team, you need to have a systemized approach to how you develop those around you. It won't just happen. You've got to invest your time to become better.

I really like Alabama head football coach Nick Saban's approach to investing time. He says:
"You can spend time doing anything. You can read a magazine, take a nap, or watch television. When it comes to work, the same holds true. You can play on the Internet or glance over a report. But *investing* your time is something much different. Investing time means spending it for a worthwhile purpose: to work toward something, to accomplish something that will help you achieve. We see the difference on the practice field. Some players—or teams—*spend* two hours in the afternoon doing drills, rehearsing plays, and going through the motions of practice. But others invest their two hours by working hard, correcting mistakes, and improving on each play. The difference between spending time and investing time can impact results dramatically."–*How Good Do You Want to Be*, p. 40.

Here are several suggestions of ways in which you can create systems that will help you invest the time you spend in your business by actually developing your team members:

1. Set up a method or process whereby members of your staff can communicate with you about challenges or crisis situations that come up.
Every entrepreneur deals with crisis and chaos from time to time. Training your team members how to communicate with you about crisis situations that come up is very helpful in getting more done instead of the chaotic alternative where everyone is running around complaining how the sky is falling and all is lost. In moments of crisis and chaos, leaders need to remain calm, cool, and collected while gathering the facts so they can come up with solutions. Leadership doesn't have to be lonely when you have an inner circle that is full of leaders who can offer perspective and potential solutions to the challenges you face.

Here is an example of a form you can use to help your team members present challenges to you (and hopefully present you with a couple of potential solutions or options of what to do).

CHALLENGE OR CRISIS: **Urgency Level (1-5):**	
Five Key Facts You Need to Know About It: 1. 2. 3. 4. 5.	What is a brief summary of your perspective or the client's perspective (if applicable)?
Possible Solution #1: Pros • • •	Cons • • •
Possible Solution #2: Pros • • •	Cons • • •
Your Recommendation:	

Having a written form like this helps your team members think on paper. They have to have to think about what's happening, the pros and cons to each potential solution, and give you better information which will help you make better decisions. In many cases, this process will allow them to come up with their own solution and actually go about solving the problem without having to bring it to you.

You could also train everyone on your team your process of how you think about and make decisions in your business. When you have a system for making decisions, you can train those around you how to think through difficult issues so you can better run your business. I have found this process of leadership development and this perspective critically important in every business I've run.

A friend of mine, Chris Hurn, once told me how his attitude about his staff actually helps them take on more responsibility within his organization. He said:
"From day-one, I've instilled in each of my employees a desire to have their own enterprises someday. I've told them repeatedly that they need to absorb all the business lessons they can at our small, fast-growing company, so they'll be better prepared to successfully run their own firm one day. Some would think that this kind of empowerment would merely lead to them leaving me sooner, but I find exactly the opposite occurs. They're emboldened to not just work here but learn here and do better, more innovative work here. We work at developing this entrepreneurial spirit in all of our employees so that decisions can be made quickly at all levels. This fosters more speed while breeding more accountability."

He continues:
"Routinely pushing decision-making responsibilities back toward my employees gives them more autonomy and saves me time. It doesn't do them any good if I make all of the decisions ALL of the time. Sometimes they'll make mistakes, but that's just fine, as I never want to punish smart people for taking, smart calculated risks. A lack of the pursuit of excellence is a far greater sin in my company. If you want to be innovative, you're going to have to take risks and experiment and test. This means you'll deal with failures regularly or, as I like to think of them, obstacles to be overcome. Minor failures are merely learning opportunities, but the important thing is that we're taking action—most don't. You can't set the pace of innovation in your industry without constantly testing the edges of the possible." That's great advice.

2. Create a learning culture in your business.

One of my favorite things that Chris does to develop his employees is that he has twice-a-month 'reading meeting' over lunch, where he buys a book for a different employee who then presents and summarizes a famous business book for the rest of his staff. He says:

"That same employee is then expected to facilitate discussion in an effort to reflect and relate important points back to our company—what we're doing right, what we're doing wrong, and what we need to be doing. We spare no one from this exercise, not even our interns. This allows the entire firm to share in the knowledge from these books, while the employees gain practice presenting, defending ideas, and managing a meeting. And of course, it's a quick way to disseminate information most people would have a hard time getting through in several years time. It also subtly forces our people to view work as more than just a place to earn a paycheck and demonstrates to them that learning is a lifelong experience. All of this is part of a very deliberate learning culture I've crafted in our business since I first came to appreciate one when I worked at GE Capital for a number of years while Jack Welch was still the CEO."

I really like that idea. I have had many of our top sellers present what is working best for them at our sales training meetings in the past. I like this idea of buying and assigning a book to be read and then having one of our team members report back on a chapter or an idea for one of our sales training meetings. The important idea here is that you've got to create a learning culture if you want to develop everyone on your team to be a better leader.

John Maxwell talks in his books about the importance of having a plan for how you will learn. In his book *The 15 Invaluable Laws of Growth*, he describes the questions he uses to prepare for any time he will spend with other leaders he wants to learn from. I think these are some great suggestions. He says:

"Another way I've challenged myself—both when I started and still today—is to look for one major growth opportunity every week, follow through on it, and learn from it. Whether it's a meeting with friends, a learning lunch with a mentor, a conference I'm attending, or a speaking event where I might get time with high-profile leaders, I always prepare the same way—by asking five questions before the learning time. I ask:

- **What are their strengths?** This is where I'll learn the most.
- **What are they learning now?** This is how I can catch their passion.
- **What do I need to do right now?** This helps me to apply what I learn to my situation.
- **Who have they met, what have they read, or what have they done that has helped them?** This helps me to find additional growth opportunities.
- **What haven't I asked that I should have?** This enables them to point out changes I need to make from their perspective."

He continues:

"A better growth environment won't help you much if you don't do everything in your power to make the most of it. It's like an entrepreneur being given money for new opportunities and never using it. You must seize the growth opportunities you have and make the most of them by challenging yourself." –p. 94.

Here are three additional ideas for how you can help members of your team grow:

- ***Develop yourself.*** Let others see how important your own personal growth is by letting them see you read and study. I learned how to read and the importance of study because every morning when I woke up I saw my father studying. There is a powerful example. All of my children are excellent readers. I believe this is true because they see how much Heather and I value reading. They see us reading and they emulate the example.
- ***Assign members of your team to read a book and pay them to do so.*** I've paid my oldest son Mason $10 for every business book he has read since he was nine years old and another $10 for any book report he does on it. I'll do the same for my other children as they get older.
- ***Set a goal to be more curious about other industries.*** Give several of your team members the assignment to go out and study how other industries are dealing with the biggest challenge that you are facing today in your industry. It likely exists in other industries and you can learn valuable insights from what they are doing to successfully deal with it. Offer a $100 reward to those who bring back at least five ideas on companies who have successfully reinvented their businesses to succeed with specific challenges.

In his book *Smart Retail*, author Richard Hammond offers the following encouragement about members of your team that I think really illustrates the type of environment you want to create:

- "Reward people for improving things.
- Consider issues from your team's perspective.
- Don't get mad with people for trying.
- Let grown-ups think for themselves- empower people to make their own improvements.
- Encourage talk, talk and more talk – leave every feedback channel open all the time.
- Recognize people contributions.
- Don't rip off your staff.
- Never criticize employees in front of anyone else.
- Build a great culture founded on trust and respect.
- Tell people you are chuffed with them whenever they make you feel that way.
- Are your job descriptions a jargon-filled sack of nonsense?
- Feel free to build friendships but never forget that you are the boss—keep a perspective.
- Encourage the team to be open with mistakes.
- Have a laugh together.
- Always, always celebrate success.
- Be human in your relationships—if someone is going through a life crisis help them cope with it.
- Share the numbers—let the team own them as much as you do.
- Pay a profit related bonus.
- Pay a customer service related bonus.
- Smile when you walk through the door every morning even if you don't feel like it.
- Put aside cash for training.
- Use training as a reward.
- Be specific with instructions.
- Challenge people and encourage them to challenge themselves.
- Teach by example.
- Show people that the best way to do things is to consider solutions rather than dwell on problems.
- Get the team involved in all the big decisions.
- Help employees to see that it is customers, not you, who pay their wages.

- Hold regular one-to-one appraisals but be prepared to allow employees to tell what they think of you, of your business, and of the team too.
- Have a team meeting every single day—just 15 minutes' worth but make those minutes count." –pp. 84-85.

What great advice about leadership development and creating a culture of learning! What are you *doing* to create a learning culture in your business?

3. Give everyone a number.

Gino Wickman makes this point about the importance of measuring what you want with numbers in his book *Traction*:
"The founder and chairman of a large Michigan mortgage company and a leading online mortgage lender once gave a talk at our Entrepreneurs' Organization Chapter. This was 16 years ago, when I was running my first company and he had 75 employees. He's a fanatic about measuring everything; at one point he told us that 'everyone has a number.' He went on to explain how every employee in his organization has a number, even his receptionist. Hers was two, as in 'two rings good, three rings bad.'

"His speech was a wake-up call for me. Back at my office, I came up with and implemented a number for everyone. I have since taught this discipline to every client, and it has produced tremendous results. Dale Carnegie's book *How to Win Friends & Influence People* contains an example illustrating the power that numbers can generate among your people: Charles Schwab ran Bethlehem Steel Company in the early 1900s, and he had a mill manager whose people weren't producing their work quota. One day Schwab asked him, 'How is it that a manager as capable as you can't make this mill turn out what it should?' The mill manager didn't have an answer. He had tried everything. This conversation took place at the end of the day, just before the night shift came on. Schwab asked the manager for a piece of chalk and asked the nearest man how many heats (i.e., batches of refined steel) his shift had made that day. The man said six. Without another word, Schwab chalked a big figure six on the floor and walked away.

"When the night shift came in, they saw the six and asked what it meant. The day people explained that Charles Schwab, the big boss, has asked how many heats they'd made, and chalked the number down on the floor. The next morning, Schwab walked through the mill again, and he found the night shift had rubbed out the six and replaced it with a big seven. When the day shift reported to work that morning, they too saw the seven chalked on the floor, and decided that they would show the night shift a thing or two. The crew pitched in with enthusiasm, and when they quit that night, they left behind them an enormous 10. It wasn't soon before this mill, which had been lagging way behind in production, was turning out more work than any other plant.

"This shows the power of giving everyone a number. In fact, there are eight distinct advantages to everyone having a number (with my comments in italics under each point).

"1. Numbers cut through murky subjective communication between manager and direct reports.... Numbers aren't just for the person. They become a communication tool between manager and direct report, creating the basis of comparison, unemotional dialogue, and, ultimately, results."

Whenever I have explained our productivity worksheet to anyone, they are amazed that there can be buy in from any of our employees to measure the results in each of these areas. The truth is that if you aren't getting the results that you want, it is because you aren't clear about what you want others to help you achieve. Numbers are the ultimate form of clarity. If you are clear with your expectations, it is difficult for anyone to misunderstand what you want. Remember, great leaders don't just explain something so it is understood, they also explain it so clearly that they can't be misunderstood. Ned Hill, a great educator and teacher, taught me this principle when he was my supervisor at one of my college jobs. He said: "Great teachers don't just cover material. They uncover understanding." That is the kind of perspective that great leaders have as well.

"2. Numbers create accountability. When you set a number, everyone knows what the expectation is. Accountability begins with clear expectations, and nothing is clearer than a number."

What are the numbers that you expect in your business? Here are a few to help you get started with your team:
Receptionist:
  • *Answer the phone after the second ring, never the first.*

- *Don't leave someone on hold for more than 60 seconds.*

Sales consultant:

- *Sell at $150/hour, no excuses*
- *Take no longer than 90 minutes for each appointment*
- *Make at least two outbound marketing phone calls every day*

Customer Service:

- *Have every email or social media complaint addressed within 24 hours after it is given.*
- *Use at least these three methods to solve a situation before asking a manager for additional help*
- *Be sure you meet each of our criteria for our 5-point inspection process before a client sees or picks up her order*

You can't improve what you aren't measuring. Do you have numbers for each member of your team that you expect them to hit?

"3. Accountable people appreciate numbers. Wrong people in the wrong seats usually resist measurables. Right people in the right seats love clarity. Knowing the numbers they need to hit, they enjoy being a part of a culture where all are held accountable."

You can always see who shouldn't be on your team by the degree of resistance someone shows to the numbers you expect them to achieve. Those who are lazy or resistant to change are not those who you want on your team, period. Replace them as soon as possible.

"4. Numbers create clarity and commitment. When an employee is clear on his or her number and agrees that he or she can achieve it, you have commitment. There is no gray area."

It is up to you how long you will tolerate the inconsistency of any member of your team who isn't hitting their daily targets and numbers. My criteria is based on how committed and how much effort each team member puts into making their numbers happen. When they are committed and are doing whatever it takes, I am much more willing to invest time and resources towards helping them get better. If they are not committed (even though I've been clear about what I expect), a change is necessary.

"5. Numbers create competition. Charles Schwab was able to create competition by making a target number known to all teams. Sure, they might experience some discomfort and a little stress, but there is nothing wrong with a little pressure.

It never ceases to amaze me how much better things get when a little healthy competition is involved. Team members and sales consultants work harder to hit their sales goals and everyone on the team is a little bit more excited (especially those who are winning and finally win when the day or the contest is over).

"6. Numbers produce results....What gets watched improves."

Do your team members know that you're watching? Is there a consequence if a result doesn't happen? If not, what's the point of measuring the numbers?

"7. Numbers create teamwork. When a team composed of the right people in the right seats agree to a number to hit, they ask themselves 'how can we hit it,' creating camaraderie and peer pressure. When a team of technicians are challenged to perform their service in four hours or less collectively, they will all pull together to figure out ways to achieve that number. The ones that aren't pulling their weight and hitting the number will be called out by the other team members that are."

No one wants to be on a losing team. Also, no one wants to be on a team where everyone isn't pulling their own weight. If you permit this to happen, you'll lose the enthusiasm of your best performers. They won't tolerate this for long before leaving.

"8. You solve problems faster. When an activity-based number is off track, you can attack it and solve the problem proactively, unlike with an end-result based number that shows up after it's too late to change it. In addition, the use of hard data cuts through all of the subjective and emotional opinions that create murkiness and lengthen the amount of time it takes to make the right decision."–*Traction*, pp. 122-125.

As a leader, you must pay attention to the critical numbers that fuel your business on a daily, weekly, and monthly basis. I wholeheartedly agree with his comment that you don't want to get caught up getting the information too late to make meaningful changes. You've got to not only measure the results, but understand what those numbers mean and where

you'll need to make changes to get meaningful changes in your results.
Again, it is completely up to you whether you'll manage your business better
with numbers or not.

Know your numbers and act on what you find quickly. This is the only
way to better manage for results. Ignoring numbers or not measuring
them is a quick way to begin or accelerate a decline in your business.

4. Be authentic and willing to admit your weaknesses. Help others
to move up the accountability ladder in your business.
David Novak wrote a great book entitled *Taking People with You* that
details how you can stay true to who you are and stay authentic (so you
remain yourself even in the toughest situations). David is the CEO of
Yum! Brands which operates in more than 117 countries and employees
1.4 million people. All three of the company's restaurant chains—KFC,
Pizza Hut, and Taco Bell—are global leaders in fast food and I think
there is a lot to be learned learn from such a leader that can be applied to
your business.

David explains why authenticity is so important in leading and how it
has impacted him and his company. He says: "To inspire as a leader,
you need to know your stuff, but you also need to be able to admit when
you don't know stuff. You need to be both confident and vulnerable at
the same time. I struggled with that paradox myself when, in 1996, at
the age of forty-three, I was given the job of president of KFC. It was
the first time I'd been the president of anything, and because it had been
a career long goal to be in charge of running a business, I was excited to
get started. I really wanted to be good at it, to have a positive impact on
the brand and the people working with me, and I wanted to turn around
what had been a business in decline and have some fun along the way.
But like many people with the best of intentions, I learned the hard way
what I wasn't good at." *–Taking People With You*, p. 31.

In Novak's case, he tried to make a video with him telling jokes to all of
two thousand of the company's restaurant general managers. The video
bombed badly and no one laughed at his jokes. He appeared stiff and
completely out of his element. He still shows the video today when he
conducts one of his leadership seminars to show that it is okay to point
out your weaknesses, because it makes you more real.

One of the challenges that any entrepreneur faces is being more consistent at follow through and being more accountable for results. When you make a mistake or aren't following through as well as you should (and you're willing to admit it), you'll get more buy in from your team members that they should make improvements as well. It takes daily discipline to do the little things that will help your business get to the next level. Being open with your reasons why everyone must be committed to follow up and being willing to admit you've made a mistake when you haven't is a big key to being a better leader.

Too often in our society, it is easier to blame someone else or something else instead of taking personal responsibility for your mistakes. One of the reasons why skepticism is so high today is because people are sick and tired of people not taking responsibility for what they have agreed to do.

I had an interesting experience once when one of our team members accepted an assignment to help find models for an upcoming trade show. She promised that she would get the models all lined up. Three days before the event, I asked her if it had been done. She said it would be. Unfortunately, she didn't get anyone lined up. On top of that, she didn't tell anyone. As a result, when my wife showed up at the event, there were no models there. We scrambled and were able to put together a few models in a short period of time, but we ended up cancelling the first show of the day. It didn't reflect well on our business that we ended up cancelling the show, but in my opinion it was better to cancel the show than to only have a couple of models who would have had to rush and drop everything to be there at the last minute and do the show.

When I confronted the team member about what had happened, she didn't even apologize and tried to place the blame on the schedules of her friends who she had tried to line up for the show. Her attitude of trying to shift the blame when she had accepted responsibility for lining up the models is unfortunately one that is way too prevalent today. When something happens that isn't supposed to, it is easy to get mad and place blame. But, if we can recognize our own failings and set goals to improve (and let everyone else know of our desire to get it right), we become much better and more valuable leaders.

I should have followed up with her again to ensure that it had been done and I admitted as much to all of our team members when we talked about this issue at our weekly training meeting the following week. I explained that we all have to do our part on our team to make our events and every part of our business work. I also explained that if someone doesn't do their part and everyone else is depending on you to get something done (and the ball is dropped) it affects everyone on the team. At that meeting, I shared two sports stories that are instructive and I want to share them with you as well. There are a lot of great and positive accomplishments in sports, but these two stories are about bad performances and the lessons that can be learned from them.

The first one is that of Fred Snodgrass who famously dropped a fly ball in the last game of the World Series of 1912. The series was between the Boston Red Sox and the New York Giants. The game was tied 1-1. The Boston Red Sox were at bat, the New York Giants in the field. A Boston batter knocked a high-arching fly. Two New York players ran for it. Fred Snodgrass in center field signaled to his associate that he would take it. He came squarely under the ball, which fell into his glove. It went right through his hand and fell to the ground. A howl went up in the stands. The roaring fans couldn't believe it. Snodgrass had dropped the ball. He had caught hundreds of fly balls before. But now, at this crucial moment, he dropped the ball. The New York Giants lost. The Boston Red Sox won the series. Snodgrass came back the following season and played baseball for nine more years. He lived to be eighty-six years of age, dying in 1974. But after that one slip, for sixty-two years when he was introduced to anybody, the expected response was, "Oh, yes, you're the one who dropped the ball."

The second story is that of Roy Riegels who played center for the University of California Berkley during the 1929 Rose Bowl. Midway through the second quarter, Riegels, picked up a fumble by the opposing team Georgia Tech's Jack "Stumpy" Thomason. Just 30 yards away from scoring, Riegels was somehow turned around and ran 65 yards in the wrong direction. Teammate and quarterback Benny Lom chased Riegels, screaming at him to stop. Known for his speed, Lom finally caught up with Riegels at California's 3-yard line and tried to turn him around, but he was immediately hit by a wave of Tech players and tackled back to the 1-yard line. His wrong-way run in the 1929 Rose Bowl is often cited as the worst blunder in the history of college football. He lived to be eighty-four, but from that point on he was always remembered as the man who ran the wrong way.

What can we learn from these two individuals who had two bad performances? Even though both of these individuals continued to play well throughout the rest of their careers, they became known as the one who dropped the ball and the one who ran the wrong way.

In your business, every action you take, especially every sale you make or don't make can be characterized as a defining moment for your business. Every day you are either making the sale or dropping the ball. Thinking that one sale doesn't really matter will cause other sales to be lost as well. Remember, the secret to your future success is hidden in your daily routine. Take care of each day and the weeks, months, and years will take care of themselves. If you continually let the same objection stop you from making a sale, you are dropping the ball. If you aren't putting a pre-sales strategy in place to build trust and rapport with prospects before they hear your presentation and offer, you're dropping the ball. If you're not continuously training and helping your team improve their sales skills, you are dropping the ball. If you're not following up with every customer who buys or doesn't buy from you to invite her to come back to do business with you, you are dropping the ball. Don't be known as the one who dropped the ball. Stay focused on the fundamentals. Continuously strive for improvement. Everyone can improve and get better especially at selling and marketing. Having systems in place ensures that you and your team members aren't dropping the ball.

You must know the direction your business is going in and that following that course will lead you to where you really want to go. Don't be like Roy Riegels who thought he was doing a great thing when he was really running the wrong way. Knowing where you are heading is so important.

Here are five suggestions for ensuring that your business is on track:

1. **Define what you want.** If you aren't clear on your goals, how can you expect anyone else on your team to be clear about the direction you are headed? I am often reminded of one of my favorite quotes from the great philosopher Winnie the Pooh. He said, "It is wise to ask someone—perhaps yourself—what you are looking for, before you begin looking for it." Wise words.

2. **Understand how what you want fits into the goals you have for your business and your life.** Many mistakes in direction can be corrected simply by understanding the correlation between what you

want in your business and your life. Not clearly understanding the two can lead to a life without balance and fulfillment.

3. **Once you know what you want, take time to envision it in your mind.** Everything is created twice. Once in the spiritual realm and once in the physical realm. Clearly seeing where you are going in your mind first can allow you to think backwards to determine what needs to be done to help you get there. If you get knocked down, be sure you get your bearings before you start running down the field again. If you don't, you may find out you are running the wrong way and end up where you didn't think you would.

4. **Take action.** The more compelling your vision, the easier it will be to take the first steps. The clearer you are about what it is that you want (your goals), the easier it will be to take the first steps. Lack of clarity is usually the culprit of indecision and inaction.

5. **Stay focused.** Don't allow distractions to dissuade you from achieving what you want. As entrepreneurs, it can be easy to get distracted by shiny objects that can take our focus off what we really want. Spending profits on unnecessary distractions won't help you be profitable and reach your end goals.

At that training meeting, I encouraged our team to never forget the lessons of the guy who dropped the ball and the man who ran the wrong way. I encourage you to remember these lessons as well and ensure that you and every member of your team are focused on the daily activities that will help you reach your goal. Knowing where you are going will help you stay on track and run the right way.

It takes relentless follow-up and accountability to ensure that this happens. David Novak makes this point in his book *Taking People with You*: "To get the results you want, you're going to have to follow through with daily intensity. Jack Welch talked to me about 'the relentless drumbeat for performance.' A constant awareness of what needs to be done and the energy to make it happen are essential for any leader. What's also essential is that you hold people accountable for their part."–p. 167.

One of the best parts of Novak's book is something he learned from Larry Senn called the accountability ladder. Novak describes it as follows:

"Larry Senn taught us something called the accountability ladder to drive a sense of personal responsibility. At the bottom of the ladder is the person suffering from complete obliviousness; he or she doesn't even know what's going wrong or what needs to happen. You move up from there to blaming others for what's not working. The ideal rungs are at the top, where a person takes responsibility for finding solutions to a problem and then gets on with executing those solutions. You always want to be moving yourself and your people up that ladder." –p. 169.

Novak then shared a great example of how he learned how to let others take responsibility for their actions when he worked at Pepsi. One day, he went to one of their bottling plants in Baltimore. The plant was in a tough neighborhood and when he arrived he could see bullet holes in the Pepsi sign in front. Novak shares this experience about how he dealt with the challenges of the plant.

He said: "I went in and had my usual meeting with the crew. I started off by asking what was going well there. 'Nothing,' they said. 'Ok,' I responded, 'then how can this place be more effective?' Well, the floodgates opened after that. Some guys said they didn't have all the equipment they needed; others said it took too long to get the route trucks out in the morning. They just went on and on, until one finally piped up: 'You seem like a pretty good guy. What are you going to do about all this?' That shut everybody up. They all turned to me and waited. 'Nothing,' I said. 'Absolutely nothing. You're the ones who are going to fix all this. I'm going to bring the plant manager in here and together we're going to make a list of all of the things that you talked about. In fact, I've already started.' Then I showed them the pages of notes I had taken. 'The only thing I'm going to do is, I'm going to come back, in six months, and you all are going to show me what sort of progress you've made when I get here.'

"Six months later, I did go back, and it was as though I had entered a whole new plant. They were waiting for me at the door and led me around, showing me all the various improvements and talking about their plans. They still had more work ahead, but they had done a lot. And what's more, they were darn proud of themselves for doing it. You could just see it on their faces." –pp. 169-170.

He continues:

"Sometimes the worst thing you can do as a leader is to solve all the problems yourself. You've got to assign responsibility where it really belongs. Even if I had known everything there was to know about operations, I still wouldn't have been around that one plant long enough to fix everything that needed fixing. But those guys could. And they did. Follow-through, like a lot of things I've talked about, is leader led. You have to keep people climbing up that accountability ladder, and don't let them stop until you've accomplished all that needs to be done." –p. 170.

In one of our businesses, I had a similar conversation with our manager. She told me of some of the challenges they were facing. I asked her for some numbers and statistics and for her to provide a plan of how the challenges could be overcome. She emailed me the numbers I requested and I had my own thoughts about what should be done as I reviewed them. When we talked again, I listened to her plan and it was exactly in line with what I thought. She led the team to overcome the challenge we discussed and the team worked hard and accomplished the goals that had been set. She is a great leader and by giving her the opportunity to make decisions and be accountable for those decisions, she has accomplished great things. You should do the same for your leaders.

I would encourage you to be more vulnerable when you make mistakes and be willing to admit them. We all need to be a little more transparent and authentic as leaders. We also can lead better by helping those on our teams climb the accountability ladder.

5. Pay attention to the little things.
Leaders pay attention to the little things and they teach their team members to do the same. The little things can make all of the difference in whether or not you make the sale and whether or not your business stays focused on the goals you've set for yourself.

One of my favorite stories about the little things comes from the first practice John Wooden would conduct with his freshmen basketball players. Don Yaeger tells the story in his book *Greatness: The 16 Characteristics of True Champions*. He says:

"Prior to the first on-court practice, Wooden would gather his new players and tell them to take off their shoes and socks. Each player in the room would look around, bewildered, but obliged. Wooden's first lesson went down to the basics: how to put on socks and shoes properly. 'I want you to make sure that there are no wrinkles or gaps,' he'd tell them. 'Make sure your heel is fully seated in the heel of the sock; run your hand over the toes and make sure to smooth out any bumpy areas.'

"Over the next half hour, he would show each player how to properly lace his shoes and tie them snugly so that there was no room for the shoe to rub or the sock to bunch up. 'That's your first lesson.' Wooden would then start to walk away, but, after about a dozen steps, he'd turn around and explain the life lesson to the puzzled players. 'You see, if there are wrinkles in your socks or your shoes aren't tied properly, you will develop blisters. With blisters, you'll miss practice. If you miss practice, you don't play. And if you don't play, we cannot win,' he'd tell them. 'If you want to win championships, you must take care of the smallest of details.'"–p. 69.

What are some of the small details that you may be neglecting in your business? Here are a few for you to consider:

- How well you are approaching every prospect? 30% of prospects make a decision of whether they will buy from you within one minute of entering your business. 60% of prospects make that decision within five minutes of meeting you and hearing your offer. Are you ensuring your success by making sure your approach builds trust and causes prospects to want to buy from you?

- Are your products displayed in such a way that a prospect can quickly and easily distinguish which one is right for them through a systematic approach that educates him or her to be more confident in a buying decision?

- Is your business cluttered in any way? What impression does your business give prospects when they first walk through the doors or when they interact with you?

- Have you observed the traffic patterns of prospects in your business lately? Are there areas of your marketing funnel where prospects clump together and you drop the ball? What could you do to make the traffic flow better in these areas?

- Are clients feeling welcomed once they've made the initial transaction to buy from you?

- Does your warm greeting cause a prospect to feel that he or she has arrived at the business where they'll find the solution to the challenge their facing? If not, what could you do to engage him more in the process of discovery within the first few moments of visiting your web site or after she sets foot in your business?

- Do prospects sense a genuine desire from each of your sales consultants to help them (regardless of what he or she has said their stated budget is)?

- Are customers greeted on the phone with answers to their questions? Have they learned something and been invited to take action to do something (schedule an appointment, etc.) before they hang up the phone?

Remember, the little things are the foundational things that help your business to grow quickly. Richard Hammond makes this point in his book *Smart Retail*:

"The best [businesses] do not stand still when successful. They strive to keep the momentum, to keep growing and to keep moving forward. That growth and movement is inspired by tiny little everyday improvements just as much as it is by sweeping change."—p. 81.

Adam Lashinsky makes this observation about Apple when they began to open their own retail stores in his book *Inside Apple*: "Apple executives didn't just look at existing stores for inspiration. They asked themselves: What are the best consumer experiences people have? Hotels in general—and specifically concierges—came up in response again and again, and the concierge became the inspiration for the Genius Bar. They also talked about what turns people off in stores—clutter, bad design, unfriendly or pushy salespeople. The look of the stores shows Apple's obsession with detail."–p. 152. Focusing on the little details that matter transformed Apple into a retail powerhouse.

Be the kind of leader that trains each of your team members that the little things *really* do matter. Break down the component parts of what each team in your business does as clearly as John Wooden did for his beginning basketball players. If and when you make a mistake, make it up to the client as quickly as possible. The little things have a way of becoming big things if they aren't taken care of quickly and your ability to respond to these issues quickly as a leader will make a dramatic impact on the growth of your business.

6. Control your emotions.

There will always be situations, clients or team members who make you upset. I had an experience a couple of years ago that illustrates the importance of staying in control when this happens. I had a wedding consultant who I had met with previously show up at our business with one of her clients while I was not there. After she left, she called me and gave me a lengthy list of things that my consultants had done wrong and how disappointed she was in my staff. It was an embarrassing situation and compounded by the fact that my team members knew better. I was angry. I had to compose myself. I vented to my wife and then went into the store and handled the situation by talking with each team member about the situation that happened and what I expected going forward. Each of the consultants reaffirmed their commitment to live up to the standards we had. I was mad enough I could have fired everyone on the spot, but what good would that have done? Instead, because I was able to regain control, I was able to have a meaningful conversation with each one of our consultants to help our business improve and get better.

Probably the greatest lesson I've ever learned about control happened before I ever got into business for myself. My freshman year in college, I worked at a chemistry lab to pay for my schooling and expenses. One day, I came into the lab and began to clean up as I often did. Unfortunately, I threw away an experiment that one of my bosses had been working on for three days and that probably cost the company tens of thousands of dollars. My boss was furious, but I'll never forget his kindness to me. He knew I felt terrible about it and he didn't rub it in and make me feel even worse. There was nothing that could be done about it then. He regrouped and restarted the experiment. Years later, I had a member of my staff make a mistake that cost me tens of thousands of dollars. While I was upset, I remembered the lesson of my previous boss. The mistake had been made. We ended up working overtime for weeks (and I lost a lot of sleep), but we rectified the problem. Being angry and livid and taking it out on someone else when you are mad rarely helps solve the problem. Instead, learn from the mistake, put better controls in place to ensure it doesn't happen again and begin again.

We all feel the emotion of fear from time to time. To be a great leader, you must fight your fear with action until you achieve results. Opportunities are seldom labeled as such. Ask yourself: How can I take action now when others may be hesitating because of their fears? When you can control your own fear by taking action, you will accomplish great things. Be the leader in your business and act when others are cowering in fear. Your team looks up to you. You must lead them forward with faith and action.

Leadership is often described as lonely, because you alone are responsible for the decisions you make. Everyone may not agree with what you've decided, but if you have made your decision with facts and with your own instincts, you will rarely make the wrong choice. I've made decisions to let sales consultants go that were selling, but who were causing contention and unhappiness amongst other members of our staff who were also selling. That choice has always been hard, but in the end, it has proven to be the right one (and one that I should have made sooner).

I've always believed that there are a few critical success factors that drive the bottom line of any business. As a result, I expect certain things to be done on a daily basis. I can get a good pulse for each of my businesses by looking at daily reports that measure these things. Recently, I showed up in one of my businesses unannounced and saw some things that I wouldn't have seen if I had told my staff that I was going to be there. This helped me end a potential problem before it became one and reminded my staff that they always need to be on their toes and follow the systems we have in place. The little things do matter and measurement of these things is critical to your success as a leader. The more successful you become, the more you've got to keep a pulse on the small things and think about what they mean to your organization.

7. Have high expectations and be demanding. Rewarding mediocrity won't get you very far.
I strongly believe in the motto that there is no limit to how much good you can do if you don't care who gets the credit. Nothing will destroy morale faster than taking credit for something you didn't do. Instead, reward those who achieve exceptional results and let every member of your team know what it is that you truly value. I once had a sales manager who always said: "I don't reward mediocrity." That was a great lesson to me about how every person on the team played their part.

When someone did something great, he was the first to congratulate him or her and acknowledge the contribution that was made to the entire team. However, he would never acknowledge mediocre efforts. He knew that we would work harder to get his approval and that it would help us achieve what really mattered instead of being content with a meaningless trophy that everyone received for achieving little to nothing.

Where do you want to end up? If you don't know your purpose then it is impossible for your team to figure it out. Some may say that I am demanding in what I expect our team members to do. Yet, I've found that most people love working in an environment and being a part of team that knows where they are going. I have two friends who have a very successful fitness business. There is an excitement around their growth. It is infectious and everyone wants to be a part of it. I've learned a lot from watching how they use that vision and energy to get everyone on their team even more excited to go out and do what needs to be done on a daily basis. Have a vision and expect those on your team to make it happen. If you are slack and lack discipline, everyone on your team will too.

There is nothing more inspiring than being a part of a team that believes, that comes to work everyday determined to make a difference for every client they work with and to make the day's goals happen. I love being on teams where there is a sense of purpose and excitement. As the leader, you've got to believe first. You've got to set the pace and set the standard by being optimistic yourself and doing the work everyday. When you lead with optimism, there are few if any obstacles that will slow you down towards the accomplishment of your goal.

I started out this chapter by talking about the difference between unilateral control and mutual learning approaches as explained by Roger Schwartz in his book *Smart Leaders, Smarter Teams*. I want to end by offering this summary of the difference from his book.

He explains:

	Unilateral Control	**Mutual Learning**
Who leads and who follows?	There is 'one leader in the room'—the formal leader. Team members follow.	There is 'leadership from every chair.' At any point, any team member may lead and others may follow.
Who is accountable for how the team works together?	The formal leader.	Every team member.
Who are team members accountable to?	The formal leader.	Every team member.
Who or what determines the basis for effective team action?	The formal leader.	The team's guiding principles.
How are team structures and processes designed?	Congruent with unilateral control core values and assumptions.	Congruent with mutual learning core values and assumptions.
How are decisions made?	In a range of ways, but driven by a unilateral control mindset.	In a range of ways, but driven by a mutual learning mindset.

--*Smart Leaders, Smarter Teams*, p. 222.

Here is an assessment for your leadership development systems:

#	Rank yourself from 1-10 based on your current business behaviors.	1	2	3	4	5	6	7	8	9	10	Rank yourself from 1-10 based on your current business behaviors.
1	Leadership is lacking in our business.											Our leaders have strong leadership capabilities.
2	If a manager or assistant manager leaves, there is not another person on our staff that I can easily promote to this position.											We have a strong culture of developing leaders around us at our business.
3	We do not provide learning resources to our staff members to help them develop their leadership qualities.											We provide learning resources to our staff members to help them develop their leadership qualities.
4	I don't offer encouragement to members of our team. They don't know how I feel about the work they are doing (unless it is bad).											I continuously offer hope and encouragement in our staff's ability to reach our business goals.
5	I feel like the only one who cares about what happens in our company. No one else seems willing to help share the load.											Leaders in our organization have been trained and are adequately prepared to help carry the load.
6	No one rises to help out when a challenge is presented. As the leader, I feel very alone.											Expectations are clearly laid out so that everyone knows what is expected and rises to their potential.
7	Our team is like a thermometer. We are currently losing momentum and we are concerned.											Our team environment is like a thermostat. Our goals, mission, and agenda are clear and team members rise to make them happen.
8	Our management team feels alone. There is not a sense of shared purpose, vision, and goals.											We are surrounded by great leaders who exhibit strength of character, leadership, and results orientation.
9	We are scared to leave our business for any length of time.											We are confident that any leader at any level on our team could handle any situation as well as we could if we were gone.
10	Top performers feel like they have to support others who aren't pulling their weight.											Production and results are expected and delivered by each member of our team.

Here is a task list to help you implement better systems for you and your team:

1. Explain and implement a better process so that every member of your team who deals with difficult situations is trained how to bring problems AND solutions to your desk. Train others to think as you would think and most importantly ACT.

2. Adopt a learning culture at your business by immediately starting these three activities:
1) Pick a skill that you want to develop and start learning more about it.
2) Assign members of your team to read a book and discuss it with everyone else on your team in an upcoming training meeting as my friend Chris Hurn does.
3) Write down a problem you are currently facing and start researching what other growing companies in other industries are doing to solve the same problem. Report your findings to those on your team.

3. Write down your numbers so that everyone is clear about their job responsibilities.
For example:
Receptionist:
- Answer the phone after the second ring, never the first.
- Don't leave someone on hold for more than 60 seconds.
Sales consultant:
- Sell at $150/hour, no excuses
- Take no longer than 90 minutes for each appointment
- Make at least two outbound marketing phone calls every day
Customer Service:
- Have every email or social media complaint addressed within 24 hours after it is given.
- Use at least these three methods to solve a situation before asking a manager for additional help
- Be sure you meet each of our criteria for our 5-point inspection process before a client sees her order

4. Consider the accountability ladder and where each member of your team is on the ladder between powerless and powerful. What can you do to move everyone to take more accountability for their actions and present solutions to you for what should be done to help your business grow?

5. What key activities could you assign to ensure that everyone is committed to helping your business succeed? For example: Change the measurement of making two phone calls per day to scheduling 2 or 3 appointments per day. This goal is much more results focused and everyone then becomes engaged and takes ownership for helping your business hit your targets..

6. Have each member of your staff who is over a specific department or area of your business submit to you their top five suggestions for how they will hit the targets you've set and their recommendation of what the reward should be if the goal is achieved.

7. What causes you to lose control of your emotions? What behaviors trigger that loss of control? What can you do to pause, take a deep breath and choose a different response instead of anger?

8. Read *Develop the Leader Within You* and *Develop the Leaders Around You* by John C. Maxwell to learn more about leadership development systems.

You will have much more leverage and grow your business on a more solid foundation when you choose to develop leaders like I've been describing here. Make the choice to develop leaders around you and you'll find that the process of improving your business systems sticks and becomes a part of your business culture.

CHAPTER 14

CRISIS MANAGEMENT SYSTEMS

"If you don't have time to do it right, you must have time to do it over."
—John Wooden

Every business will experience problems, an unexpected reversal, or a crisis of some kind as it grows. Unfortunately, such crises rarely come at opportune times. When you have challenges or problems come up, you need a system for dealing with and managing the situation.

Noted author and trainer Mark S.A. Smith shares this fantastic advice about what he does when he experiences a stressful event or moment in his business. He says: "When you feel overwhelmed immediately do these three things:
1) Stop and take a breath. Unless you're in the middle of a life or death situation, you can take five minutes to take a break. You can't be resourceful when you feel overwhelmed, so stop and get your feet on the ground.

2) Make a list of what you know about your situation. Look for information and resources that you can use to move forward. One of the biggest opportunities: renegotiate the deadline to get more breathing room.

3) Identify the next logical step. You don't have to have every step identified, just the next one. You'll be delighted to find that what you need lines up at the right time. Movement relieves overwhelm.

The best way to beat overwhelm is to learn to say, "No!"

What great advice. Perspective also helps you look at every problem or crisis that comes up in your business as a valuable lesson or an opportunity in disguise. While this is much easier said than done, it does help to deal with challenges when you are simultaneously looking for the valuable lesson in every setback or difficulty.

Brian Tracy in his book *Crunch Point: The 21 Secrets to Succeeding When It Matters Most* says: "No matter who you are or what you are doing, every person and organization experiences problems, difficulties, unexpected reversals, and crises that knock you off balance and must be dealt with right away. It is estimated that every business has a crisis every two to three months that, if not handled quickly and effectively, can threaten the very survival of the enterprise."

He continues:
"But when the going gets tough, the tough get going. It is only by facing the challenge of a crunch point that you demonstrate to yourself and others what you are really made of....By their very nature, sudden challenges, problems, and crises come unbidden. They are unwanted, unexpected, and often serious in their implications. They also are unavoidable and inevitable. You can never stop them completely. The only part of the challenge-response equation that you can control is your *response*. All that you can determine is how you are going to respond to the inevitable ups and downs of business and personal life. Your response is under your control."

It is easy to get discouraged or beat down when one problem after another seems to wear you out or wear you down and that is usually how such business problems arrive (one after the other). In such moments, it can be easy to lose control of your thoughts and feelings and be overwhelmed by whatever crisis you are experiencing in your business or personal life.

Brian Tracy says:
"The natural tendency when things go wrong is to react or overreact in a negative way. You may become angry, upset, disappointed, or afraid. These stressful thoughts and negative emotions immediately start to shut down major parts of your brain, including your neocortex, the thinking part of your brain, which you use to analyze, assess, and solve problems and make decisions. If you do not immediately and consciously assert mental and emotional control in crunch time, you will automatically resort to the fight-or-flight reaction. When things go wrong, you will want to either counterattack or retreat, neither of which may be the right strategy in a crisis situation."

Let me give you an example. Several years ago, I had to make a difficult decision about a business my wife and I owned in another state. Our manager who had worked for us for four and a half years was burned out. She didn't want to admit this and to be honest, neither did I. I knew that going back into the business to manage it and run it would be very time consuming. After a lackluster weekend in sales (when our numbers were very far down from what they had been the previous year), I had an interesting insight and I made a decision. I realized that there was lesson that I needed to learn from what was happening. That lesson was simply this: No amount of coaxing, fixing, or trying to improve the situation would be able to happen unless a change was made at the management level first. I realized that the poor sales numbers I didn't want to see would continue unless I made the change. I had just traveled to be in the business and had put some new marketing initiatives in place, but nothing seemed to be making a difference. I finally realized when I stepped back from the emotion of the situation that I needed to make a change and so I did. Sales immediately turned around and I found out that many of our team members were relieved about the change and were re-energized when I took back over the business.

That lesson has been a good reminder to me. Sometimes the answer to our challenges and crises are not what we want to hear, but tough situations can help us do what needs to be done so we can actually make the changes necessary to get our businesses back on track.

Brian Tracy has a four part "worry-buster formula" that I have used often when I have encountered a difficult situation. Here is his formula:
1) "Stop and identify the worst possible outcome of the problem or crisis. Be perfectly honest with yourself and others. Ask, 'What is the worst thing that can happen in this situation?'
2) Resolve to accept the worst, whatever it is, should it occur. This action calms you down and clears your mind. Once you have mentally decided that you can live with the worst possible outcome, you will stop worrying.
3) Determine what you would do if the worst possible outcome occurred. What actions would you take?
4) Begin immediately to improve upon the worst possible outcome. Identify everything you could do to minimize the damage or reduce your losses. Focus all your time and attention on

achieving the very best outcome you possibly can."--*Crunch Point*, p. 12.

Being paralyzed by fear doesn't do much to help you overcome your problems. When you can objectively look at the situation and follow these steps, you can move forward with purposeful action to fixing the challenges you are facing.

I've heard it said that the answer to most of the problems that a business faces is a great sales offer. In other words, if you invite a group of prospects or clients to take action now, what will the financial result be for you and your business?

There are four types of challenges that can come up in your business followed by a few possible challenges in each category. Of course, there are more possible challenges, but they all fall into one of these four categories. These are:

1) **Anticipated Changes** – this category includes challenges such as:
   o Knowing that you will need to add additional inventory or team members at certain times of year
   o Knowing a key employee will be leaving because of a move, pregnancy, etc.
   o Knowing what months are slowest in your business so you can prepare ahead of time to market for these slower times
   o Knowing when you are busting at the seams and need additional resources (a bigger place or more team members) to take care of the new prospects and clients coming in

2) **Sudden & Unexpected Changes** – this category includes challenges such as:
   o Discovering that a key employee is leaving or has to be fired
   o Discovering that your credit card processing company is cancelling your merchant account
   o Discovering that an employee has been stealing from you or that inventory has been stolen from you
   o Discovering that critically important data to your business is lost (or has been wiped out in a computer crash)

3) **Crisis (Forced on You Changes)** - this category includes challenges such as:

- o Dealing with a cash flow crunch where you're not able to make payroll (or you have to cut your own payroll out causing stress in your family situation)
- o Dealing with customer service issues (especially ones that cost you big money)
- o Dealing with any crisis in your family
- o Dealing with negative review by clients online that causes you stress (especially when it is wrong and not true)
- o Seeing expenses go up without a corresponding increase in sales

4) **_Competitive Changes_** - this category includes challenges such as:
- o Discovering that a big competitor is moving in by you or has just acquired one of your biggest clients
- o Discovering that a competitor builds an alliance with a vendor or partner that you have heavily relied on and have been doing very well with
- o Discovering that a key employee is going to leave to work at a competitor
- o Discovering that a competitor is copying what you have done and is profiting from it
- o Discovering that a competitor is badmouthing you online

When you experience any kind of challenge (especially when you or one of your team has made a mistake that will cost you money), it is best to ask yourself the following ten questions so you can get the facts:

1) What is the situation exactly?
2) What has happened from different perspectives?
3) How did it happen?
4) When did it happen?
5) Where did it happen?
6) What are the facts?
7) How do we know that these facts are accurate?
8) Who was involved?
9) Who is responsible for doing (or not doing) the things that set in motion the challenge we are facing today?
10) What can be done to ensure that this situation doesn't happen in the future?

Sometimes, we make assumptions that get us into trouble without getting all of the facts. It is best to question your assumptions, determine what would happen if they were wrong before making any concrete decisions about doing something different in your business.

When you make a BIG mistake that causes you to lose money or your business experiences something shocking that you weren't expecting, you go through the five stages of grief as outlined by psychologist Elizabeth Kübler-Ross. These are the same stages you go through when you lose someone close to you. When you understand these emotions, you can better bounce back from the disappointment and frustration you feel when something doesn't go your way in your business.

These stages are:
1. *Denial* – basically what happens here is you are shocked because you can't believe what is happening is *actually* happening *to you* and it will now seriously disrupt you and your business. In denial, you mentally try to shut out what you are feeling and pretend that it really isn't happening.
2. *Anger* – once you realize that the situation is indeed happening (such as losing a valuable employee or finding out about a mistake that will cost you money), the natural tendency is to lash out in anger against someone else that you feel is responsible for the setback that you are experiencing. When you do this to members of your team, you may say something that you really don't mean and which you can't take back.
3. *Blame* – anger turns into blame very quickly where you try to track down the person that caused the problem in the first place. Sometimes in really bad situations, someone may end up getting fired.
4. *Depression* – when the reality sets in that you can't avoid the setback takes place, it is common and easy to get depressed and tremendously discouraged. You feel let down, cheated and betrayed by someone else. Very often, you may feel sorry for yourself (especially when you look around at others and see that they don't seem to be experiencing the same challenges that you are).
5. *Acceptance* – At some point, you realize that the setback has happened and that it doesn't do any good to be angry about what is going on. You accept what happened and start looking to the future again. In some cases, this may take several weeks or months before this feeling is reached.

The thing I would mention about these five stages (and why it is important to understand them) is that when you recognize what stage you are in, you can take control of your emotions and get through the next step. This isn't easy, but it is a lot harder if you don't have a road map to guide you through the challenges.

Brian Tracy says that "when a crisis occurs, there are four things you should do immediately.
1) Stop the bleeding. Practice damage control. Put every possible limitation on losses. Preserve cash at all costs.
2) Gather information. Get the facts. Speak to the key people and find out exactly what you are dealing with.
3) Solve the problem. Discipline yourself to think only in terms of solutions, about what you can do immediately to minimize the damage and fix the problem.
4) Become action-oriented. Think in terms of your next step. Often any decision is better than no decision." –p. 31-32.

The process for making any of the types of decisions mentioned above are triggered when you are dissatisfied with a situation and you start asking "What If" questions, you discover an opportunity and begin investigating how it could affect you, you meet a talented or exceptional individual, and you are looking and thinking about ways to turn some kind of challenge into an opportunity.

If you are going to get out of a crisis situation and get more done in your business, you've got to decide AND act. Those who are most successful decide and get into motion right away. There is little or no time gap between decision and action. They get to implementation right away.

If you want to grow your business out of a crisis situation, there are five critically important actions that you must take:
1) Take simultaneous actions, not sequential ones.
2) Anticipate trends and direction. Work on your opportunities; don't just react to what's going on around you.
3) Be quick and agile. Respond quickly. Work to minimize the time between your decision and action.
4) Take massive action. Implement quickly. When you look at anyone who is super-successful, it is no surprise. Just look at *everything* that they're doing.

5) Don't expect perfection. When something is wrong, fix it. Don't wait to pull the trigger on something until it is perfect. If you do, you'll never accomplish much and the crisis may overtake you.

Here is the process and system I use when I'm faced with a difficult challenge and the sequence of questions I force myself to answer. I first learned the sequence of these questions from Lee Milteer and have used it many times to come up with solutions to tough challenges. Use this process with a big issue you face and you'll be amazed at how well it works.

Your Biggest Concern
1. What is your biggest concern in your business right now (what keeps you up at night)?

2. What's the cause of the concern?

3. Can you realistically do anything to solve it?
        A. No, I can't. I will not worry about it any longer. If I think about it at all, I will be sure all my thoughts are constructive.
        B. Yes, I can and will take care of this problem.
4. What is your strategy to overcome this concern?
First I will:

When?
Then I Will:

When?
Then I Will:

I will complete solving this problem by Day/Date/Time:

In times of crisis, it is natural to turn up our performance to ensure that we get the results we want. Here are eight areas where you must raise your effort while dealing with a crisis situation in your business:
1) **Your most important profit generating items**– what is selling best and what is helping you make the most profit now? If you only focused on selling those items (and incentivized your clients and prospects to buy them), could you sell even more of them over the

next 90 days?

2) **Your best team members** - Who are the 20% of your staff that produced most of your results (80%)? What should you do to reward them and help them buy into what needs to be done to climb out of your crisis situation? What incentives or rewards will you put in place to get them excited about what you are doing?

3) **Your core marketing activities** - What are the three to five things that are working best right now to bring in prospects? In other words, if you found out today that you could only do one thing to get prospects into your marketing funnel, what would that core marketing activity be? Then, over the next 30, 60 and 90 days, work on accelerating your efforts in that area (or at the most 3 areas) so you can bring in the right kinds of prospects now. This doesn't mean you stop doing the other marketing things you've already got in place. What you are doing is focusing on what is working best and accelerating your performance in those areas. For example, if you are spending $300 a month on Google Ad Words now, and that is bringing in prospects, why not increase that to $500 or $1000 over the next 90 days (and cut back somewhere else if necessary)?

4) **Sales strategy** – What is working best for you to close the sale now? What seems to get your sales consultants excited and your prospects excited to buy now? Put your best sales strategy in place to ensure the maximum number of dollars to enter your business every day.

5) **Profit centers** – What 20% of your business is generating 80% of your profits? What can you do in the next 90 days to ensure that you are selling more of what is making you the most money?

6) **Top clients** – who are your top clients? Who has already bought something from you? What can you do to get those clients to return and buy something else from you in the next 30 days? The key question: How can you get more of the clients who have already purchased something from you in the last 90 days to buy something from you again in the next 30 days?

7) **Your own skills, qualities and attributes** – What is the one thing that you and only you can do that would have the biggest impact on making the next 30, 60, and 90 days your best ever? Does that mean you should be out talking with prospects and selling yourself several hours each day? Does that mean that you go out and generate revenue from existing clients in some other way in your business?

8) **The key result areas of your business** – what is your daily goal in order to make your next 30, 60, and 90 days your best ever? Where

are you the strongest right now? Where are you the weakest? Where should you put your focus in the next 30, 60, and 90 days? What one thing could you do in the next 24-48 hours that would strengthen and reinforce your weakest key result area?

Transformation out of a crisis is possible for you. It is up to you to decide that you will persist through any difficulty you are facing now in order to make a major transformation in the next 30, 60, and 90 days. James Whitcome Riley once wrote: "The most essential factor is persistence, the determination never to allow your energy or enthusiasm to be dampened by the discouragement that must inevitably come."

When your back is against the wall, it is easy to motivate yourself to do what needs to be done when you have a *reason why*. If you aren't up against the wall, then you need to manufacture your why so you take the actions necessary to create optimal results. You don't have to wait for a crisis to get out and make it happen.

The key is that if your reason why is not compelling enough, you will give up to soon. Where are you heading? Where do you want to end up? These are important questions that you must take time to stop and think about. In all of the hustle and bustle of your business, are you taking time to readjust your direction and get on track to where you want to go?

If not, you will likely end up in a much different place than what you thought when you got into your business. Why not choose to make the next 30, 60, and 90 days your best ever?

Why not manufacture your reasons why you will make these periods of time exceptional?

Ask yourself the following four questions:
- What will be my why?
- What reward will I give myself if we hit our outrageous goal in the next 30, 60, and 90 days?
- What would I have to start doing now in order to make this vision a reality?
- What do I need to stop doing that is wasting my time and taking me away from doing what I must be doing to hit this goal?

It is time for you to be proactive about what you want from your business. When you have a reason why and can clearly articulate that purpose to others, you will find that you will attract better individuals to your team. The secret to fast growth and conversely beating any challenge you face is to remember that people want to be a part of a team and around those who *know* where they are going. Your sales consultants will buy into your vision for your business when they buy into you as a leader and they see that you clearly understand why you are committed to make your next 30, 60, and 90 days your best ever.

If they constantly hear you grumbling about everything that is wrong with your business instead of staying focused on where you are headed, they will lose faith in what you and they are doing. Be the kind of leader who knows exactly what you stand for and those who surround you will also stand up with you to help you accomplish the goals you have for your business.

I love this statement by Dr. C.E. Welch:
"Many fail because they quit too soon. People lose faith when the signs are against them. They do not have the courage to hold on, to keep fighting in spite of that which seems insurmountable. If more of us would strike out and attempt the 'impossible,' we very soon would find the truth of that old saying that nothing is impossible. Abolish fear, and you can accomplish anything you wish."

If you are going through a challenging time right now, realize that fear, panic, and worry are not going to make your situation any better. Worrying is not going to help you create money or sales. Follow the crisis management system I've outlined here with your own modifications. When you are singularly focused on achieving results through revenue producing activities, you won't waste time doing anything else and you'll be able to get your business back on track.

Here is an assessment for your crisis management systems:

#	Rank yourself from 1-10 based on your current business behaviors.	1	2	3	4	5	6	7	8	9	10	Rank yourself from 1-10 based on your current business behaviors.
1	I find myself blindsided by the changes that happen in the marketplace and in my business.											I anticipate changes that are changing in the marketplace.
2	When a crisis we weren't expecting is forced upon us, I get frustrated and find myself responding in a negative way without looking for a good solution.											When a crisis we weren't expecting is forced upon us, I am resolved to come up with a successful resolution quickly. I bounce back quickly from my initial negative reactions and focus on the problem at hand with determination.
3	We respond to what our competitors are doing. They are in the lead and we are following them.											Our competitors are chasing us.
4	I spend the majority of my day putting out fires. At the end of the day, I feel exhausted and don't have much enthusiasm for new opportunities.											I spend the majority of my most productive time working on opportunities for my business.
5	I wing it and hope for the best. I don't plan or prepare for change and don't deal with it well at all.											I have a process I use to anticipate and prepare for opportunities that can benefit our business.
6	The decisions I make are often forced upon me. I find myself reacting more than being proactive about the direction of my business.											I take time to think about the future of my business weekly and proactively plan and make decisions before they must be made.
7	I feel like I am alone most of the time. Few, if anyone else on the team, understands the extent of the stress and decisions I make daily.											I have surrounded myself with others who care deeply about our success and are committed to the decisions and direction I help navigate for our business.
8	I work constantly and don't take time for renewal (because I don't feel I can). My perspective is often clouded with my worries and concerns.											I take time to relax and rejuvenate my body and spirit so I can see things with clear perspective.

CHAPTER 15

FINANCIAL SYSTEMS

"Watch the little things; a small leak will sink a great ship."
—*Benjamin Franklin*

In this chapter, I'll cover several of the challenges of profitability and several specific strategies you can use to be more profitable and put financial systems in control in your business. Having financial systems and the right accounting partners can make or break your business. If you don't have great systems and controls in this area, it's time to do so.

Great financial advice and the specifics of what you should do should regarding your financial systems should come from a financial professional who knows the ins an outs of your business. Financial specifics involving spreadsheets, numbers, taxes, and *what* to do and *when* are beyond the scope of this book. My goal in this addressing these systems is to primarily help you analyze your business profitability and pricing.

The fastest way to increase your profitability is to raise your prices, lower your expenses, and sell to more affluent clientele. You may feel that you are in a business or an industry where you can't raise your prices. However, there are six challenges with selling solely on the basis of price in any business. These are:

1) **It is hard to sustain.** There will always be someone who will enter your market and try to compete with you solely on the basis of price. Even if that business loses money, they will stay around long enough to become a problem for you. They will likely force your prices down.

2) **Your sales staff becomes so accustomed to selling for less that they don't know any other way to sell.** As a result, shifts in the economy have woken many entrepreneurs up to the realization that their sales skills aren't as sharp as they thought they were.

3) *It is much more difficult to create a great experience for prospects and clients coming into your marketing funnel without profits to create and market the experience.* For example, Disney charges more than any other amusement park experience in the marketplace. As a result, they can provide a better experience with better rides, better employees, and better training to help employees interact well with their guests.

4) *You can't afford to spend more money on marketing to get future prospects into your marketing funnel since you may just be barely breaking even or losing money to bring in the clients coming into your business now.* By trying to be the cheapest, you won't have the profits necessary to create the great experience for the next group of clients coming to you.

5) *You have to grow your business more slowly.* Your ability to buy inventory and sell it to niche market groups is limited if you don't have the profits to reinvest back into your business.

6) *You can only afford to provide an ordinary experience that can easily be copied by other competitors.* Your best business ideas will always be copied by other competitors. Make it so it is difficult to copy. Don't be ordinary or boring.

To build a solid foundation for your financial systems, you have to be willing to look at the things in your business that may not currently be a pretty picture. Your business finances may be frightening, disappointing, and even downright discouraging for you to think about. If so, that's likely why you've been avoiding it.

George Cloutier makes this observation in his book *Profits Aren't Everything, They're the Only Thing*:
"Taking a cold, hard look at yourself and your business can be the toughest thing for an owner to do. But the truth test is necessary. You have to understand where the leaks are in your business, and exactly how, as the boss, it's your fault. You have to wake up before you can make more profits. Denial is the small business owner's worst enemy. End it now. Face whatever it takes to build a stronger business."—p. 17.

When is the last time you carefully analyzed every product you are selling in your business to determine which ones are profitable and which ones are not? If you have an underperforming product, do you have the courage to drop it and invest in more profitable options? Or do you live in denial and continue to sell it ignoring the fact that it isn't making you money? To be profitable, you have to make tough decisions. There will be some sales reps who won't like that you selling their products. But the reality is that it isn't their business, they don't have to pay your bills, and continuing to sell an underperforming or unprofitable product is cutting into your profits and your own personal income.

Remember that procrastination is denial's best friend. Saying or thinking that someday you'll get around to dropping a product is a belief that will hold you back from being profitable. Have you ever found yourself continuing to sell unprofitable products longer than you should? If so, you are guilty of denial. You have to run your business as a business and that means making tough decisions. Living in denial and making the decision to continue selling unprofitable products in this new economy is a sure recipe for hastening the death of your business. A business needs profits to stay in business and you have to make the tough choices to help you remain or become profitable. Not making those tough decisions or procrastinating them reveals inadequacy in leadership.

If you need to fire a sales consultant who isn't performing, you need to do it now. Procrastinating the decision isn't going to make lower sales improve. Trying to help someone else out isn't going to help your business if your business can't pay its bills or employ you.

Here are seven questions for you to evaluate as you think about the hard realities of where you are at and what you must change to get to where you need to go:

- Do you have sales consultants on your staff that aren't meeting your minimum standard? When will you talk with them to get them on the right track or let them go?
- You hired a sales consultant who isn't selling and isn't putting forth the effort to learn how to get better. How much longer will you keep him or her? Procrastinating this decision will cost you thousands of dollars of lost revenue and profits.
- When you hear excuses from sales consultants about why they aren't closing sales, how long do you let this go before you do training to overcome the objection? If they aren't improving quickly and keep

giving you excuses, how long is it before you make a change and let someone go?

- If your business isn't making a profit, who is to blame? What are you doing about it?
- How is your business doing? Are you where you want to be?
- What are you currently doing to increase your business profitability this year and next year?
- What will your profitability be in 5 years? What steps are you currently taking that will help you get there?

These are hard questions, but avoiding them and continuing to live in denial won't help you get your business where it needs to be. You have to be a leader and take these questions on to help you get to where you want to be. Don't lose sight of why you are building and running a business in the first place—to make your life better. You took on the risk and created your business to pay you. When sales are down and profits are low, you may not feel like you can pay yourself anything. That has to change. You've got to fix your business model so your financial systems are set up in such a way that you can pay yourself for the work you do. Of course, there are always sacrifices in the beginning of any enterprise, but at some point you've got to fix your systems so you can pay yourself.

I think Cloutier says it best:
"Focus on fixing your business model. It doesn't matter if you own a restaurant, a construction company, or a limo service. Lack of sales or quality controls, bloated overhead, and other financial woes are the real reasons you're not taking a salary. Shame on you, not your employees, for failing to make sufficient profits." –p. 23.

He continues:
"Most business owners underpay themselves...Instead of accumulating wealth, they've slaved at a job for decades just to cover payroll and pay the bills. Always work to make a good salary. Then cover the expenses. Not the other way around. If the numbers don't line up, don't even start because you'll always be fighting an uphill battle to stay ahead of your expenses. This is a basic issue of survival. How are you going to make that climb if you are not setting aside enough cash for your own well-being?"--pp. 23-24.

Of course, you have to be smart about this. You can't reward yourself too much. You should still be making profits after paying yourself so you can reinvest back into your business with marketing, new inventory, and growth. I have known some individuals who have overpaid themselves, put their business into financial difficulty, and lost their business as a result.

The key thing is that you should pay yourself and not live in denial or sacrifice forever to get your business going. If you have been in your business for a while and still aren't taking a salary, it's time to sit down and figure out how to increase your sales, increase your profits, and decrease your overhead and get the systems in place to ensure that everything runs smoothly.

Cloutier outlines six great principles about paying yourself. He says:
- "For small business owners, what venture capitalists call 'sweat equity' is no more than working for nothing and being a fool.
- "Take care of yourself first and the rest will follow. You can't lead the way if you're behind the pack.
- If things are tight, don't be the only one to take a pay cut. You're not in business to be everyone else's benefactor.
- If you can't afford to pay yourself the first few cents on every dollar, there's something seriously wrong with your business model. Fix it!
- Money talks. Show who's the boss by paying yourself like one.
- Remember, there are no rich martyrs."--*Profits Aren't Everything, They're the Only Thing*, p. 33.

If you are looking for a great book that will cause you to serious look at your business, this is one I would highly recommend. There are a lot of questions asked in this book that will cause you think very differently about your business and motivate you to set up the systems required to be profitable. Don't live in denial. Raise your prices, lower your expenses, and increase your profits. That should be your mantra and your focal point for running your business.

Here are six ways you can build great financial systems:

1. Be aware of your financial position at all times. Have ironclad fiscal discipline on your spending and expenses.
I want to share this sobering thought from George Cloutier from his book entitled *Profits Aren't Everything, They're the Only Thing*. He says:

"Owners always say they have a financial and operating plan, but few do. Most of these are on the back of an envelope or gathering dust in the bottom drawer, never to see the light of day again. Some owners say they have one in their head, but it only serves to clutter their brains. Most of these plans are never reviewed or modified, and changes are rarely implemented."

He continues:
"If you don't have a strong and evolving plan for profits, don't bother to come to work, because you will fail. Running your business month-to-month, week-to-week, and day-to-day, you'll always be playing catch-up to meet expenses. But if you choose to live by our creed that 'profits are the ONLY thing,' then a disciplined plan is the only way you are going to get there. You should be focused about where you stand on your plan every hour that you're working and implement the required changes without mercy." –pp. 71-72.

Closely monitor with ironclad discipline your operating costs. Everything counts in today's market and if there are operating costs that are unnecessary or things that can be done for less, make these changes as soon as you can. Knowing your costs and carefully cutting out unnecessary expenses will help you be more profitable as well. You are in control of what you spend.

In addition to carefully monitoring expenses, you have to carefully think about what you will do each day and week to generate cash flow. Cash flow is the lifeblood of any business. When the cash stops flowing, the business stops growing. As small business owners, cash flow is vital.

2. Position and leverage yourself to gain power. A great way to do this is to look at new segments or niches of the market where you can sell and build a powerful brand.

A fascinating business you should study is the Barkley Pet Hotel and Day Spa (www.thebarkleypethotel.com). They originated in Cleveland, Ohio. You should study their web site and how they have used the media to promote their 16,000 square foot facility that offers bedtime stories, grooming, special accommodations, private swimming areas, play time, meals, treats, chew toys, etc. all for an upgraded price. Their stated goal is to serve your pets so they don't even miss you because they are having such an enjoyable experience. They have a positioning statement that shows what end of the market they are catering to: "America's Premier Pet Care Facility." They have a limo service that can pick up your dog or you can drop off your pet on the way to the airport. There are cameras that constantly monitor what the pets are doing which can be accessed online and viewed on your cell phone.

Aspiring clients have to pay for their pets to take an assessment to see whether or not they can be accepted to stay there. They even have a day camp for pets. In the assessment, they can see if your dog plays well with the other dogs or if it is territorial. This allows them to eliminate problems before they come up so they can focus on their best clients.

They have three types of suites you can choose for your pet to stay at: the poolside suite, the garden suite, or the deluxe suite and the highest priced suites always sell out first. Some of the dogs even have dinner catered in at night from a local steakhouse. The extra charges can include cuddle time, play time, walking, bed time, story time (you can pick the story your dog hears).

What can you learn from this example of taking a pet kennel business and turning it into a high priced resort with extraordinary profits?

What kind of leverage and power do they have over their competitors because of how they have positioned and are promoting their business?

The important point is this: Their profits allow them to provide a much better experience than any other business in their market niche and haven them the opportunity to expand (they have another facility in Westlake Village, California).

How can you position your business to be the premier provider of what you offer in your market niche? Can you cater to a higher clientele and offer additional services that make the experience of shopping with you more unique than any other business who offers what you do?

Think about how you can raise your prices to provide unique experiences in your market. If you will do this, you may find hidden profits that no one else in your market niche even realized were available (and your clients will thank you for providing the extraordinary service and value to them). There is a powerful advantage in selling to more affluent buyers. They are out there, but you may not currently be positioned correctly to sell to them.

This is something you should be working on in your business: to sell better to the affluent buyer. I sometimes hear from entrepreneurs that they can't get their clients to spend money on high end products. While every market is different, the one truth is that it takes the same amount of time to sell a $2,000 or a $4,000 product as it does a $500 one. The difference is in the kind of client you attract and the value you provide.

Where do you really want to be? Choose to focus on creating products that offer value to more affluent clientele in ways that none of your competitors have previously thought about.

A great example of this is found in the contrast between Omaha Steaks (www.omahasteaks.com) and Allen Brothers Steaks (www.allenbrothers.com). Allen Brothers started after Omaha steaks, yet they decided to sell their steaks for more money than the premium vendor who was already selling at the highest place in the market. Most businesses who come into a market look at what everyone else is doing and then price themselves for less than what others are selling for. This company took the opposite approach. They priced higher (where there are fewer competitors) and built a very nice business by creating more value for their affluent customers. There is a lot you can learn from studying how these two mail order steak companies are doing business in a commodity market where many people only buy steak at the lowest price they can get it for from Wal-Mart.

The key is this: **No one is forcing you to sell exclusively to the market you are currently selling to.** Look for opportunity to sell to another market in your area and you can increase your higher end sales and your profits.

There is one final reason why you should raise your prices that you need to remember and that is this: **In the mind of the prospect, a higher price equals greater quality.** The difference between a high priced product and a lower priced one is in perception. In the prospect's mind, a higher price equals greater quality. I first became exposed to this idea in the sale of furniture. When a price is higher, the buyer assumes that the quality is higher. Recently, there was a study done by Stanford and MIT that proves this point. Their findings were published in the November 2005 *Journal of Marketing Research*. What this group of researchers found with an energy drink they studied was that the satisfaction of the customer related to perceived results could be shaped by price and what they believed about the price.

For example, the findings showed:

1. Two groups of bodybuilders were given an energy drink. One group was told the product was sold at a discounted price and the other group was told that the drink was sold for a premium price. Those who viewed the drink as a discount product reported having a less intense, effective workout.

2. They also did a test with two groups of consumers who were told that the drink improved mental function. Those who believed that the drink was sold at a discounted price were less effective at solving the same word puzzles as those who were told the drink was a premium priced product. *--Journal of Marketing Research*, Vol. XlII (November 2005), pp. 410-414.

If you want to position yourself so that you have more power than your competitors which allows you to beat your competitors in your business, you have to do the following:

- Understand the prospect's perceptions about *your* business in connection with other competitors in your market niche.

- Understand your competitive *difference* and articulate it to prospects and clients.

- Position yourself as an authority with valuable expertise. When you are an authority, you can charge more because the experience of dealing with you is perceived as being more valuable.

- Position yourself as the preferred source of what you sell in your market niche and use written and video testimonials to validate your claims.

- Improve your systems so that you can run your business more effectively and smoothly. Improving your sales and marketing systems will have a big impact on your financial systems.

3. Rethink and reconsider how you formulate your prices in the context of who will buy it and the story behind what your client will actually experience when buying from you. Consider how you can offer a premium option to what you sell.

Everyone in every business has some type of formula they use to set their prices. Most often people calculate price by some cost plus formula from what others in the industry are doing or by talking to peers and some let the manufacturers tell them how to price their product, strictly going by the published MSRP. Some entrepreneurs simply look at what their competitors are charging and try to sell their offering for a little less without regard for how this will affect their overall profitability.

Dan Kennedy makes this observation:
"At the forum shops at Caesar's Palace in Las Vegas, they are selling a watch for $180,000. What you have to know about a $180,000 watch is that it isn't ten times more expensive to manufacture than an $18,000 watch. It's darn sure not 100 times more expensive to manufacture than the $18,000 watch. The cost maybe went up but the price went up exponentially. What does that tell you? It tells you that there should be no relationship between what it costs to make something and what we sell it for. Yet it is so ingrained in us that there should be some relationship."--*Price Elasticity*, p. 95.

"Another example: Craft Steak, the restaurant at the MGM Grand, it is owned by one of the guys on Bravo's Top Chef show. Here is an 8 ounce platinum filet mignon which is $184. The nicer cut is $240. And nothing comes with it. Soup, salad, appetizers, all that stuff is ala carte. That is the slab of beef on the plate. Do you really think it costs proportionately more in cost of goods and overhead for the fancy restaurant than it does at Outback to put their steak on a plate? No, it doesn't. It costs more, but not proportionately more."--*Price Elasticity*, p. 95.

The two things that allow you to build value that way are the "who" and "context". The *who* is who you are selling to and the *context* is the result or the end benefit the client is going to get from doing business with you. Remember, you choose who you go after. If you really want to raise you prices and accelerate your profitability, you have to think differently about this segment of the market and how you can attract that buyer to buy from you as opposed to someone else. If you don't like the "who" that you are currently selling to, you are to blame. Only you can change who you market to and who you sell to.

"The context is the premise of what is being sold. There are lots of ways for example to sell estate planning, tax planning, tax service, there are all sorts of context from 'stay out of jail,' to at the low end, 'get the biggest refund you can as fast as you can and we'll give you that refund right now.' There are all sorts of context for every product and service. You create the context and the context has more to do with price than does the product or service. How does Allen Brothers get two to three times as much to deliver a box of steaks to your house as Omaha Steaks does? There is a different context. Allen Brothers, for example, gets to brag about being the supplier to restaurants like Craft Steaks...There is a story to these steaks. There is no story to those steaks. You control context."--*Price Elasticity*, p. 97.

I've mentioned this before, but this is why it is so important for you to build a story around you and your team and create context that has deep meaning to the clients you serve. Then, you no longer just sell products. You become the premier location to buy your products and clients in your market niche get to brag about how they got to work with you. This is why celebrity appeal is so important.

Lastly, you should add a premium option to what you sell. In the right market niche, you will find that 10 to 20 percent of clients will take the premium option because it is available and because they want the best. It won't be everyone, but it will allow you to be more profitable for a certain segment of the market.

Think more about how to disconnect the price of what you sell from what it costs to make and focus instead on the experience, the story and the intrinsic, personal and unique value you offer that will help you be more profitable.

4. Upsell the minute a client says yes and bundle your accessories to force a larger transaction size.

In a fascinating book entitled *Selling Luxury*, the following four scenarios and the language patterns used by the sales consultant ensure the upsell. Notice that this approach and sales scripting system engages the customer without appearing threatening or condescending. You'll also notice there is a specific suggestion, not a general inquiry like, "Anything else?"

First, a couple, where the man has just purchased for the woman is told: "Now, Sir, let's take a look at something for yourself!"
Second, when a hand bag is sold, the salesperson says: "I have just the shoes to go with it."
Third, when a gift is purchased for a friend, the consultant asks: "What would *you* like to see from our new collection?"
Fourth, when a gift is being bought for a new mother, the consultant says: "We also have beautiful charms for babies."

Robin Lent and Genevieve Tour, authors of *Selling Luxury* say: "The proposal for an additional sale should always make sense. It should avoid being a closed question like "Anything else?" because it loses every time. When is the ideal time to propose the additional sale? Obviously, each situation varies somewhat. But most sales ambassadors feel the best time is after they have concluded the first sale. It may be a situation where a customer promptly indicates that she does not wish to buy anything else, and it should be left at that. Other times, a proposal is seen as a positive continuation of what she has just bought. A Sales Ambassador is sensitive to these issues, always proposing when appropriate."

Then this important key: "Make the additional sale purchase part of the pleasure." –*Selling Luxury*, pp. 126-127.

A bundled upsell allows you to make more profits on every sale you make. Let's say you sell 50 of a particular product a month. If you add on a $100 upsell package to ½ of those sales, that will be an additional $2,500 in sales per month. If your cost of goods on that $100 upsell package is $33, your gross profit will be $1,675. If you multiply that across 12 months, you can add $20,100 in gross profit to your bottom line.

If you sell 100 products a month and add a $100 upsell package to half of those sales, that will be an additional $5,000 in sales per month. If your cost of goods on that $100 upsell package is $33, your gross profit will be $3,350. If you multiply that across 12 months, you can add $40,200 in gross profit to your bottom line.

Increasing your sales closing percentage by having and following a great sales system can help that number be even higher. If you increase the price of every product and force the larger transaction size while simultaneously building the value to your clients, you could increase your profitability even more.

Obviously, if you sell a higher priced upsell package or have more profit built into the upsell, you can do even better. You should be asking for the upsell with every sale you make just like most fast food places ask you to upsize your meal when you order it. Ask the question, "And you would like the _____ (upsell package with your _____*product they are purchasing*____, right?" and you can add more to your overall sales and profits.

Don't forget this important area of your business. Make a list of the things you can upsell to your clients when you make the first sale. If you can bundle these, offer a premium option for these, or sell them individually, you will be so much farther ahead than the competitor who is content to just have the first sale. As part of your financial system, have a strategic plan for upselling and bundling with every sale. Your profits depend on it.

5. Focus on your sales. Every sale matters.

George Cloutier makes this statement in his book *Profits Aren't Everything They're the Only Thing* about the importance of sales. He says: "If sales are down, there's always something, or someone else to blame: incompetent sales staff, a declining economy, an ever-shrinking niche market, the government, and politicians. Yes, these factors have an impact on everyone's sales levels, but if you're losing sales and heading for financial trouble, it's your fault. Large or small, if your business doesn't have a disciplined, aggressive, and accountable sales program, it will fail. And that's exactly what's happening to thousands of small businesses, where making sales requires constant, disciplined effort."--p. 128.

He continues:

"You are only as good as your sales personnel. Most business owners don't have a clue how to conceive and construct a disciplined sales effort....I'm afraid there's just no way around this one. If you don't have your sales strategy down pat, if you haven't built a disciplined sales team with telemarketing, customer support, and regular reports that you look at every day, then you aren't covering even the basics of your business....Making your sales effort stronger is the easy answer and the one profit strategy that works. You have got to do the basics for the market you are in."

The bottom line is that you can't afford to have mediocre sales consultants. They are too expensive in potentially lost sales. If you have mediocre workers and they aren't improving after you talk with them, you have to let them go. Every sale matters.

6. Don't tolerate excuses, especially from yourself.

I mentioned at the beginning of this chapter many reasons or excuses that entrepreneurs make for not raising their prices and their profits which also means cutting out unnecessary expenses. You'll notice that all of these "reasons" are based on the owner's own fears and false assumptions.

David J. Schwartz in his book *The Magic of Thinking Big* makes this statement: "Go deep into your study of people, and you'll discover *un*successful people suffer a mind-deadening thought disease. We call this disease *excusitis*. Every failure has this disease in its advanced form. And most 'average' persons have at least a mild case of it. You will discover that excusitis explains the difference between the person who is going places and the fellow who is barely holding his own. You will find that the more successful the individual, the less inclined he is to make excuses. But the fellow who has gone nowhere and has no plans for getting anywhere always has a bookful of reasons to explain why. Persons with mediocre accomplishments are quick to explain why they haven't, why they don't, why they can't, and why they aren't. Study the lives of successful people and you'll discover this: all the excuses made by the mediocre fellow could be *but aren't* made by the successful person." –p. 29.

My encouragement to you is that you can put financial systems in place that will help you increase your profitability. Now is the time to retake control of your business and make it what you want it to be with these systems in place.

Here is an assessment for your financial systems:

#	Rank yourself from 1-10 based on your current business behaviors.	1	2	3	4	5	6	7	8	9	10	Rank yourself from 1-10 based on your current business behaviors.
1	I rarely look at and analyze my inventory looking for trends, weaknesses, and opportunities.											I have a good control over my inventory at all times. I look at reports to familiarize myself with trends, weaknesses, and opportunities.
2	Unprofitable areas of our business are stealing from profitable areas. I allow these areas to continue instead of cutting them back or out of our business.											Each category of what we sell at our business is profitable.
3	We don't have a system to eliminate unprofitable items from our business. We typically hold onto unprofitable items until they can't be moved or sold.											We systematically eliminate unprofitable inventory items from our business.
4	I don't have reports or surveys to give me an accurate of picture of what is selling in my business.											Through reports and surveys, I have an accurate pulse on what is selling in my business at all times.
5	I know what our best sellers are but I am not planning for what's next.											I am aware of our best selling products and plan accordingly bringing in more of those products to sell and preparing for future best sellers.
6	I rarely look at sales and revenue reports. If I do, I don't take action to maximize turnover. I often end up losing profitability that I wouldn't lose if I planned and prepared better.											Sales and revenue reports are closely monitored to ensure maximum turnover and minimal financial outlay.

#	Rank yourself from 1-10 based on your current business behaviors.	1	2	3	4	5	6	7	8	9	10	Rank yourself from 1-10 based on your current business behaviors.
7	I accept whatever terms I am given with any suppliers and occasionally pay more than I should.											Terms are negotiated with all suppliers including early payment discounts.
8	My debt keeps growing from year to year.											Debt service as a percentage of gross profit decreased last year.
9	I buy by gut instinct and don't buy with a budget when buying supplies and inventory. I allow myself to spend more than I should.											I have and utilize a budget when making purchase or inventory expenditures.
10	I may know what our hottest sellers are but I don't take action so that I have more of those items available to sell.											I stay on top of our hottest trends in our market niche and make sure they are available to sell. I create new products.

Chapter 16

Improving Your Personal And Team Productivity Systems

"Time waste differs from material waste in that there can be no salvage. The easiest of all wastes and the hardest to correct is the waste of time, because wasted time does not litter the floor like wasted material."—Henry Ford

In this chapter, I'd like to discuss systems that will help you and each member of your staff be more productive and get more done. If you struggle with being consistently productive or find yourself interrupted often by members of your staff so that it is difficult for you to focus, you'll find this chapter extremely helpful. I want to explain how you can systematize your productivity so you can get more done.

One of the biggest challenges you will face as an entrepreneur in the area of productivity is how you control and deal with interruptions. It is so easy to get distracted away from your most important priority and the task you are working on because there are so many ways to get interrupted on a daily basis today. It is easy to be busy all day long, yet not feel like you've accomplished much. When you end up reacting to all of the situations around you instead of proactively working on your goals, it is nearly impossible to stay focused on what you set out to accomplish. You've got to put proactive systems in place so you can stay focused on the priority and task you have in front of you that *you've* determined is the most important. If you don't make that decision and implement effective systems for you, you *will* be controlled by someone else's agenda.

There are a lot of reasons why we are interrupted. Some of the reasons may appear legitimate, but the reality is that *you* are in control of your time. Ultimately, allowing yourself to be interrupted is your fault if you permit or invite interruptions. If you're going to get more done, you've got to learn how to stop interruptions and have your own self defense mechanisms that allow you to stay on top of your own productivity.

Here are ten tactics and systems I use to be more productive in my business and that I would encourage you to implement so you can get more done.

1. Don't physically be in your business all of the time. If people can't find you, they can't interrupt you.

Now, this may seem kind of silly, but I have discovered that when I'm traveling between my different businesses or when I'm out speaking or training, my team can figure out what to do in a situation when I'm not there. If they didn't, they were able to call me and if I wasn't available, they were able to put a temporary fix in place *until* we were able to put a new process in place. Then, we made sure that everyone in the business knew the answer to the perplexing question that came up and what to do in the future (and a place they could go to that referenced the exact process of what to do for the future). The reality is that you shouldn't be the only one at your business who knows the answers to every single situation that comes up. That is what systems are all about. It turns out in the rare care where our team wasn't aware of what to do in a situation that came up in my absence that more than eighty percent of all of the situations were handled correctly, and the other percentage was handled with a quick text message or phone call when I was available.

I've been in businesses where I have been conducting a consulting day and have been amazed at how little control and effort goes into ensuring that interruptions don't happen. I remember having a meeting with one business owner who told me she couldn't get anything done because she was constantly interrupted. I told her I could solve her problem. I told her to close the door, put a sign on it that said "Available at 1:00pm." Then, if anyone opened her door and interrupted her, they would have to buy her lunch. Guess what? The interruptions stopped and she found she was much more productive. I've given this advice to many entrepreneurs and now I'm sharing it with you.

It is amazing what we *permit* to happen to ourselves. It doesn't do a lot of good to complain about it if you have no system and no consequences for yourself or others if you permit yourself to be interrupted. For example, you choose to have your cell phone with you and if you are constantly interrupted by calls, text messages, Twitter and Facebook updates, etc. with beeps, whistles and chimes, you can choose to stop the insanity by simply choosing to turn off your phone for a 60 or 90 minute block of time when you are focused on getting something done. You may argue that you need to be constantly connected to your business via these tools. The reality is that this is an excuse. If you're not willing to do anything about putting processes and systems in place to protect you so that you can be more productive, you have little room to complain.

If you are constantly being interrupted because someone doesn't know something in your business, like a price on an item, or if isn't in the computer, teach someone on your staff how to enter that information in the computer. If you don't want anyone else to know how to do this, I would question why that would be necessary, but even if you did, block some time off for yourself so that you can get these details entered into your computer so others on your staff can access it when they need to **without** interrupting you from your most important priority.

Some people feel like they can't close their door because they have an open door policy and always want their staff to feel like they can ask them anything. My response to that is that an open door policy doesn't mean that your door has to be open all of the time. If you don't have an office door, maybe you need to schedule time away from your business when you can work on the marketing or other systems within your business so you can be focused and more productive.

2. Have a time when you return calls. Just because someone calls you doesn't mean that you have to answer your phone at that very moment.
I read recently that there are a lot of 'dumb' people who hold 'smart' phones. They have their phone with them at all times and can't break free from the phone when someone calls. If I'm in the middle of something, I'm not going to answer my phone every time that it rings. It may be someone on the other line who wants me to drop everything and talk to them for 15-20 minutes and I can't do that on their schedule if I'm going to be productive in my business and get done everything that I need to do.

You don't have to answer the phone unless you want to. There is very little that can't wait for ninety minutes. For example, when I'm in the middle of consulting with someone, I don't answer my phone for someone else. I am focused on what I am doing and that client deserves my attention and my time. When I'm working in the middle of a ninety-minute block on a priority I've chosen, I focus on what I'm doing and I get a lot more done because of that.

If you take phone calls every time your phone rings, you will always be stopping what you are doing to interrupt something that you obviously consider a priority. When you choose to answer the phone, you also choose to let someone else control your day, your time, and your life. Choose not to do this. Instead, have a set time everyday when you return calls. My daily time when I do this is at 1pm. You can choose your own time but when any sales rep, advertising rep, business associate, etc. calls you, you don't have to and shouldn't answer your phone. If you allow yourself to be constantly interrupted, you won't get much done.

You've got to control how accessible you are if you want to get more done. If someone is annoyed because they can't get a hold of you, it is their problem, not yours. You'll get back to them as soon as you can, but don't feel like you have to jump up and answer the phone every time it rings. Some people are time vampires. They will suck your energy and your life out of you. You can turn off the ringer on your cell phone or turn it off. When I write, I go to a location where I can't be found and I leave my phone in the car. When I return, I get my messages and call back those who want to get in touch with me. This approach has helped me be much more effective in the control of my time.

It wasn't that long ago that it was rare to have a cell phone and business went on without such devices. Now, people allow cell phones to consume their lives and allow themselves to constantly be distracted by the latest breaking news update, text message, app update, or whatever else you have programmed your phone to interrupt you with. Choose to be a smart person with a smart phone and use it as a tool to help you get more done. Choose not let it dictate what you can or can't do.

One last thing about the telephone. There are sneaky salespeople who ask for you by name (who you don't know) and tell your team members that their call is important. When you pick up, they offer you the latest credit card, better merchant account, or whatever. They will sometimes say, "She is expecting my call. Or "It's a private matter."

I instruct my staff to tell anyone who calls the following:

"He takes time at 1pm to call back all those who call. I'll be sure to have him give you a call then."

If it is a sales call, they say: "He would be happy to look at your proposal. You can email it to him at _____(they provide my email address)___. If he is interested, he will contact you."
Then, on *my* schedule, I look at their email and decide if it is something that I need or don't need. Most often, it is something I don't need and I am not being interrupted or wasting my time on something that doesn't help me reach my most important priority that I'm working on.

I have a few individuals who know my system. These individuals (including sales reps that I know) are respectful and send me an email with any proposal that they believe may be beneficial to me. Then, he or she waits for me to return their email and then we schedule a time to meet if it is necessary.

This is particularly important if you are in the middle of meeting with a client. When you are doing so, don't stop to take a phone call. Instead, have your receptionist say:
"_____ is in a meeting with a client right now, but will be happy to return your call if you can give me your name, phone number and a brief message."

If you must, have a VIP list of those who you will stop what you are doing to take a call for, but this list should be short and only for those who truly respect your time and what you are getting done each day.

Even then, you should tell whoever calls you (should you choose to answer the phone) that you've only got 2, 5, or at the most 10 minutes because you are about to step into a meeting. If you don't put some kind of time constraint on your call or meeting, some people will take as much or more time as you give them. That won't help you get done what you need to.

Remember, you are in control of your schedule. If you let yourself be interrupted by everyone around you on the phone, you won't be very effective or productive in getting a lot of things done.

3. Have two or at the most three times when you look at and answer emails everyday.

Just because someone sends you an email doesn't mean that you have to answer it within 30 seconds to an hour of receiving it. Letting someone else dictate your schedule when you first walk into your business and deal with the flood of messages in your inbox is a recipe for losing control of your day quickly. Have a set time when you answer emails. Maybe it is at 10:30am, 1:30pm and 5:00pm. You set your times. Then, close your email program and leave it off. Focus on what you have to do. If you need to send an email, write it down and then send that email on your next scheduled email time.

4. Teach your team how to deal with a busy and productive person.

Most people have never spent time around anyone who is highly productive. As a result, they think it is okay to constantly interrupt you. If you want to be interrupted less, the key is to be busy and let it be known that you are busy and that you don't tolerate interruptions. Don't allow others to be a thief of your time.

5. Have a daily script where your day has start and end times.

I find it best to do this the night before I leave my office. Then, I can map out and plan my day. I also have a daily and weekly calendar that helps me prioritize what I will or won't do on certain days. I would encourage you to do the same: Have a daily or weekly calendar where you detail what you will do and won't do on certain days. You can tag certain tasks by colors on your calendar or create a 3x5 card system which I'll explain in the next paragraph with start and end times for each day. Then, don't deviate from that pattern or behavior once it has been scheduled.

You don't have to have software installed on your computer to be productive although you can use your smart phone to schedule start and end times for you. I've found it helpful to use a planning book or 3x5 cards with tasks on them. You can use different colors of cards for different tasks and then put them on a cork board in the order you will do them with start and stop times. You can have different colors coded for different activities.

For example, you could categorize your activities into six areas with a corresponding color:

- Compiling and sending proposals = yellow

- Marketing = green
- Training and staff improvement = purple
- Evaluating reports = pink
- Selling = gray
- Planning = light blue

Think on paper. Make and use lists. We all know that we are much more effective when we think through our day on paper first. We don't do this more often because *it is easier to begin and get distracted* on other activities than it is to take five minutes to plan out your day first and focus on these things systematically throughout the day. Remember, there are 1440 minutes in every day. Take at least fourteen minutes (less than 1% of the total time in your day) to plan out what you will do the night before or early in the morning before you begin working on your first task.

The biggest reason why we don't work off of lists very well is because we have too many things on the list in the first place and it is easier to get distracted by easier things than it is to focus on all of the many activities on the list itself.

Chet Holmes explained it very well in his book *The Ultimate Sales Machine*:
"The key to being productive is to stick to the six most important things you need to get done that day. You'll find that when you have a long list, it becomes the management tool for your time. When you want to feel productive, you go to your list and just pick something and do it. It feels good. When you have a long list, you generally do the easier, less productive tasks just to trim down the list. At the end of the day, you find that the most important things on the list didn't get completed because they are either the hardest, the most time-consuming or both. Long lists also mean that you will never finish your list. There is a negative psychological impact to not finishing your list. But there is an enormous psychological boost to crossing off that sixth item on your list, especially when all six of them were the most important things you needed to do that day. So here's the rule: list the six most important things you need to do and, by hook or by crook, get those six things completed each day. That doesn't mean you don't keep a side list of running items that need to be done. When you plan each day, you can go to your long list and use that as a menu of items from which to build

your list of the six most important things for that day." – *The Ultimate Sales Machine*, p. 14.

That is great advice. When you plan, write down the six most important priorities you need and *will* get accomplished that day before you stop working for the day. When you do get interrupted, do your best to get back on task as quickly as you can. Remember, productivity is about control. The discipline of putting the six items you will do each day (at a maximum) with their start and end times is a key skill.

6. Detail what specific objectives are for any meeting or activity with another person(s) BEFORE you meet with them.
Otherwise, you will spend more time than you planned in that meeting and your day will get away from you very quickly.

7. When beginning work on a certain task, remove ALL distractions.
Turn off your phone, close your email program, turn your Wi-Fi off on your computer so you're not tempted to browse the news, sports scores, your favorite blog or forum site, etc. Controlling distractions is a system that you've got to set up and control.

8. Make sure each activity you do has a dollar figure attached to it. In other words, a given activity can only be given the amount of time its monetary or compensation value permits.
Dan Kennedy says: "If you end up spending more time on something that the activity pays for, you WILL end up missing your income targets. Have and keep your own rules. It is hard to waste time if there is no time to be wasted."

You can use the following example of how time can add up quickly just by thinking what will happen if a phone call, email you're writing, or time spent perusing social media sites goes more than 3 minutes over its allotted time. If you have four phone calls a day and each goes more than 3 minutes over their allotted time, you will lose two full eight hour business days a year (4 calls x 3 minutes x 261 work days = 3,132 minutes a year). 3,132 minutes = 52.2 hours per year or nearly a week of time. This means that you're now down to 51 weeks a year instead of 52 to accomplish all of your goals. Do you know what your time is worth? If you want to make $100,000 per year and you work 40 hours per week (50 weeks per year), every activity you do during that hour of time should be producing at least $50. If you only want to work 30 hours per week, that number goes up to $56.67 per hour. If you work, 50 hours per week, the number goes down to $40 per hour, but you are spending more time. It is better to spend less time to make more, right? So, treat the activities on your schedule with the respect they deserve.

9. Have a monthly snapshot where you evaluate your schedule and look at ways you can better use your time. Choose to do things in your personal life during non-peak hours.

One way I've found to be more productive is to do things during off peak hours. For example, my wife and I usually go on a date on Tuesday evenings. Why? There is no wait. On Friday evenings when I travel, I see literally hundreds of people waiting sometimes for an hour or more to eat at a restaurant. On Tuesday evenings, we are able to get into the restaurant, enjoy our meal and then do something we want to because we plan our lives around doing things at non-peak times. We also shop for groceries on any night other than Friday or Saturday night for the same reason. There aren't any lines at the supermarkets on Tuesday evenings. I don't go to the bank on Friday afternoons or on the 1st or 15th of each month because there will always be a line.

The bottom line is that you can choose how you will organize and spend the time in your life. Looking for patterns in the way people behave and choosing to do things differently in your own life will save you tremendous amounts of time.

10. Block your key areas of accomplishment that repeat from week to week on a consistent daily pattern. You can batch activities into specific times that you can repeat again and again. If you let it, your work will expand to fill the time you have each day. Start and end times for every activity are critical.

Break your day into 90 minute blocks. As an example, you could set up five 90 minute focus blocks as follows:
- Block 1 (8:00am-9:30am)
- Block 2 (10:00am-11:30am)
- Block 3: (11:30am-1:00pm)
- Block 4: (1:00pm-2:30pm)
- Block 5: (3:00pm-4:30pm)

The priorities of the day can then be written in and scheduled based on the key priorities to be completed in the empty spots on the calendar. You can also schedule breaks where you do activities that don't require such complete focus. Figure out what blocks of time that will work best for you and then schedule out activities that you can do on each of those days. For example,

In Block 1, you could work on marketing on Mondays, plan training meetings on Tuesday, etc....
In Block 2, you could prepare a list of delegated assignments and activities to members of your staff on Monday, meet with staff members about their performance on Tuesday, etc.
In Block 3, you could eat lunch, return emails and phone calls on each day, etc.
In Block 4, you could work on a marketing project on Mondays, do business paperwork on Tuesdays, do systems work on Wednesdays, pay bills on Thursdays, develop a new product line on Fridays, etc.

The point is to have a consistent time that you work on key priorities in focused blocks of time. It takes discipline to outline and schedule your time this way, but the dividends are tremendous.

Consider this statement by Dan Kennedy about the discipline it takes to be more productive:
"Success isn't much of a mystery. In that respect, it's actually disappointing to a lot of people who want it to be very complicated, who, as discussed earlier, prefer a good alibi. But it's just a reflection of what you are doing with your time."

He continues:
"I can do a good job predicting what your bank balance will be a year from now, if you'll give me the following information:
- What's in the account today
- A list of the books you read and the CDs you listened to last month
- Some information about the five people you hang out with most
- A little analysis of how you spend your time during an average week

"For 90% of all people, by the way, making this prediction is a no-brainer. The correct guess is: same as it was last year. If you happen to be "stuck," then just taking some action to change isn't even enough. Jim Rohn calls this 'The principle of massive action.' And when you look at highly successful people, you'll find they are massive action takers. They don't just try one solution to a problem, they implement 20 all at the same time."

Let's say that you wanted to grow your business unlike anything it had ever been and you read *The System is the Secret* and decided that there were 200 things that you needed to change in your business.

If you worked on ten things a week for twenty weeks, you would complete them all and transform your business. Most people never make the list or are disciplined to follow the list consistently to get the results they want. If you are going to be more productive, you've got to be absolutely focused on implementation and getting more done in your business. Make the list. Then, get it done.

John Maxwell makes this statement in *Today Matters*: "Successful people conquer their feelings and form the habit of doing things unsuccessful people do not like to do. The bookends of success are starting and finishing. **Decisions help us start. Discipline helps us finish."**

He continues: "Most people want to avoid pain, and discipline is often painful. But we need to recognize that there are really two kinds of pain when it comes to our daily conduct. There's the pain of self-discipline and the pain of regret. Many people avoid the pain of self-discipline because it's the easy thing to do. What they may not realize is that the pain of self-discipline is momentary but the payoff is long-lasting."— pp. 26-27.

Have the self-discipline to do what you know you need to do to put a time blocking system into your schedule. Make up your own chart that you can use to plan out your 90 Minute Time Blocking System (where depending on your day you can set up six or seven blocks of time per day for your most focused, productive work).

Now, let's discuss some specifics about your systems for getting more productivity out of yourself and those around you.

Getting more done in your business hinges on four things:
- Your ability to control yourself because distractions are continuous if you allow them to be
- Your ability to control your working environment
- Your ability to control others (to avoid them from distracting and interrupting you)
- Your ability to control your time and priorities

This will require that you are willing to disappoint, frustrate, and inconvenience others to get your priorities accomplished. It also means that you must compartmentalize your time so you can focus on what you need to get done one thing at a time. Have your own rules that you will NOT violate. You may need to put your rules up on your wall so you and others can see them. Remember, you must stay in control of your time if you want to be more productive. Real time management is not about time or management. It is about your goals and your determination to have clear plans and clear boundaries.

The biggest problem you face as an entrepreneur everyday is taking control of your time and your productivity. When you have personal clarity about what you want to do with your business and your life and the outcomes become important to you, *then* you will set up the boundaries in your business that will allow you to get done what needs to get done.

When your boundaries are set, your ability to get done what you want will accelerate, because you will be able to focus on it **without interruption**.

Here are nine questions to help you evaluate your personal boundaries and how your productivity habits are working for you:
1) Where are you weak? What is your productivity kryptonite?

2) What boundaries are working for you?

3) What habits are you repeating that may no longer serve you?

4) Are there those who step over your boundaries so long and so often that you have forgotten what your own personal boundaries are? How can you set better controls in place so you can focus on what must be done?

5) What are your biggest obstacles to your productivity and what are you going to do about them?

6) List your three biggest time wasters. What is your productivity kryptonite?

7) How will you compensate for these going forward? What will you eliminate?

8) List three areas where you are most productive?

9) In what area of your business are you currently best using your time?

Here are some tasks that you should work on to improve your business systems so you and each member of your staff can be more productive.

1. *List all of the business activities at your business that take up your time **and** that require your talent (things no one else can do but you).* Be specific, clear, and brief. Then, list the obstacles that prevent you from getting these things done. Third, list what conditions you will put in place to ensure that you can focus on these activities in 90 minute blocks. Finally, write your goal and action steps you will put in place to be more productive.

2. *List the three to five ways in which you wish your sales consultants were more productive with their time. Now, grade your own*

performance in each of these areas. If your own scores are low, you can't be surprised if your consultants are the same or worse. You must raise your own performance and be the example of what you want your consultants to be. If your own scores are low, then you need to make your example more visible to your consultants. Model the behavior and customer service situations you want to see in your business.

3. *Evaluate how you use every fifteen minutes of your time this week at your business. Look for patterns where you get interrupted, where you are ineffective (because of your own choices and what you will do to change this going forward).*

4. *Decide who you will delegate the following activities to:*

   • Sending and Receiving Emails
   • Browsing Internet sites
   • Taking and Making Phone Calls
   • Errands (going to the bank, picking up supplies, going to the post office, etc.)
   • Bill paying
   • Going through the mail

5. *Choose to minimize the amount of time you spend in the following areas:*

   • Sending and Receiving Emails
   • Browsing Internet sites
   • Taking and Making Phone Calls

Here are eight additional questions for you to reflect on about your productivity:

1. What have you found is the best way to stay focused on the goals you've set for yourself and your business with all of the distractions you face?

2. What have you found is the best way to let your team members know that you are unavailable during parts of the day so you can focus on what you really need to implement in your business?

3. What do you do when you've experienced a day filled with distraction and you've gone home frustrated that you didn't get more done? How do you reset and refocus so you're able to get more done the next day (and get back on track with your goals)?

4. What has been your biggest distraction in your business and how have you learned to keep this under control?

5. What has been the biggest lesson you've learned about resistance and distraction and what you must do to beat it and stay on track with what *you* want to accomplish? What advice would you give to another entrepreneur who continually finds themselves distracted and what they can do to get back on track with their goals and agenda?

6. In what ways has distraction helped you manage your time and life better?

7. How do you beat the battle of procrastination to get more done in your business (specifically to focus on opportunities instead of problems)?

8. Describe an average day in your business and what processes you've put in place to help you and each of your team members stay on task to get more done. What areas for improvement do you see?

Here is an assessment for your productivity systems:

#	Rank yourself from 1-10 based on your current business behaviors.	1	2	3	4	5	6	7	8	9	10	Rank yourself from 1-10 based on your current business behaviors.
1	I often spend time each week looking for papers I need.											I waste no time looking for papers I need.
2	I waste time looking for electronic files I need (emails, attachments, etc).											I waste no time looking for electronic files I need (emails, attachments, etc).
3	I would be majorly stressed out if I were notified of an impending audit.											I would be totally calm if I were notified of an impending audit.
4	I don't have a system for managing articles/resources that come across my desk.											I have a system for managing articles/resources that come across my desk.
5	I have piles of papers I've accumulated all over my office. It is hard to find what I'm looking for.											I have a system for getting rid of outdated materials I no longer need (so they don't accumulate with time).
6	I don't plan my day and I just go from fire to fire dealing with whatever comes up.											I use a time planner / organizer (on paper, computer, or phone) effectively to stay on top of my appointments and deadlines.
7	I find myself finishing a lot of things last minute and am often late getting things done.											I have a system to manage work in progress (so I am not stuck trying to get it all done at the last minute).
8	I would hate for clients to see my office.											My office reflects the quality of service I provide in our business.
9	I don't feel in control of my time or what I do each day and am frustrated with where I am going.											My daily life is in control and reflects the quality of life I want to life.
10	I often catch myself doing things that I could be paying someone else to do for me so I could focus on my high priority activities.											I spend time on my highest value activities.
11	Our sales consultants and team members aren't very productive when things slow down in our business.											Our sales consultants and team members are very productive and fully effective.
12	I feel like I'm so busy at my business that I don't have time to do the things I want to do.											I have time to do the things I want to do.
13	I typically work 60+ hours per week.											I work less than 50 hours a week.

#	Rank yourself from 1-10 based on your current business behaviors.	1	2	3	4	5	6	7	8	9	10	Rank yourself from 1-10 based on your current business behaviors.
14	I wish I had more time to get everything done.											I have more time than I need to get things done.
15	I don't delegate much because I don't feel anyone can do things as well as I can.											I effectively delegate the details of my business ensuring I have time to focus *on* the business instead of just being *in* it.
16	I rarely exercise and spend time in front of the TV when not working. I find I don't spend much quality time with the people I care about.											I exercise regularly and spend quality time with the people I care about.
17	I am barely making ends meet and constantly stress about the next bill that needs to be paid.											I am putting aside funds regularly with which to become financially independent.
18	I don't have a daily personal success ritual.											I have daily well-being habits and I do them consistently. I have a daily personal success ritual.
19	My days get away from me and I feel my stress rise throughout the day.											My days are well planned and I never run on adrenaline.
20	I am constantly interrupted and find it very difficult to stay focused.											I have systems in place to prevent me from being interrupted and to help me stay focused.
21	My behaviors don't indicate that I understand the value of my time. I am often busy doing things that don't pay me my desired hourly rate.											I know the value of my time and don't do activities that don't pay me my desired hourly rate.
22	My list of things to do continually grows and I never feel like I get much done on it.											I have no more than six key items on my daily "to do" list each day.
23	I spend my peak performance hours each day on stress relieving activities instead of goal achieving activities.											I spend my peak performance hours each day on profit producing activities and opportunities.
24	I don't track my time and know where it goes. I rarely plan *before* I begin anything.											I track my time and spend time each day planning about how to best utilize my time *before* I begin.

#	Rank yourself from 1-10 based on your current business behaviors.	1	2	3	4	5	6	7	8	9	10	Rank yourself from 1-10 based on your current business behaviors.
25	I spend more than an hour a day online looking at Facebook or monitoring websites that don't help me achieve my goals.											I limit the amount of time I spend online each day looking at my favorite web sites (Facebook, favorite blogs and forums, etc.) to 30 minutes or less/day.
26	I am aware of my productivity kryptonite but still find myself being unproductive in those activities.											I am aware of my productivity kryptonite and have systems in place to help me stay on track.

Another way to look at this exercise is to score yourself with your personal productivity on the following report card.

Read the statement and then determine what grade you would give yourself.

Scoring Your Performance with Your Personal Productivity	Your Grade
1. I waste no time looking for papers I need.	
2. I waste no time looking for electronic files I need (emails, attachments, etc).	
3. I have a system for managing articles/resources that come across my desk.	
4. I have a system for getting rid of outdated materials I no longer need (so they don't accumulate with time).	
5. I use a time planner / organizer (on paper, computer, or phone) effectively to stay on top of my appointments and deadlines.	
6. I have a system to manage work in progress (so I am not stuck trying to get it all done at the last minute).	
7. My office reflects the quality of service we provide in our business.	
8. My daily life is in control and reflects the quality of life I want to live.	
9. I spend time on my highest value activities.	
10. Our sales consultants and team members are very productive and fully utilized.	
11. I have time to do the things I want to do.	

Scoring Your Performance with Your Personal Productivity	Your Grade
12. I work less than 50 hours a week.	
13. I have more time than I need to get things done.	
14. I effectively delegate the details of my business ensuring I have time to focus *on* the business instead of just being *in* it.	
15. I spend quality time with the people I care about.	
16. My days are well planned and I never run on adrenaline.	
17. I have systems in place to prevent me from being interrupted and to help me stay focused.	
18. I know the value of my time and don't do activities that don't pay me my desired hourly rate.	
19. I have no more than six key items on my daily "to do" list each day.	
20. I spend my peak performance hours each day on profit producing activities and opportunities.	
21. I track my time and know where it goes. I spend at least 14 minutes each day planning and thinking about how to best utilize my time *before* I begin.	
22. I limit the amount of time I spend online each day looking at my favorite web sites (Facebook, favorite blogs or forums, etc.) to 30 minutes or less/day.	
23. I am aware of my productivity kryptonite and have systems in place to help me stay on track.	
24. When was the last time you felt in control of your time? A = last week; B = two weeks ago; C = 3 weeks ago; D = a month or longer; F = I can't remember	

It would be a great idea to have each of your team take this quiz and report back to you on their own grades for their report card and how they can improve and use their time better in your business. I'll close this chapter with this great statement by author John C. Maxwell: "The secret of your success is determined by your daily agenda...You will never change your life until you change something you do daily." Make sure your productivity systems are influencing what you do daily by scheduling your priorities into time blocks with start and end times. If you don't, someone else will dictate your priorities for you and you won't accomplish the goals you've set for yourself.

Chapter 17

Staying on the Cutting Edge with Business Reinvention Systems

"To doubt everything or to believe everything are two equally convenient solutions; both dispense with the necessity of reflection."—Jules Henri Poincaré

In this chapter, I'd like to discuss how you evaluate the direction of your business so you can find concealed and unseen opportunities that others may not be able to see. Many businesses have very detailed and organized systems around how they track and control the flow of items that move through their business, yet they don't really take time to evaluate how well they plan the direction of where they are going. When a business first gets started and as it grows, mistakes here can lead you in directions that you might not have originally planned on going.

I'd like to help you analyze your systems around reinventing your business when challenges and unforeseen obstacles threaten to distract you from the direction you were going. Most people have a hard time seeing opportunities in their own business, especially when they find themselves in the midst of challenging times. It is much easier to be paralyzed and wonder what to do next without taking any action at all.

However, inaction won't help you move forward. An opportunity for re-invention may prove to be very beneficial in the long run when you feel stuck and aren't where you want or need to be. Since you may be dealing with your own set of challenges and crises in your business, I want to discuss in this chapter the topic of reinvention and what you can do going forward to prune your business back to have it grow to become what is best for you.

It is difficult to see opportunity in the midst of challenges, especially when those challenges force you to re-evaluate your business and what you are doing. Here are ten reasons why it is hard to re-invent yourself (even though it may be time or past time that changes were made).

1. You are used to seeing your business the same way all of the time so you overlook what is *really* there.
Looking at your business with a fresh perspective allows you to seeing things that perhaps you don't want to see or consider whether what you are doing is taking you in the right direction. When things have been the same way for a long time, this is particularly true. Sometimes it is impossible for you to see what others may already see because it has been a certain way for a long, long time.

When problems come up (as they undoubtedly will when you own your own business), you've got to take action. Live by Gandhi's mantra that "Action is my domain." Sometimes when you start, you are going the wrong direction. Making a mistake or experiencing a failure in a painful, public, and embarrassing way is not something anyone ever wants to have happen. Yet, it can help you re-evaluate and refocus on what matters most.

Walt Disney said: "While the worriers are worrying, the planners are planning, and the accountants are figuring out why we can't afford it, I'm busy getting it started." Action is key to success. If you want to succeed at anything, you've got to take action. These actions should be simultaneous, not sequential and anticipatory, not just reactive.

To succeed, you've got to be quick and agile on your feet. As you take actions, you may need to modify what you are doing, but be sure that you are taking steps in the right direction. There may be pain associated with change and adjustments, but in a long journey, it is best to get started as soon as possible.

I have a friend who is paralyzed by thinking. It is never easy for him to take action. He would much rather analyze and think about it some more before he does anything. As a result, he doesn't really do much. He is too worried about making an imperfect decision so he doesn't make one at all.

Making decisions and taking actions are so important. Actions that are hard and painful in the short term may be required and can be painful and embarrassing. Yet, some choices are not only obvious, but necessary when you choose to reinvent and rethink your business. You may even question what you've decided to do when you hear criticism from others.

Take for example the reinvention of movie characters. Remember when Daniel Craig was cast as the new James Bond in 2005? Some people were absolutely adamant that he was not the right choice. However, time has shown that he was a very effective casting choice and that has benefited the producers immensely. More recently, there was controversy over Ben Affleck being cast as Batman. The point I'm trying to make is that when you choose to reinvent yourself, there will always be those who question you, mock you, and try to tear you down.

You have to be comfortable with who you are. You have to be confident about your own skills and abilities even though you may not yet have the entire journey mapped out. However, when you are confident in your own skills and abilities and surround yourself with those who can help you make your goals and dreams happen, they *will* happen. Eventually, the naysayers will be proven wrong because of your decisions and your actions.

It can be a big challenge as an entrepreneur to look at things with a fresh perspective. It is so easy to see things how they have been. Many opportunities are overlooked because they aren't seen for what they are. It is easier to see what *is* instead of what *could be*.

To change this, you must look at your business from time to time with fresh eyes as though you weren't the owner and ask, how would you change it? In other words, if you were hired to be a consultant and come in and evaluate your business, what questions would you ask?

What advice would you give the owner if you were to objectively look at numbers (what is up, what is down, what is not improving)? Would you act on those recommendations if you felt they could help you improve things overall?

2. You are stuck with your own bias and think little can be done in a certain area or region.

Over the years, I've faced multiple challenges with managers and crises that have come up in business. With the benefit of hindsight, I've realized that I accepted some things that I didn't have to accept. It is amazing how freeing it can be to be objective about your business and have no biases. It is much easier to accept things that you don't have to accept.

If you are struggling with your own set of challenges, I would invite you to consider what would happen if that challenge didn't exist any more at all. If you think out of the box, many times you can come up with solutions because you aren't tied down by the bias you have about what you have done in the past or what you think you must do. I was once forced with an unpleasant and embarrassing reality about having to close a business. That decision opened up new possibilities that I didn't even realize were there because I had been completely closed off to them before. You may have to end something to begin something better.

Seth Godin explains this principle in his book *The Dip*. He says: "You and your organization have the power to change everything. To create remarkable products and services. To over deliver. To be the best in the world. How dare you squander that resource by spreading it too thin. How dare you settle for mediocre just because you're busy coping with too many things on your agenda, racing against the clock to get it all done. The lesson is simple: If you've got as much as you've got, use it. Use it to become the best in the world, to change the game, to set the agenda for everyone else. You can only do that by marshaling all of your resources to get through the biggest possible Dip. In order to get through that Dip, you'll need to quit everything else. If it's not going to put a dent in the world, quit. Right now. Quit and use that void to find the energy to assault the Dip that matters. Go ahead, make something happen. We're waiting!"—pp. 74-75.

In business, you must occasionally ask: What will happen if I stick with this in the long term?

When you fail (which <u>will</u> happen to you as an entrepreneur), it is hard to face the future seeing new opportunities. It is much easier to look to the past and see the failures. However, by failing, you're in good company. That perspective is invaluable. Evaluating what you've learned from the failures you experience can help you think about where you'll go next and will propel you forward. If you don't, you'll be passed up by those who do.

Henry Ford once remarked: "Anyone who stops learning is old, whether at twenty or eighty." I remember reading a statement about Bill Gates that came out when he built a home in 1992 that his library had 14,000 books. Who knows if he has read them all? I'll bet that he has read a vast majority of them. There is a fascinating connection in the lives of successful business leaders I've studied and the books they read.

One of the best statements I've ever read about the importance of continuous learning and education and the perspective it will give you is this one I read by Brian Tracy soon after I graduated from college and first got into selling. He said:

"Some things in life are optional, and some things in life are mandatory. Taking your next vacation to the Caribbean is optional. Building a personal library and becoming an excellent reader is mandatory. It is no longer something you can choose to do or not do. It is absolutely essential and indispensable for your success. A great many people do not read very much. Fifty-eight percent of adult Americans never read a nonfiction book from cover to cover after they finish school. The average American reads less than one book per year. In fact, according to a Gallup study of the most successful men and women in America, reading one nonfiction book per month will put you into the top 1 percent of living Americans. It takes regular, persistent reading and studying for you to improve, to move to the front of your field. It is not optional.

"One of the best tests for compatibility with your work is your desire to read and learn more about it. If you are doing the job that is right for you, you will naturally be eager to read everything that you can possibly find about your field. You will want to get better and better. You will be hungry for new knowledge. You will be determined to become excellent. And every single bit of new information motivates and stimulates you and makes you excited about learning even more. However, if you are in the wrong field, you will look upon reading about it as drudgery. If the reading and studying is a required condition of your job or profession, you will do it, but only under duress. You will want to get it over with, like a visit to the dentist. If, for any reason, you are not eager to learn more about what you are doing, it could very well be that you are wasting your time and your life in the wrong field.

"In one 22-year study of self-made millionaires, the researchers found that one of the common characteristics of those special men and women who went from rags to riches was that they were absolutely fascinated by their work. They didn't think so much about making a lot of money. They were more concerned about becoming better and better at what they did. Their work absorbed them completely. In almost no time at all, because of their commitment to reading and self-development, they were paid more and more. And once they reached a high level of income, their fascination with their work still continued. Instead of drawing extra money from their business and spending it frivolously, they reinvested it in themselves and in their career. As a result, they became more and more proficient and wealthier and wealthier. Then, one day, they opened their eyes, looked around and found that they were worth more than $1 million. And the continuous learning, the nonstop reading, was the key ingredient."

He continues:
"If you want to get ahead, you must read things that give you new ideas and insights, not merely things that confirm what you already know. Becoming a proficient and persistent reader may not be easy to do so, but it's certainly possible. The future does belong to the competent. Those who know more will always win out over those who know less. The more you read, the better you get. The more you learn, the easier it is for you to learn. And the more you challenge your mind, the smarter you get." --http://www.personal-development.com/brian-tracy-articles/discipline-of-reading.htm

Jim Rohn once said:
"Ignorance is not bliss. Ignorance is poverty. Ignorance is devastation. Ignorance is tragedy. Ignorance is illness. It all stems from ignorance."

Read and think more. Schedule time to do this. Have the discipline to make this an important system in your business and your life. If you aren't reading and learning something new each day, resolve today that you will begin. Even if you feel like you are not a very good reader, you can learn. There is a world of information and opportunity that awaits you when you decide to learn and think more.

3. You don't pay attention or listen to what others in different industries are doing.
In his book *Smart Retail*, author Richard Hammond offers the following suggestions about improvement and ways you can force yourself to

think differently about your business by how you look at what others are doing. He offers the following list:

- "Read stuff
- Get involved in the business community – join your street or shopping centre advisory committee or the chamber of commerce
- Talk to your business neighbors
- Ask people about your management style (and listen openly when they tell you)
- Learn from those below you as well as above you
- Seek out examples of great retailers and learn from them
- Sign up to every Internet resource you can find—here are three corkers for a start-off (in the retail niche): www.theretailbulletin.com, www.nrf.com and the fashion-biased but still very useful www.racked.com. Equally, there are loads of great Twitter feeds...
- Get a subscription to Retail Week and learn to read between the lines (Why did so and so make that choice? Why is X thriving? Why is Y on its uppers?)
- What things do you do outside of work that might be useful inside?
- Make an honest list of your strengths
- Then one of your weaknesses
- Go on courses
- Sign up to every training and seminar resource you can initially—the more you go on the better you will become at recognizing which ones are going to be truly useful in the future
- Set life goals and then yearly goals for yourself—what do these goals tell you about the areas in which you will need to concentrate to make personal improvements?
- Listen to people more than talk to people
- Open your eyes!
- Go shopping more often—do things your customers do
- Read the trade press
- Learn from competitors
- Listen from people outside your sector
- Maintain your standards
- Get rid of the 'yes' men and surround yourself with people who challenge and inspire you

- Appoint an honest and strong assistant manager—they will soon let you know where you have room for improvement
- Improve the balance of your life: you look after shops— shopping is fun, try to see it more that way." –pp. 83-84.

You may not be a retailer, or have any interest in ever having a retail business. But, there are things that retailers are dealing with now that may very well happen in your industry in the future. Paying attention to what happens in retail or in other in other industries will give you a wide array of input and ideas into your business.

Hammond makes this observation about the importance of looking at others for ideas. He says:
"Ideas are the fuel for organizations. What you do with those ideas, how you convert them into action and improvements, is what then makes the organization grow and prosper. Space for improvement can be readily found in all areas...All retailers can benefit from a culture of everyday performance improvement but few try to."—pp. 75.

4. Your own experience is limited. You can only see what you observe. If you are going to see more opportunity, you've got to look for ideas and seek the input of others who can help you recycle, transfer and apply ideas from other businesses or industries to your business.
A great example of a brilliant businessman who looked beyond his challenges and adversity is that of Soichiro Honda. He was born in Japan on November 17, 1906. He spent his early childhood helping his father, Gihei, a blacksmith, with his bicycle repair business. At the time his mother, Mika, was a weaver. At 15, without any formal education, Honda left home and headed to Tokyo to look for work. He obtained an apprenticeship at a garage in 1922, and after some hesitation over his employment, he stayed for six years, working as a car mechanic before returning home to start his own auto repair business in 1928 at the age of 22.

In 1937 Honda began producing piston rings for small engines, which led to manufacturing small engines to be used in motorcycles. "He did this during the war until a bomb crippled his factory and then in 1945 an earthquake destroyed it completely." –*Profiles of Genius*, p. 184.

Can you imagine how you would respond if your business was bombed and then destroyed by an earthquake a few years later? Would you persist and keep on going or would you give up?

"Honda was dismayed, sold out, and went into semi-retirement. His entry into the motorcycle market occurred quite by accident. Honda was faced with no gas for his car in 1946, so this visionary took one of the many surplus motors left by the GIs and attached it to his bike for transportation. The engine was fueled by kerosene. This simple but elegant solution to a fundamental problem was Honda's way. His friends asked him to make them one of his motorbikes. After a dozen such requests, it occurred to the ever-innovative Honda that there must be a larger market for such a machine. He incorporated Honda Motor Company in 1948 with a charter to design and build motorbikes." – *Profiles of Genius*, p. 184.

"Honda launched his company into the crowded motorcycle industry in the early fifties and within five years had successfully eliminated 250 competitors in that industry (50 were Japanese). His 'Dream' machine, introduced in 1950, was a realization of his childhood fantasy of building a better machine....[His] unique products, coupled with an inspirational advertising promotion ("You Meet the Nicest People on a Honda"), made Honda an instant success and changed this one-time stagnant industry. By 1963, Honda had become the dominant force in the motorcycle business in virtually every country of the world, leaving Harley-Davidson and the Italian bike companies in the dust." –*Profiles of Genius*, p. 183.

"Honda's excellent engineering and clever marketing resulted in Honda motorcycles out-selling Triumph and Harley-Davidson in their respective home markets. In 1959 Honda Motorcycles opened its first dealership in the United States.

"Honda remained president until his retirement in 1973, stayed on as director, and was appointed "supreme adviser" in 1983. His legendary status was such that *People* magazine placed him on their"25 Most Intriguing People of the Year" list for 1980, dubbing him "the Japanese Henry Ford." In retirement Honda busied himself with work connected with the Honda Foundation. He died in 1991 from liver failure." -- http://en.wikipedia.org/wiki/Soichiro_Honda

Honda took a series of problems he had and turned them into opportunities because he looked beyond his own experience. You and I must do this as well if we are going to grow our businesses.

5. You may have skills registering at a "10" level, but you are stuck in a "1" or "2" opportunity. This situation will cause you to do less and less over time because of discouragement. When you are discouraged, you personalize failure, you identify it as pervasive in other areas of your life, and finally you accept failure as permanent. As a result, you don't take actions that could help lift you out of the challenges in which you find yourself. Constantly be learning new skills and look for new opportunities where your skills can be utilized.

6. You are a generalist and are ignoring niche/target marketing. Be sure your message matches your market. Focus on areas where you can be the very best in your market niche.

7. You don't have any offering for top 20% of premium price clients in your niche who are able and willing to spend more to get what they want. Pay attention to and market to more affluent clientele.

8. You are used to doing things exactly the same way as you've always done them. When you make mistakes and fail, you've still got to believe in yourself.
Jeff Bezos, the founder of Amazon.com said that your belief in yourself is so important in any new business operation (especially where you're doing something new that hasn't been done before) and that three things are required to succeed:
1) "You must be willing to fail
2) You have to be willing to think long-term
3) You have to be willing to be misunderstood for long periods of time."
–*Success*, August 2011, p. 50.

Bezos also warned his team at meetings during the dot-com bubble from 1995 to 2000 that you can't allow yourself to feel '30 percent smarter this month because the stock price is up 30 percent because you'll feel 30 percent dumber when it declines.' –*Success*, August 2011, p. 50.

Amazon.com was once referred to as Amazon.bomb. Bezos overcame tough obstacles through the ability to sell as well. His belief in what he was doing and his focus on business metrics has allowed him to create a massive company that continues to affect nearly every industry the world over.

Bezos started his business when he observed that usage on the Internet was growing at a 2300 percent increase a year. He quit his promising job and typed a business plan in his car while his wife drove to Seattle. He told his original investors that there was a 70 percent chance they would lose their entire investment. His parents signed on for $300,000, a substantial portion of their life savings. His mother said, "We weren't betting on the Internet. We were betting on Jeff." Today, as six percent owners of Amazon.com, Jeff's parents are billionaires.

I think the same thing could be said of you. You have clients who believe in you and are betting on your success. There are prospects out there who need what you offer and who will be so grateful when they get in touch with you, hear your message, and discover the benefits of your offering. I hope you have the kind of belief that allows you to push forward even in tough times and that you passion sustains you when things are tough. In the midst of failures and adversity I've experienced, there have been those who have reached out and offered their support and their help. This has been very meaningful to me. When you have failures and disappointments, it can be easy to turn inward and miss the opportunities available to you. Keep going. Things will get better.

Long-term success is about belief, passion, and selling more. You will have failures along the way. It doesn't matter if you are just starting a small boutique or a large business. If you don't believe in yourself and have passion to get you through the tough times, you won't. When you struggle, you can learn to sell your way through difficulty. One of the big lessons I've learned through adversity is that you've got persist in what you start instead of beginning lots of little projects while actually implementing very few of them. If you get to the point where you have too many things going on, it is a good idea to simplify your life and refocus on what is most important.

George Wright, the marketer behind the BlendTec videos campaigns said this in a recent interview about the importance of belief: "I believed in it. I knew it was going to work. When I saw the first videos I knew it. Although I thought it might take years to get traction. But the technology proved me wrong and it took a week to get a million views on YouTube. Powerful tools are there for free. If you try them they will work for you. However, you have to change the way you think from a traditional advertiser or marketer to make it work." –Jim Kukral, *Attention!*, p. 186.

Tom Monaghan, the founder of Domino's once said of himself of his early years in business: "'I was shy but I had a lot of self-confidence.' He told his wife on their engagement, 'I am going to be a millionaire by the time I am thirty,' and he meant it." --*Profiles of Genius*, p. 102. He actually accomplished the goal when he was thirty nine in 1976.

Marie Curie, the winner of Nobel prizes in Physics and Chemistry said: "Life is not easy for any of us. But what of that? We must have perseverance and, above all, confidence in ourselves. We must believe that we are gifted for something, and that this thing, at whatever cost, must be attained."

People who achieve their dreams experience a lot of failures on their way to success, but they don't let their failures get the better of them. They get knocked down and get back up again. They think of themselves as successful—even when things go wrong.

Jim Rohn said: "How long should you try? Until."

I've got confidence that you can do it. I believe in you. I believe in myself. I believe that you are making a great difference to the clients you serve in your market area. Get good at selling and you'll be able to raise yourself out of any difficulty you may experience. As George Foreman once told me, "Learn to sell and you will never starve."

9. Nothing is being done to address problems and complaints of clients. This happens because you get stuck in the status quo.
Too often, we accept what is in front of us instead of looking for new opportunities to rise above challenges. When you notice trends where clients and prospects are complaining, look for ways in which you can help these individuals overcome their challenges and find less stress and more fulfillment as they benefit from your products and services.

10. You have assets that remain un- or under-utilized.
Make a list of your current assets often and look for ways you can exploit them to help your business reach its goals.

Here are several examples of assets that you have. Take time to evaluate these from time to time as part of your system so you can look for ways you better utilize the assets you have.

- Your prospect and customer lists that you can market to again to have them return and buy an additional product from you.
- Your marketing funnel / process (making sure prospects and clients aren't dropping through the cracks) – The better your follow up, the better utilized and valuable this asset is for you.
- Your access and influence with other well-known professionals in your area. Are you networking with those that can help you build your business?
- Your status as an authority figure, celebrity specialist. It is hard to break free from being a commodity when you are a generalist.
- Your sales consultants and staff. The better trained, the more valuable they are in helping you bring in new and additional business. Conversely, poorly trained employees can quickly destroy your business.
- Your clients (who have already purchased from you). One way your clients can be considered an asset is by having other businesses that want access to these individuals have to pay for the privilege to do so. An example of this would be an affiliate relationship with another business who pays you a percentage of sales based on your recommendation.
- Your knowledge about your business and industry that others could benefit from. You can teach others how to profit and benefit from what you know and build your own audience with books, special reports, conferences, podcasts, etc.
- Your brand identity and all of your intellectual property (business name, brand identity, logo, etc.) It is amazing how valuable of an asset this can be over time if a business is built properly.
- Your inventory (time, product, property, etc.) - How well are you turning your inventory for a profit? Time alone won't make an asset more valuable. For example, some inventory in a grocery store will go bad in a short period of time. Ensure your future success by building inventory assets that will increase in value.

Before we talk about some specific steps you can take to reinvent your business, I want to just talk about one other really important idea. When you make mistakes and you have to reinvent your business, it is easy to get angry at yourself for why you are in the situation you are. It can be difficult to balance reality about where you are with optimism about where you are going in the future.

I think it is really important that you are working everyday on something that will help you get to where you are going. In other words, it is easy to be consumed with problems and allow a crisis to completely take over your life. However, you also need to work on what you can actually affect and get done. Sometimes things are out of your control. When something doesn't go like you think it should, you can choose to be mad about it, be consumed by it, or you can work and move forward focusing on what you do have and not beat yourself up about the mistakes and the failures you've had.

It is okay to have the emotions of grief, anger and frustration about any crisis that has happened. Yet, remember, we are not our mistakes. We have to separate who we are from the situations we are in. This does not mean that we abdicate responsibility. We have to do what needs to be done.

That may mean scheduling out time in your block schedule everyday where you only work on what can be done to generate more revenue for your business. The point is that you must work on what only you can do and delegate the rest to others. At some point you will have to reinvent your business. It is just a matter of time. Having a system to periodically evaluate what is working and what is not is a great way to ensure that you are reinventing your business and not waking up to discover that your market has shifted, leaving you behind.

Jason Jennings author of *The Reinventors* makes this startling assertion: "Your job as you know it and your business as it is currently run will eventually change. The only chance any of us have for prosperity is to constantly reimagine, rethink, and reinvent everything we do and how we do it in order to remain relevant. We must all become reinventors, and we'd better do it quickly. Compare the list of the top twenty-five companies in the Fortune 500 in the year 2000 and the year 2010. The results are shocking. Sixteen of the top twenty-five companies fell off their lofty perches in the span of only ten years. That's almost two-thirds! Dig a little deeper and you'll find that since the Fortune 500 list was first published in 1955 more than 90 percent of the companies on it have been mopped up by smaller rivals, gone bankrupt, shrunk so small that they have become inconsequential, or simply closed their doors.

These companies were once the largest and most stable businesses in the nation....All of these companies failed to constantly evolve, change, grow, and reinvent themselves, and eventually they were kicked to the curb."

He continues:
"Today, a combination of stagnant Western markets, former third world nations embracing technology and becoming manufacturing powerhouses with middle classes larger than that of the U.S., technology that makes everything increasingly transparent, and customers who believe that they can get exactly what they want when they want it at a price they're willing to pay all add up to a game-changing business environment. Anyone who thinks that they'll get a free pass and that they don't have to constantly reinvent their business has their head in the sand." –pp. 3-4.

I've met and talked with a lot of entrepreneurs who have their heads in the sand. They've seen their businesses shrink or stay even with past years (which weren't great to begin with) yet they're hopeful and optimistic that things will get better even though they aren't changing anything. In many cases, they're going back to what they used to do instead of figuring out what it takes to reinvent themselves and succeed in today's new economy.

I hope you'll take this system of your business seriously. The 2010 IBM Global CEO Study showed why this is so important. According to this study, 67 percent of worldwide CEOs think their current business model is only sustainable for another three years, while another 31 percent believe their current financial model might have as long as five years. In other words, 98% of global CEOs believe that their current business models are ultimately unsustainable. This means that your business, my business, and all of these businesses are going to need to undergo some form of reinvention.

Jason Jennings says: "Good business is about making sure you're providing something of value to someone willing to pay you enough to make it worth your while. Reinventors make certain their *continually* providing something of value to someone willing to pay them enough to make it worthwhile." –p. 7.

In other words, there is no time to rest on your laurels when you arrive at any destination. You've got to be ready to move to the next stage and learn the skills necessary to continually grow your business in an environment of rapid change. Most business owners would rather make excuses than figure out how to change and get better.

So, how do you go about reinventing yourself? Here are eight steps to doing this for your business according to Jennings in his book, *The Reinventors*, which I highly recommend you read and study.

1. Let go.
In order to see your business differently, you've got to let go of your previously conceived notions. Most people have a really hard time doing this.

Jennings shares three examples of the difficulty of letting go.
1) Toyota vs. Ford – Toyota invited Ford to see one of their new manufacturing plants in Japan. Their engineers went, but doubted they had really seen a manufacturing plant. In their words, the demonstration was "staged like a movie." In reality, Ford's engineers missed what they should have seen because they had in their minds what a manufacturing plant should be. They missed that Toyota had figured out a way to streamline production and completely reinvent how cars were manufactured.
2) Smoke jumpers holding on too long to their equipment. "Smoke jumpers are highly trained, highly evolved elite firefighters who parachute into dangerous terrain to put out wildfires." More than 50 years ago, "fifteen of the bravest smoke jumpers were battling in a deep canyon when suddenly the inferno turned and raced right at them. The men tried to retreat, scrambling up the steep walls to get away. Tragically, twelve souls were lost; only three were able to escape. The testimony of the three survivors and a review of the scene revealed a surprising finding. Large poleaxes, shovels and twelve heavy backpacks, in all some 115 pounds per man of professional gear, were on the ground hundreds of yards from where the smoke jumpers first turned from fighting the wildfire to race away. Only three dropped their gear early; the rest couldn't let it go until it was too late."—p. 34.
Jenning says: "When we've got something we want in our tightly clenched hands, we'll resist like hell before letting go."—p. 35.

3) Monkeys trapped by refusing to let go of the nuts inside the gourd they have and getting captured as a result. The monkeys could avoid capture by simply letting go, but their greed prevents them from doing so.

According to Jennings there are eight reinvention killers that prevent you from changing yourself and your business to adapt with the changing times. I've included his comments followed by mine in italics. The eight reinvention killers you need to let go of are:

1) **Yesterday's breadwinners.**
   Jennings says: "Every product or service has a natural life cycle that begins with an introduction, followed by growth, maturity, and inevitably a decline as it becomes yesterday's breadwinner. There are no exceptions."

   The example everyone is familiar with that Jennings discusses is that of Kodak. He says: "Almost thirty years ago the leadership of Eastman Kodak was warned by its own engineers that one day digital photography would replace film. The company couldn't let go and continued unprofitably producing and selling film while enduring countless rounds of layoffs and downsizing, managing to stay alive only by the benefit of proceeds from lawsuits against other companies. It couldn't let go of a legacy product."—p. 36.
   Other examples include:
   - Universal Music Group, BMG, and EMI who refused to let go of the old traditional music business model (instead being overtaken by Apple and the iTunes store)
   - Blockbuster being overtaken by Redbox and Netflix
   - AOL couldn't let go of dial up access (went from 30 million customers to a few million) – their service became irrelevant with high speed internet service
   - Sony CEO Sir Howard Stringer once observed: "Great companies [inevitably] develop a rowboat mentality. They are always looking behind to past successes with awe and admiration as they row into the future." –pp. 36-38.

   It is hard for many entrepreneurs to let go of a product that has performed well for them in the past (even though they see the writing on the wall). For example in the retail business today, there are many competitors including Internet vendors and Chinese manufacturers who are going straight to the end user customer. This cuts out the retail business which has a lot bigger overhead. It would seem that entrepreneurs would be able to make better choices about letting go of products that are no longer selling or working—but many find it very hard to let go of what they see as their legacy to provide. As a result, they frequently hold onto a product offering for too long which ends up causing decline and destruction. If a product isn't producing for you, you've got to let it go to find a better one that will.

Now is the time to figure this out for your business by asking yourself the following questions:

- What's selling now and where do the trends seem to be heading?
- What product will give me the greatest visibility, exclusivity and margin?
- What is needed to meet the demands of the marketplace?
- How often am I taking time to monitor what's selling and why?
- What reports am I looking at and what are they telling me about what's selling and what's not?
- What are of my business is selling best?
- What area of my business is not selling as much as it used to? Could / should I shrink the amount of time, space, or effort devoted to this area?
- What opportunities are available to me?

Staying on top of your business and what is selling is so critical. One of the biggest mistakes you can make is to not evaluate what has happened at your business and figure out new ways to make improvements. Work in this area can be tedious, but it is a critical component of understanding what has made your business work and projecting where you will be in the future. Relying on yesterday's breadwinners for too long is a certain recipe for slow decay and death.

Do you know where your customers are coming from now? And how that compares with where they used to come from? What changes are you making as a result?

Jennings says: "Recently it was revealed that American Express is now able to forecast with eerie accuracy (based on customers' spending habits and where and what they're charging on their credit cards) which of its members will file for divorce within the next twelve months. You can and should know as much about your customers. Given how inexpensive technology and analytics have become, it's inexcusable for any business not to know every customer—who's returning, who's new, their purchasing habits, the gross margin and profits they generate, those things they're buying more of, those they're purchasing less of, and if you are meeting or exceeding their expectations. If you lay that kind of analysis over every individual product or service you offer, you'll be able to quickly see what's winning, what's losing, where everything stands, and when it's time to go." –p. 38.

2) **Ego.**
No one wants to admit what they don't know or what goes counter to what they've already decided in the past. When you are in charge, it is easy to think you have all of the answers or that your answer is the best one. To succeed at reinventing your business means that you have to be humble and recognize that you don't have all of the answers. Pushing for what you want can alienate you from others and can cause you to reject new knowledge because it contradicts your past beliefs.
Jennings gives two great questions to know if you are making decisions based on what's right for your company or whether you're making them to satisfy your ego. These are:
- "Is it all about you, or are you truly doing what you do for the interests and greater good of the organization?"
- "Am I doing this for my need to be the center of attention or because it's in the long-term beneficial interests of the company?" –p. 41.

Jennings quotes Mel Haught, CEO of Pella Corporation, which reinvents five hundred manufacturing processes and operating systems every year as saying: "There are three beliefs common to people with strong egos that they must constantly work to let go of: that they're the smartest people in the room, that the goal is to be perfect, and that they're too busy for dumb questions. Any boss who has to be the smartest person in the room hijacks the dialog, signaling 'correct' comments and conclusions that stifle good ideas. Perfectionism opens the door to doing nothing while committees study a strategy to death." –p. 41.

I had a boss whose ego got in the growth of the company. His attitude stifled any kind of creative approach to new problems and it led to the eventual death of the company. I learned a lot about what not to do in a company by watching him and his leadership style. All of us have to watch our egos. We've got to let go of what we think and what we know for the better good of our businesses.

3) Same Old, Same Old.

Oren Hatari is quoted as saying that "If it ain't broke, don't fix it is a slogan for the complacent, the arrogant, or the scared." The problem with this statement is that by the time you figure out it's broken, it's been broken for a long time and may not be repairable. Jennings says: "The net effect of not challenging or changing anything until it's obviously broken is that a culture is created in which workers and managers become firefighters instead of proactive change agents."

In other words, if you're always putting out fires, you don't have to proactively work on opportunities that could yield better results for you and your business. It is so easy to get caught up in a routine and breaking yourself out of that routine is very difficult. Set a goal this week to spend 20 minutes every day thinking about opportunities you may have been neglecting in your business. This may need to be away from your business, but you should do it so that you can get away from your normal routine and figure out what you should be working on, instead of which fires you should be putting out.

4) Conventional wisdom.

Following conventional wisdom will yield a conventional result. You have to be willing to expose yourself to and embrace new ideas to break free of conventional restraints. Most people aren't even aware of other ideas, much less taking time to embrace them. For example, I've been studying several of top retailers in the country who are growing right now and studying what they are doing different that is causing them such great growth. Among these companies are Hobby Lobby and Nordstrom. Each of the companies who are experiencing rapid growth now sell different products, but I've discovered some great new by studying what they're doing that is different. I'll share some of these lessons in upcoming podcast episodes. Most aren't even taking the time to study what other businesses are doing, much less implement these ideas into their businesses.

Jennings says that two questions you should ask yourself frequently are:

- "Why do we do it this way?
- Isn't there a better way to go about doing this?" –p. 47.

5) Entitlement

Jennings says: "Few things stand in the way of radical change and reinvention as much as a sense of entitlement. It's not the sense of entitlement shared by spoiled rich kids. Instead it's the misguided and arrogant belief shared by so many business owners and executives that their business has a right to continue to exist and do well simply by virtue of either being in business or having been successful at some point. There's no letting go of a sense of entitlement. People who have it are incapable of letting go of anything. They'll spend all of their time pointing their fingers at people they think should be doing it for them. People with a sense of entitlement have no place in a leadership position in business. Let go of them.

Several years ago, I had to fire a manager at one of my businesses. It was a hard decision, but it had to be done because I couldn't rely on what she was doing a year ago, or three years ago. What matters is what you are doing now. You've got to be able to let go of this kind of philosophy. Excuses that stem from entitlement are the worst kind because they are the easiest kind to believe and more importantly they don't help you get closer to reaching your goal.

Grant Cardone makes this point in his book *The 10 X Rule*: "...Ask yourself, will any of [your] excuses ever improve your condition? I doubt it. So why, then, do so many people make them so often? Does it even matter? An excuse is just an alteration of reality; nothing about it will move you to a better situation." –p. 156.

It is easy to whine and complain about what you don't have or feel like you should have. But, as Cardone says, excuses or a sense of entitlement don't get you any closer to improving your situation or helping your business reach its goals. You've got to buckle down and remember that "Nothing happens to you; it happens because of you."

6) Greed

The worst manifestation of greed in my opinion is wanting something for nothing. In order to succeed in your business and in life, you've got to let go of this philosophy. It takes work to implement what works in business. You can't just assume because you know something that it is going to be a part of your business. You've got to work hard to systematize what you know so the right things are done, no matter what. To be a success, you've got to embrace reinvention as a habit and let go of greed.

7) Short-timers

Jennings says:

"The term short-timer refers to someone who is planning on leaving but is still on the job. Predictably, nobody counts on much actual work or productivity from these people, because their heads and interests are elsewhere and they've already emotionally checked out."

He continues:

"No organization deserves to have short-timers on the job paying scant attention to detail, possessing bad attitudes, and infecting others with what they have, getting them to fantasize or think about leaving. Short-timers should immediately leave of their own volition or be very quickly shown the door. Unless there are extenuating circumstances, it's good policy that when it's time for those people to move on they do so immediately." –pp. 49-50.

How many employees do you have working for you at your business who are just waiting there until they can get a different (or better in their opinion) job?

When I have discovered employees who aren't happy for one reason or another, I know I have to make a decision. Leaving these kinds of employees in your business is poison and will affect other employees.

Shortly before I fired that manager, three of our employees left over a period of a month. Two more followed shortly after that because I had to let them go. I ended up having to fire the two who left because it was infecting the entire attitude of the staff. You can't afford to have short-timers on your staff who are just biding their time until they get another job. They will coast through the motions and will annoy any "A" players you have on your team. You can't afford to hold onto these employees one more day. If you have any members of your staff who are short-timers, who have informed you that they are leaving to a different job in a month or two, you will be better off to let them on their way now than to hold onto the poison that comes from letting them stay on and infect the members of your team. Otherwise, you are in for a major situation where you will have to hire new members of your staff. It didn't make me happy to lose five employees so quickly. I found out when I fired my manager that she hadn't worked to bring up leaders behind her, and so I really started over and it took me several months rehire and retrain our team. Take it from me, this is one way to reinvent your business, but it isn't one that I would recommend because it is very time consuming and painful.

8) **Risk averse**

Jennings says:

"Being afraid of taking a chance is common....It's irrational to be paralyzed by the fear of risk taking....It's [often] a matter of getting a checkup from the neck up. The only guarantee in business is if you do nothing, nothing will happen. Also, as the school of hard knocks teaches, most good strategy is made by doing. Once you've figured out how you're going to deal with the reinvention killers in your life and business, it will be time to pick up a destination and let the radical change begin." –pp. 51-53.

> *Here are five questions for you to consider:*
> *What decisions are you postponing because of fear?*
> *Are you hoarding cash right now instead of looking for opportunities to grow your business?*
> *What is it that you fear most right now?*
> *Will waiting make it better?*
> *Will doing nothing help you get what you want?*

These eight reinvention killers may be holding you back now at this stage in your business. Too many entrepreneurs are risk averse when they should be considering what they are actually going to do. Standing still and doing nothing is not a great business strategy. You'll be passed up for sure by those who are faster and who are less risk averse to moving ahead now.

2. Pick the destination. Do you know where your business is going?

Jennings says this about the importance of the leader being able to pick and see the destination. He says:

"Pat Hassey, who retired in May 2011 as CEO of Allegheny Technologies, is average height but still stands head and shoulders above most other CEOs in the Fortune 1000. He reinvented his company, taking a confused victim of the commoditization of metals manufacturing on the edge of bankruptcy and helping it become one of the nine best performing publicly traded companies from 2001 to 2008. Hassey told me how he made that happen: 'My main job is one thing...to be the destination expert. I have to be able to see through the fog, see far enough to connect the dots between near and far, and let everybody know where we are going. And people don't want to wait forever to find out the destination.'"

He continues:
"Not having a clear destination means never knowing the steps you need to take to get to where you want to go, never knowing if you've arrived or if you've achieved what you set out to accomplish. But if you have your destination in sight, those things that need to be reinvented will become obvious...The destination is partly what the organization does and where it is going, but it also addresses why the organization is headed where they are." –pp. 59-60.

Jennings makes this statement:
"How do you land on a bright idea that's ahead of what your customer thinks he or she needs or wants? One way is to follow the lead of Ted Taylor."

"Ted Taylor was the son-in-law of pioneer Salinas, California, produce grower and reinventor Bruce Church. In 1926 Church became famous for using ice to keep his lettuce crisp as it traveled by rail from California to Maine, creating a national business for himself. (He's the guy responsible for 'iceberg' lettuce.) Ted followed in his father-in-law's footsteps by using a recipe of nitrogen, oxygen, and carbon dioxide in chilled railcars to extend freshness even longer. But Taylor's deepest desire was to get his family business out of the commodity marketplace altogether. In those days growers squeezed a paltry one or two cents' profit out of every head of lettuce. Taylor invented a way to sell that same head of lettuce for five times more, making considerably more money."

"He washed it, chopped, it, mixed in some shredded carrots or other kinds of greens, and put it all in a high-tech twelve-ounce bag that would keep everything delicious for weeks instead of days. Families got healthy salad, ready to eat; stores got a more profitable, more popular item while cutting down on spoiled produce; and Taylor reinvented his company as a six-hundred-million-dollar player, in the process creating a brand-new business category, selling salad instead of just lettuce."

"What Taylor did was first written about as a best practice back at the turn of the twentieth century. It was called the Law of the Situation. A window shade manufacturer was advised by the first female business consultant, 'Don't look at your business as being a maker and installer of wooden blinds. See yourself through your client's eyes. You are actually in the lighting control business.'" –pp. 71-72.

What lessons can you learn from Ted Taylor? Here are a few:
- Get out of the commodities business. Look for ways to dress up what you sell to make it more unique and meaningful to your clients.
- Always be looking for ways you can spruce up what you offer so you can make it more unique and more profitable. People are busy today—provide more done-for-you services so they can spend more time doing what they want to do or relaxing (and let them know that you are the one that is making it so easy for them). Taylor took the step of preparation out of making salad for families and charged a premium for doing so. Busy shoppers could now save time because of this added convenience and were willing to pay for it.
- Taylor invented a way to reduce spoiled produce to extend freshness. This made the businesses that bought his salad excited to buy his product because he reduced their inventory turnover rates while increasing their profitability.

Remember, you are in charge of the destination where you want to end up. Not taking time to think about your end destination ensures that you'll float along with every other business and end up being mediocre instead of rising above the pack. Focus on providing something different and truly amazing that will cause clients to brag about you and the experience they've had when they've worked with you.

3. Make lots of small bets instead of one big bet.
Jason Jennings says:

"People are 120 times more likely to die by being hit by lightning and twelve hundred times more likely to die from a bee sting or snakebite than to win the lottery, but they still line up to buy lottery tickets. While its one thing to occasionally wager a dollar on nearly impossible odds, it would be insane to sell your house and cash in your life savings to place a single bet on impossible odds, but that's what many people in business routinely do."

He continues:
"Businesses that do the best job of constant radical change and reinvention simply don't get blinded by the fairy tales of the biggest bets generating the biggest paydays. They realize that successful strategy is discovered by doing, and that doing has to be learned from making lots of small bets." –p. 81.

Dot Foods is an example of a business that Jennings highlights that has done an amazing job of making lots of small bets on little opportunities that they saw could pay off down the road. Current chairman John Tracy says: "When the recession hit we immediately started investing even more money in more initiatives. We promoted a bunch of people who we thought had a lot of potential and gave them each some money and some people and started immediately chasing new opportunities and making some small bets we thought could become big parts of our business down the road."

Those opportunities included working in the health and beauty business with their supermarket customers, the cheese business, and the beef and pork business. In each case, they talked with their customers and found opportunities where they could expand and provide better options to their customers and others who weren't yet their customers. Tracy says that "Innovation and constant change got us to where we are and are still what drives the business."

Jennings cautions that you should only take on as many small bets as can "adequately be handled without disrupting the core business or putting it at risk." He gives the following criteria when making your small bets:
- "Don't plan on only hitting home runs.
- Make as many small bets as you have people responsible for making them happen and sufficient financial resources to maximize the odds of success. If there aren't enough resources to give the small

bet a chance, you'll never know if it might have worked out or been a possible home run.
- Make as many small bets as you're able with enough time available to analyze and learn from each.
- Have some general backup ideas in mind, but don't let the backup plan be carved in stone." –pp. 88-89.

Your team members will be more excited about showing up for work and being a part of your vision and your team when they see little things happening that signal that good growth and change is happening.

4. The right people are your only resource. Do you have the right people on your team?

Jennings says:

"Companies committed to constant radical change and growth recruit and retain workers who exhibit the following six traits:
1) Basic smarts and eager lifelong learners.
2) A good work ethic.
3) They truly like working at your business and want to climb some mountains.
4) Optimistic.
5) They think like the owner.
6) They belong here." –pp. 103-113.

He also says that "the people chosen for leadership roles in companies committed to constant radical change and growth share all the previous traits and the following five attributes:
1) Good leaders treat people well.
2) Good leaders are good communicators.
3) They lead by example.
4) They build trust.
   Four guiding principles for building trust quickly:
   - We trust those who speak our language.
   - We trust those who ask good questions.
   - We trust those who share our values.
   - We trust those who listen.
5) They attract and keep talent." –pp. 114-120.

Here is the big lesson: "If you have workers or leaders who don't fit the preceding criteria, they will slow you down and confound you in your efforts to create an organization that embraces constant change and growth. Add up the countless time and resources that are utterly wasted by having the wrong leaders recruiting and hiring the wrong people. Then, fix the people thing and get the right leaders and workers on board, and constant change and growth will become your culture and will be achieved." –p. 121.

You've got to have the right people on the bus in the right seats if you are going to successfully arrive at your destination without crashing or getting lost. When everyone is going in the same direction and wants to climb mountains, it is amazing what you can accomplish.

5. Get and keep everyone on the same page.
Here are some suggestions for getting everyone on the same page:
    1)   Be interested instead of interesting.
    2)   Listen with your full attention.
    3)   Make sense first; make judgments later.
    4)   Read between the lines. –pp.142-146.

"[When everyone is on the same page], work is more fun, morale is high, and when one workday ends people look forward to the next one....teams [also] get lots done without anyone barking orders down their necks, hard work isn't as draining, and sacrifices aren't a big deal. Problems get solved without too much fuss, but not because everyone always agree. It's just that everyone does their best to communicate and cooperate...." –Jason Jennings, *The Reinventors*, p. 125.

6. Be frugal. You are much more frugal with your own money than you are with someone else's money.
Here are some tips on being more frugal:
    1)   Make everything simple.
    2)   Edit every 'to do' list. Keep your priority list small – have an average of 21 priorities instead of 372 (like most companies).
    3)   Celebrate frugal reinvention.
    4)   Be more disciplined and ask: What's the good business reason for spending this money?
    5)   Blow up any bureaucracy. How many people does it really take to get the work done?--pp.174-179.

7. Systematize everything.
Here are some things you should systematize:

- In the first hour of your day, go over the workload and delegation assignments for the day; discuss potential problems; goals and rewards, etc.
- How you go about expressing appreciation
- Your marketing process
- Operations
- Customer service concerns and issues

Work with each team member over each area to ensure that the right priorities are in place.

Here are some suggestions for systematization:
1) Don't let systematization become an excuse for getting rule bound.
2) Don't go with anything but the BEST idea.
3) Don't rely on anyone's memory for systems decisions—use data.
4) Don't create mean systems. Make sure you can understand and get the information you need to make decisions. If the system is too mean, you may not discover problems before they become too big.
5) Don't insist on going it alone. –pp. 197-205.

8. Don't hesitate.
Jennings outlines nine reasons why people hesitate to act:
- Gotten too comfortable
- Study thing to death
- Lack of confidence
- Think the big deal will fly in the window
- Think it's already too late for them
- Fear of losing what they have
- Afraid nobody will pitch in
- Family pressures to not take the risk
- Lack of financial safety net –p. 218.

Don't hesitate. Focus on these eight principles to help you reinvent your business so you can be more competitive and rise above the challenges you are facing. Staying where you are won't get you where you want to go. Remember, if you aren't improving, you will be average.

Here is an assessment for your business reinvention systems:

#	Rank yourself from 1-10 based on your current business behaviors.	1	2	3	4	5	6	7	8	9	10	Rank yourself from 1-10 based on your current business behaviors.
1	I'm oblivious to coming changes in the marketplace and don't have a systematic approach to help me think about how my business can improve.											I look at my business from time to time with fresh eyes as though I weren't the owner to consider how it could be changed to better help clients get the results they want.
2	I am trapped in my own bias and think little can be done to improve that we haven't already done.											I look for ways to change recognizing that the way we currently do things may not be the best way.
3	I don't pay attention to what is going on in other industries much less implement the best ideas.											I listen to what is going on in other industries and think about how to apply the best ideas.
4	I only see what I observe. I don't have a systematic approach or time to look for new ideas.											I have a system for looking for new ideas so I can recycle, transfer and apply what's working elsewhere.
5	I don't have time to learn new skills. I can barely keep up with what I'm doing now.											I seek to learn new skills that will help our business find new opportunities for growth.
6	We try to be all things for all people and as a result we often ignore our best and most profitable niche markets and future opportunities.											Our message matches our market and our clients consider us the best in our niche.
7	We're happy to get whatever business we can. We aren't looking for ways to attract more affluent clients.											We're looking and actively seeking ways to attract more affluent clientele to our business.
8	We ignore any other distribution channels other than what we're doing now.											We find new distribution channels to distribute our products and services.
9	Nothing is being done to address the complaints of our clients. We are stuck in the status quo.											We hear complaints from our clients and work to implement new solutions to solve them.
10	We have assets that are unutilized or underutilized.											I often look at our assets and think about how they could be better utilized to exploit new opportunities.

Here is a task list to help you implement better reinvention systems for you and your team:

1. Schedule 30 minutes or more of time to think and plan your business this week. Ask yourself questions that challenge your assumptions. Think about where you are going and how you can get there.

2. What can you do to reinvent your business without having actions forced upon you by competitors or market forces?

3. Think about the ten things that limit entrepreneurs from seeing opportunities within their own business. Which areas are you guilty of? What will you do differently about your business going forward?

4. Analyze your list of assets. Where do you see opportunity? Where do you see liability? What can you do to eliminate liabilities and increase your assets?

5. Go through the list of 11 areas of your business that you should know something different about this week as opposed to last week. What have you learned by going through this exercise?

6. Have you gotten angry at yourself lately for your mistakes? Are you guilty of personalizing your mistakes which can paralyze you even further? What can you do to break free of this cycle so you can truly reinvent your business?

I hope that this chapter has been helpful to you as you consider this important system to ensure that you are reinventing your business by eliminating what isn't working so you can in turn focus on what is.

Every business has stages and cycles in it. What you want to do is focus on creating systems that allow you to evaluate your assumptions so you can constantly reinvent your business before circumstances or the market force you to. Then, you'll be able to anticipate where trends are taking the industry before you have to respond in a more drastic way. You can do it. You can overcome your challenges, your obstacles, and your adversity. Better opportunities lie ahead on the horizon. You must keep riding and moving forward and not let frustration or disappointment get in the way of the actions you must take to do what needs to be done.

CHAPTER 18

SYSTEMS FOR BALANCING WORK AND FAMILY

"When solving problems, dig at the roots instead of just hacking at the leaves."
—*Anthony J. D'Angelo*

Balance is such an interesting topic. Sometimes we feel like we have it, other times we don't. And, when we don't, we often feel guilty for what we feel we should or ought to be doing. Every person reading this has different situations going on in their lives. Some reading this have young children, some have grown children, and some have no children. There are those reading this who are married and those who are not. Regardless of your personal situation, I hope that you'll think carefully about what you can do better set up this critical business system in your personal and professional life.

Gary Keller shares this truth about balance in his book *The One Thing: The Surprisingly Simple Truth Behind Extraordinary Results.* He says:

"Nothing ever achieves absolute balance. Nothing. No matter how imperceptible it might be, what appears to be a state of balance is something entirely different—an act of balancing. Viewed wistfully as a noun, balance is lived practically as a verb. Seen as something we ultimately attain, balance is actually something we constantly do. A 'balanced life' is a myth—a misleading concept most accept as a worthy and attainable goal without ever stopping to truly consider it. I want you to consider it. I want you to challenge it. I want you to reject it. A balanced life is a lie.

"The idea of balance is exactly that—an idea. In philosophy, 'the golden mean' is the moderate middle between polar extremes, a concept used to describe a place between two positions that is more desirable than one state or the other. This is a grand idea, but not a very practical one. Idealistic, but not realistic. Balance doesn't exist.

"This is tough to conceive, much less believe, mainly because one of the most frequent laments is 'I need more balance,' a common mantra for what's missing in most lives. We hear about balance so much we automatically assume it's exactly what we should be seeking. It's not. Purpose, meaning, significance—these are what make a successful life. Seek them and you will most certainly live your life out of balance, criss-crossing an invisible middle line as you pursue your priorities. The act of living a full life by giving time to what matters is a balancing act. Extraordinary results require focused attention and time. Time on one thing means time away from another. This makes balance impossible."-- pp. 72-73.

That is a pretty fascinating statement. I can't tell you how many times I've had coaching calls with entrepreneurs with young children who were going back and forth about how to balance their business and their lives. Recently, I talked with one couple who told me that they worked hard in their business for a number of years, built it up and then took some time away from the business. Over the past couple of years, they've been able to spend time with their young children and their business is still successful, but it has dipped in recent months as the attention and focus that was once there in abundance has waned.

I really like Keller's statement: Time on one thing means time away from another. You can't escape that reality. This is again why systems are so important. As your business grows and expands, you need to be able to "see" what's going on in your business with a little bit of information so you can make decisions even though you may not be in every aspect of it. However, you do still have to spend time in the business. Believing that it will endlessly grow higher and higher with little to no effort on your part is a myth and a lie.

Keller continues:
"The desire for balance makes sense. Enough time for everything and everything done in time. It sounds so appealing that just thinking about it makes us feel serene and peaceful. This calm is so real that we just know it's the way life was meant to be. But it's not. If you think of balance as the middle, then out of balance is when you're away from it. Get too far away from the middle and you're living at the extremes. The problem with living in the middle is that it prevents you from making extraordinary time commitments to anything. In your effort to attend to all things, everything gets shortchanged and nothing gets its due.

Sometimes this can be okay and sometimes not. Knowing when to pursue the middle and when to pursue the extremes is in essence the true beginning of wisdom. Extraordinary results are achieved by this negotiation with your time."

He concludes with this thought:
"The reason we shouldn't pursue balance is that the magic never happens in the middle; magic happens at the extremes. The dilemma is that chasing the extremes presents real challenges. We naturally understand that success lies at the outer edges, but we don't know how to manage our lives while we're out there. When we work too long, eventually our personal life suffers. Falling prey to the belief that long hours are virtuous, we unfairly blame work when we say, 'I have no life.' Often, it's just the opposite. Even if our work life doesn't interfere, our personal life itself can be so full of 'have-tos' that we again reach the same defeated conclusion: 'I have no life.' And sometimes we get hit from both sides. Some of us face so many personal and professional demands that everything suffers. Breakdown imminent, we once again declare, 'I have no life!' Just like playing to the middle, playing to the extremes is the kind of middle mismanagement that plays out all the time." –pp. 75-77.

Sheryl Sandberg, the COO of Facebook, devotes an entire chapter to this subject in her book *Lean In*. She says:
" 'Having it all.' Perhaps the greatest trap ever set for women was the coining of this phrase. Bandied about in speeches, headlines, and articles, these three little words are intended to be aspirational but instead make all of us feel like we have fallen short. I have never met a woman, or man, who has stated emphatically, 'Yes, I have it all.' Because no matter what any one of us has—and how grateful we are for what we have—no one has it all. Nor can we. The very concept of having it all flies in the face of the basic laws of economics and common sense...."

"'Having it all' is best regarded as a myth. And like many myths, it can deliver a helpful cautionary message. Think of Icarus, who soared to great heights with his man-made wings. His father warned him not to fly too near the sun, but Icarus ignored the advice. He soared even higher, his wings melted, and he crashed to earth. Pursuing both a professional and personal life is a noble and attainable goal, up to a point.

Women should learn from Icarus to aim for the sky, but keep in mind that we all have real limits."

She continues:
"Instead of pondering the question 'Can we have it all?,' we should be asking the more practical question 'Can we do it all?' And again, the answer is no. Each of us makes choices constantly between work and family, exercising and relaxing, making time for others and taking time for ourselves. Being a parent means making adjustments, compromises, and sacrifices every day. For most people, sacrifices and hardships are not a choice, but a necessity." –pp. 121-122.

A fascinating story told in the book is of Tina Fey who commented that when she was promoting her movie *Date Night* with Steve Carrell that she was asked how she balances her life, but the same reporter didn't ask this question of Carrell. She commented that this "is the rudest question you can ask a woman."

Sandberg says:
"Fey nails it. Employed mothers and fathers both struggle with multiple responsibilities, but mothers also have to endure the rude questions and accusatory looks that remind us that we're shortchanging both our jobs *and* our children. As if we needed reminding. Like me, most of the women I know do a great job worrying that we don't measure up. We compare our efforts at work to those of our colleagues, usually men, who typically have far fewer responsibilities at home. Then we compare our efforts at home to those of mothers who dedicate themselves solely to their families. Outside observers reminding us that we must be struggling—and failing—is just bitter icing on an already soggy cake. Trying to do it all and expecting that it all can be done exactly right is a recipe for disappointment. Perfection is the enemy." –pp. 122-123.

I really like what Sandberg says:
"One of my favorite posters at Facebook declares in big red letters, 'Done is better than perfect.' I have tried to embrace this motto and let go of unattainable standards. Aiming for perfection causes frustration at best and paralysis at worst. I agree completely with the advice offered by Nora Ephron in her 1996 Wellesley commencement speech when she addressed the issue of women having both a career and family. Ephron insisted, 'It will be a little messy, but embrace the mess. It will be complicated, but rejoice in the complications. It will not be anything

like what you think it will be like, but surprises are good for you. And don't be frightened: you can always change your mind." –p. 126.

Sandberg shares a really interesting insight in the book that I teach in my management mastery course. She talks about something she learned from Larry Kanarek who was her boss at McKinsey and Company in Washington D.C. She says: "One day, Larry gathered everyone together for a talk. He explained that since he was running the office, employees came to him and wanted to quit. Over time, he noticed that people quit for one reason only: they were burnt out, tired of working long hours and traveling. Larry said he could understand the complaint, but what he could not understand was that all the people who quit—every single one—had unused vacation time. Up until the day they left, they did everything McKinsey asked of them before deciding that it was too much."

"Larry implored us to exert more control over our careers. He said McKinsey would never stop making demands on our time, so it was up to us to decide what we were willing to do. It was our responsibility to draw the line. We needed to determine how many hours we were willing to work in a day and how many nights we were willing to travel. If later on, the job did not work out, we would know that we had tried on our own terms. Counter-intuitively, long-term success at work often depends on *not* trying to meet every demand placed on us. The best way to make room for both life and career is to make choices deliberately— to set limits and stick to them." –p. 125-126.

Do you do this? Do you choose to not take breaks from your business because you think it can't run without you? If so, it is just a matter of time before you burn out and lose your energy so you won't be able to do much of anything going forward.

I have talked with many entrepreneurs who have lost their motivation or their initiative to continue as things became harder and harder and they refused to take a break. As a result, the business became less and less important while they just went through the motions until it got to the point where they HAD do something to save it.

This chapter in Sandberg's book *Lean In* was a fascinating read because it illustrates how so many feel a struggle between balancing their life and their family and yet how many really feel like they don't do this well. As a result, they beat themselves up and feel guilty about it. This in turn affects their performance in every other area of their business and their life.

Life is too short to beat yourself up and to feel guilty over what you haven't done. You've chosen to be an entrepreneur. You're business is very demanding. In addition to all you do in your business, you've got to take time for you and choose to draw the line so you have some time off.

Gary Keller explains that counterbalance is the key to balance. He says: "So if achieving balance is a lie, then what do you do? Counterbalance. Replace the word 'balance' with 'counterbalance' and what you experience makes sense. The things we presume to have balance are really just counterbalancing. The ballerina is a classic example. When the ballerina poses en pointe, she can appear weightless, floating on air, the very idea of balance and grace. A closer look would reveal her toe shoes vibrating rapidly, making minute adjustments for balance. Counterbalancing done well gives the illusion of balance.

"When we say we're out of balance, we're usually referring to a sense that some priorities—things that matter to us—are being underserved or unmet. The problem is that when you focus on what is truly important, something will always be underserved. No matter how hard you try, there will always be things left undone at the end of your day, week, month, year, and life. Trying to get them all done is folly. When the things that matter most get done, you'll still be left with a sense of things being undone—a sense of imbalance. Leaving some things undone is a necessary tradeoff for extraordinary results. But you can't leave everything undone, and that's where counterbalancing comes in. The idea of counterbalancing is that you never go so far that you can't find your way back or stay so long that there is nothing waiting for you when you return." –pp. 79-80.

He continues:
"There are two types of counterbalancing: the balancing between work and personal life and the balancing within each. In the world of professional success, it's not about how much overtime you put in; the key ingredient is focused time over time. To achieve an extraordinary result you must choose what matters most and give it all the time it demands. This requires getting extremely out of balance in relation to

all other work issues, with only infrequent counterbalancing to address them. In your personal world, awareness is the essential ingredient. Awareness of your spirit and body, awareness of your family and friends, awareness of your personal needs—none of these can be sacrificed if you intend to 'have a life,' so you can never forsake them for work or one for the other. You can move back and forth quickly between these and often even combine the activities around them, but you can't neglect any of them for long. Your personal life requires tight counterbalancing.

"Whether or not to go out of balance isn't really the question. The question is: 'Do you go short or long?' In your personal life, go short and avoid long periods where you're out of balance. Going short means you stay connected to all the things that matter most and move them along together. In your professional life, go long and make peace with the idea that the pursuit of extraordinary results may require you to be out of balance for long periods. Going long allows you to focus on what matters most, even at the expense of other, lesser priorities. In your personal life, nothing gets left behind. At work it's required." –p. 81.

A recent article in *Inc.* magazine discusses Tim Ferris and his book *The Four Hour Work Week* and the myth that there is an easy path to big rewards. Ferris is touted as taking one month vacations completely unplugged from what he does. He works hard and he plays hard but it is obvious from the article that he sure doesn't work a four-hour workweek. That is a myth. Ferris works hard for his success. He has great ideas for being more productive. One quote in particular from this article is quite insightful. The author of the article, Tom Foster says:

"One of the key ways Ferriss tries to disrupt how people think about productivity is by urging them not to think in terms of time management. 'I think time management as a label encourages people to view each 24 hour period as a slot in which they should pack as much as possible,' Ferriss says. For maximum productivity, in his view, people should focus on doing less, not more. The point is to maximize the outcome, not the amount of work." –*Inc.*, April 2013, p. 74.

Russell Ballard once observed: "Sometimes we need a personal crisis to reinforce in our minds what we really value and cherish...Perhaps if you, too, search your hearts and courageously assess the priorities in your life, you may discover, as I did, that you need a better balance among your priorities. All of us must come to an honest, open self-examination, an awareness within us as to who and what we want to be. As most of you know, coping with the complex and diverse challenges of everyday life, which is not an easy task, can upset the balance and harmony we seek. Many good people who care a great deal are trying very hard to maintain balance, but they sometimes feel overwhelmed and defeated."

Keller says:
"The question of balance is really a question of priority. When you change your language from balancing to prioritizing, you see your choices more clearly and open the door to changing your destiny. Extraordinary results demand that you set a priority and act on it. When you act on your priority, you'll automatically go out of balance, giving more time to one thing over another. The challenge then doesn't become one of not going out of balance, for in fact you must. The challenge becomes how long you stay on your priority. To be able to address your priorities outside of work, be clear about your most important work priority so you can get it done. Then go home and be clear about your priorities there so you can get back to work. When you're supposed to be working, work, and when you're supposed to be playing, play. It's a weird tightrope you're walking, but it's only when you get your priorities mixed up that things fall apart." –p. 82.

I remember coaching an entrepreneur several years ago who really struggled with taking time off. She told me in one of our initial coaching sessions that she hadn't taken a day off from work in nearly 13 years. She was worn out, exhausted and felt like she couldn't take any time off because the business would collapse if she wasn't always there. We had many conversations about this and she finally agreed to take off an afternoon from her business for lunch and then away from her business. When she reported back, she told me she was only able to take time off for lunch before she felt she had to return. It took a couple of weeks, but she finally was able to take an entire afternoon off and then she worked up to an entire day off which gave her a new perspective on her life and helped her return back to work with a renewed perspective and vision.

In fact, I created a chart and exercise for her and now I use it to help others plan, balance and counter-balance their lives as well. The exercise allows you to evaluate what provides renewal, relaxation and rejuvenation and then forces you to schedule the activities that best provide the opportunity to counter-balance into your scheduled day off.

To complete it, you've got to make a list of all of the things that you enjoy doing that allow you to renew and rejuvenate yourself so you can relax. Then, you've got to analyze how much time you currently spend on each of those activities every week. Then, you need to set goals based on how much time you would like to spend on each of these activities per week. Then, you've got to schedule those activities into your schedule just like you would a meeting with an important client (or it won't get done).

You've probably schedule out the activities you do on an average day in your life. The point of this exercise is to allow yourself to schedule time for you so you don't get burned out to the point that you can't function as well as you could if you just took some time to recharge your batteries and clear your mind of what you've been so worried about. I've found that these occasions are when I most often receive ideas and inspiration for what to do next. If you don't take the time to do these things, you will be wound up like a spring and will experience stress fractures over time. It isn't a matter of if, but when.

Take time to better structure your time each day and your rejuvenation time each week by completing this exercise.

Leonardo da Vinci once observed this truth:
"Every now and then go away, have a little relaxation, for when you come back to your work your judgment will be surer. Go some distance away because then the work appears smaller and more of it can be taken in at a glance and a lack of harmony and proportion is more readily seen."

Keller has three ideas about how to better balance your life in his book *The One Thing*. These are:
1. **"Think about two balancing buckets.** Separate your work life and personal life into two distinct buckets—not to compartmentalize them, just for counterbalancing. Each has its own counterbalancing goals and approaches.
2. **Counterbalance your work bucket.** View work as involving a skill or knowledge that must be mastered. This will cause you to give disproportionate time to your ONE Thing and will throw the rest of your work day, week, month, and year continually out of balance. Your work life is divided into two distinct areas—what matters most and everything else. You will have to take what matters to

extremes and be okay with what happens to the rest. Professional success requires it.

3. **Counterbalance your personal life bucket.** Acknowledge that your life actually has multiple areas and that each requires a minimum of attention for you to feel that you 'have a life.' Drop any one and you will feel the effects. This requires constant awareness. You must never go too long or too far without counterbalancing them so that they are all active areas of your life. Your personal life requires it." –p. 83.

Keller says:
"Start leading a counterbalanced life. Let the right things take precedence when they should and get to the rest when you can. An extraordinary life is a counterbalancing act." –p. 83.

Your system for balance should ensure that you build personal and family time into your calendar first.

When I first started coaching entrepreneurs, I coached one retail store owner who was also a doctor. She was extremely busy. She told me that the advice I shared with her to schedule her family time first on her calendar and then schedule everything else around that was a revolutionary idea for her and extremely helpful in her quest for a more balanced life.

Be sure you do this for your calendar as well. Take time for the ones you love most. Even though I am always extremely busy with our businesses, I have to take time to spend with my wife (on at least a weekly date) and with our five children. Sometimes that means inviting them to activities that I are planning on doing and finding moments to share with them that will be meaningful for them.

Everyone I've ever spent time coaching has always shared with me that they would like more vacation time. My advice to them is the same as my advice to you: schedule it and make it happen! It should be the first thing you plan on your calendar.

I've always liked this statement by Charles J. Givens:
"Your personal time is your mental-health time. The big mistake that many people make with their personal time is to say to themselves, 'Well, when I get all the business done, then I'll spend some time with my

family.' Business is *never* done. Therefore, there is seldom any real time to spend with the family. It's the same as saying, 'Well, when I get my bills paid, then I'll start to invest the extra money.' Have you ever noticed that there is never any extra money? Well, there's never any extra time either, so it must be created. Scheduling your personal time with the same priority as your business time is an absolute must for balanced, successful living. When there is a conflict, business can often wait, but not your family and friends. Your attitude should be: 'No matter what comes up in business, I will not change the time I've scheduled for myself or my family.'"--*SuperSelf*, pp. 197-198.

Schedule your personal time with the same priority or with a higher priority than your business time and then stick to your schedule. You don't want to look back on your life in 10 or 20 years and regret that you didn't spend more time with your family.

Remember what B.C. Forbes once said: "The business of life is not business, but living." In his book, *The Seven Habits of Highly Effective People*, Stephen R. Covey wrote: "The challenge is not to manage time, but to manage ourselves." The problem that most people have is not inadequate discipline, but rather that they have not deeply internalized their priorities. As Covey said, "It is easy to say no, when you have a deeper yes burning within."

Bob Buford explains this principle another way in his book *HalfTime*: "Your life is like a teacup, flowing over. There's no room for anything new. You need to pour out, not take more in."--p. 126. He recommends ten ways to better balance your life and your work. These are:

1. **"Delegate—at work, play, and home.** You cannot do everything and shouldn't try. This becomes especially important for those whose second half involves keeping their present job but doing it at half speed. Work smarter, not harder.
2. **Do what you do best; drop the rest.** I tend to be a visionary, so I'm less motivated to do hands-on implementation, though I can and have done it. Not anymore. Go with your strengths.
3. **Know when to say no.** The more successful you are, the more you will be asked to help others. Don't let others talk you into doing something you don't want to do or don't have time to do; it will become a chore. You want to pursue your mission, not someone else's.

4. **Set limits.**....If you normally stay an hour after work, go home on time. If you take twelve business trips a year, cut back to six or eight. Reallocate time to your mission, to your core issues.

5. **Protect your personal time by putting it on your calendar.** I like Ken Blanchard's advice to start your day slow. It is much easier to maintain control over your life if you have a regular quiet time. This time should be more than devotions...Leave time for absolute silence, for deliberately looking at your life to see that it is in balance. This is probably the most vital activity for me in terms of staying in control.

6. **Work with people you like.** One of my friends, Karol Emmerich, who quit a year ago as treasurer of Dayton-Hudson, says, 'I want to find all the people I like being with and find some beneficial work we can do together. In my second half, I want to work with people who add energy to life, not with those who take energy away.

7. **Set timetables.** Your mission is important and, therefore, deserving of your attention and care. If you do not put your second half dreams on a timetable, they will quickly become unfulfilled wishes.

8. **Downsize.** When Thoreau moved into a cabin on Walden Pond, he lightened up on the nonessentials in his life. Think about all the time and energy that are drained by owning a boat, a cottage, a second or third car, or a country club membership. None of these things are bad by themselves and are, in fact, designed to provide some fun in your life, but they can very easily become master controllers. Most people I know who own a boat feel they have to use it to make it a worthwhile investment. I also know people who do not particularly enjoy spending four hours on a golf course, but do it because they belong to a club. If these kinds of things stand between you and regaining control of your life, get rid of them.

9. **Play around a little.** Not in the sense that would get you in trouble, but as a way to keep a handle on who's in charge. There is something about skipping out of the office to catch a baseball game in the middle of the week, or taking your spouse to a movie instead of attending a church committee meeting, that reminds you who's calling the shots. Play ought to be a big second-half activity, not so much in terms of time spend, but in importance.

10. **Take the phone off the hook.** Not literally (at least, not all the time), but learn how to hide gracefully. I don't always like talking to voice mail when I call someone, but I wouldn't live without one myself. It lets *me* control who I talk to and when....Unless you're a

brain surgeon on twenty-four hour call, I don't think it is necessary to let people know where you are all the time." –p. 132-135.

If we don't take control of our time, time will control us. Here are indicators that you are in control of your day:
- You plan your daily activities each day in advance.
- You finish each day with a sense of accomplishment.
- You prioritize your daily activities.
- You start on time.
- You show up on time.
- You refuse to get sucked into confrontations.
- You eliminate interruptions.
- You separate your emotions from the events and the difficult situations you deal with.
- You maintain a positive, can-do attitude that encourages your team members.
- You plan your work, then work your plan.
- Your complete your day by prioritizing your activities for the next day.

Now, contrast that with indicators that you've lost control of your day:
- You feel exhausted and depleted by the end of the day.
- You rarely plan or prioritize your daily schedule.
- You start late for work or an appointment.
- You arrive late, making excuses.
- You let unforeseen events (especially big customer service issues with upset clients) completely turn your day upside down.
- You allow interruptions to detour your planned activities.
- You become rushed and pressured, and therefore, under stress.
- You measure your day in terms of what didn't get done instead of what did.
- You become the victim with thoughts like "Why me?"
- You finish your day by complaining about what went wrong.

Which do you *really* want?

Productivity and counter-balance are within your control. You've just got to decide and then put systems in place to ensure that you day stays in control.

Here is a task list to help you implement better systems for yourself and how you balance your life:

1. Think about the analogy of the two buckets. How can focusing on what you are doing in each bucket while you are there and moving back and forth between the two of them help you better prioritize your life? Write down your priorities for both buckets and then prioritize your weekly schedule so that you are truly counter-balancing your activities between the two buckets. It may be painful at first to actually schedule time off for you, but you MUST do this if you want to maintain your sanity, your relationships and your health.

2. Complete the exercise where you detail what you do in a focused day and what you will do on a focused day off. Plan a day this week where you will take off at least ½ of a day and actually do something you want to do that will bring you rejuvenation and help you relax from the stress you have been dealing with in your business. Only you can actually schedule and make sure these activities are done so do it and make it happen. Schedule a trip with your spouse and then actually buy the non-refundable tickets so you can GO and actually have time away from the business that is not related to it.

3. Think about the advice of Sheryl Sandberg. Where are you going to draw your line? What priorities will you set for your personal life boundaries so you have a chance to reset and refocus back on these important areas throughout your day and your week?

4. Evaluate the chart indicating whether you are in control or out of control with your time. What indicators do you see that you need to change in your life. Make a list and start drawing lines with how you will use your time.

5. Go through the ten recommendations of Bob Buford. What do you need to start doing and conversely stop doing to better feel in control of the balance and counterbalance needed to feel successful in your business and your life? Set a goal for what you are going to star and stop.

Balance is a sensitive topic. I want to share some advice from Sheryl Sandberg from her book *Lean In* because it shows how hard this struggle is and why it is important to give yourself a break so you are not beating yourself up over what you are or aren't doing.

She says: "I still struggle with the trade-offs between work and home on a daily basis. Every woman I know does, and I know that I'm far luckier than most. I have remarkable resources—a husband who is a real partner, the ability to hire great people to assist me both in the office and at home, and a good measure of control over my schedule. I also have a wonderful sister who lives close by and is always willing to take care of her niece and nephew, occasionally at a moment's notice....

"If there is a new normal for the workplace, there is a new normal for the home too. Just as expectations for how many hours people will work have risen dramatically, so have expectations for how many hours mothers will spend focused on their children. In 1975, stay-at-home mothers spent an average of about eleven hours per week on primary child care (defined as routine caregiving and activities that foster a child's well-being, such as reading and fully focused play). Mothers employed outside the home in 1975 spent six hours doing these activities. Today, stay-at-home mothers spend about seventeen hours per week on primary child care, on average, while mothers who work outside the home spend about eleven hours. This means that an employed mother today spends about the same amount of time on primary care activities as a non-employed mother did in 1975.

"My memory of being a kid is that my mother was available but rarely hovering or directing my activities. My siblings and I did not have organized playdates. We rode our bikes around the neighborhood without adult supervision. Our parents might have checked on our homework once in a while, but they rarely sat with us while we completed it. Today, a 'good mother' is always around and always devoted to the needs of her children. Sociologists call this relatively new phenomenon 'intensive mothering,' and it has culturally elevated the importance of women spending large amounts of time with their children. Being judged against the current all-consuming standard means mothers who work outside the home feel as if we are failing, even if we are spending the same number of hours with our kids as our mothers did. When I drop my kids off at school and see the mothers who are staying to volunteer, I worry that my children are worse off because I'm not with them full-time. This is where my trust in hard data and research has helped me the most. Study after study suggests that the pressure society places on women to stay home and do 'what's best for the child' is based on emotion, not evidence. Although I know the data and understand intellectually that my career is not harming my children, there are times when I still feel anxious about my choices. A friend of mind felt the same way, so she discussed it with her therapist and, later, shared this insight: 'My therapist told me that when I was worrying about how much I was leaving my girls, that separation anxiety is actually more about the mom than the kids. We talk about it was though it is a problem for children, but actually it can be more of an issue for the mom.'

"I always want to do more for my children. Because of work obligations, I've missed doctor's appointments and parent teacher conferences and have had to travel when my kids were sick. I haven't missed a dance recital yet, but it probably will happen. I have also missed a level of detail about their lives. I once asked a mother at our school if she knew any of the other kids in the first-grade class, hoping for a familiar name or two. She spent twenty minutes reciting from memory the name of every child, detailing their parents, siblings, which class they had been in the year before, and their interests. How could she possibly know all this? Was I a bad mother for not knowing *any* of this?

"I knew the answer to that last question. It bothered me because like most people with choices, I am not completely comfortable with mine. Later that same year, I dropped my son off at school on St. Patrick's Day. As he got out of the car wearing his favorite blue T-shirt, the same mother pointed out, 'He's supposed to be wearing green today.' I simultaneously thought, *Oh, who the hell can remember that it's St. Patrick's Day?* and *I'm a bad mom.*

"Guilt management can be just as important as time management for mothers. When I went back to my job after giving birth, other working mothers told me to prepare for the day that my son would cry for his nanny. Sure enough, when he was about eleven months old, he was crawling on the floor of his room and put his knee down on a toy. He looked up for help, crying, and reached for her instead of me. It pierced my heart, but Dave thought it was a good sign. He reasoned that we were the central figures in our son's life, but forming an attachment to a caregiver was good for his development. I understood his logic, especially in retrospect, but at the time, it hurt like hell.

"To this day, I count the hours away from my kids and feel sad when I miss a dinner or a night with them. Did I have to take this trip? Was this speech really critical for Facebook? Was this meeting really necessary? Far from worrying about nights he misses, Dave thinks we are heroes for getting home for dinner as often as we do. Our different viewpoints seem inextricably gender based. Compared to his peers, Dave is an exceptionally devoted dad. Compared to many of my peers, I spend a lot more time away from my children. A study that conducted in-depth interviews with mothers and fathers in dual-earner families uncovered similar reactions. The mothers were riddled with guilt about what their jobs were doing to their families. The fathers were not. As Marie Wilson, founder of the White House Project, has noted, 'Show me a woman without guilt and I'll show you a man.'

She concludes: "I know that I can easily spend time focusing on what I'm not doing; like many, I excel at self-flagellation. And even with my vast support system, there are times when I feel pulled in too many directions. But when I dwell less on the conflicts and compromises, and more on being fully engaged with the task at hand, the center holds and I feel content. I love my job and the brilliant and fascinating people I work with. I also love my time with my kids. A great day is when I rush home from the craziness of the office to have dinner with my family and then sit in the rocking chair in the corner of my daughter's room with both of my kids on my lap. We rock and read together, just a quiet (okay, not always quiet), joyful moment at the end of their day. They drift off to sleep and I drift (okay, run) back to my laptop....I would never claim to be able to find serenity or total focus in every moment. I am so far from that. But when I remember that no one can do it all and identify my real priorities at home and at work, I feel better, and I am more productive in the office and probably a better mother as well."-pp.134-138.

I hope this chapter has helped you see where and how you can systematize your business to be more successful in balancing or counterbalancing your actions at your business and in your personal life. Do the assignments and set up systems for counter-balance in your life. Feeling in control of your life and that you have a life are critical components of maintaining the energy necessary to continue to grow your business and be happy and fulfilled in what you've accomplished.

To evaluate how well you are doing with balancing and counterbalancing your work and family life, rate yourself in these areas:

#	Rank yourself from 1-10 based on your current out of business behaviors.	1	2	3	4	5	6	7	8	9	10	Rank yourself from 1-10 based on your current out of business behaviors.
1	I rarely spend any quality time with my spouse or other members of my family.											I spend at least 10 hours of focused time with my family each week.
2	I don't go out with my spouse on a date once a week (without children).											I get together with friends at least once a week. I go out on a date without children with my spouse once a week.
3	I feel stress and anxiety because of the anger I feel towards someone else.											There is no one in my life that I haven't completely forgiven.
4	I am pretty happy with where I am in my relationships. I don't feel like I need to improve anything.											I am actively engaged in learning how to be a better spouse, parent, and/or friend.
5	I am so consumed in everything that I am doing that I don't take much time to support the activities of my friends or family. I wish I had more time, but I don't.											I actively look for ways to support and help advance the success of my friends and family.
6	It is always someone else's fault. I am rarely wrong.											I take complete responsibility for all relationship conflicts when they arise.
7	I used to be more trusting of others, but since I've been burned on more than one occasion, it is hard to be trusting of anyone.											I easily trust those I live and work with.
8	I have secrets that I would prefer others never found out about me.											I am 100% honest and open with all those I live and work with.

#	Rank yourself from 1-10 based on your current out of business behaviors.	1	2	3	4	5	6	7	8	9	10	Rank yourself from 1-10 based on your current out of business behaviors.
9	I have a really hard time living up to my commitments. I can't remember what I've promised to whom.											It is easy for me to commit to others and honor those commitments.
10	I don't need help from anyone and if someone suggests that I do, they probably have the issue.											I recognize when I need support and am continually seeking help.

Section 3:
Secrets of Implementation

## Chapter 19

How to Set Up Your Business Systems and Build Your Business Blueprint

"If your business depends on you, you don't own a business—you have a job! The business owner should be devoted to business development, not doing business."
—Michael E. Gerber

Systems make up the blueprint that runs your business day in and day out. A blueprint is required to build anything. This book has laid out the blueprints you need to build a solid foundation for your business. Changes in systems are tweaks that you will continuously make in your similar to changing out the furniture or repainting the walls in a home. However, the basics of the foundation remain the same. Occasionally, with the growth of your business, you may have to push out a wall and expand. However, it is rare when a foundation of a home or a business is completely torn out. When, this happens, you are usually building a new house or a new business.

In today's competitive environment, many entrepreneurs feel like the foundation they have built has been completely ripped out from under them. The blueprint they felt confident in following for years has changed. They want to move forward yet they are paralyzed by the continuous changes in the economy, regulations, and the attitudes of competitors and clients. Today there are more competitors (especially on the Internet) and prospects in general are more distracted and disenchanted with the whole buying experience.

In the midst of such dramatic changes, many entrepreneurs have chosen to continue on in the same vein of what they have always done or have reverted back to what they used to do. They feel overwhelmed and frustrated with a continual unpredictability about their daily, weekly and monthly results. The solution goes back to what I talked about in

Chapter 1 regarding the E-Myth. You've got to learn new skills of vision and seeing the big picture (as the entrepreneur), improving work flow and ensuring it gets done through systems (as the manager), and then actually doing the work or hiring others to do the work (as the technician).

This change reinforces the power of systems and why creating a business blueprint that will help you not only stand out to *your* customers and apart from your competitors is so important today. Building effective systems will help you ensure that you are happy with your result as you construct your business.

Your business, like any business, needs a solid foundation to provide stability. If corners were cut when the foundation was built, cracks may appear and in time the structure will crumble and fall. Great systems and a solid blueprint ensures that you create a business that is built to last, not just one that will look pretty on the outside, yet have unsightly cracks and problems in the basement.

This is a hard lesson for many to learn. Neglecting important details in the foundation while spending money on paint and varnish can give the appearance of sustainability, yet under the surface danger lurks. In this chapter, I want to talk about your business blueprint and putting all of the systems you've been working on together. This is what makes up the foundational elements of your business. As an example, it is much easier to rely on others to build your brand than it is to build your own brand. It is easier to rely on the new paint and shiny varnish of a trendy new product you are selling than it is to look under the hood of your business and find out if you are *really* profitable with what you are selling day in and day out.

I read an interesting statement by Dan Kennedy recently that gets to the core of this issue. He said: "Business growth requires new customer acquisition. And if you aren't waking and working on this at least half your days, your business will not grow and will inevitably be in jeopardy....This is ONE of the chief responsibilities: creating, split-testing, changing up, mixing up such Magnets; different ones for different markets; and having full marketing funnels attached to each. If you aren't generating, maturing and managing leads, and working only with Buy Now Customers, you are never going to rise above 'kill today to eat today', above constant uncertainty and vulnerability."—*No BS Marketing Letter*, March 2014, p. 1

In the midst of running your business, it is easy to confuse revenue growth with business growth. As stated, business growth requires new customer acquisition. Kennedy continues: "There are three money questions tied to customer acquisition. What will you invest? What can you invest? How can you make it possible to invest more per customer acquired without burying yourself in debt (although debt incurred for this purpose can be good debt) or leaving yourself with empty pockets? How good you are at figuring out creative answers to these questions determines how successful you can be at business growth."

I talk a lot about customer acquisition strategies in my books, webinars, and my various monthly training calls. Yet, few are willing to look closely at the blueprints and do the hard work required to actually build a solid foundation and a business worth emulating. Most business owners are more interested in the harvest, yet aren't willing to do what it takes each day consistently to plant, water, fertilize, nurture, and put in the work necessary to actually yield a harvest that will sustain them through the tough and challenging times. It is much easier to look for shortcuts that may appear to yield a result at whatever cost, yet that may not sustain long-term growth.

Discounting for the sake of discounting because of fear of losing customers is a real phenomenon. Customers today are demanding discounts and with the explosion of choice available via the Internet and similar businesses offering the same or similar products, they are often finding those deals. Businesses who assume that things will just get better without putting viable solutions in place are seeing rapidly expanding cracks in their foundations. It is our responsibility as business owners to communicate our value and why we are different and better than the other options out there that a prospective client may be considering before buying.

To build a business blueprint with systems that will withstand the tests that are placed on it, you must be aware of and fix the small hairline fractures that happen when mistakes are made. Every business has areas of strength and weakness. You've got to focus on the areas of strength and ensure that they remain strong. You can't just spend all of your time working on just the weak areas of your business. If you do, you risk losing the strong areas to other aggressive competitors.

In this chapter, I want to share with you seven things that are required to create the systems and business blueprints you need to be strong in your business. These systems will help you appeal to today's disenchanted, distracted and busy prospects who are being pulled in many different directions.

1. **Recognize your strengths. It is better to be strong somewhere than weak everywhere.**

If you try to be all things to all people, you weaken your brand, weaken the depth of your offering and weaken your business area of strength. It is impossible to have everything a prospect will want in every single category. This means you've got to choose. When you stand for something, you become unique.

Here are four ways you can make your business stand out in your market:

1) **Find the uncontested space. Look for ways to make your competition irrelevant.**

This is a challenging thing to do, but can really set you apart from your competition. The best way to do this is to have a unique edge and build your brand around it.

Rohit Bhargava in his book *Personality Not Included* explains that this is hard to do "because as soon as you create a new industry there will be other challengers entering and ready to take you on. [But], Nintendo's Wii, Cirque du Soleil, and Crocs are all examples of others that have created a new niche for themselves by forging into new areas to make their competition irrelevant."--*Personality Not Included*, p. 85.

Here are two great questions for you to consider:
- What can you do to make your competition irrelevant?
- How can you position yourself so that you are a perceived authority, celebrity, and have exclusivity so that clients can't find what you offer or have anywhere else?

2) **Don't be a "me-too" business. Position yourself and promote your uniqueness.**

Jack Trout observes: "Many people believe that the basic issue in marketing is convincing the prospect that they have a better product or service. They say to themselves, 'We might not be first but we're going to be better.' That may be true, but if you're late into a market space and have to do battle with large, well established competitors then your marketing strategy is probably faulty. Me-too just won't cut it.

"Consider the efforts of Pepsi in the lemon-lime category. Even though supermarket soda aisles are overcrowded and sales growth is flat, Pepsi [launched] Sierra Mist, a competitor to Sprite and 7UP. This is after two failed prior attempts (Slice and a product called 'Storm'). Their introductory strategy is, what else, a 'better' soda. Dawn Hudson, Pepsi's senior vice president of strategy and marketing, boasted to the Wall Street Journal that Sierra Mist will have a"cleaner, lighter, more refreshing lemon-lime."--*Big Brands, Big Trouble*, pp. 2-3.

Sierra Mist was discontinued in 2010 and their new version of it Sierra Mist Natural is still struggling. It is easy to make the "me-too" mistake in business but as is shown here, sales haven't supported the product and its different versions.

In your business, do you make the "me-too" mistake? Do you try to promote yourself as being a better business than the other ones in your market?

Jack Trout makes this point: "When you're a me-too, you're a second class citizen. Marketing is a battle of perceptions, not products."--*Big Brands, Big Trouble*, p. 3.

Differentiation is the key. Don't adopt the me-too approach. Don't just watch your competitors and instantly mimic everything they are doing (or you think they are doing).

Instead, be different. Be unique. Position yourself in your area of strength. Yesterday, we had four prospects come into our business. Three of them bought products from us. Every single one of them had been to other businesses, yet they were all excited about being in our business (which had a unique offering) and which provided an amazing experience that they hadn't experienced anywhere else. Positioning is the art of defining how you want to be perceived without necessarily changing what you do. Marketing is about perception. Are your perceptions working for you? How do your systems and your business blueprint reflect your uniqueness?

3) Create a twist.

Do things a little bit differently than other businesses. Think about what makes you unique. Focus on developing these areas of expertise.

4) Think outside the box.

See if there are new ways to promote you and your business. My wife and I wrote a book entitled *The Ultimate Insider's Guide to Planning the Perfect Wedding* to promote our wedding business. The book is a great resource and helps couples plan their wedding with informative resources and generates new leads. Lead generation and sales efficiency are the two most important systems that you have in your business. Are there things you do in your area that can help you more successfully stand out to your clients?

Theodore Leavitt from Harvard Business School said: "The greatest asset a company has is how it is known to its customers." Reputation, brand, words, your story and how you are perceived and known by your prospects and clients are all important aspects of your systems and business blueprint.

What do your marketing messages say about you and your business?

Don't blur your difference by trying to be all things to all people. Remember, if everyone offers the same products you do, are you really that different?

As Al and Laura Ries point out in *The 22 Immutable Laws of Branding*: "Good things happen when you contract rather than expand your business. Most of the retail powerhouses today followed the same five-step pattern.
1) **Narrow the focus.** A powerful branding program always starts by contracting the category, not expanding it.
2) **Stock in depth.** A typical Toys "R" Us carries 10,000 toys versus 3,000 toys for even a large department store.
3) **Buy cheap.** Toys "R" Us makes its money buying toys, not selling toys. This is true of successful entrepreneurs as well. We make our money when we buy, not when we sell.

4) **Sell cheap.** When you can buy cheap, you can sell cheap and still maintain good margins.

5) **Dominate the category.** The ultimate objective of any branding program is to dominate the category."--Al Ries and Laura Ries, *The 22 Immutable Laws of Branding*, p. 20-21.

The companies Bench and Zara are great examples of fashion businesses that understand their uniqueness that we can all learn from:

"To cater for the immediacy demanded by fashion-conscious customers, UK street-wear fashion branch Bench has focused on 'Place'—in this instance the speed at which the product can reach retail outlets. Rather than relying on the usual trade-show route and showroom invitations, Bench uses a more direct approach. Sales people take samples to retailers, and send orders directly to headquarters while still with the retailer. An automated system then generates purchase orders to the manufacturing site within hours. From the customer's point of view (both individual consumers and retail outlets), styles arrive quickly, keeping the brand fresh. For the company it means greater efficiency, more accurate revenue forecasting, and a greatly reduced risk of being overstocked at the end of the season. The marketing mix of fashion chain Zara embodies the four Ps. Because of an emphasis on 'Place' (distribution), new products are delivered twice a week, and there are only 10-16 days from the sketching of a new design to the item's arrival on the store floor. Such a streamlined approach to 'Place' means that 'Product' reflects immediate trends; 'Promotion' happens on the instant channel of the Internet; and 'Price' is kept low due to the emphasis on 'Place.'...Zara [as] a company...has kept 50 percent of manufacturing in Spain rather than subcontracting it to Asia. Not only can the business react more quickly to changing fashions, it can also be applauded for keeping employment local."—*The Business Book*, p. 283.

Developing systems to lower costs and bring products quicker to your marketplace are both ideas that you should be focusing on in your business.

2. Your systems and business blueprint should be built on the basics of what makes a valuable, successful business.

Dan Kennedy says: "Let's review the basics of a successful, valuable business. A key factor is the affordable acquisition and assembly of a sufficient number of customers who can be retained and who will engage in on-going or repetitive transactions at price points producing net profitability."

That's a great point. If a business isn't profitable, there isn't much difference between a $25 million company with zero profits and a $100,000 a year company with zero profits. Net profitability is the foundation that any valuable, successful business is built on.

Years ago, I read this statement by Al and Laura Ries in their book *The 22 Immutable Laws of Branding* and I've never forgotten its powerful lesson. They say:
"Let's say that you really want to be rich. Now ask yourself: Can I get rich by doing what rich people do? Rich people buy expensive houses and eat in expensive restaurants. They drive Rolls-Royces and wear Rolex watches. They vacation on the Riviera. Would buying an expensive house, a Rolls-Royce, and a Rolex make your rich? Just the opposite. It's likely to make you poor, even bankrupt.
"Most people search for success in all of the wrong places. They try to find out what rich and successful companies are currently doing and then try to copy them.
"What do rich companies do? They buy Gulfstream jets. They run programs like empowerment, leadership training, open-book management, and total-quality management. And they extend their brands.
"If you want to be rich, you have to do what rich people did before they were rich—you have to find out what they did to become rich. If you want to have a successful company, you have to do what successful companies did before they were successful. As it happens, they all did the same thing. They narrowed their focus."--Al Ries and Laura Ries, *The 22 Immutable Laws of Branding*, p. 21-22.

Focus and profitability. Both are key components of a valuable, profitable business. Are these part of your business?

One area of focus all successful businesses have is the ability to keep your hands dirty or to keep your ear close to the marketplace. Jason Jennings calls this keeping your hands dirty when he explains the contrast between a CEO of a big hotel chain and Jim Cabela, the CEO of Cabela's in his book *Think Big, Act Small* on page 31.

As part of a reality television show entitled *Now Who's Boss?*, "the CEO spent five days working in one of his hotels while taping the show. 'It got me closer to the people,' he said in an interview with Hotel Magazine. 'I learned that housekeeping is physically demanding, uniforms are polyester and uncomfortable, and that many people don't tip the housekeepers.' But his biggest surprise occurred when he got stiffed while serving as a bellman. He carried fifteen bags for one customer and received no tip! This person, who has been chairman and CEO of the hotel chain for fifteen years says he was so inspired by this experience that he made a decision to implement an annual event for hotel general managers and executive committee members to spend one day doing line-level jobs. Whoosh...whatever he learned went right over his head."--*Think Big, Act Small*, pp. 31-32.

Now, contrast that with Jim Cabela:
"Each morning when Jim Cabela, cochairman, walks into his office at world headquarters in Sidney, Nebraska, there's a tall stack of eight by five sheets of white paper awaiting him. Each sheet contains a customer comment or complaint from the previous day, the customer's name and contact information, and the Cabela's representative who took the comment. Cabela spends his mornings reading each of them, noting his comments, and separating the complaints into smaller piles. Then before heading home for lunch, he walks around the company and personally delivers the small stacks to the responsible parties for their immediate action and follow up."

Then, Jason Jennings asks this question:
"How many chairman of multibillion-dollar firms do you think spend several hours each day reviewing all of the previous day's comments and complaints and personally directing an immediate follow-up? A jealous competitor might cynically mutter, 'What the heck else is there to do in Sidney, Nebraska?' At Cabela's with a string of 40 years of consistent revenue growth, Jim Cabela's response would be a benign smile and a question, 'What could be more important than listening and responding, to customers and doing whatever else you have to do to make and keep them happy?'"--*Think Big, Act Small*, p. 33.

I love this statement from Al Ries and Jack Trout in their book *Marketing Warfare*: "Strategy should evolve out of the mud of the marketplace, not in the antiseptic environment of an ivory tower."--p. 188.

As an entrepreneur in today's challenging business environment, you likely feel like you're up to your neck in the mud of the marketplace. *Yet,* you must step out of the "mud of the marketplace" enough to stay in touch with the prospects and clients coming into your business and offer them a personal touch because it is one of the most powerful things you have to offer with your business brand that will help your message spread faster.

Creating an experience where you have more of a personal interaction with your customers will set you very far ahead of the competition when it comes to the experience they tell their friends about.

3. The essence of your systems and business blueprint should show detail in a systematized way how your customers can do business with you next.
The way you attract prospects and clients into your business and the way you treat them once they are there is the key to establishing brand loyalty and getting the next sale..

Consider this example of how a supermarket attracts new customers into their stores as detailed by Guy Kawasaki in his book, How *to Drive Your Competition Crazy.* He says: "Dick's Supermarkets, a chain of eight markets in Wisconsin and Illinois, uses a comprehensive direct mail program to establish brand loyalty with new customers.

"Store employees create a list of people who recently moved into the area, newly married couples, and families with newborn children. These lists are compiled from newspaper announcements, utility company new account information, chambers of commerce announcements, and personal knowledge.

"Newly arrived and newly married couples receive a welcome or congratulations letter from the general manager of the nearest Dick's store. There are six coupons included with the letter that are good for two free items each week for three weeks. "If we can bring people in six times we feel we can convert them into regular customers, says William Brodbeck, the president of Dick's Supermarkets.

"Two and a half weeks after the first letter, Dick's sends a second letter from Brodbeck, another six coupons, and a self-addressed, postage paid survey about the store. In this letter Brodbeck thanks people for using the coupons. How does he track coupon usage? He doesn't. He assumes that the recipients have used the coupons and send his thank you letter to all of them.

"Finally, one year after the first letter is sent, Dick's sends a third letter with another survey and a coupon for a discount on items such as baked goods or flowers.

"Newborn children receive a letter containing coupons that starts out with "This is your first business letter." Parents can redeem the coupons, and on the child's first birthday, a letter is sent to his or her parents along with a coupon for $2 off a birthday cake from Dick's."--*How to Drive Your Competition Crazy*, pp. 114-115.

How could you use this idea in your business?

Is there a sequence of correspondence you could develop and use as part of your business blueprint to impress your overall experience onto those who come into your business and buy from you?

In Chapters 7 and 8 of *The System is the Secret*, I discussed twelve specific lead generation systems. Many of these have sequential elements that can help you focus on what the prospect or client needs to do next. For example, the referral system you utilize in your business is one example of telling clients who have had a great experience with you how they can specifically invite their friends to do business with you.

4. Create a community where you can get the word out about your business.

One way you could do this is to create an online community where your prospects and clients can share helpful tips with one another about how to better utilize the products and services you provide. This online community can not only help you share helpful information to prospects, but it will be a place where you can see what your prospects and clients are talking about and what is important to them. This will allow you to create better experiences for your clients in the future. This will help you create and utilize your own media to spread the word about your business. This online community is one example of how you'll be able to position yourself as an authority and expert in your market niche and get a sense for how prospects and clients are actually using your products and services. This feedback can help you discover new product opportunities as well as discover how clients are best utilizing what you offer so you can create better testimonials.

The credibility you'll get from such testimonials and from creating such a place where your community can interact with you and with others will go a long way towards helping you sell more of your products and services. Let me share with you an experience I had when I was in high school that taught me the importance of credibility. The principle is as true now as it was then. I met with a banker in our small local town in Northwest Missouri with the purpose of selling him some fundraising tickets for a dinner that our scout troop was hosting. He was a little annoyed that I was meeting with him and completely brushed me off. I never forgot how he made me feel and I never went by that bank without thinking about that experience. He wasn't inspired by our cause and didn't see me as credible. A good friend of mine's father knew that banker and took his son in to see him and sell him the exact same fundraising tickets. The same banker bought ten tickets from him. That experience is a good reminder to me of why credibility is so important. An online community where you share and help prospects and clients is a powerful way to create and build long-term credibility for your business. I learned about the power of credibility when my friend Robert got a sale because he had a referral and most importantly the credibility of his father to get the sale.

Here are some questions for you to ask to determine how well your systems and overall business blueprint is helping you project credibility to prospects in your area:

- Are you educating prospects about what they most need to know about buying what you offer?
- Are you promoting your experience and what it will mean for them (that they can't get anywhere else)?
- Do you come across as being knowledgeable about what it is that you are selling or do they seem to know more than you?

- Are you communicating clearly with him or her? It has been proven that seven out of ten marketing communications are misunderstood today.
- Do prospects and clients sense that you are an expert?
- Are you likable?
- Are you inspiring? Do you borrow the credibility of others to enhance your own?

These are great questions to carefully consider as you promote your credibility. Remember, credibility is the pivot point of influence. It is what will help you build the foundation to be more persuasive. This is just one example of how you can position yourself as an expert and be aware of what is happening in your market community.

Other ways you can benefit prospects in your market niche community would be to offer:
- Tips and advice for prospects
- Events at your business
- Awards you've received
- Information, articles, and advice
- Place for prospects to post pictures and their experience in your business
- Recommended resources and vendors

Prospects should be able to access from your site in such a community forum sections of your book, tips to help them utilize your product or service, and interviews with other happy clients who have enjoyed working with you.

The benefits of doing this are huge:
- Lower cost than having radio station or TV station interview you. You can create your own video and put it on YouTube and you can record your own content right on your computer.
- Additional income stream for your business – you can charge advertisers to be on your web site or do be a part of your interview series as opposed to you paying to be on radio shows. You can put it right on your web site for clients to download.
- You can position yourself as an authority and a celebrity in your market.

A powerful way to create a community where prospects and clients want to be is to have a unique and memorable edge that your competitors don't.

Robyn Spizman and Rick Frishman make this astounding claim in their book *Where's Your Wow?*:
"If your product or service has no unique or meaningful edge, no amount of marketing is going to make it a success."--p. 33.

When you have a unique edge and an authentic story, you can differentiate yourself from your competitors. A good reason to do this is so that you don't get lumped into the commodity classification.

Consider this statement from Laura Ries who with her father wrote *"The 22 Immutable Laws of Branding"* *"The Fall of Advertising and the Rise of PR"* and *The Origin of Brands*. She said recently:
"Brands do matter. Brands are what enable you to make profits. If you don't have a brand, then you have a commodity, and everybody knows there is no money in selling commodities."

Author Seth Godin makes this observation in his book, *Purple Cow*:
"Remarkable marketing is the art of building things worth noticing right into your product or service. Not just slapping on the marketing function as a last minute add-on, but also understanding from the outset that if your offering isn't remarkable, then it's invisible."

You don't want your business to be invisible, so it is critical that you make your brand authentic and have an edge.

A big part of your systems and business blueprint is to reinvent yourself and tell your story in unique ways as we talked about in Chapter 17. I like how authors Chip and Dan Heath explain this in their book *Made to Stick*. They explain:

"A sticky idea is a simple, unexpected, concrete, credible, emotional story. Lots of sticky ideas have only a few of these traits, but some have all six like John F. Kennedy's famous call to put a man on the moon and return him safely before the end of the decade. It's simple—easy to understand, easy to explain. It's unexpected – in 1961, putting a man on the moon sounded like science fiction. It's amazingly concrete—notice how easy it is to visualize the moment of success, the moment when a human being sets foot on the moon. It was credible because it came from the mouth of a popular president. It's emotional—it appealed to our yearning to reach the next frontier (and let's not forget, our desire to beat the Soviets). And it's the story of a journey in a miniature."-*Where's Your Wow?*, p. 35.

The number of people viewing viral content online is what drives advertising revenue and studying what makes something go viral and then acting on those ideas to create your own viral content is an important part of your future business blueprint. David Letterman is losing in a dramatic way to new thinking and a better blueprint that is capturing more viewers and is one of the reasons why NBC is betting big on Jimmy Fallon and Seth Meyers in their late night lineup. No one wants to be caught being the dinosaur that goes extinct.

5. Be clear about what you want and be sure that everyone on your team understands their role AND their part in achieving the goal. Bill Walsh, one of the most influential head coaches in the history of the NFL explains this in his book *The Score Takes Care of Itself.* He says:

"Former Cleveland and Cincinnati head coach Paul Brown taught me a lot during the eight years I worked for him as an assistant coach. Among his many talents was direct communication. He was clear, specific, and comprehensive without an ounce of ambiguity. I like his approach and recommend the same for you. Here's an example of how he insured that everyone was on the same page. On the first day of each season's training camp, Brown would give a lecture to the squad that covered his own Standard of Performance—what he expected (demanded) in all areas. Of course, a leader's personal example is perhaps his most powerful teaching tool, but words have their own power and specificity.

"Brown would start each season with the phrase, 'Gentlemen, let's set the record straight,' and then proceed to do exactly that. Step by step by step, specific after specific, he would cover every aspect of being on the Cincinnati Bengals football team.

"He discussed how to wear the uniform, how to dress for meals, how each player was expected to keep his locker in order. He told players how he wanted them to respond to coaching, how to take notes during lectures, how teaching would be done, and what to expect from each assistant coach.

"Brown covered such specifics as punctuality, the training-room rules, what would happen when players were waived (this always sent a chill through the group), and the overall environment he intended to create. Furthermore, he shared his policy of treating each player—starts, backups, veterans, rookies, free agents—equally, with the same high level of respect and dignity.

"Each year his lecture, and this was only a sampling of topics, lasted about four hours (and voluminous printed material supplemented the lecture). Paul Brown was thorough enough that when the Bengals personnel left the meeting room they knew precisely what they were supposed to do in the coming weeks and that their head coach expected them to enthusiastically adhere to every procedure, policy, and timetable he had specified. Needless to say, he continued with that kind of direct and clear communication in the months that followed—in practice, during games, and elsewhere. What he laid out was measurable. And he measured it on a regular basis—his version of your company's year-end review. (You will note that I included some of Brown's material in my own Standard of Performance and expanded greatly on it. Like Paul Brown, I attempted to be clear, specific, and direct in putting forth my own requirements concerning actions and attitude.)

"Vince Lombardi had a similar appreciation for the benefits of direct—specific—communication. Supposedly, he started each season's training camp by assembling the team and announcing, as he held it over his head, 'Gentlemen, *this* is a football.' That's how Vince began his introduction of the fundamentals of his particular system, with clear communication. Both Brown and Lombardi understood the necessity of spelling out in detail what you expect from employees and doing it in a manner that is unambiguous and comprehensive.

"It is an important element in why these great coaches succeeded. Employees can thrive in an environment where they know exactly what is expected of them—even when expectations are very high. When it comes to telling people what you expect from them, don't be subtle, don't be coy, don't be vague. What's your version of 'Gentlemen, this is a football'?

"There's another story about Vince Lombardi worth mentioning because it points out a high-priority responsibility of any leader. During a game in which his Green Bay Packers were giving up one gain after another, as the opponent marched down the field, he screamed out at his defensive players, 'Grabbin', grabbin', grabbin'! Nobody's tackling!!! What the hell is going on out there?'

"Lombardi could see that this defensive players were not getting it done, were not really doing the hard job of *tackling* runners. He let them know that 'grabbin'' was not their job description and simply going through the motions was going to get them beat. A leader must know when his team is making a lot of noise signifying nothing. UCLA's coach John Wooden summed it up like this: 'Don't mistake activity for accomplishment.' (John Wooden, *Wooden on Leadership*) Lombardi was more graphic in his language but was addressing the same issue."—pp. 109-111.

Don't be vague about what you expect yourself and those on your team to do. A clear system or blueprint outlines exactly what must be done as a business or a project it is based upon is being built. If you lack clarity, you will probably end up with something you didn't expect.

6. Don't be content with where you are. Have the courage to attack yourself before your competitors do.
A great example to me of the courage it takes to attack yourself is found in the life of Diane von Furstenberg and how she has reinvented her company by necessity.

"In 1970, von Furstenberg created her own line of printed cotton knit dresses and brought them to New York. She was seven months pregnant, she recalled, pulling a heavy suitcase full of samples up flights of stairs, taking one rejection after another from the buyers. Her friends thought she had lost her mind. That spring, during New York's famed Fashion Week, she hired some young women from a modeling school to present her work at the Gotham Hotel. A few small shops bought her designs, then Bloomingdale's, then a store on Rodeo Drive in Beverly Hills. She hit the road, lugging her suitcase full of samples from one mom-and-pop clothing store to another....By the end of 1975, von Furstenberg was selling 15,000 of her figure-hugging 'wrap dresses' a week. Retail sales from her clothes, branding licenses, and a new fragrance and cosmetics line hit $60 million. A few months later she was on the front page of the Wall Street Journal—and then, the cover of Newsweek. 'Von Furstenberg: The Princess Who is Everywhere,' the New York Times proclaimed. And she was still just twenty-eight years old. But in 1977, the bubble burst: The company was overextended, the market saturated with her products. Women's Wear Daily declared the wrap-dress craze history. Von Furstenberg was stuck with $4 million in inventory—and a factory in Italy pumping out 25,000 new dresses a week. The company was sliding quickly toward bankruptcy.

"But von Furstenberg fought back. She sold the entire dress business, despite the emotional toll, and restructured the company top to bottom. She refocused exclusively on cosmetics and perfumes while continuing to make millions a year by licensing her famous DVF brand name. The company took off again—only to overheat and overexpand once more in the early 1980s. The company was nearly lost, until the cosmetic business was sold. Now, with a cash-positive position, von Furstenberg set out to build DVF all over again.

"In 1992, she made her most unexpected leap: She brought her DVF signature goods to QVC, the dowdy home shopping network. One night, she recalls, she sold more than $750,000 worth of her goods in just fifteen minutes. When Barry Diller bought QVC, von Furstenberg got 10 percent of the company as a kind of finder's fee.

"Since then she has continued to fight for the survival of her firm....Now, some 40 years after setting off a fashion revolution with her wrap dress, von Furstenberg is president of the Council of Fashion Designers of America, the highest seat at the most prestigious fashion association in the nation. 'Isn't it hard,' I asked her one day, 'fighting one battle after another, to keep your dream alive?'

" 'My mother was in the concentration camps,' Diane replied quietly, 'at Auschwitz-Birkenau and Ravensbruck. When she was freed she weighed forty-nine pounds. Sixteen months later she gave birth to me. Compared to that, my hardships are nothing."–Erik Calonius, *Ten Steps Ahead*, pp. 80-82.

Oftentimes, the best way to stay on top in any business is to attack your own core business with something unique that makes what you used to sell obsolete. If you don't have the courage to do this, the marketplace may shift and you will be left behind. One interesting observation about the late-night host battles that are heating up is that shifting demographics and shifting behaviors of how people consume media are changing the landscape in that industry. Things are shifting and changing your industry as well. How you adapt to those changes will be a big part of whether you will continue to grow and prosper or whether your business will decline as your client's behaviors shift and change.

In order to determine where to attack your business, ask:
- What is your number one strength in your business?
- What is your biggest weakness?
- What is your biggest opportunity?
- What is your biggest threat?
- If you were your competitor, where would you attack?

Taking time to think about how to attack yourself is a great way to stay on top and to look for better ways to stand out in the marketplace.

7. Be committed enough to continually look for ways to improve and get better and get back up one more time.
Ask the clients you work with: How can I improve my service to you next time? How can I be better next time? If you just ask clients, "How is everything going?", they will invariably answer "Fine." To have the edge, learn more, and set yourself apart, you could ask: "How can I improve my service to you next time?" Then look for meaningful ways to act on what you've learned.

It takes commitment to change and learn new things. It is hard to beat resistance everyday. It takes courage and a willingness to do what hasn't been done before.

I'm inspired by this great statement by Sterling Sill about Julius Caesar in his book *How to Personally Profit from the Laws of Success*. He said: "Pompey the Great was ruler of the vast Roman Empire half a century before Christ. His most important field general was Julius Caesar. Caesar had some differences with Pompey, and was considering marching on the capital to take matters into his own hands. In forty nine B.C. Caesar came to the Rubicon, a small river in Northern Italy that served as his territorial boundary line. The Rubicon was called 'the sacred and inviolable.' It was the line across which no general was ever allowed to pass without special permission from the Senate. If Caesar crossed the Rubicon it would be with the idea of making the entire Roman Empire subject to his will.

"That was a momentous decision. It would immediately precipitate a civil war and divide the world between Pompey and Caesar. Caesar knew what the consequences would be if he tried and failed. He knew that many lives would be lost, in any event. Surely he must have hesitated before arriving at so great a decision, for he knew there could be no hesitation after the decision was made. Caesar carefully considered every angle. He explored every possible alternative. Then he made up his mind. He would march on Rome.

"One part of Caesar's power came because of his ability to analyze a situation: another part came because of his habit of always finishing what he started. He was not starting the biggest undertaking of his life, to strike down the very heart of the world. Caesar said, 'The die is cast.' That expression marked the point where deliberation ended and action began. There would be no turning back. Then Caesar threw himself into the waters of the Rubicon at the head of his legions and the whole history of the world was changed."–pp. 49-50.

What have been the moments in your life where you have made a momentous decision and stuck with what you started out to do? Perhaps, you are experiencing your own "crossing the Rubicon" moment in your business right now.

What have you decided to stick with or eliminate to help you get back on track or stay on track towards the accomplishment of your goals? When you are sure and determined, your commitment will be seen by everyone around you.

This important quality of leadership is what will give you the courage to continue and motivate those around you to give a little bit more and to be a little more focused on the accomplishment of your daily, weekly and monthly goals. After all, you can't lead anyone somewhere that you aren't committed to get to yourself. The decision to get there and stay on track is at the heart of any successful business blueprint.

As an entrepreneur, you may be hurting and stressed out from the continual pressure placed on you. It takes courage to go back into the game one more time for one more sale when the chips are down and you don't know if you have what it takes to succeed.

I love this statement by B.C. Forbes about this quality that you and I need to hold onto every day of our lives: "History has demonstrated that the most notable winners usually encountered heartbreaking obstacles before they triumphed. They won because they refused to become discouraged by their defeats."

Few individuals had as many reverses of fortune in business as Walt Disney. There is a lot we can learn from his life and more importantly his perseverance when others had all but given up on him or thought he was crazy. The story of how he created *Snow White and the Seven Dwarfs* is a particularly inspiring example of what it takes to persevere when others don't believe in what you are trying to do. A great summary of this story is told by Darcy Andries in her book *The Secret of Success is Not a Secret*. She says:

"The film *Snow White and the Seven Dwarfs* was not Walt Disney's first business venture. In fact, at least three of Disney's previous businesses had failed and, and after one such failure, he was forced to file for bankruptcy. Disney had once been fired by a newspaper editor who told him he 'had no good ideas.' Somehow, Disney knew that the Snow White venture would be different and that this idea was a good one. Not everyone agreed with him, and early in production others warned him that he was going too far. The whole concept of creating such an extravagant family film seemed ludicrous to his critics. For four years, Disney ignored the skeptics and critics as he worked. Costs for the film exceeded $1.5 million and pushed his company to the edge of bankruptcy before he was done. *Snow White and the Seven Dwarfs*, the first full-length animated feature presentation, became the most successful motion picture of 1938 and earned an honorary Oscar in 1939, in part because it 'pioneered a great new entertainment field.' Since its release, the film has earned more than $400 million. Disney holds the record for having received the most Academy Awards, twenty-six, including four honorary awards. He was nominated for sixty-four awards during his lifetime." –pp. 172-173.

This is an important reminder. Even a consistent hit maker like Disney has failures and disappointments. Disney had two notable failures in 2013 with *John Carter* and *The Lone Ranger* at the box office. However, nobody is talking about those disappointments with the massive success of *Frozen* in late 2013 and throughout 2014. Your business is no different. You may be experiencing difficulty, challenge, and failures in your business right now. Persevere through the difficulties you're facing. Someday soon, you'll look back on your challenges, the failures, and the criticism you've experienced as the stepping stones that led to your success. Do what it takes to learn to develop the business blueprint and systems that will lead you to the success you desire.

The late Chet Holmes tells a fascinating story at the beginning of his excellent book *The Ultimate Sales Machine* that I want to share here because it gets to the core of the kind of commitment it takes to implement systems into your business. He said:

"When I was 15 years old, I tried a new method for increasing my karate skills. I had a high vaulted ceiling in my bedroom. I screwed a cowhide rope into the peak of the ceiling and attached a softball to the other end, at chest level. My intent was to kick and chop the ball and then to be able to deflect it, block it, kick it, or chop the ball again when it came bouncing back.

"With my first karate chop at the ball with my hand, the ball bounced out to the edge of the rope and back fast, smacking me in the head. This wasn't going to be as easy as I thought. I tried all kinds of kicks—hook kick, front kick, back kick, side kick—but again and again the ball flew to the end of the rope and then bounced back, hitting me in the head, elbow, shoulders, or chest.

"I worked on this for several weeks and made very little progress. After a month, there were a couple of times when I could actually block the ball from hitting me. After three months of doing this every single day, I could hit the ball with any one of the body's weapons—my hands, my feet, my elbows, and my knees. I could even do a spinning back kick and hit it again, then block it expertly as it flew at me from a different angle.

"After six months, the ball never touched me. I could spin artfully in the air, flawlessly blocking the ball at every angle. It was amazing. I could literally catch, kick, or swat that ball with every move any time I liked and faster than I would've ever thought possible. My body was operating like a machine, responding to the ball as if preprogrammed to anticipate every possible move the ball could make.

"Imagine my skill level when that ball would ricochet around the room with lightning speed and my reflexes were even faster. It was thrilling. I felt such power. I realized that becoming a master of karate was not about learning 4,000 moves but about doing just a handful of moves 4,000 times. The repetition trained my body to run like a machine—and that's what constant and focused repetition will do for your business. No matter what comes up, your responses are automatic because you've prepared for and developed the skills to deal with every possible scenario....It is the same with any business; there are basics that you can do over and over again until every aspect runs like a machine." --pp. xix-xx.

One of the best parts of the book is the part where he explains the need for repetition in sales training and the same applies for implementing your business systems. He says:

"When designing your training programs, remember that repetition is the key to preprogramming your company or department to run like a machine...No one gets good at anything without repetition....Just how serious are you about your company? Are you playing at business or taking care of business? According to Sun Tzu in *The Art or War*, one of the five essentials of victory is this: 'He will win whose army is animated with the same spirit throughout all its rank.' How are you going to animate your whole team with the same spirit? Three words: training, training, training.

Most of the better training programs come in and blitz an organization with a lot of information and then they leave. The staff has a nice healthy glow for about a week afterward....But in reality, without continuous follow-up, very little sticks from a one-shot training. That said, one-shot training is better than no training, but you're about to learn that there is a better way.

By rotating core material regularly, the same concepts are constantly reinforced and reiterated. Skills are impacted immediately in either training method; yet, over time, skills are impacted immediately with constant repetition......[When you] constantly teach the same information again and again until the skill is permanent, the skill improves [with less falloff] because it's the same material being covered....With each training session mastery is that much closer."-- *The Ultimate Sales Machine*, pp. 28-29.

In this book, I have outlined the systems and strategies you need to grow your business to new heights. When you implement better systems in your business, you will turn your business into a cash-producing machine.

It's time to take care of business and put better systems into your business. Your commitment to keep at it and push through your challenges and fears will help you make it work no matter what it takes. The ability to forge on when you feel fear is what makes champions. That kind of perseverance and tenacity is something that can't be written in any blueprint. It is what makes you who you are and why you will win in the fight you are now waging each and every day. I wish you the best of success as you continue to work on, develop, and refine your systems into a clear blueprint that will build your business for a long, sustainable, and profitable future.

<u>Chapter 20</u>

Why You Haven't Built and Refined Your Systems and What to Do About It

"Time is a created thing. To say, 'I don't have time' is like saying 'I don't want to.'"
—*Lao-Tzu*

Most entrepreneurs know they need to create, refine and better implement systems in their business. However, a force called resistance prevents you from actually doing what it takes to do what you know you need to do. Resistance is the powerful force that stops us from doing what we know we need to do every day. In order to get anything done and to stay focused on your personal and business goals, you have to beat resistance every day of your life.

Stephen Pressfield in his excellent book, *The War of Art* makes this observation: "Most of us have two lives. The life we live and the unlived life within us. Between the two stands Resistance."

If you've ever started an exercise routine and haven't followed through for more than a few days, you've experienced resistance. If you've ever set a goal to follow a new routine or start a new habit (or eliminate a bad one), you've experienced resistance. If you've set the goal to finally write down and implement better systems, you've experienced resistance. The reality is that if you've ever tried to change anything or do anything outside of your comfort zone, you've experienced resistance.

Breaking through resistance is the only way we can really get ahead and move up to the next level in anything. As Steven Pressfield points out in *The War of Art*, "Resistance obstructs movement only from a lower sphere to a higher." That means that staying stagnant or plummeting to a lower level won't cause much resistance on the way down. You do feel resistance when you *recognize* how far you've fallen and how much harder you'll have to work to get to where you used to be, or where you really want to be.

I sincerely believe that our inability to break free of resistance is at the heart of why we don't achieve more in our businesses. It is easier to *stay* where you are than it is to battle the resistance necessary to climb to the next level. It is easier to *accept* where you are now than it is to battle the resistance you will continually encounter on your way up.
The truth is that all of us let resistance beat us much more than we would care to admit. In this chapter, I will show you five specific ways you can beat resistance so you can get back on track and create better systems so you can be more productive, focused, and successful.

1. Get around others who can help you. Break free of your own inertia.
Marshall Goldsmith that outlines why most people don't succeed at what they set out to do in life and this applies to why you may have been delaying the systems work necessary in your business as well. He says: "As much as we all claim to want happiness and meaning in our lives (very few people say that they want to live miserable, empty lives), there's a paradoxical catch that thwarts us at every turn. I call it the Mojo Paradox and I want you to burn it into your memory:
Our default response in life is not to experience happiness.
Our default response in life is not to experience meaning.
Our default response in life is to experience inertia.

In other words, our most common everyday process—the thing we do more often than anything else—is *continue to do what we're already doing.*

If you've ever come to the end of a TV show and then passively continued watching the next show on the same channel, you know the power of inertia. You only have to press a button on the remote (an expenditure of less than one calorie of energy) to change the channel. Yet many of us cannot do that. Quite often, inertia is so powerful that we can't even hit the remote to turn the TV off! We continue doing what we're doing even when we no longer want to do it.

Inertia is the reason I can say the following with absolute certainty about your immediate future. The most reliable predictor of what you will be doing five minutes from now is what you are doing now. If you're

reading now, you'll probably be reading five minutes from now. The same is true for almost any other daily activity. If you are drinking or exercising or exercising or shopping or surfing the Internet now, you will probably be drinking or exercising or shopping or surfing the Internet five minutes from now. Take a minute to let that sink in and weigh the statement against your own life." –*Mojo: How to Get It, How to Keep It, How to Get it Back If You Lose It*, pp. 34-35.
He continues:

"Very few people achieve positive, lasting change without ongoing follow-up. Unless they know at the end of the day (or week or month) that someone is going to measure if they're doing what they promised to do, most people fall prey to inertia. They continue doing what they *were* doing. They don't change their behavior, and as a result, they don't become more effective."—Marshall Goldsmith, *Mojo*, p. 36.

Many entrepreneurs fall prey to this trap of going with the flow (of doing things the way they've always been done) instead of looking for new ways to improve. It takes a conscious choice to break free of your own inertia. Get around others who can help you.

In his book *8 Ways to Great*, author Dr. Doug Hirschhorn shares this insight from how Roger Bannister broke the four-minute mile. The lesson shows why having a systematic process for achievement is so important and why getting around others who can help you achieve your goals is critical. He says:

"One of the most compelling illustrations of how setting short-term goals and committing to the process leads to extraordinary achievement is the story of how Roger Bannister became the first person to ever run a mile in under four minutes. At the time, many people believed that running a sub-four-minute mile was humanly impossible, but Bannister had a plan. He ran with two pacemakers. The first pacemaker, Chris Brasher, ran under the four minute pace with Bannister slotted to run behind him for the first mile. Then, when Brasher began to tire, Bannister signaled to his second pacemaker, Chris Chataway, to take over. Chataway moved up and ran under the pace with Bannister right behind him until they were two hundred yards from the finish, at which point Bannister sprinted ahead and crossed the finish line in 3 minutes, 59.4 seconds. The point is, Bannister didn't start out saying he had to

run the mile in under four minutes. Instead, he had short-term goals—
keeping up first with Brasher and then with Chataway—and when those
two things were added together, Roger found himself being the first
person to break the 'impossible' four minute mile."

I love that story because it illustrates what you must *do* to build and
create systems. You think through the process and challenge in front of
you. Bannister succeeded, where many others had failed, because he
broke down his goal and then had others around him set the pace for his
achievement. In your business, you have to figure out what will work
and what you need to do to reach your goals. When obstacles arise, as
they always do, you have to remain optimistic and lead by taking action.
Great leaders, like great systems, rely upon a plan and a process. They
make adjustments and improve.

Over my desk, I have a signed picture of Roger Bannister breaking the
four minute mile along with my favorite quote by him which says: "The
man who can drive himself further once the effort gets painful is the
man who will win."

Reading this book and acting on what you've learned is one way you've
chosen to learn new ways to grow your business. Making the choice to
overcome your own resistance to implement new and better ways of
promoting your business can be painful, yet that sustained effort will
make all of the difference to help you get to where you want to be.

2. Have vision. Know what you want. Don't let the fear of failure hold you back.

My favorite example of vision is in the life of Erik Weihenmayer, who is
the first blind person to reach the 29,035 foot summit of Mount Everest,
the world's highest mountain. I would like to tell you a little bit about
Erik and use his story to talk about the importance of vision in your
business from Brian Souza's book *Become Who You Were Born to Be*:

"When Erik Weihenmayer was six months old, doctors learned that he
had retinoschisis, an eye disorder that would slowly destroy his retinas.
He grew up knowing he didn't have long to see the world, and by the age
of thirteen, he was totally blind."—p.105

How would you respond to such a crisis? Would you draw inward, setting limits on what you could accomplish in the future or would you push outward looking for new ways to accomplish your dreams?

Erik is one who chose to expand his horizons and look for new ways to accomplish his dreams. As Souza says: "Today, Erik has broken through boundaries few people—let alone those who are blind would even dare to approach. He's a marathon runner, skydiver, long-distance biker, skier, scuba diver, and member of the college wrestling Hall of fame. More amazing yet, he's accomplished the three highest mountains the world [including his summit of Mount Everest]."

"'All my life,' he wrote in his book *Touch the Top of the World*, 'fear of failure has nearly paralyzed me.' The operative word is *nearly*."

"Even as a boy when his sight was ebbing, he rebelled against falling into the trap of retreat and self-pity. He would go with his friends to a forty-foot cliff, below which flowed a shallow stream with only one small deep spot. Miss that spot and you could be killed. But in what would later become one of his signature habits, he faced down his feats and went for it."

"Failure, as Weihenmayer sees it, is a learning opportunity, not a disgrace. Once, for instance, while scaling Washington's Mount Rainier, a warm-up for the Everest ascent, he had to set up a tent on a freezing snowfield. When he took off his glove so he could feel the tent pole, sharp splinters of ice sliced into his hand. It went numb, and when it regained feeling, the pain was so intense he almost vomited. His teammates had to finish putting up the tent for him."

"Stung by this setback, he resolved to turn it to his advantage. Back home in Phoenix's hundred-degree heat, he put on his thick winter gloves and practiced setting up his tent again and again. Today, he can do it faster than any of his sighted comrades."

"Innovations and small acts, he's found, together can spell success. When he decided to climb El Capitan's 3,300-foot vertical wall in Yosemite National Park, he spent a month learning how to haul equipment up the mountain, place pitons in cracks, sleep overnight on a ledge, and perform dozens of other complex skills. While other climbers can see where they're going, he finds his way by raking his fingers across rock faces to find even the tiniest cracks. He has become so attuned to sounds that he can plunge his ax into an icy wall and actually hear which routes seem safest."

"Unlike Weihenmayer, many people are afraid to even attempt to achieve their lifelong dreams and thus become emotionally paralyzed, daring neither to succeed nor to fail. They may exist in this world, but they're not really *living*. They're surviving, not *thriving*. But, as Weihenmayer's father put it after his son's Everest climb, 'A meaningful life is all about taking constructive risks, whether you succeed or not.'

"Erik Weihenmayer has proven that no matter how outlandish it may seem, any *dream* is possible."—Brian Souza, *Become Who You Were Born to Be*, pp. 105-107.

What about you? Do you allow yourself to dream bigger or have you shut down your dream factory? Hearing about Erik Weihenmayer has hopefully inspired you to begin dreaming again. You should imagine what you could do or accomplish in your life if you had no limitations and begin dreaming again. Successful people in every walk of life dream big dreams.

The one thing you need more than any other in your life is vision. None of us sees far enough, clearly enough, or soon enough. Don't get so caught up in focusing so much on the present that your future is out of focus. The biggest difference between those who have vision and those who don't is that the person with vision thinks about and prepares for their future, while the person who lacks vision lives each day as it comes. Vision is the ability to see, but it is also the ability to imagine what others cannot see.

Shortsightedness is caused when we are more interested in what is going on in the present than we are in looking to the future. The proverb "where there is no vision, the people perish" is still true today. In order to succeed long-term in business, you must develop the ability to project your plans and dreams for the future beyond your present situation. Those who have vision that motivates them to take action have used their imaginations to picture their distant goals so large in their conscious mind that they seem even more important than the goals of the present.

Author J.K. Rowling made this statement about how she conceived her character Harry Potter and there are several things you can learn from what she says about dreams and vision. She said: "My boyfriend was moving to Manchester and wanted me to move, too. It was during the train journey back from Manchester to London, after a weekend looking for a flat, that Harry Potter made his appearance. I have never felt such a huge rush of excitement. I knew immediately that this was going to be such fun to write...I didn't know then that it was going to be a book for children—I just knew that I had this boy, Harry. During that journey I also discovered Ron, Nearly Headless Nick, Hagrid, and Peeves. But with the idea of my life careering round my head, I didn't have a pen that worked! And I never went anywhere without my pen and notebook. So, rather than trying to write it, I had to think it. And I think that was a very good thing. I was besieged by a mass of detail and if it didn't survive that journey it probably wasn't worth remembering."

Don't be shortsighted. Look to the future. Have vision. Learn to dream again. Leonard Lauder (president of Estee Lauder) probably said it best:

"We were a tiny company, but I dreamed someday of being able to run a large company....I came to realize that fantasizing, projecting yourself into a successful situation is the most powerful means there is of achieving personal goals. That is what an athlete does when he kicks a field goal with three seconds on the clock, and 80,000 people in the stands and 30 million people watching. As the kicker begins to move he automatically makes the thousand tiny adjustment necessary to achieve the mental picture he has formed in his mind so many times: the picture of himself kicking the winning field goal."

Are your thoughts focused on who you need to be and how you need to act to get what you want?

How great is your desire to be proactive (have vision) instead of reactive (stay in the present) in your business?

John Maxwell wrote in *Failing Forward*:
"Not *realizing* what you want is a problem of *knowledge*.
Not *pursuing* what you want is a problem of *motivation*.
Not *achieving* what you want is a problem of *persistence*." –*Failing Forward*, p. 97.

Mystery author Rita May Brown made this observation: "A life of reaction is a life of slavery, intellectually, and spiritually. One must fight for a life of action, not reaction."

Don't be someone who has the ability to see, but has no vision. Fight for your dreams. Focus on the future and you *will see* great things you can achieve and do in your business and in your life.

3. Persist through difficulty. Live by the mantra: Profit or perish.
It isn't easy to persist when no one believes in you, but yourself. It isn't easy to be patient when you hold out for what you want. Yet, persistence and patience are two extraordinary qualities that are at the heart of all success. I never imagined that I would be in the bridal business when I was growing up. I had "friends" of mine laugh at me when I told them I was going to get into the bridal business. Some even thought I was opening a horse bridle business. Those who laughed and those who were encouraging weren't there through the early years of the store when my wife and I barely saw each other and worked insane hours just to keep things going. I worked a sales job in the mornings before I opened the store to help pay the bills. We steamed dresses together on our date nights. We persisted and believed in what we were doing. We didn't give up when things were tough.

It is easy to look at someone's success and see the end without realizing that the beginning was much different. When you are working through challenges and problems in your business, don't give up. Be persistent. Develop patience. Have the courage to endure when times are tough.

I've always loved this poem by Edgar A. Guest. He said:

"Stick to your task till its stick to you;
Beginners are many, but enders are few.
Honour, power, place and praise
Will come, in time, to the one who stays.

Stick to your task till it sticks to you;
Bend at it, sweat at it, smile at it too;
For out of the bend and the sweat and the smile
Will come life's victories, after awhile."

Your determination to succeed and your ability to hold tightly onto your dreams will help you have the courage and the motivation to make one more sale or to improve one more system in your business when you are completely exhausted and don't know how you will do it anymore. With patience and persistence, you'll be able to the overcome obstacles that stand in your way and make your goals and dreams realities.

Big changes are happening in business in all industries today. It is so important to live by the mantra of Profit or Perish more than ever today since big and costly mistakes can mean the end of your business. If it isn't making you money, why are you still selling it? It isn't just about making sales. It is about how much money you get to keep after **all** of the expenses are paid. If you see shifts in the marketplace, what will you do about it? What will you do to ensure that your systems are set up to maximize profitability?

When I think about all of the challenges that face entrepreneurs, I think about this poem by Edgar A. Guest:

"The easy roads are crowded
And the level roads are jammed;
The pleasant little rivers
With drifting folks are crammed.
But off yonder where it's rocky,
Where you get the better view,
You will find the ranks are thinning
And the travelers are few.

Where the going's smooth and pleasant
You will always find the throng,
For the many—more's the pity
Seem to like to drift along.
But the steps that call for courage
And the task that's hard to do,
In the end result in glory
For the never-wavering few."

Persist through difficulty. You can do it. Kenneth Cole's story of his ingenuity and resourcefulness when launching his shoe line is another inspiring example of what it takes to succeed.

"In December 1982, footwear buyers from all over the country converged on New York City for market week. More than 1,100 smaller companies vied for the attention of shoe buyers at the Hilton hotel on Sixth Avenue. Christmas lights were already lining the streets, and larger shoe companies had set up showrooms within the hotel's twinkling four-block radius.

But in 1982, Kenneth Cole didn't have the money for a showroom. Or a hotel room, for that matter. And he didn't think that lining up with hundreds of other small to medium-sized footwear designers was the way to make his products stand out.

So, he called a friend in the trucking business. 'Sure, you can borrow a truck,' his friend said. 'But good luck getting permission to park. This is New York.'

Then Cole called the mayor's office. They told him the only way to get a permit to park along the street in New York City was to be a utility company...or a production company shooting a full-length motion picture.

Cole ran to the stationary store, changed the name on his business cards and boxes from Kenneth Cole Inc. to Kenneth Cole Productions Inc. and applied for a permit to shoot the full-length movie The Birth of a Shoe Company.

On December 2, across the street from the Hilton and surrounded by footwear showrooms, Cole parked a 40-foot trailer filled with his new designs, painted his company name on the side and put a staircase at the back. He unloaded klieg lights, a film camera, a director, models as actresses and two policemen sent by the city to control traffic—and soon to be employed by Cole to control the crowd at the velvet rope. Every important buyer in town for market week visited that trailer over the next few days to see what all of the fuss was about. The longer they waited behind the velvet rope outside the police-guarded 'movie set' trailer, the more intrigued they became. And the more they bought. Kenneth Cole Productions sold 40,000 pairs of shoes in two and a half days. And a shoe company was born." –Amy Anderson, *Success*, July 2010, pp. 41-42.

What are you willing to do when things don't go your way? Are you willing to creatively approach the challenge or the problem from a new angle? Are you willing to persist when others don't believe in you?

I am reminded of writer J.K. Rowling's persistence to get her first book published. She persisted through a three-year process of writing the first Harry Potter book and persisting through twelve rejections by publishers.

"Joanne Rowling had always dreamed of being a writer, yet she failed to complete any of the adult novels that she had started. One day, during a delayed train trip, she got another idea; she would write a children's book. It took her three years to finish writing the book. At the time, she did not own a computer—or even a typewriter—and did all of the writing longhand. When she had completed the book, she typed in on a second-hand manual typewriter and contacted an agent.

"Her agent immediately sent the manuscript out to twelve publishers, but each rejected the work. He tried other publishers, and finally, Bloomsbury agreed to publish the book, *Harry Potter and the Philosopher's Stone*. Rowling received an advance of just $3,000. The head of the company's children fiction division warned her that there was no financial reward in children's books.

"With money she received from a grant from the Scottish Arts Council, Rowling purchased a word processer and steadied her turbulent finances while she finished a second book in the series, *Harry Potter and the Chamber of Secrets*. Even before *Harry Potter and the Philosopher's Stone* had been published, it garnered the attention of Arthur Levine, the editorial director of Scholastic Books. After a bidding war, Scholastic secured the American rights for *Philosopher's Stone* for $100,000. In June 1997, Bloomsbury published Harry Potter and the Philosopher's Stone with an initial print run of only one thousand copies, half of which were distributed to libraries. More than a year later, the book hit American shelves under a slightly different title, *Harry Potter and the Sorcerer's Stone*, to highlight the book's magical theme.

"Sales of the book greatly exceeded expectations. Almost half a billion of Rowling's books about the young wizard Harry Potter have been published in more than six hundred languages. In 2004, Forbes magazine estimated that she had earned more than $1 billion from her books, making her the first person ever to become a billionaire as a writer. In 2006, Forbes placed her as the second richest woman entertainer in the world, right behind Oprah Winfrey." –Darcy Andries, *The Secret of Success is Not a Secret*, pp. 256-257.

Rowling once wrote "It's important to remember that we all have magic inside us." You have magic inside of you to keep getting up and doing the things every day to make your business succeed. Never give up. You can do it. Every one of us has the magic of persistence inside of us that helps us push through the difficulties to get it all done.

4. Ignore naysayers who criticize, mock, or doubt what you have set out to accomplish.

A big key to being successful in anything is to move forward with action when you feel strongly about it and feel there is a tremendous opportunity that others are missing. This often means that you *will* be criticized by others. A great example of the power of persistence and refusing to let the criticism of others hold you back is found in the life of Jennifer Hudson. Jennifer auditioned to become a contestant on American Idol and landed a spot as one of the show's top performers.

"Simon Cowell, a judge for the show, told Hudson that she was 'out of her league.' As if to prove his point, she twice landed among the bottom three, but then received enough votes to remain on the show. On the sixth episode, she sang 'Circle of Life,' impressing Cowell as well as the song's writer, Elton John. Revising his initial opinion, the judge proclaimed that Hudson had 'finally proved why she was among the top twelve.'

"She was stunned and disappointed when voters cast her once again among the bottom three contestants, ending her role on the show. 'I cried all the next day,' she later admitted. 'It definitely hurt.'

"About a year later, after Hudson had finished touring with other American Idol contestants, a New York casting agency asked her to try out for a role in an upcoming movie, *Dreamgirls*. After two auditions and two rejections, she was asked to try out once more. The third time was definitely the charm—she landed the role of Effie White in Dreamgirls. Hudson beat out almost eight hundred people—including Fantasia Barrino, who had appeared with Hudson on American Idol and had eventually won the title. After the movie proved to be a huge success, Cowell admitted on national television, 'I'd like to be the first to admit a massive dose of humble pie. That was extraordinary, Jennifer, and I feel very proud of you.'

"To date, Hudson has won more than eighteen awards for best supporting actress or 'best breakthrough performance' from organizations such as the New York Film Critics, the Los Angeles Film Critics Association, the Southeastern Film Critics Association, and the National Board of Review. She has also won an Academy Award for Best Performance by an Actress in a Supporting Role, a Screen Actors Guild Award for Best Supporting Actress, an NAACP Image Award for Best Supporting Actress in a Movie, and British Academy Film Award for Best Actress in a Supporting Role."—*The Secret of Success is Not a Secret*, pp. 338-339.

Jennifer later said, "Simon [Cowell] said to me that you only get one shot at the big time. But you know what, Simon, I got shot number two." Don't let your past failures discourage you from getting back up and making it happen. If you haven't set up systems in your business, yet, it's okay. You can begin now. Persistence and creativity are two important qualities that can help you turn failures into successes. Don't give up. You can do it!

All successful individuals at one point in their lives have had to ignore naysayers that criticized, mocked, and doubted what they set out to accomplish. You have to make the conscious choice to ignore this criticism and choose to persevere instead. This is one of the most common characteristics I've observed as I've read numerous business biographies throughout my life. Some have become motivated by hearing others laugh at them and then they have chosen to rise above that criticism to succeed. Others have experienced reverses and misfortunes and have chosen to rise above them.

I recently read about Cordia Harrington who is the founder of Tennessee Bun Company, Nashville Bun Company, and Cornerstone Baking Company. She is known as "The Bun Lady" and her companies make the English muffins on an Egg McMuffin at McDonald's, the buttery rolls at O'Charley's and the biscuits at KFC, among a host of other buns and bakery products.

She bought a McDonald's franchise as a single mom in 1990 (after applying and training for two years) in hope of offering a better life to her three sons. Her story is a great example of the creativity and ingenuity it take to succeed at anything. The restaurant was in a poor location and sales weren't what she had hoped they would be.

Harrington didn't place the blame on her poor location. She went out and did something about it that transformed the restaurant and gave her another big opportunity years later. She purchased a Greyhound bus franchise and moved the routes so they would stop at her restaurant. Talk about ingenuity!

She said:
"I needed to grow sales in this small town (Effingham, Illinois), so I purchased a Greyhound franchise and moved it to my restaurant parking lot. It worked. In the winter, we averaged 68 buses a day, and in the summer, over 100 buses a day—all stopping for food."

When challenges arise in your business, do you have the courage and the initiative to look for new ways to generate business? Or is it easier to place the blame on external situations or factors? I recently discovered this great quote by former President Lyndon B. Johnson that I think identifies the easy way out of problems, but not the one that will help you achieve lasting success. He said: "There are plenty of recommendations on how to get out of trouble cheaply and fast. Most of them come down to this: deny your responsibility."

Don't deny your responsibility. Take the initiative to make things happen. Harrington had an opportunity years later at her McDonald's franchise when she heard of their need of a bun supplier and decided to take the initiative to provide the buns to all of their franchises.

"She landed a spot on the restaurant's corporate bun committee. Learning of their need for a bun supplier, she fought like mad (calling regularly and even sending photographs of herself in a chef's uniform) to land the supplier job, even though her résumé included no baking experience."

"When she earned the position, she sold her franchises, cleaned out her bank accounts and borrowed $13.5 million to create Tennessee Bun

Company in 1996. Today, it is one of the fastest automated bakeries in the world, producing 1,000 buns a minute." –*Success*, August 2010, p. 34.

I really like this comment she makes:
"There are going to be tons of naysayers who will tell us not to take risks. They'll tell us to keep the comfortable job where there is income and insurance. But if you believe in something, then you should go for it. The real key is that you have to have passion and enthusiasm for the product or project you are going to sell." --*Success*, August 2010, pp. 34-35.

Have you had others laugh at you or doubt what you are trying to do? Do you have the resolve to believe in what you are doing in your business when others don't?

Never forget that the resolve to succeed even when others don't believe in you is one of the most important ingredients in the recipe that leads to success in anything.

Are you motivated by what naysayers have told you about your business? Are you motivated to do what it takes to prove them wrong? Will you build systems that will inspire awe of others in your industry?

I love this statement by B.C. Forbes about this quality that you and I need to hold onto every day of our lives: "History has demonstrated that the most notable winners usually encountered heartbreaking obstacles before they triumphed. They won because they refused to become discouraged by their defeats."

5. Resistance to changing anything that affects the status quo or stepping outside of your personal comfort zone.

If you've ever felt resistance to changing how things have always been done in your business, you have experienced this type of resistance. Everyone knows that change is the only way we really make progress but we all resist it.

A closed-minded approach to new ideas is one of the most common manifestations of this type of resistance. You have likely experienced or thought these things before. For example, have you ever heard yourself say:

- " We don't do it that way."
- "We don't care what anyone else is doing. We have all of the answers right here."
- "We're doing okay. That may get results for them, but it would never work for us because...."

The problem with this kind of thinking is that the things that have worked in the past won't always work in the future. It is a good idea to be constantly seeking out new ideas to old and challenging problems.

A great example of this comes from the life of Henry Ford, who invented the automobile. He was once asked about customer demand for the automobile. He said: "If we had asked the public what they wanted, they would have said faster horses." Because he was willing to reach out of his comfort zone and think differently, he achieved legendary success during his lifetime. Later in his life, he became closed to new ideas. He thought he had all of the right answers. This attitude started him on the path of decline. He once famously said that the public could have their Model-T car in any color as long as it was "black." His closed minded approach allowed competitors to gain the upper hand and shatter the momentum that Ford had created in the marketplace.

Think about the resistance of the big three automakers in the past to making different types of cars and continuing to make gas-guzzling SUVs when other competitors were offering alternatives. These companies are in trouble largely for their inability to get outside of the comfort zone that they got used to. As a result, they have been declining for years.

The question to ask yourself is: Are you open to new ideas or do you close yourself off to suggestions by others who are successful saying, "That will never work here."?

For example, I know many entrepreneurs who invest in privately labeled products that give them a higher profit margin. Many resist this and other strategies to get new customers by saying or believing that only branded merchandise would sell in their businesses. Today, smart entrepreneurs look for new ways to make their business work. When they discover that their old way of doing business is no longer working, especially in the case where they are being shopped solely on the basis of price, they change what they are doing to get the results they seek. The best way to avoid becoming closed minded is to ask questions: find out what others are doing and how you can do the same.

I have five children. I've always been amazed how children ask better questions than adults. They aren't afraid of looking dumb or silly. And they don't try to impress with the quality or caliber of their questions. They sincerely want to know the answers. Most questions that kids ask are "How Come..." questions like "How come the sky is blue?" or "How come dogs have cold noses?" or "How come we don't have dessert after breakfast?"

Avoid the resistance to change by being open to new ideas. Ask questions of others who are where you want to be. As Charles Steinmetz once observed: "No person really becomes a fool until that person stops asking questions." Many times we resist change because that is the only way we know to do things.

There is a story told of a family who moved into a new neighborhood. One morning they got a late start, and the six year old missed her bus to school. Though it would make him late for work, the father agreed to take her to school if she could give him directions. They left the neighborhood, and the young girl began directing her father to take one turn after another. Following twenty minutes of circuitous driving, they arrived at the school, which turned out to be only eight blocks away. Steaming, the father asked the kindergartener why she had him drive all over the place when the school was so close to home. "We went the way the bus goes," she said. "That's the only way I know."

How many of us are like this young girl? We go where we go in our business—because that is the only way we know how to do it. We can't be like Alice in Lewis Carroll's *Through the Looking Glass*, who asks for directions in this way during her encounter with the Cheshire Cat: "Would you tell me please, which way I ought to go from here?" she asks.

"That depends a good deal on where you want to get", the cat replies with a grin.

"I don't care much where", she answers.

"Then it doesn't matter which way you go", the cat responds.

If you are undecided about the direction of your business, you will merely *drift* along (and will likely not achieve the success you could if you would just focus in on what you need to do).

What do you *really* want your business to do?

Are you focusing on the right things that will lead you to that goal moment-by-moment and day-to-day or do you get easily distracted and lose your focus?

You can overcome this resistance by recognizing what you don't know and asking lots of questions of those who do. Drifting with the status quo or just going with the tide can give the false appearance of *motion without direction*. Drifting is dangerous because you feel as though you are making progress (and sometimes you are), but you will never get to your desired goals with the speed and momentum you could if you just focused in on the actions required to get you where you want to go.

I like what Mark Sanborn says in his book *You Don't Need a Title to Be a Leader*: "Without focus, it is impossible to move forward to achieve your goals. Effective leaders...are able to keep themselves and those around them on task. Those who lack focus in their personal lives and in their careers tend to drift.

"Years ago, on one of the first cruises my wife and I ever took, I visited the bridge of the behemoth ocean liner we were sailing on and spoke with the captain. I asked him about the biggest seas he had ever sailed in with that ship. He told me he had been in seas with ninety-foot waves. Impressed, I inquired about how he had managed to keep the ship intact. He told me that while ninety-foot waves were daunting, the ship could negotiate them quite handily as long as it didn't lose power.

'If you lose power in big seas in any boat, you're in serious trouble. Under power,' he explained, 'the boat can stay perpendicular to the waves. Without power, the boat would drift parallel to the waves and be capsized or swamped.' That is the danger of drifting.

"In acting as a leader, you can handle just about anything that comes your way as long as you don't lose power and drift. Power, in this sense, is the ability to stay engaged in what is going on. It doesn't mean that you have control over every situation, any more than a boat has control over the waves. Rather, it is the ability to engage the situation with intent, with *focus*. Drifting and waiting are very different things. Waiting is an intentional choice. It requires patience and deliberation. Drifting takes away your power of choice.

"When you wait, you believe that something will happen, although you may not know when. Instead of acting rashly or impetuously, you pause to gather information and seek insight. Drifting results from rudderlessness and lack of direction. When you drift, it doesn't even take particularly large waves to capsize the boat. It's all too easy to become distracted or lulled into complacency. Before you know it, you are drifting. A simple lack of attention can cause you to lose the power of purpose and engagement. Instead of initiating action, you become paralyzed. Rather than acting, you find yourself acted upon." —pp. 42-43.

Resistance has both positive and negative aspects to it. It has been said without resistance a person or vehicle could not move about, or if already in motion, could not be stopped except by collision. Simple things like nails, screws, and bolts would not stay in place; a cork would not stay in a bottle, a light globe would drop from its socket; a lid would not stay on a jar.

Yet, if you let resistance prevent you from doing what you know in your heart you should do, especially when it comes to refining the systems in your business, you will be stopped in your progression. Learn to break through resistance and let it be what propels you to achieve your goals.

A great analogy of how you can use resistance to propel you forward is that of a boat. When you pull the oars against the resistance of the water, it creates the force that causes the boat to move forward. Well-designed boats also have a prow that helps the boat cut through and divide the water in order to help overcome the resistance that slows down the speed of the boat.

Don't give in to resistance as you are building and refining your systems. Learn to overcome these five areas of resistance in your life and in your business. When you overcome its daily assault on your life, you *will* rise above it. When this happens, you will utilize the time and resources necessary to create and implement systems in your business.

Chapter 21

Take Action and Do It Now

"You are surrounded by simple, obvious solutions that can dramatically increase your income, power, influence, and success. The problem is, you just don't see them."
—*Jay Abraham*

"I always look to the system for a solution. If a challenge arises I use a system correction before I look for a people correction."—*Brad Sugars*

There is power in taking action. With the ups and downs of the economy over the past several years, many businesses have cut back, retreated, and as a result have lost market share. Others have expanded and are increasing their market share. There is a great lesson to be learned form the two very different responses of Kellogg and Post during the Great Depression.

"In the late nineteen-twenties, two companies—Kellogg and Post—dominated the market for packaged cereal. It was still a relatively new market: ready-to-eat cereal had been around for decades, but Americans didn't see it as a real alternative to oatmeal or cream of wheat until the twenties. So, when the Depression hit, no one knew what would happen to consumer demand. Post did the predictable thing: it reined in expenses and cut back on advertising. But Kellogg doubled its ad budget, moved aggressively into radio advertising, and heavily pushed its new cereal, Rice Krispies. (Snap, Crackle, and Pop first appeared in the thirties.) By 1933, even as the economy cratered, Kellogg's profits had risen almost thirty percent and it had become what it remains today: the industry's dominant player.

You'd think that everyone would want to emulate Kellogg's success, but when hard times hit, most companies end up behaving more like Post. They hunker down, cut spending, and wait for good times to return. They make fewer acquisitions, even though prices are cheaper. They cut advertising budgets. And often they invest less in research and development. They do all this to preserve what they have. But there's a trade-off: numerous studies have shown that companies that keep spending on acquisition, advertising, and R. & D. during recessions do significantly better than those which make big cuts." –James Surowiecki, "Hanging Tough", *The New Yorker*, April 20, 2009

The difference between financial success and mediocrity in any business is action and implementation. All of us know more than we do. As General H. Norman Schwarzkopf once observed, "The truth of the matter is that you always know the right thing to do. The hard part is doing it."

The key to thriving and not just surviving the troubled times we find ourselves in is to do more of the right things and then create systems to better run those areas of your business. Here are seven ways you can take action and get more done now:

1. Stay focused on your top priority every day. Eliminate productivity killers.
There is so much that needs to be done in our businesses every day. If we don't have a plan and priorities for action, we are likely to get sucked into the day's activities and merely drift through each day instead of focusing on the most important priorities of each day.

Why don't more of us get things done more productively in our lives and in our businesses? The problem in large measure is us. We don't clearly define what it is that we want and make sure that every activity we do moves us closer to that goal. Jim Rohn was once asked why more people don't become millionaires. His answer is very interesting. He said, "The reason more people don't become millionaires is because they don't have enough reasons to."

Do you have enough reasons to keep you productive? Or do you allow yourself to get easily distracted from the things that you do that create profit in your business?

What this really means is that you have to control yourself and many people really have a challenge with this. As I mentioned in Chapter 16, most people have never been around someone who is extremely productive. They haven't observed the success habits of those who get more done than others do. But, if you study this, you'll find that the most productive people are those who have learned to control themselves and what they do. They put themselves in an environment where they can focus and where distractions are eliminated. In many cases, they use their environment to control their behavior.

To help you be more productive, you must learn to eliminate distractions that will prevent you from accomplishing the tasks you need to get done. This may mean working on marketing campaigns or other projects you need to get done out of your business or by coming in earlier before anyone else arrives. You have to discipline yourself to unplug the phone, turn off your cell phone, not connect to the Internet, and avoid anything that will distract you from the priority in front of you.

Distractions today are incredible. Many are completely consumed by technology and have an automatic tendency to constantly be checking email, text messages, voice mail, Facebook and Twitter updates, phone calls, updates on their favorite web sites, etc. Even if you are the most productive person on the planet, you will still have productivity issues with those around you who interrupt you or who aren't as focused on the task at hand as they could or should be. You must first learn to control yourself and your environment and then help members of your team to do the same.

Everyone has some form of productivity kryptonite—something that interrupts you and prevents you from performing at peak productivity. Just like Superman, you have to shield yourself from these productivity killers so you can get done what must be done.

What is your productivity kryptonite? Once you've identified it, determine what you can do to shield yourself from this deadly productivity killer. To get more done, what changes will you have to make to your behavior or your environment to ensure maximum productivity?

For example, if you know you should have a Monthly Morning Marketing meeting with yourself every Monday morning and you are being interrupted, what changes will you have to make in order to make this meeting more productive so you can focus and get things done?

The other thing you need to think about is this: What is the productivity kryptonite of your staff?

For example, if looking at and constantly updating Facebook or another online forum is your productivity killer, what constraints do you have to put in place to prevent you from constantly getting online?

Here are three suggestions if your productivity kryptonite is getting online instead of focusing on the work at hand:

- Limit yourself to 1/2 hour every day when you will get online
- Install software on your computer that blocks Facebook unless you enter a password. This will help you get out of the electronic OCD loop (where you do something without even thinking about it).
- Unplug your Internet connection when you are working on your priority.

A big part of increasing your productivity is to put constraints on others. If you are your own biggest enemy, everyone else in your business, and outside your business that wants to talk to you is your next biggest enemy. You have to let people know how you work so that you can get things done. For example, if you are the primary salesperson in your business, you can't be constantly interrupted by sales reps or others constantly calling you on the phone.

You need to have some controls in place as we discussed in Chapter 16. For example, you may decide that you will return phone calls from 1:00 to 2:00pm every day. Then, you have to train your staff when they answer the phone to tell the other party that you aren't available then, but will return their call sometime that day between 1 and 2pm. This will disappoint, frustrate, annoy and inconvenience some, but you will disappoint, frustrate, annoy and inconvenience yourself if you don't have these types of parameters in place since you will have fewer sales and less productive time in your office and in your business.

I would strongly encourage you to work on this. To be more productive, you must understand and control yourself and those around you. Be clear about your priorities. When you are clear, you can stay focused on the task at hand. You may need to write down what your rules will be and post them on your wall.

For example, during my Monday Morning Marketing meeting that I work on in my business, I will not:

- Answer the phone or take phone calls (I turn off my phone or take the phone off the hook before I start working to ensure the environment is conducive to this type of focus).
- Check my email (my email browser will be closed)
- Be distracted by web sites that don't pertain to my specific objective or focus
- Get up from this meeting with myself until I have a comprehensive plan in place with lists and steps for what needs to be done next, who will do it, and when it will be completed by so I can stay on track for launching and creating a successful event).

In addition to my weekly Monday Morning Marketing meeting, I have numerous time periods each week that I have blocked off to focus on specific areas of my business that I want to work on. My staff knows not to interrupt me during that time. Things can wait 90 minutes while I finish what I am working on.

The key to being more productive is to focus on one thing at a time and compartmentalize your thinking so that you allow yourself to focus on one thing at a time. The other part of this is being really clear about why you are staying focused. In other words, what is the reason behind the need for increased focus? Are you really motivated to stay on task because of the goal you have set for yourself?

The questions you should ask are:

- What is driving me?
- Does it really motivate me to stay on track?

Until you gain clarity on this issue, you will never have the personal discipline to control yourself, your environment and others around you because the priority won't be strong enough to overcome the resistance you'll feel.

2. Delegate more.

Face it – you can't do it all. Trying to do it all will burn you out and prevent you from reaching your true potential. Instead, get good at assigning the right job to the right person in the right way. This means that you think through the job *before* you delegate it. Determine who the best person to delegate a task to will be. Ask them to write down what you've asked them to do and have them summarize for you what needs to be done. Then, set up a time to review progress or completion.

One of the biggest mistakes made when delegating is to think you can forget about something once it has been delegated and believe that it will still be done. Instead, help others remain accountable to the task you've delegated by carefully explaining and overseeing what needs to be done. To help you find out what activities you can delegate, carefully think through these five questions.

1) List all of the business activities in your business that take up your time. Include everything (including five minute tasks). Be specific, clear, and brief.
2) Describe three things that you are brilliant at doing in your business (that only you can do).
3) Name the three most important activities that produce revenue for your business.
4) Briefly outline your daily schedule. What do you spend most of your time doing? Can you delegate out some things you are weak at so you can focus more on what you are brilliant at?
5) Name the three most important activities that you don't like to do in your business or that you feel you are weak at doing. Then ask yourself, "Who could do these for me?"

Now that you've determined what time consuming activities you can delegate, what is the *first* thing you are going to say 'No' to or delegate right away? Don't put it off any longer. Delegate this activity now. There will be an immediate benefit to your business because of your choice to delegate and focus on what you are best at.

3. Spend more time every week working on marketing your business. Stop guessing and start tracking results.

How much time do you really spend on marketing your business to gain new leads or to guide those leads so they can move to the next step? If you're like many entrepreneurs, it is not nearly enough as it should or could be. Everyone can do better at this and if you have the right framework with a marketing calendar planned out for the year and you put in the time, this will have a dramatic impact on the number of prospects coming into your business through your marketing funnels.

The best marketing strategies in the world won't work if you don't utilize them. As I already mentioned, you should be having a meeting weekly where you plan your marketing promotions and strategies. You should also set aside at least 5-10 hours a week where you can work exclusively on the marketing of your business. If you find that you are too busy, find someone who can help you with this critical function of your business. This can be one of the most profitable things you'll ever do for your business.

In every successful business, someone takes time to carefully evaluate the numbers. You should take time to carefully evaluate how successful each campaign you have done has been. Here are two reasons why you should track your results more closely:

1) If you know what works and what doesn't, you will know what to do to increase your business.
2) Once you see an increase in sales due to good marketing decisions, you will see a drop in client visit cost.

In other words, let's say you spend $1,000 on an advertising campaign that brings in 10 prospects. The cost of attracting each of these prospects is $100 ($1000 divided by 10). On the other hand, if you use proven strategies that will help you bring in 30 prospects and you spend the same $1,000, these prospects now only cost you $33.33 each ($1000 divided by 30). When you track your results, you can make better decisions about how to spend your advertising budget.

As an assignment, here are four questions for you to consider about your marketing and advertising decisions:
1) What has been the most successful marketing promotion you've done this past year?
2) Why was it so successful?
3) When can you run this promotion again? Is there any way you can change it to make it even more effective?
4) What promotions do your competitors use that are successful?

Which ones can you adapt and use now? Find out what works and keep repeating it. The bottom line is that if you want to be successful in marketing your business, stop guessing, start implementing, and track your results to determine how you can be even more effective.

4. Build and take control of your unique difference with your personal brand. Do everything it takes to become an authority figure in your market niche in your area.

As an entrepreneur, you must quickly define what it is that give you a unique or meaningful edge in your market niche. If you don't and your prospects and clients can commoditize your product, you will see your business decline and suffer.

Consider this statement by Robyn Spizman and Rick Frishman on page 33 of *Where's Your Wow?*:

"If your product or service has no unique or meaningful edge, no amount of marketing is going to make it a success."

When you brand your business and you, you can create clients that are loyal to *your business* and *the experience* they will have working with you as compared to anyone else. The most important part of branding is to stand for something. You can only stand for something when you specialize. Many businesses today try to be all things to all people. As a result, the products and services they offer become commoditized because there isn't anything unique about them.

I first learned how power and authority are related and tiered from marketing expert Dan Kennedy. He says: "At the bottom of the hierarchy of any business is a generalist. A generalist has very little authority and they have very little power. Why? Because they are fundamentally interchangeable and generalists are viewed as interchangeable by everybody who does business with them. A great example of how this works is in medicine. If you go to a general doctor or a general practice (you may not even see your doctor), you can get the care you want from pretty much any doctor there. If your doctor isn't in, you can get help from someone else. The doctor is interchangeable with any other doctor because they are not a specialist.

"If the doctor is out on vacation when you come, you can still find someone else to give you service. This means that you as the patient have the power. You can decide if you like that group of doctors or not. If you don't, you can go down the street and find a new group of doctors (provided that your health insurance covers their care). However, if you need cardiac surgery or brain surgery, you go to a specialist. You go to the best one in the business. How are you treated when you call a specialist? You have to have an appointment. They can't just see you anytime (in other words, they are in control). The people who have the most power in any market are those who have specialized their businesses into a specific niche."

I want to encourage you to become a specialist in your business. Why? Because when you are a specialist instead of a generalist, you will be more valued, remembered, and clients will value doing business with you to a much higher degree. Your goal should be to move up the hierarchy where you will have more power and control and where you'll also be the most profitable.

So, in order to build a powerful business brand and be more successful in selling more of your product or service, you need to have more power as a business *and* as a person. There are so many personal tools that you can use to build your brand in today's crowded marketplace. In order to expand your outreach and build your authority and celebrity, your business should have a blog, a business Facebook and Twitter account, and a good website to start. You can also build an audience with your own book and a podcast. Each of these tools gives you a coordinated place to showcase your business, why you're different and your specialized knowledge in your market niche.

5. Pay the price. Be willing to change and make sacrifices to reach your goals.
Even if your business is already doing very well, you always have to be willing to make changes. John Maxwell has four ideas in his book *The 17 Indisputable Laws of Teamwork* that explain the price you have to be willing to pay if you want to keep improving and get better.

He says:
1) The price must be paid by everyone.
"It is so critical that every member on your team is willing to pay a price and that they pay the price to win. Because if they don't, then you will pay the price of losing." You are in your business to win. I know this is true or you wouldn't have gotten this far in this book.

I like what former Notre Dame coach Lou Holtz once said, "The freedom to do your own thing ends when you have obligations and responsibilities. If you want to fail yourself you can but you cannot do your own thing if you have responsibilities to team members.""

2) The price must be paid all the time.

John Maxwell observes: "Destination disease is as dangerous for a team as it is for any individual. It makes us believe that we can stop working, stop striving, stop paying the price—yet still reach our potential."

Dwight D. Eisenhower once said: "There are no victories at bargain prices."

3) The price increases if the team wants to improve, change, or keep winning.

John Maxwell writes on p. 139 of his book *The 17 Indisputable Laws of Teamwork* that "there are few back to back champions in sports. And few companies stay at the top of *Forbe's* magazine's lists for a decade. Becoming a champion has a high price. But remaining on top costs even more. And improving upon your best is even more costly. The higher you are, the more you have to pay to make even small improvements. World champion sprinters improve their times not by seconds, but by hundreths of a second."

Are you constantly striving to improve or do you sometimes stop to admire the view?

If you want to improve, change, and keep winning in your business, you always have to be making improvements and pushing the envelope. Otherwise, you will start to decline.

4) The price never decreases.

Maxwell observes: "Most people who quit don't give up at the bottom of the mountain; they stop halfway up it. Nobody sets out with the purpose of losing. The problem is often a mistaken belief that a time will come when success will suddenly get cheaper. But life rarely works that way."

He concludes with this thought:

"When it comes to the Law of the Price Tag, I believe there are really only two kinds of teams who violate it: those who don't realize the price of success, and those who know the price but are not willing to pay it. No one can force a team member to have the will to succeed. Each person must decide in his own heart whether the goal is worth the price that must be paid."

What about you? Are you willing to pay the price to succeed in your business? Do your actions demonstrate that commitment?

Today is the best day to take action to get what you want. In his book *Action! Nothing Happens Until Something Moves*, author Robert Ringer says:

"There are two kinds of actions. One is proaction, which puts you on the offensive and, all other things being equal, gives you a great deal of control over events. The other is reaction, which puts you on the defensive and relegates you to an inherent position of weakness. An interesting way of looking at inaction is that it's really just a negative form of action—a sort of black hole of action that sucks energy away from you much the same as the black holes of the universe pull matter into the deep recesses of their cosmic bowels. This is why inaction often yields consequences by default. Nothing happens until something moves, so if you wait for something, or someone, to act on you, you likely will be unable to control the consequences."

To stay on track with your goals, you should take time out of your schedule to get away from your business and write down business goals for yourself for the upcoming month, quarter, 6 months out, and a full year ahead. Determine what it is that you want. The clearer you can be, the better. Once the goals are set, the big challenge is to get everyone around you who will help make the goal happen buy into the goal and do the work necessary to accomplish the goals. This is always a challenge because you typically have to go against the grain to get things done. Change is always required and when change is required, there will be resistance. The greater the change with your goals over the previous year's accomplishments, the greater the resistance you will experience. You willingness to pay the price and make sacrifices as they are translated into meaningful actions will ensure that you overcome the resistance you face.

6. Accept the responsibility to motivate yourself. Accepting responsibility means being creative and initiating change where it is needed.

If you are thinking that next year is going to be more of the same of last year, you are likely going to move slower towards accomplishing it.

Why?

Because if you don't have something to jump-to or feel like you don't have something to jump-to, you won't have much of a desire to jump-start your business. You won't jump up and do what it takes if you feel beaten down and have lost hope for the future.

Take the initiative to jump-start your life and your business. Overcome the tendency to procrastinate from what you know you need to do. Now is the time to align or re-align your business with the energy you had when you started. Every day you choose to stay in your business by how you show up in it. Choosing to be an owner of anything requires responsibility. Besides being responsible to your employees and your clients, you have a responsibility to yourself. When anyone accepts responsibility in their life, they simultaneously embrace initiative. When you get into a rut or a routine and don't continue to be creative and initiate change, you have dumped your responsibility and are looking to someone else to bail you out. Choose to motivate yourself and build your systems now.

7. Stop doing the stuff that isn't helping your business achieve your goals and start doing what will.
You likely got into your business because you were passionate about it and it was something that you really wanted to do. Along the way, you may have started focusing on something that has taken you away from your goals. Perhaps this was a product or service that you thought your clients would want that hasn't turned out to be very successful or profitable.

Focus on what works. The most powerful word for accomplishing more of what you want is to specialize. Specialization requires us to simplify down what we do to the core elements that will bring us the greatest profitability, the highest return on our time and energy, and to focus on what really matters. If it isn't making a difference in your business, stop doing it and start doing something that does.

John Maxwell says: "Winners stop doing things that are not good for them and losers stop doing things that are good for them."

That's a great statement. If you are going to win in today's hyper-competitive environment, you can't do things the way you've always done them. In order to win the sale today, you've got to stop what isn't working and start doing more of what does. You've got to have better lead flow systems, better sales and persuasion systems and better follow-up systems. You've got to be clear about the results you are after.

Asking great questions such as: "How can we sell more now?" or "Why aren't our prospects buying now?" help you gain the clarity you need to take action in the right areas. Great questions help you discover great answers. The questions I just posed on improving sales and understanding why prospects aren't buying are "focusing questions" as Gary Keller explains in his book *The One Thing*. He says:

"The Focusing Question helps you identify your ONE Thing in any situation. It will clarify what you want in the big areas of your life and then drill down to what you must do to get them. It's really a simple process: You ask a great question, then you seek out a great answer. As simple as two steps, it's the ultimate Success Habit".

He continues: "The Focusing Question helps you ask a great question. Great questions, like great goals, are big and specific. They push you, stretch you, and aim you at big, specific answers. And because they're framed to be memorable, there's no wiggle room about what the results will look like....A big, specific question leads to a big, specific answer, which is absolutely necessary for achieving a big goal.

"So if 'What can I do to double sales in six months?' is a Great Question, how do you make it more powerful? Convert it into the Focusing Question: *'What's the ONE Thing I can do to double sales in six months such that by doing it everything else will be easier or unnecessary?'* Turning it into the Focusing Question goes to the heart of success by forcing you to identify what absolutely matters most and start there. Why? Because there's where big success starts too." –pp. 119-123.

I think this perspective is very important in taking the focused action necessary to build systems. It can be overwhelming if you try to do it all at once. Instead, you've got to ask great questions with as much specificity as possible.

Here are some examples based on the systems we've discussed together:
*   What's the ONE Thing we can to improve our inbound lead flow system so we have a steady stream of leads?

- What's the ONE thing we can do to increase trust with our prospects to make our pre-sales and marketing systems more effective?
- What's the ONE thing we can do to improve our sales and persuasion systems so we double our current closing rate?
- What's the ONE thing we can do to improve our follow-up systems so we don't leave money on the table?
- What's the ONE thing we can do to improve our customer service systems so we can prevent our most common issues from ever coming up again?
- What's the ONE thing we can do to improve our hiring and training systems so we hire the right people and train them to succeed from day one?
- What's the ONE thing we can do to improve our leadership development systems so everyone is working together to accomplish our goals?
- What's the ONE thing we can do to better plan and prepare against having a competitor coming in and take one of our biggest and best clients (or any other specific crisis situation)?
- What's the ONE thing we can do to improve our financial systems and ensure more consistent cash flow?
- What's the ONE thing we can do to increase our productivity so that every day is moving us closer towards the accomplishment of our goals?
- What's the ONE thing we can do to reinvent our business this year so we aren't blindsided by an upcoming trend?
- What's the ONE thing we can do to better counter-balance our scheduling systems?

If you aren't asking the right questions you aren't going to be able to get to the right answers. Keller explains it this way in *The One Thing*: "The challenge of asking a Great Question is that, once you've asked it, you're now faced with finding a Great Answer.

"Answers come in three categories: doable, stretch, and possibility. The easiest answer you can seek is the one that's already within reach of your knowledge, skills, and experience. With this type of solution you probably already know how to do it and won't have to change much to get it. Think of this as 'doable' and the most likely to be achieved.

"The next level up is a 'stretch' answer. While this is within your reach, it can be at the farthest end of your range. You'll most likely have to do some research and study what others have done to come up with this answer. Doing it can be iffy since you might have to extend yourself to the very limits of your current abilities. Think of this as potentially achievable and probable, depending on your effort."

Keller continues:
"High achievers understand these first two routes but reject them. Unwilling to settle for ordinary when extraordinary is possible, they've asked a Great Question and want the very best answer. Extraordinary results require a Great Answer.

"Highly successful people choose to live at the outer limits of achievement. They not only dream of but deeply crave what is beyond their natural grasp. They know this type of answer is the hardest to come by, but also know that just by extending themselves to find it, they expand and enrich their lives for the better.

"If you want the most from your answer, you must realize that it lives outside your comfort zone. This is rare air. A big answer is never in plain view, nor is the path to finding one laid out for you. A possibility answer exists beyond what is already known and being done. As with a stretch goal, you can start out by doing research and studying the lives of other high achievers. But you can't stop there. In fact, your search has just begun. Whatever you learn, you'll use it to do what only the greatest achievers do: benchmark and trend....The research and experience of others is the best place to start when looking for your answer."—pp. 123-125.

This is another way of looking at the minimum, target and optimal goals that I've discussed in Chapter 6. I really like Keller's explanation that you've got to stretch beyond your current reality to find the answers to the big questions that you have.

All entrepreneurs are being forced to ask tough questions today in order to win in today's hyper-competitive business environment. To successfully build better systems, you'll have to reject complacency and do your very best day in and day out. You have to get out of your comfort zone and learn new skills. I've discovered that there are four I's that hold you back from getting things done and from accomplishing more in your business. These are ignorance, indecision, indifference, and intention.

Let me share with you a quick story about something I learned about ignorance in my first sales job. When I graduated from college, I couldn't get a job in my field to support my family. I ended up working in construction for a while and hated it. I couldn't afford to go back to school and so I wound up in sales. During my first day in that job, I learned a valuable lesson from Brian, who was training the six of us who were in his class, how to sell the company's product.

During Brian's training, he asked the question, "Why aren't more people financially independent?" He asked all six of us for a response. My answer was that "people didn't know how." Then, he asked me, "Why aren't *you* financially independent?" My simple answer was, "I've never been taught how." He then said, "You mean to tell me that in this day and age where information is literally available at the click of a button that you don't know how?"

His sobering question caused me a lot of reflection. I realized that day that ignorance is no excuse for remaining where you are. I committed to seek out others who could help me learn to sell and become financially successful. As I mention in the introduction of this book, I was terrible at sales when I started. I was so committed to learn how to sell that I went to a local Barnes and Noble at night and read books (since I couldn't afford them) and took notes on ideas I could use to be successful. I listened to what the top salespeople at our office were saying. I asked lots of questions of them at lunch. I studied and practiced like crazy. My first year in selling I read over 60 books. As I listened to what other successful salespeople were saying and doing, I became an excellent salesperson.

I have had that approach ever since in everything I have attempted. If there is something I want to learn, I know there is no excuse for saying I don't know something, I choose to make the choice to get up, get information, and get around others who are where I want to be.

There are laws in selling and business that must be learned and applied to become successful. If a person is ignorant of the law of gravity and decides to step off of a building, their ignorance doesn't prevent them from experiencing the consequences of falling to the ground. Likewise, simply not knowing something doesn't prevent you from escaping the consequences of your failure to take certain actions.

Don't fail in your business because you say, "I've never been taught how." Take the initiative to seek out the best information and best individuals to help you get to where you want to be. If you are not actively seeking solutions to the challenges you are facing in your business, you are guilty of this "I". With the explosion of information available today (on virtually every subject), there is *no* excuse for ignorance. As John Maxwell says: "You can look at others to place the blame, or you can look at yourself to discover your opportunities."

The second "I" is that of indecision. Oftentimes, we may know what to do but we don't take action. This may be due to fear, an inability to make up our minds about what to do, or simply postponing action or procrastinating what needs to be done.

Many prospects and clients that you and I work with allow procrastination and vacillation to paralyze them so badly that they can't even make a decision by themselves or without the approval of others. This can be very frustrating. Don't let this poison slowly kill you as well.

No one deliberately chooses to fail who gets into business for themselves, yet many do fail precisely because they simply keep postponing what needs to be done (for whatever reason). The fear of taking action or waiting to take action can cause your competitors to pass you by. Everyone wants to be a success but many aren't willing to consistently take the hard steps and *do* the work necessary to get there.

What one thing do you know you need to be doing in your business that you aren't currently doing? Start there. Do something about it today. When will you start? Answering those questions and having the courage to act on the answers will change the direction of your business.

The third "I" is that of indifference. Indifference or apathy prevents you from either enthusiastically acting or skeptically choosing to do anything at all. This isn't being hot or cold, but lukewarm. When someone is indifferent, they remain apathetic and detached from action.

Most challenges in our lives arise from indifference and our struggle to overcome its resistance. If you think about it, ignorance is really indifference to learning. Laziness is indifference to work. Weakness is indifference to strength. A prospect's indecision to buy now is indifference to making a decision. The path to failure in anything is usually greased with the slime of indifference.

What are you indifferent to in your business? What has that indifference cost you? This book has taught you what to do to build your systems. Get involved in the details. Make it happen.

The fourth "I" is intention. This is where someone says they are going to *do* something—so they have technically made a decision—but they put it off for some reason. All of us struggle with procrastination in one way or another. As the old saying goes, "The road to ruin in life or business is paved with good intentions."

True leaders realize that intentions don't pay the bills and so they eradicate "someday" and "tomorrow" from their vocabularies. True leaders are like the mule in a story Jim Tressel retells in his book *The Winner's Manual*. They take action even when everything and everyone seems to not go their way. As Tressel says, "[this story] concerns a farmer whose mule fell into a dry well. The farmer heard the mule making noise and discovered the poor animal's misfortune. After assessing the situation, the farmer decided the mule wasn't worth the time and expense it would take to save it. Essentially, he lost hope in the old mule. So he called his neighbors together and asked them to help him haul dirt to bury the animal and put it out of its misery.

"When the shovelfuls of dirt came down, the mule became hysterical and began to kick. But as the dirt continued to hit his back, it dawned on the creature that he should shake it off each time and step up on the growing mound of dirt beneath him. Load after load of dirt hit him square in the back, but no matter how painful it was, he shook the dirt off and stepped on it.

"Before long, the accumulation of dirt was such that the old mule, battered and exhausted, stepped triumphantly over the wall of the well. The dirt that had been mean to bury him had actually saved his life because of the manner in which he had responded to the situation." – *The Winner's Manual*, p. 228.

Don't let indecision or indifference paralyze you from taking action. As in this story, taking action instead of being resigned to fate can help you rise above your difficulties. Your ability to overcome these four I's will make a huge difference in your business. Don't let the killer of ignorance or the poisons of indecision, indifference, and intention stunt your growth and block you from achieving your goals.

Everyday, you stand in front of five doors of opportunity that determine where you will end up in life. The first door is the door of ignorance. You can blame others for what you don't know or you can do something about it. The second door is the door of indecision. You can worry and ponder about what needs to be done so much that you end up suffering from decision constipation or you can decide and take action. Behind the third door is indifference. This poison kills you slowly, but eventually you will wake up to the fact that you have been apathetic and detached and haven't accomplished much of anything. Behind the fourth door lurks intention. This is one of the most dangerous of all because even though you *have decided* to do something, you don't take action because of your fears. The fifth door is the door of action. It is only behind this door that you will accomplish anything.

Choose to do eradicate ignorance. Be a leader, a reader and a learner. Learn to make good decisions. Love getting out of your comfort zone. Don't procrastinate what you know needs to be done. Stamp out indifference by taking action and do it now.

Don't wait on what you know you should do. Take action. Ask better questions that will help you know and focus on what to do next. Nothing will happen at your business *until* you move. Carefully consider the seven actions I've recommended in this chapter and keep moving forward as you build your systems. Being proactive every day on the critical success factors of your business will help you get what you want.

CHAPTER 22

USING SYSTEMS TO GET FROM WHERE YOU ARE TO WHERE YOU WANT TO BE

"In order for any business to succeed, it must first become a system so that the business functions exactly the same way every time down to the last detail."
—*Rick Harshaw*

Entrepreneurs experience challenges and difficulties on the way to success. It doesn't matter what business or endeavor you've chosen to pursue. All great companies were once small. Now, that you've just about finished *The System is the Secret*, I want to talk with you *why* having a long-term vision / plan for your life is so important. This is especially true when you feel like you are holding on to what you have by the skin of your teeth and aren't sure how you are going to get from where you are now to where you want to be.

To help you along your journey, here are ten ways you can use systems to develop a long-term vision and plan for your business and your life.

1. **Break free of the negative vision you are replaying in your mind. Instead, utilize affirmations and positive thoughts as part of your daily system to replace any negative vision with a clear vision of what you do want.**

You attract into your life what you think and reflect on. Earl Nightingale said it best: "You become what you think about most of the time." For example, if you are focusing on how you aren't making sales or aren't selling, or are struggling constantly, you will attract more of this into your life.

Here is my question for you: Is that what you *really* want?

Then (as gently as I can possibly ask this question), why do you allow yourself to spend so much time thinking about what you don't want?

Now, I know your answer is because that is what is in front of you everyday. I have experienced the same emotions as well. When we opened our first business, we felt those emotions all of the time. The key is to put them in the back of your mind and focus on what you want and start attracting more of that into what you do in your business.

Abraham Hicks in his book *Money and the Law of Attraction: Learning to Attract Health, Wealth and Happiness* makes this statement and I think it is very illustrative of what I'm trying to say. He says:

"Continuing to tell stories of shortage only continues to contradict your desire for abundance, and you cannot have it both ways: You cannot focus upon unwanted and receive wanted. You cannot focus upon stories about money that make you feel uncomfortable and allow into your experience what makes you feel comfortable. A different story will bring different results: My thoughts are the basis for the attraction of all things that I consider to be good, which includes enough money, and health, for my comfort and joy."

Henry Ford once famously said: "Whether you believe you can do a thing or not, you are right."

So, if thoughts are the basis for the attraction of all good things you want to bring into your business and into your life, how can you start visualizing the right way?

To start with, I think it is important to understand what visualization is. The term visualization simply means making a mental picture of something. It is your ability to vividly imagine or see what you want in your own mind's eye. In other words, everything is created twice: once in the spiritual realm and once in the physical realm.

Lee Milteer, a good friend, personal coach, and mentor of mine and the author of the book *Success is an Inside Job* shared with me at a mastermind meeting I attended that:
"When you use visualization, you are literally taking your intentions and creating a living picture for your mind (the most sophisticated computer on earth) to find ways to manifest. As human beings, we are visual creatures. One quarter of the brain's entire processing power is devoted to the sensory stream that comes in through your eyes. Scientists say that visual images have a massive impact on your brain, both consciously and subconsciously, and this is why vision boards are extremely powerful tools for imprinting your goals and aspirations deep into the

subconscious brain."

Lee has taught me a lot about visualization. I've also done a lot of my own study and research on this topic. I would encourage you to do so as well. Here are two key points from my study and research that I think are critically important to understand.

1) *There are two parts to the brain: the conscious and subconscious functions.*
The conscious part of our brain thinks logically, focuses on one thing at a time, constructs logical sequences , imagines things (but isn't good at getting things done), and is easily distracted. The conscious mind cannot remember more than three or four things at a time. Yet, it is like the director of a movie. It directs the actors, makeup artists, musicians, and editors what to do as they follow the script that has been decided on in advance.

The subconscious part of our brain on the other hand sees a complete picture of everything happening at once, carries out the commands of the conscious mind, can remember billions of things in perfect sequence (for example, there are ten quadrillion different biochemical processes happening in your body every second and your subconscious keeps track of them), and most importantly never gets distracted.

2) *What your conscious mind imagines, your subconscious delivers.*
The reason so many people never achieve their goals is because they depend on their conscious mind to do it for them. Goal setting and goal achieving is really accomplished by your subconscious mind. Visualization is so important because your subconscious sees whatever you visualize in your head as real. Your subconscious can't tell the difference between what is true or imagined.

When you use the technique of visualization, you are actually empowering yourself to reshape your inner reality. When you do that, your outer reality will conform to that new shape.

The law of attraction works in the positive sense but it also works in the negative. If you're constantly focused on what you don't want, you will tend to attract more of those unwanted things into your life. This is why having a system that allows you to program your subconscious mind with positive affirmations is so important. It allows you to direct your mind to seek out solutions to create the realities you've imagined through visualization.

So, here are a couple of questions for you to think about and reflect on about your business:
1) What are you focusing on in your business?

2) What daily positive commands do give to your subconscious mind?
- For example, *Every day, we reach $_____ in sales* or *Our sales consultants are the very best trained and most successful sales people in our industry in the entire world.*

As an assignment, list some of the positive commands you *want* to give to your subconscious mind:
-

-

-

3) Now, what daily negative commands are you feeding to your subconscious mind? When you hear or think these thoughts, you want to immediately repel them with positive affirmations of what you do want.
- *For example, when you hear yourself saying thinks like: Our sales are down...Why can't we get our prospects to buy what we're selling?, replace those thoughts with the affirmations of what you do want such as: We're attracting more qualified prospects to our business everyday. We listen to our prospects and deliver solutions to the challenges they are looking for.*

-

-

-

Stop feeding your mind with negative visions of your future. Instead, focus on the positive things you want to have happen and visualize what you want. Then, your subconscious mind will help you attract the things you want in your life.

2. **Know where you are going. As a system, write a letter to yourself each month detailing all of the accomplishments you'll be congratulating yourself on completing the following month. Then, open the letter on the first of the following month.**

A great example of the importance of knowing where you are going can be found in the story of Tamara Mellon who founded Jimmy Choo shoes.

"Designer-shoe mogul Tamara Mellon was born with a bent for both fashion and business. Her mother, Ann Yeardye, was a former Chanel model; her father, Tom Yeardye, was a successful entrepreneur and co-founder of the Vidal Sassoon hair company.

"Mellon began her career with a short stint in public relations and retail sales before transitioning to the editorial side of the fashion business. In 1990, she became accessories editor at British *Vogue*.

"While she was at *Vogue*, Mellon's entrepreneurial instinct and eye for fashion led her to perceive a gap in the luxury shoe market: She believed the offerings of the time lacked both style and variety. Mellon saw the potential for developing her own ready to wear brand, in collaboration with a talented—yet relatively unknown—Malaysian shoe maker named Jimmy Choo.

"Mellon launched the business in 1996 and soon became her own company's muse, generating a glamorous global image for the little known brand. And it wasn't long before Hollywood took notice. Beyonce sang about them, Sex and the City women drooled over them, and A-list actresses considered them good-luck charms on Oscar night. In eight short years, Mellon turned a 150,000 pound loan from her father into a $100 million global phenomenon." –Michael J. Berland and Douglas E. Schoen, *What Makes You Tick?*, pp. 25-26.

Her book *In My Shoes* details a fascinating account of how she pushed through difficulty to expand and grow her business. Here's one early experience of how she overcame the resistance of dealing with factories who didn't want to work with her because her volume was too small. Listen to her words:

"Very early on, I opened a store in London. Then I opened one in New York...Usually, it takes British brands twenty years to make that move. We did it within a year.

"The hardest thing was getting factories to work with us, because they aren't interested in small volumes. They want to work with big brands that can give them orders for ten thousand pairs of pumps in black. When I was doing it, you had a lot of color, a lot of accessories on the shoes, and in the beginning we were ordering small quantities. So it was a real fight to get good-quality factories to work with us. I had to convince them that this would be a long-term project that eventually would pay off."

Mellon succeeded because she persisted and was willing to go through a constant barrage of challenges on the way. There is a price to success. As Tamara reveals in her memoir, you've got to know what you *really* want. If you don't know where you are going, you will end up somewhere else. You will let others dictate where you end up instead of going in the direction of your own dreams.

Do you *know* what you really want? How will *your* system keep you on track with that vision?

3. Avoid obstacles to achieving your vision.

There is always resistance to anything you want to accomplish in your life as I discussed in Chapter 20. How you deal with this resistance in large measure determines where you will end up. Here are three obstacles you need to be very careful to avoid in your life.

1) Negative association.

Choose to be around positive mentors and individuals who believe in you and can help you get where you want to be.

Some people are like crabs in a bucket. They hate to see someone they know doing well and becoming more successful than them. Instead of helping them, they keep pulling them down. I once heard Brian Tracy say: "Avoid toxic people. If you meet them, introduce them to each other and run!"

Pursue relationships with people who stretch and encourage you. Do you need to change any of your associations to get what you want?

2) Embracing your past failures as reasons why the vision isn't possible.

Don't be a victim of your past. Learn from your failures instead of embracing them as reasons why you can't do, be, or have more.

Don't give into self-defeating emotions like guilt or anger that distract you from clearing focusing on the dream in front of you.

3) Your limiting beliefs.

Our subconscious mind looks for what it is programmed to seek out. If you continually focus on what you don't want, you'll get more of it. Instead, replace the negative thoughts with positive affirmations of what you do want and your subconscious mind will seek that out.

Some of your limiting beliefs may be:

- Limited time
- Limited money
- Limited knowledge, talent, and ability
- Limited opportunity
- Limited self-confidence
- Limited support from spouse or family

Dan Kennedy tells an interesting story about an interaction he had with a seminar attendee that reveals how _we_ are really the limiting factors in many cases to why we aren't more successful. He said (and I know this is a little crass, but he has a great and valid point):

"In a recent seminar, during Q&A, an attendee—with great sincerity—expressed angst, frustration, puzzlement over her situation, surrounded by co-workers, friends, and family entirely unsupportive of her ambitions, critical of her, generally unambitious and pessimistic and discouraging. What, oh what, could she do? She was, after all, stuck in her job and stuck with her family. I asked, since she was financially dependent on her job, if her company transferred her to another city, if she would go—or refuse, in order to stay in close proximity to her present co-workers, friends, and family? She said she'd have to move and leave them behind. I suggested she give herself a transfer."

He continued:

"If you have a nice home with expensive white carpet and beautiful décor, and every night at 5pm your neighbor strolls in without knocking, drops his pants, goes to the bathroom on your carpet, then steals something (vase, TV, etc.) – and walks out, how many days in a row will you let that continue? After, all you're stuck in your house, stuck with your neighbor, aren't you? So why tolerate anybody...[dumping] on you?"

Why do you let others dump on your dreams and what you are trying to accomplish when you would never let someone dump on, damage, or destroy your personal property?

If you have individuals in your life who are cutting you down, who don't believe in what you are doing and where you are going, why do you allow this? If you need to make a move mentally, do it. If you need to have different associations, start associating with those who are where you want to be and stop spending time with those who aren't where you want to be. Remember, your life is the sum total of the top six people you spend the most time around. If you need to make a move from some of these associations, do it.

Don't make excuses about this. As Benjamin Franklin once observed: "He that is good for making excuses is seldom good for anything else."

Your limits (even if you currently feel like you have them) have power over your life and your future only to the extent that *you* let them. All limits can be overcome and the best way is to write down your dreams— what which you would do, have, and be if there were no limits. Outlining your dreams is the first step to creating the blueprint of your vision for the future.

Put up pictures on a poster in a place where you can see it each day that help you visualize what it is that you want. Spend time picturing and thinking about what it is you want and let these emotions sink deep into your subconscious. It is best to do this early in the morning or late at night right before you go to sleep. Your subconscious mind will motivate you towards taking action and responding to opportunities that will bring you closer to your goals and your vision.

When you make mistakes, don't let discouragement affect your vision. Instead, learn from your mistakes and use your frustration to help you accomplish what you want. See disappointments as feedback that can help you change direction and make course adjustments on the way to what you really want in life.

4. **Understand how what you are doing in this moment will contribute to your long-term plan. Your productivity systems will help you stay on track with your daily goals.**

Jim Rohn once observed: "If you don't design your own life plan, chances are you'll fall into someone else's plan. And guess what they have planned for you? Not much."

Understand where you are going and design your own plan around this thought. How does what you are doing *now* fit in with the rest of your overall vision and goals for your business?

A great way to way to visualize what you should be doing daily is found in how much time you spend on the core systemic areas of your business.

According to author Dan Kennedy there are six core entrepreneurial competencies. These are:

1) "The ability to provide appealing products, services, and offers.
2) The ability to affordably acquire customers (marketing).
3) The ability to manage those customers for maximum profit.
4) The ability to retain customers and maximize value.
5) The ability to develop value and equity.
6) The ability to meet personal and lifestyle goals.

The first two are functions of sales and marketing.
Numbers 3 and 4 are functions of profit and stability.
Numbers 5 and 6 are functions of building long-term wealth."

Where are you spending your time?

According to Kennedy: "The business owner typically gives 70% of his attention to Competency #1, 20% to #2, 9% to #3, and 1% to #4. Ever so gradually, over time, if he gets smarter, and if he's making money, the ratios shift. Late in the game, he tackles #5. He hardly ever thinks about #6. If he does, it's in the context of retirement. The business owner is often most comfortable with #1, having gotten into business in the first place to do the thing (not to market it). A more accurate visual depiction of the business owner's relationship to these competencies would be #2 through #6 as small boxes inside one big box identified as 'The Business' with #1 as its function.

"For the entrepreneur, the six competencies [are] an 'overlay' for any business, moved from one business to another as warranted. While the business owner may work to implement these competencies inside a particular business, the entrepreneur works to master these competencies, period.

"If given a shoe store, the small-business owner will manage and promote that shoe store well. But ten years from now, it will still be a shoe store. Give that same shoe store to a true entrepreneur and, ten years from now you probably won't recognize it!" –Dan Kennedy, *No B.S. Business Success in the New Economy*, pp. 109-110.

You have control over what you do at every moment by where you choose to place your priorities and focus. Be sure your productivity systems ensure that your daily activities fit into the big picture of where you want to be. Remember, your future success is hidden in your daily routine.

5. Allow yourself to dream again.

How long has it been since you dreamed, really dreamed about what you could do, be or have?

Has it been too long? Have you been trapped in the present moment completely consumed with the daily activities you are doing that aren't helping you get to where you want to go?

Instead of dreaming about your future, are you worrying about:
  * Making payroll this week?

- How you are going to come up with the money to pay a vendor this week?

- What to do about declining sales closing ratios and percentages and the person you thought who would totally work out in your business (who no longer is)?

- How to deal with your cash flow issues?

- And any other array of problems?

If so, that's okay. All successful entrepreneurs stress and worry about these things – but they also take time to dream.

I want to encourage you to dream bigger. Successful people in every walk of life dream big dreams. Great men and women allow themselves to dream. Too many adults shut down their dream factory as they get older. Yet, all children dream big. It's time for you to dream again.

Howard Schultz, the founder of Starbucks made this statement about why you and I should dream bigger: "If you want to build a great enterprise, you have to have the courage to dream great dreams. If you dream small dreams, you may succeed in building something small. For many people, that is enough. But if you want to achieve widespread impact and lasting value, be bold. Who wants a dream that's near-fetched?" –*Pour Your Heart Into It*, p. 106.

Here is a great assignment for you to complete: Imagine no limitations and take twenty or thirty minutes this week to write down your dreams.

Break this down into five different categories:
1) What would you like to have or own?

2) What would you like to do or create?

3)   Where would you like to go or travel?

4)   What would you like to be or become?

5)   What would you like to contribute or put back?

Now, create a dreams list for your business. Project your business ahead to where you want to be. Imagine 5 years have passed and everything is exactly where you want it to be (it is perfect in every way).

What is your take home income? What are your gross revenues? What are your net revenues? What do you sell? What is your profitability?

Then, write down what you would have to start doing now in order to make this dream a reality. Be clear and specific.

-
-
-
-
-
-
-
-

Then, prioritize your tasks by asking:
1) Which of these are closer to realization than others?
2) Which are the most exciting?
3) Which could you put off until later?

You must have a systemic process where you project and think about the future. The time you spend building your dreams mentally has a big impact on what you do and create daily. The process of dreaming and daily action towards those dreams can restore hope and give you the energy to propel yourself forward.

6. **See your vision in your mind and then write it down so you can articulate your vision to others.**

In 1952, Walt Disney wrote down his vision statement for Disneyland to help his board members approve the project. As I share this with you, I want you to think about what he actually created on paper and how it compares with the experience you've had at Disneyland or Disneyworld.

"The idea of Disneyland is a simple one. It will be a place for people to find happiness and knowledge. It will be a place for parents and children to share pleasant times in one another's company: a place for teachers and pupils to discover greater ways of understanding and education. Here the older generation can recapture the nostalgia of days gone by and the younger generation can savor the challenge of the future. Here will be the wonders of Nature and Man for all to see and understand. Disneyland will be based upon and dedicated to the ideals, the dreams, and the hard facts that have created America. And it will be uniquely equipped to dramatize these dreams and facts and send them forth as a source of courage and inspiration to the entire world. Disneyland will be a fair, an exhibition, a playground, a community center, a museum of living facts, and a showplace of beauty and magic. It will be filled with the accomplishments, the joys, and the hopes of the world we live in. And it will remind us and show us how to make those wonders a part of our own lives. Sometime in 1955, Walt Disney will present for the people in the world—and children of all ages—a new experience in entertainment."

What stands out to you about this vision statement? Four things stand out to me:
- It is vivid and compelling.

- It is inspiring. You can see how this written vision statement would attract people and resources to help make it a reality.
- You can feel the enthusiasm and commitment to making it happen. This helped Walt continue towards his dream when things were tough.
- The date wasn't specific when it was written, but the year was.

The vision statement was clear, but consider this statement he made when he presented it to his board.

He said:
"There's nothing like it in the entire world. I know, because I've looked. That's why it can be great; because it will be unique, a new concept in entertainment. And I think—I know—it can be a success."

Walt Disney died before Disney World in Orlando, Florida was completed. His brother, Roy, came out of retirement and finished the project. On the opening day of Disney World, a young reporter came up to Roy and said: "Isn't it a tragedy that Walt never got to see Walt Disney World?"

Roy Disney replied: "You're wrong, young man. Walt did see it. He saw it in his imagination first. That's why you're seeing it physically here today."

Author James Allen wrote:
"The greatest achievement was at first and for a time a dream. The oak sleeps in the acorn, the bird waits in the egg, and in the highest vision of the soul, a waking angel stirs. Dreams are the seedlings of realities."

Here is an assignment for you: **Write a vision statement for your business.** It should contain the following elements:
- Exactly what the vision is
- Why the dream or vision is so important to you
- What's in it for those who help you make the vision a reality? How will they benefit? How will helping you achieve your dream help them achieve their dreams?
- What you expect from those who read it
- A simple plan for the achievement of the vision

- A call to action – What do you want others to do after they hear or read your vision? If you remember, Walt asked for the loan after sharing his vision. You should have a call to action as well.

Take the time to write down your vision for what you want your business to become. Take the time to envision in your mind what your future will look like. All great enterprises are seen in the mind first and then articulated to others.

I really like the idea Andrew Fitzpatrick shares in this statement: "We are told never to cross a bridge until we come to it, but this world is owned by people who have crossed bridges in their imaginations far ahead of the crowd."

Does your vision motivate you and others to cross the bridge in your imagination to accomplish the daily activities that will propel you toward your goals?

7. **Visualize what you want. Remember, what you focus on, expands. Put your vision in front of you on a dream board so your subconscious mind can seek out attract to you the ideas, people, and information you need to help you accomplish what you want.**

You have to allow yourself to think big. If you don't, no one else will do it for you. What you focus on does expand, and it doesn't matter if it is positive or negative.

Walt Disney had many failures prior to his successes. For example, "In Kansas City, Walt had a small cartoon company that failed. He decided to start over in Hollywood. To raise money for the train ticket, he went door to door, photographing babies. He left Kansas City wearing a checkered coat and pants that didn't match. He had $40 in cash. His imitation leather suitcase contained one shirt, two pairs of undershorts, two pairs of socks, and some drawing materials. But when he paid for his fare, he bought a first-class ticket. Walt Disney had a dream. He knew where he was going. He wanted to arrive in style." –Nate Booth, *Tiger Traits*, p. 26.

On another occasion, Disney declared:

"We're in the *happiness* business. Disneyland will bring more happiness to millions of people in ways that movies never could."

There were a lot of people who couldn't see what Walt saw. They laughed at him and doubted his ability to make this happen. This will be the case with you as well. You have to visualize your vision and work to make it happen.

So, don't put limits on yourself. Give yourself permission to figure out exactly what you want and then use the process of visualization to help attract the ideas, people and information to you.

The best way I've found to do this is to create a vision board with pictures of wealth, abundance, health, and happiness that embody what you want to have in your life.

There is no wrong way to make a vision board. The key is to find great images that represent the big dreams that you have in your head. Remember, your subconscious mind records all the images you put on your own board. If you like, you can organize your board into quadrants (similar to the exercise on goals and balance). You can also have a vision board organized by category:

- What you would like to have or own.
- What you would like to do or create.
- Where you would like to go or travel
- What you would like to be or become.
- What you would like to contribute or put back.

One way to do this is to create a bucket list of everything you want to do before you die. Here are some examples of what you should put on your dream board and bucket list:

- Relationships
- Your Health
- Your Family
- Your Wealth
- Your Accomplishments
- Your Career
- What impact do you want to have on the world- what legacy would you like to leave?
- Your spiritual life

- Places you would like to travel

Here is your assignment: Write your "Bucket List". This should include a list of all of the things you want to accomplish before you die. Then, work on crossing items off this list each year of your life.

Here are three tips to keep in mind about visualization:
1) Make visualizing your goals a regular habit (especially at night right before you go to bed).
Get into the emotions and feelings you will have when you have accomplished the goal. Visualizing your goals with emotion and enthusiasm accelerates the speed of the programming of your subconscious mind. It also allows you to focus on what you want and the mind can only focus on one thing at a time.

2) Visualize your goals as if you have already achieved them.

3) Work a little bit harder. You can't just imagine yourself to success. You have to put in the work too. So, since you and I are so busy already, I want to invite you to put in just 15 minutes more per day towards the accomplishment of one of your goals. 15 minutes per day adds up to 91 hours (nearly 4 days a year).

Here is a great story of Olympic gold and silver medalist Peter Vidmar about how fifteen minutes a day can really add up. He said:

"My coach taught me a great lesson in my early development as a gymnast. I was leaving for my first national team training camp. Before I traveled to the camp, my coach told me only one thing. He didn't tell me to learn any new maneuvers at the camp. He didn't tell me to try to perform my routines better than the rest of the team. He told me that when I returned from that training camp that he wanted to hear me tell him, with all honesty, that I had worked harder than anyone else on the national team.

So I remember making it a point to be the last one out of the gym every day; and that didn't mean just waiting at the door for everyone else to leave! Also, I remember that at night, when some team members would occasionally relax with their pizza and beer, I would go back to my room and do more exercises.

When I returned home two weeks later, I was proud to tell my coach, "Yes, I worked harder than everyone else." I didn't work twice as hard, just a little bit harder. But it was enough to help me to improve greatly. Sometimes, just a little bit is all that matters.

Let's realize what the margin of victory was in a few of the events in [1984's] summer Olympics. In women's cycling, after the 79.2-kilometer race, the difference between the gold medalist and the silver medalist at the finish line was just the length of a tire. In a pressure-packed swimming relay, the difference between the first-place team and second-place team was only .04 of a second. In many of the gymnastics competitions, the difference between first place and second place was as minute as .025 of a point.

The champions didn't win by running twice as fast, by jumping twice as far, or by scoring twice as many points as their opponents. In many cases they won by just a fraction of a second, a fraction of an inch, or a fraction of a point. Likewise, and more important, the champions didn't win by training twice as hard as their opponents. If another gymnast trains six hours a day, I can't train twelve hours a day. Twelve hours a day in a gym just isn't healthy! But I can train six hours and fifteen minutes a day. This is where giving it that little extra and going the extra mile makes the difference.

In whatever you want to improve upon, whether it be schoolwork, athletics, music,...[business] just give a little extra—every day. Fifteen minutes a day for one year add up to over ninety-one hours. I only use fifteen minutes as an example of how time well-spent can add up."

What a great example! We can all use 15 minutes better each day. There are 1,440 minutes in each day. 15 minutes is just 1% of the total amount of time we have in each day. Be committed to work on your MOST important priority for at least 15 minutes more each day and you'll be amazed by what happens.

8. Help others buy into your vision.

Howard Schultz shares this experience about his first day at Starbuck's (which he bought and combined with his idea from another company Il Giornale, which he had worked at previously). He had created a hundred page business plan that he and his partner had written that clearly spelled out what he intended to do with Starbucks once he bought it. The first morning, he had a meeting with everyone who worked at the company. His experience is a great example of why it is so important to share your vision with everyone. He said:

"At 10 A.M., I called everyone together for a big meeting on the roasting plant floor. It was the first of many. I was more excited than nervous. I had written just a few points down on a 5-by-7 note card, to remember as I addressed the group. They were:

1) Speak from the heart.

2) Put myself in their shoes.

3) Share the Big Dream with them.

Once I started talking, though, I found I didn't need to look at my notes....

Working together, I told them, we could take everything that Starbucks means to the people of Seattle and multiply it on a national scale. We could share our coffee mission so much more widely.

'I know you're scared. I know you're concerned,' I said. 'Some of you may even be angry. But if you would just meet me halfway, I promise you I will not let you down. I promise you I will not leave anyone behind.

'I want to assure you that I'm not here to do anything to dilute the integrity of the company.'

It was easy for me to be able to talk like that because I had been one of them.

My goal, I announced, was to build a national company whose values and guiding principles we could all be proud of. I discussed my vision of the growth of the company and promised to bring it about in a way that would add value to Starbucks, not diminish it. I explained how I wanted to include people in the decision-making process, to be open and honest with them.

'In five years,' I told them, 'I want you to look back at this day and say, 'I was there when it started. I helped build this company into something great.'....Starbucks' best days, I told them, were yet to come."

Now, here is the important point I want to make about this story and about what you will face at your business as well as you unfold the vision you've developed. Many people will doubt you and watch you and each of your team members will have to buy into you as a person, before they will buy into your vision. Here is what Howard Schultz said happened to him as he explained his vision and what it taught him:

"I watched their faces as I spoke. Some of them seemed to want to believe what I was saying, but were guarded. Others had that smug look of doubters who had already decided not to buy into this dream—at least not yet....This realization was a great lesson to me. A business plan is only a piece of paper, and even the greatest business plan of all will prove worthless unless the people of a company buy into it. It cannot be sustainable, or even implemented properly, unless the people are committed to it with the same heartfelt urgency as their leader. And they will not accept it unless they both trust the leader's judgment and understand that their efforts will be recognized and valued....The only way to win the confidence of Starbucks' employees was to be honest with them, to share my plans and excitement with them, and then to follow through and keep my word, delivering exactly what I promised—if not more. No one would follow me until I showed them with my own actions that my promises were not empty. It would take time." –*Pour Your Heart into It*, pp. 102-103.

This is the epitome of what vision is all about. Howard Schultz defines it in the introduction of his book. He says: "I saw Starbucks not for what it was, but for what it could be. It has immediately captivated me with its combination of passion and authenticity.....I became CEO of Starbucks in 1987 because I went out, as an entrepreneur, and convinced investors to believe in my vision for the company. Over the next ten years, with a team of smart and experienced managers, we build Starbucks from a local business with six stores and less than 100 employees into a national one with more than 1,300 stores and 25,000 employees....Both sales and profits have grown by more than 50 percent a year for six consecutive years (written in 1997)." –*Pour Your Heart into It*, pp. 4-5.

The joke is that Starbucks opened so many locations that they didn't have any more places to expand, so they started opening Starbucks in the bathrooms of Starbucks. It got a little out of control and Starbucks lost its way.

In recent years, they brought Howard Schultz back to get Starbucks back to its roots and back on purpose. Today, Starbuck has more than

23,000 stores in more than 60 countries and is the premier roaster and retailer of specialty coffee in the world.

I share that story with you to illustrate the importance of getting others to buy into your vision. Starbucks never would have grown from its first store to six stores and to 1,300 stores and later to more than 20,000 stores without vision and a lot of people to help make that vision come true.

Starbucks began in 1971. Ten years later, they had six stores. It took a leader like Howard Schultz with vision to build Starbucks into what it is today.

Without vision, Starbucks would likely have remained the same size or expanded into a small regional chain. I've written a special report about the lessons you can apply in your business from Starbuck's turnaround. If you would like a copy, please email me at info@soundlawsofsuccess.com with the subject: "Turnaround Lessons at Starbucks" and I'll send you a copy.

Whatever level of success or growth you desire to happen in your business, you have to be clear about what it is that you want and then articulate that for others so that they buy into you and your vision. Then, and only then, will you be able to get your business on track to become what you want it to be.

9. **When things get tough, and they always do at some point, resist the temptation to give up.**

Whenever you have a vision of something you want to accomplish, there will always be resistance to accomplish that vision. It may even be tempting for you to give up or give in.

I have always enjoyed reading biographies for this very reason. Reading about the failures and the temptations that other business owners have gone through to give up, have always inspired me when we've had a bad day or a tough week.

I particularly enjoy reading about those who succeed against all odds. Bill Rosenberg, who founded Dunkin Donuts in 1950, is one such example. Here is something that happened to him when he had been in business for a year and a half, that I recently read that was a great inspiration to me. He said:

"A year and a half into the business, I [nearly] went out of business. Due to a serious flu going around, many of the men got too sick to come to work, including my brother Leon. I couldn't believe it. I finally pulled Leon out of his sickbed and had him take a route. I pushed a cart at Tubular Rivet and Stud. Murray took a route. People were sick at the factories. We worked all night and pushed the carts all day. When I finally came back to the commissary, the man who washed the cans was out sick, too. I got so upset. I walked outside and said to myself: Who needs this?!

I stood on the curb and threw up in the gutter. My shoes were stained. I was sick to my stomach and it wasn't the flu. I had to get stuff purchased in the morning, stock the trucks and the carts, push the routes, canvass—it was too much for anybody. The pressures got to me and I said: 'Who needs this --- ---- ----? To hell with it! I'll just take a job and be happy like everybody else. I won't have all these headaches and problems. What am I going to do about tomorrow? How am I going to get these people fed? You know you convince yourself: Woe is me! I came inches from quitting the business that day. Then I said: Wait a minute! I've worked so hard. I found a way to get these things done before when everything couldn't get done. I did things when everybody told me they couldn't be done. Now I'm going to convince myself that I can't do it No, sireee!

I picked myself up and went back in, got a cup of coffee, and started to figure out what to do. I started calling people and organizing. Thank God the next day things got a little bit better. Ultimately things straightened out. I never got any closer to quitting or going out of business than I did on that day." –*Time to Make the Donuts*, pp. 78-79.

Everyone has tough days. Maybe you are going through these right now in your business and you're doubting your resolve to be able to make it. If so, take heart from this experience that a lot of others have experienced the same feelings you have. I have felt these things too. But, I am determined to make it, to succeed, and to help others make more of their businesses as well.

If you've ever felt discouraged, take heart. The very best have experienced the same emotions. Just keep on persisting. Here's another example of persistence that has been inspiring to me and I hope it will be for you as well.

"Tom Monaghan's high school grades were so low that he graduated at the bottom of his class. The local university rejected his application, but he managed to enroll at the University of Michigan. A few weeks later, he dropped out because he lacked money for tuition and books. In 1960, Monaghan agreed to buy a pizza store with his brother. When his brother decided he wanted out a year later, Monaghan traded his Volkswagen Beetle for his brother's half of the business.

For the first year, Monaghan worked all the time but barely made any money. He soon found himself deep in debt. He began simplifying the business, selling only three sizes of pizza, instead of five. The change helped Monaghan make a profit, which enabled him to expand his three stores under a new name, Domino's.

Just when life seemed to be improving, Monaghan faced a series of setbacks. In 1967, a fire destroyed his anchor store in Ypsilanti, Michigan, which supplied the other stores with food and served as the company's offices. Most of the damage was not covered by insurance. In an effort to recover his losses, Monaghan continued to expand his franchise, but was unable to keep up with the growth. Without Monaghan's guidance, many of the new stores foundered. By 1970, Monaghan was $1.5 million in debt and facing lawsuits from nearly 150 creditors, including many of his franchise owners. In the ensuring financial settlement, Monaghan lost 51 percent of his company to the bank.

Rather than focus on his losses, Monaghan concentrated on building the 49 percent of the business he still owned. Slowly, he began to work his way out of his financial difficulties. He defended himself in court since he could not afford an attorney. He sold his furniture and his car. When things started to turn around, he ordered checks printed with the name Operation Surprise and sent a payment and a thank you note to every creditor—even those who had already written off the debt. In about a year, he managed to pay off all his debts.

Those hard times taught him a valuable lesson in how to run a business. Instead of charging a franchise fee, he required people to work successfully as store managers before they could apply. He also set up a company to help finance franchise buyers. Under these new guidelines, Domino's began to flourish and, by 1978, two hundred Domino's stores had opened. By 1983, the number of stores had surpassed a thousand; by 1989, the chain had more than five thousand stores. The company had more than six thousand pizza delivery stores when Monaghan sold it for $1 billion in 1998. He has spent his retirement doing philanthropic work for Catholic charities and conservative political causes." – *The Secret of Success is Not a Secret*, pp. 150-152.

Colin Powell once observed:

"There are no secrets to success. It is the result of preparation, hard work, and learning from failure."

I could share a lot of stories with you about things I've learned from others who have had disappointments, failures, big losses, and tremendous discouragement. I've experienced failures too. The consistent theme I've learned from all of them is that you don't give up or give in. You learn from your mistakes, pick yourself back up, and go at it again. That is why having such a clear vision is so important. It will motivate and inspire you when things are tough and when times are hard. Don't give up on your vision. You have that vision for a reason. There are others who will someday be inspired by your story of success and how you rose above the challenges and difficulties you faced.

10. Once you achieve your vision and goals, reset them. Don't be content to remain where you are.

Tamara Mellon, founder of Jimmy Choo shoes makes this statement:

"You need a lot of determination and focus to succeed in a start-up business. You also need to be able to take risks. It was obviously a huge risk to start a company from scratch. I've probably always been a risk taker. I don't think you achieve true success without taking risks.

Ten years ago, I had a goal. Then, when I got there, I thought, 'Oh, it's not enough. I want to do more.' Then I thought, 'Okay, if I can achieve this, I'll retire by the time I'm forty.' And now I've got there and I'm thinking, 'I'm not ready to do that; I want to do more.' So you set your mind on something, and you get there, and you want to keep going. I'm the kind of person who always needs a challenge in my life." –Michael J. Berland and Douglas E. Schoen, *What Makes You Tick?*, p. 28.

Here are four questions to ask yourself so you can gain more clarity:
1) What do you *really* want for your business?

2) What goals, dreams, or vision do you have for *your* future?

3) What projects, products or services, or new ventures do you look *forward* to getting into?

4) Do you have a vision for your life that you've never acted on? Or, do you find yourself going through the motions because your vision has dimmed over the years?

If you have a vision for your life, write it down, and start working on making it a part of your life. If you don't, get one. Write down what you want and start working on developing your plan to get there. Remember, you are in control and responsible for developing the plan to make it possible.

Finally, ask yourself: What can I do to put the spark back into the vision of my life?

Be courageous to act on the answers to these questions. Author Joel A. Barker said: "Vision without action is merely a dream. Action without vision just passes the time. Vision with action can change the world."

Get out there and use the systems outlined in this book to grow your business into a massive success. The system *is* the secret. I look forward to hearing of your successes as you implement better systems in your business.

About the Author

James Karl Butler is a serial entrepreneur who has built four companies from the start-up phase to over a million dollars in revenue. He is the author of seven books and numerous E-books. He grew his first retail bridal store from $0 to over $1,000,000 in sales in three years and grew another retail business from $0 to over $1,000,000 in just over 18 months.

James has helped some of the most respected and largest retailers and businesses across the country to grow their sales and shatter their previous sales records. He is a celebrated systems and marketing authority who speaks and trains business owners how to create rapid and sustained growth in their business.

He is the host of the Sound Laws of Success Podcast and inspires entrepreneurs to take action in their businesses through applying these laws. He offers a coaching and training program to a worldwide audience of entrepreneurs providing insights and systems-based training designed to help business owners grow their businesses to the next level.

He and his wife Heather are the parents of five children.

Visit his web site at: www.soundlawsofsuccess.com

Made in the USA
Middletown, DE
28 March 2017